The Ravenscroft
School in Asheville

CONTRIBUTIONS TO SOUTHERN APPALACHIAN STUDIES

1. *Memoirs of Grassy Creek: Growing Up in the Mountains on the Virginia–North Carolina Line.* Zetta Barker Hamby. 1998
2. *The Pond Mountain Chronicle: Self-Portrait of a Southern Appalachian Community.* Edited by Leland R. Cooper and Mary Lee Cooper. 1998
3. *Traditional Musicians of the Central Blue Ridge: Old Time, Early Country, Folk and Bluegrass Label Recording Artists, with Discographies.* Marty McGee. 2000
4. *W.R. Trivett, Appalachian Pictureman: Photographs of a Bygone Time.* Ralph E. Lentz II. 2001
5. *The People of the New River: Oral Histories from the Ashe, Alleghany and Watauga Counties of North Carolina.* Edited by Leland R. Cooper and Mary Lee Cooper. 2001
6. *John Fox, Jr., Appalachian Author.* Bill York. 2003
7. *The Thistle and the Brier: Historical Links and Cultural Parallels Between Scotland and Appalachia.* Richard Blaustein. 2003
8. *Tales from Sacred Wind: Coming of Age in Appalachia. The Cratis Williams Chronicles.* Cratis D. Williams. Edited by David Cratis Williams and Patricia D. Beaver. 2003
9. *Willard Gayheart, Appalachian Artist.* Willard Gayheart and Donia S. Eley. 2003
10. *The Forest City Lynching of 1900: Populism, Racism, and White Supremacy in Rutherford County, North Carolina.* J. Timothy Cole. 2003
11. *The Brevard Rosenwald School: Black Education and Community Building in a Southern Appalachian Town, 1920–1966.* Betty J. Reed. 2004
12. *The Bristol Sessions: Writings About the Big Bang of Country Music.* Edited by Charles K. Wolfe and Ted Olson. 2005
13. *Community and Change in the North Carolina Mountains: Oral Histories and Profiles of People from Western Watauga County.* Compiled by Nannie Greene and Catherine Stokes Sheppard. 2006
14. *Ashe County: A History; A New Edition.* Arthur Lloyd Fletcher. 2009 [2006]
15. *The New River Controversy; A New Edition.* Thomas J. Schoenbaum. Epilogue by R. Seth Woodard. 2007
16. *The Blue Ridge Parkway by Foot: A Park Ranger's Memoir.* Tim Pegram. 2007
17. *James Still: Critical Essays on the Dean of Appalachian Literature.* Edited by Ted Olson and Kathy H. Olson. 2008
18. *Owsley County, Kentucky, and the Perpetuation of Poverty.* John R. Burch, Jr. 2008
19. *Asheville: A History.* Nan K. Chase. 2007
20. *Southern Appalachian Poetry: An Anthology of Works by 37 Poets.* Edited by Marita Garin. 2008
21. *Ball, Bat and Bitumen: A History of Coalfield Baseball in the Appalachian South.* L.M. Sutter. 2009
22. *The Frontier Nursing Service: America's First Rural Nurse-Midwife Service and School.* Marie Bartlett. 2009
23. *James Still in Interviews, Oral Histories and Memoirs.* Edited by Ted Olson. 2009
24. *The Millstone Quarries of Powell County, Kentucky.* Charles D. Hockensmith. 2009
25. *The Bibliography of Appalachia: More Than 4,700 Books, Articles, Monographs and Dissertations, Topically Arranged and Indexed.* Compiled by John R. Burch, Jr. 2009
26. *Appalachian Children's Literature: An Annotated Bibliography.* Compiled by Roberta Teague Herrin and Sheila Quinn Oliver. 2010

27. *Southern Appalachian Storytellers: Interviews with Sixteen Keepers of the Oral Tradition.* Edited by Saundra Gerrell Kelley. 2010

28. *Southern West Virginia and the Struggle for Modernity.* Christopher Dorsey. 2011

29. *George Scarbrough, Appalachian Poet: A Biographical and Literary Study with Unpublished Writings.* Randy Mackin. 2011

30. *The Water-Powered Mills of Floyd County, Virginia: Illustrated Histories, 1770–2010.* Franklin F. Webb and Ricky L. Cox. 2011

31. *School Segregation in Western North Carolina: A History, 1860s–1970s.* Betty Jamerson Reed. 2011

32. *The Ravenscroft School in Asheville: A History of the Institution and Its People and Buildings.* Dale Wayne Slusser. 2013

33. *The Ore Knob Mine Murders: The Crimes, the Investigation and the Trials.* Rose M. Haynes. 2013

34. *New Art of Willard Gayheart.* Willard Gayheart and Donia S. Eley. 2013

The Ravenscroft School in Asheville

A History of the Institution and Its People and Buildings

DALE WAYNE SLUSSER

CONTRIBUTIONS TO SOUTHERN APPALACHIAN STUDIES, 32

McFarland & Company, Inc., Publishers
Jefferson, North Carolina, and London

LIBRARY OF CONGRESS CATALOGUING-IN-PUBLICATION DATA

Slusser, Dale Wayne.
The Ravenscroft School in Asheville : a history of the institution and its people and buildings / Dale Wayne Slusser.
    p.   cm. — (Contributions to Southern Appalachian studies ; 32)
Includes bibliographical references and index.

ISBN 978-0-7864-7462-2 (softcover : acid free paper) ∞
ISBN 978-1-4766-0350-6 (ebook)

1. Ravenscroft School (Raleigh, N.C.)—History.   I. Title.
LD7501.N25S58 2014   371.0209756'55—dc23   2013037141

BRITISH LIBRARY CATALOGUING DATA ARE AVAILABLE

© 2014 Dale Wayne Slusser. All rights reserved

No part of this book may be reproduced or transmitted in any form or by any means, electronic or mechanical, including photocopying or recording, or by any information storage and retrieval system, without permission in writing from the publisher.

Front cover: *View of Asheville, N.C. and the Mountains from the Summer House,* Sarony & Major lithograph, published by James M. Edney, 1851; inset: part of a Ravenscroft High School advertisement, in an 1891 issue of *The Forum* (both from the collection of the author)

Manufactured in the United States of America

McFarland & Company, Inc., Publishers
Box 611, Jefferson, North Carolina 28640
www.mcfarlandpub.com

In memory of
Mary Toole Parker (1914–2012),
*whose father, Haywood Parker, was a Ravenscroft
headmaster; whose grandfather, Thomas Walton Patton,
was on the Ravenscroft Board of Fellows;
and whose great-grandparents,
James W. and Henrietta Kerr Patton,
were founders of Trinity Episcopal Church.*

Table of Contents

Acknowledgments xi
Preface 1

ONE. Mountains, Mansions and Missionaries: *1800–1849* 3
TWO. Reading, 'Riting and Rectors: *1850–1864* 18
THREE. Post-War: Postulants and Priests: *1865–1883* 31
FOUR. Redirection: Rectors and Ravenscroft High: *1884–1897* 45
FIVE. Buxton Hill, Bishops and Boarding Houses: *1898–1950* 80
SIX. Postscript: Peril or Preservation? *1951–2010* 90
SEVEN. Ravenscroft Boys: Biographical Notes of Notable Alumni 95
EIGHT. Histories of Ravenscroft Associate Mission Churches 106
    Buncombe County   107   Madison County   164
    Cherokee County   138   Rutherford County   169
    Haywood County   142   Transylvania County   172
    Henderson County   148   Missions Miscellanea   176
    Jackson County   157

Timeline 183
Appendix — Chronology of Joseph Roland Osborne 187
Chapter Notes 197
Bibliography 215
Index 221

Acknowledgments

One quickly finds that research and writing are collaborative efforts, requiring the aid and assistance of friends, family, fellow researchers, archivists, and librarians.

Zoe Rhine, Ann Wright and Lyme Kedic of the North Carolina Collection at Pack Memorial Library in Asheville were constant and invaluable assistants to my research. They not only patiently handled my numerous emails and phone calls (and occasional visits) but also often provided the "legwork" to search through material for me.

A number of staff from academic institutions were of great assistance to me in my research. Locally, I acknowledge the help of Helen Wyckle, associate professor and head librarian of the special collections at the D. H. Ramsey Library at the University of North Carolina at Asheville.Also, Jeremy Williams and Greta Browning assisted me in accessing material from the WNC Episcopal Diocese Collection in the Special Collections Library at Appalachian State University in Boone, North Carolina. I extend special thanks to my friend, Stuart Burns of Boone, for acting as my research assistant and retrieving the material for me from Appalachian State University. Rachel Howarth at Houghton Library, Harvard University, was very helpful in tracking down a photo of Judge Cocke and Thomas Wolfe, despite my giving her an incorrect call number.

Asheville's resident preservation specialists were also an invaluable source of aid. These included Rebecca Johnson and Jennifer Cathey of the Western Office of the North Carolina State Historic Preservation Office, Department of Cultural Affairs Jack Thomson and Peggy Gardner of the Preservation Society of Asheville-Buncombe County; and Stacy Merton of the Historic Resources Commission, Asheville.

I am indebted to architect and historic preservationist David R. Black, AIA of Hager Smith architects, Raleigh, for sharing his experience with the initial saving of Ravenscroft in 1978. Also, I am indebted to J. Myrick Howard, executive director of Preservation North Carolina, for sharing his experience with the initial saving of Ravenscroft as well. But more importantly, I publicly thank these two men for their foundational and instrumental roles in the preservation of Ravenscroft.

I am likewise indebted to a number of people who helped me find information about Mr. Shoenberger and Shoenberger Hall, including Jude Wudarczyk of the Lawrenceville Historical Society, Lawrenceville, Pennsylvania; the Rev. Richard W. Davies, director of Old St. Luke's Church in Pittsburgh, Pennsylvania; author Mary Brignano, Pittsburgh; architect and preservationist Mike Cox of Asheville; and John Toms, board member of the Preservation Society of Asheville-Buncombe County and archivist at St. Lawrence Cathedral,

Asheville. In addition, I would like to acknowledge the help of Margaret Hunt Landis of the Marietta Restorations Associates, Marietta, Pennsylvania, who recently helped with research on the Shoenberger family. More importantly, I would like to thank her for giving me my first opportunity to use my research skills. Thirty years ago she asked a young inexperienced college student to take on the monumental task (or so it seemed to me) of preparing the National Register nomination for an extension to the Marietta Historic District. It was then that I first learned to research, identify architectural features, prepare maps and diagrams and write concise and readable text.

I am also very thankful to Thomas M. Phelps of Bostic, North Carolina, for contacting me and sharing the results of his family research and the journals of his great-grandfather, Girard Phelps. Thanks are also in order to his wife, Christine Phelps, who had transcribed the handwritten journals into a readable format.

The Rev. Mr. Edward Chapman of Emmanuel Episcopal Church in Cumberland, Maryland, was helpful in sharing his research on the Rev. D. H. Buel, who had served at Emmanuel before coming to Ravenscroft. I am also indebted to the Rev. Mr. Chapman for scanning the portrait of Rev. Buel and permitting its use for this book. Also helpful with research on the Rev. Buel was Maggie Bowles of St. David's Episcopal Church, Cullowhee, North Carolina.

On the editorial side of things, I would like to thank my wife, Susan, for her patience during those many hours when my head was either in a reference book or racing ahead composing the next paragraph of the story. Friend and professor of business administrator/department chair at Newberry College, Dr. Joe Franklin, was a constant encouragement throughout the preparation of this book. Joe's superb photographic skills are evident throughout the book as well.

I also thank MTM Investments, the current owners of Ravenscroft, for their faithful stewardship of the building. Thanks are likewise sent to Amanda McDevitt, building manager; Lynn Burns and Rick Flemming of RPF Construction; and the staff of Biltmore Dermatology Associates for access to the many rooms of Ravenscroft.

Lastly, I acknowledge the help of Mary Toole Parker, whose family (Parker/Patton) had been a part of Ravenscroft from its inception in 1854. Mary's father, Haywood Parker, had been an instructor and headmaster at Ravenscroft High School from 1887 to 1889. Mary's mother was Josie Buel Patton Parker, who not only was named for Ravenscroft's longtime principal, the Rev. D. H. Buel, but also was the daughter of Thomas Walton Patton, longtime member of the Board of Fellows of Ravenscroft. Mary's great-grandparents (Thomas Walton's parents), James W. and Henrietta Kerr Patton, were founders of Trinity Episcopal Church, the parish in which Ravenscroft operated, and were ardent supporters of the school when it first opened. And lastly, Mary's great-grandfather's brother, William Patton, sold the original property to the diocese in 1854 to be used for a "Classical & Theological School." Mary Toole Parker was a lifetime member of Trinity Episcopal Church and an ardent supporter of many of Asheville's civic organizations, such as the Friends of the Library, YWCA, and Asheville League of Women Voters (a founding member), and in 2011 Mary was designated one of the Asheville's "Living Treasures." Mary, to whom this book is dedicated, passed away shortly before this book was completed.

Preface

In the course of researching and writing my previous book, *In the Near Loss of Everything: George MacDonald's Son in America*, the story of Ronald MacDonald and his seven-year sojourn in America, I learned a great deal about the Ravenscroft School, where MacDonald was the headmaster from 1889 to 1894, and although in the book I discussed some aspects of the history of Ravenscroft that were pertinent to the story, much of the school's history remained untold. In fact, very little had been previously written about Ravenscroft School, which operated in the oldest surviving building (29 Ravenscroft Drive) in downtown Asheville, North Carolina. Therefore I decided that a comprehensive history needed to be written.

This book is a historical account of the Ravenscroft School — its people, its buildings and its history. The "Ravenscroft" institutions (a ministry of the state and local Episcopal Church dioceses), which occupied the building for over fifty years during the nineteenth century, also included three other buildings that have since been demolished. This history will include the histories of those buildings and the people associated with the institution, which went by the various names of Ravenscroft Diocesan School, Ravenscroft Episcopal Seminary, Ravenscroft Associate Mission and Training School, and the Ravenscroft High School for Boys. The Ravenscroft School went through many vicissitudes from its inception in 1854 until its closing in the early 1900s, though mainly it had three phases: first as a "Classical and Theological School"; then, following the Civil War, as a Theological Training School and Associate Mission; and finally, in 1887, it split into two departments, a Theological Training School/Associate Mission and Ravenscroft High School for Boys. Though the institution was only in existence for about 50 years, the purview of this book is from the early days of Asheville (1820s) to the building of Joseph Osborn's mansion in the 1840s (which would eventually house the school), through the years of the school's operation, and on up to the twenty-first century.

In his textbook on historic preservation, Norman Tyler writes that historic buildings can be thought of as both "nouns" and "verbs." He further elaborates: "When buildings are viewed as objects, they are nouns. They make up a part of the physical presence of a space and are the 'subject' of that space. Thinking of historic buildings in terms of their physical structure is the most common approach to understanding their significance, but it is not the only one. They also can be seen as places of involvement — where historic events took place. From this perspective, they can be seen as verbs, based on the action that took place there, similar to the use of a verb in a sentence. In other words, buildings can be seen not only as static structures but also as essential carriers of our community's history."[1] The building at 29 Ravenscroft Drive, being an example of a Greek revival mansion, can certainly be described as a noun; however, its historical significance is equally important. In fact, although I describe its construction, style and architectural significance in this story, mostly I treat the building as a verb — as a place where people lived, studied, worked, played, and even died within its walls.

This is the story of a mission and school, but it is also a microcosm of the history of a church (Episcopal), a community (Asheville) and a region (western North Carolina). You will find no scandal or sensational dramatic escapades in this story, but rather the story of faithful men (and some women — mostly behind the scenes or at least unrecorded) who simply did what they were called to do. They were eminent bishops directing the work, and some were untiring preachers trekking from mission station to mission station, preaching the gospel of Jesus Christ, and some were college-trained teachers, instructors and headmasters, and others were widows acting as matrons, or servants who did the cooking and cleaning, but they all had a part to play in the story of Ravenscroft. It is difficult to trace all the people who were part of Ravenscroft (though I trust this book is a good start), but you will find that Ravenscroft was a real place where real people lived and worked for the good of their fellow men and women.

ONE

Mountains, Mansions and Missionaries: *1800–1849*

Surrounded by the fabric of urban life in downtown Asheville, North Carolina, stands an often forgotten old stately brick mansion known to the locals as "Ravenscroft." Although it is listed on the National Register of Historic Places and is the oldest extant building in downtown Asheville, few people seem to know of its existence, and even fewer know of its long history and myriad connections to men and women of Asheville, the State of North Carolina, the United States and even Great Britain.

Situated on a plateau high in the Appalachian Mountains of western North Carolina, early nineteenth-century Asheville was a small and rather remote settlement. Prior to the Revolutionary War, the land upon which Asheville is built was entirely occupied by the Cherokee Indians. White settlement was begun in the late 1700s by settlers who had received land grants as payment for their services in the Revolutionary War.

After the success of the Revolution and the establishment of a new and peaceful United States, the "western" lands became the center of attention as the source of our nation's potential expansion. Such was also the case for the State of North Carolina; however, its "western" lands were mostly made up of rugged and treacherous mountains. The inaccessibility of the mountains and their lack of available flat, tillable land were detriments to settlement. However, the beauty and the remoteness of the mountains attracted three types of people: rugged, adventurous, and independent pioneer settlers; wealthy established plantation owners from the deep South seeking cool respite from the harsh coastal summers; and missionaries eager to spread the Gospel of Jesus Christ to the people of the remote western Carolina mountains. All three groups were to play major roles in the history of the Ravenscroft institutions.

Asheville was incorporated in 1797 and was named for the standing governor of North Carolina, Samuel Ashe. Settlement began slowly as access to and from the fledgling city attracted only the heartiest and more adventuresome of pioneers. Scots-Irish immigrants seemed to be the most attracted to this remote region, perhaps because of its similarities to the rugged mountainous highlands of their ancestral homeland. One such early settler was Scots-Irish immigrant James Patton. James Patton was born in northern Ireland, County of Derry and Parish of Tamlacht, on the 13th day of February 1756. His father was a farmer by occupation but was in failing health and died when James was 14 years of age.[1] James immigrated to America in 1783.

He was a weaver by trade, but soon became a prosperous merchant. After his arrival in America he labored for several years at mining, well digging, working on the canals,

A stagecoach and its passengers sit in front of James Patton's Eagle Hotel on South Main Street in Asheville, North Carolina, in this circa 1870s photograph. Notice the use of paired Greek-revival boxed columns on the hotel's three-story portico. A similar configuration was used by the builder of Ravenscroft.— Stereoview photograph from Series: "Asheville and Vicinity — Illustrated Catalogue of Southern Scenery" (image C692–8 from the North Carolina Collection, Pack Memorial Library, Asheville).

grubbing, and so forth. After this he set out from Philadelphia, where he had landed, and with a small pack of goods went south as a peddler. He made his way into North Carolina and for several years traded in Wilkes, Burke and Buncombe counties, getting his supplies from the north.[2] In 1791 he formed a business partnership as a merchant with his future brother-in-law, Andrew Erwin.

In 1807 Patton & Erwin decided to relocate their families from Wilkes County to a farm on the Swannanoa (two miles east of Asheville). In 1814 Patton, being an entrepreneur, moved his family into Asheville, where, in addition to his farming, he set up a tannery, general store, and a hotel. Patton opened "The Eagle" hotel in 1814 on the west side of South Main Street (now Biltmore Avenue) about a block from the center square (now called Pack Square). It was readily identified by the golden eagle mounted on a pole in front of the building.

Patton's store and hotel catered to the men and "droves" of animals traveling through Asheville on the "Drover's Road." The Drover's Road, which followed the old Indian trails, was used by farmers in the hills of Tennessee, Kentucky and North Carolina to drive their herds of cattle, hogs, mules, ducks, and turkeys to lowland markets. Along the way were "stands" where the drovers could eat and rest indoors while the animals would be penned and fed.

Asheville's "Main Street" (now Biltmore Avenue) was laid out along the route of the Drover's Road and so, as still holds true today, much of its commerce and industry catered to the travelers, tourists, and transient visitors. Although the drovers brought much-needed commerce to the settlement, Asheville's first boom followed the 1828 completion of the state-chartered Buncombe Turnpike, which improved the old Drover's Road and connected Greeneville, Tennessee, with Greenville, South Carolina, and then connected to the State Road in South Carolina, which went all the way to Charleston. A stagecoach route was established on the new road, and now, in addition to the rugged mountain drovers with their wild flocks and herds coming from the north, was added the genteel coastal South Carolinians, seeking respite from the humid mosquito-infested coastal summers.

The Charlestonians' coming to the mountains was perhaps the most influential occurrence in the history of Ravenscroft. They not only brought key people who would be influential in founding, financing, managing, and maintaining the school, but they also brought a new social order to the region.[3] Their coming was the start of the gentrification of the western Carolina mountains that introduced the money and clientele needed for such a school as Ravenscroft to even come to fruition.

The "summer colony" of Charlestonians was first established by Frederick Rutledge and Edward King in 1828 at Flat Rock, 22 miles south of Asheville. Each man bought land and built summer cottages, with the picturesque names of "Brooklands" and "Argyle." The Kings and Rutledges, two of Charleston's wealthiest families, were soon followed by other wealthy families such as Charles Baring and his wife Susannah Tudor Heyward.[4] By 1833 the Barings had not only acquired thousands of acres but also built their own cottage, "The Lodge," and a small chapel, which later was enlarged and became St. John-In-the Wilderness Episcopal Church. A later Flat Rock resident recalled that "both Mr. & Mrs. Baring were great factors in the development of Flat Rock, being public spirited and liberal in their expenditures and noted for their generous hospitality."[5]

The colony grew rapidly and soon included over 50 "cottages" built by notable families of Charleston, such as the Draytons, Lowndes, Elliotts, Pinckneys, and Middletons. The "cottages" were built in the "picturesque-style," newly popularized by landscape designer A. J. (Andrew Jackson) Downing and architect A. J. (Alexander Jackson) Davis in their collaborative publications. Written by A. J. Downing, with architectural designs mostly from A. J. Davis, *A Series of Designs for Rural Cottages and their Gardens and Grounds Adapted to North America* was first published in 1842. Downing was a proponent of the "picturesque" estate with its Gothic cottage or Italianate villa, situated on a small rural estate. His comprehensive approach to designing a residence in conjunction with its site and landscaping was reminiscent of the ideas of fifteenth-century Palladio, although Downing combined English Gothic architecture with the Italian of Palladio. Downing's *The Architecture of Country Houses: Including Designs for Cottages, and Farm-Houses and Villas, With Remarks on Interiors, Furniture, and the Best Modes of Warming and Ventilating*, published in 1850, continued his comprehensive and popular ideals. The beautiful rural mountain scenery of Flat Rock, combined with the relaxed summer atmosphere, was the ideal setting for Downing-inspired picturesque residences. As Catherine Bishir writes, "The picturesque mode suited the life of fashionable informality in a mountain setting where summer 'cottages' stood on spacious estates, and driveways and plantings created a careful balance of privacy and sociability."[6] Though they were only in residence for part of the year, the Charlestonians' large estates, picturesque-style cottages and their elaborate balls and social functions contrasted severely with the log-cabin hardscrabble lives of their pioneer mountain neighbors. Locals soon dubbed Flat Rock the "Little Charleston-in the-Mountains."

By the 1850s this influx of "Charleston culture" had migrated north along the Buncombe Turnpike. The taste for cottages and villas continued along the turnpike to Asheville.[7] Daniel Blake and Alexander Robertson established homes in Fletcher, about midway between Flat Rock and Asheville. Blake first built "The Meadows," a large bracketed stone house perhaps inspired by Downing's "Suburban Cottage" in *The Architecture of Country Houses*, and later Blake built "Newington" (in Arden, closer to Asheville), a picturesque Gothic cottage perhaps inspired by "An Ornamental Farmhouse" in *Cottage Residences*. Robertson established a large Charleston-style plantation and built his Greek revival mansion around 1850, naming it "Struan," after his ancestral home in Scotland. As the house-building of the 1840s moved closer to Asheville and further from Flat Rock, the Downing-inspired designs were diluted with elements of the earlier, more conservative Greek revival style.

Mrs. Elizabeth Trescott of Charleston was the first Charlestonian to reach Asheville. She built her Greek revival mansion along the banks of the Swannanoa River. Shortly after its completion she sold the house to a fellow Charlestonian, William Patton, who named it "Azalea." Like the threads of a woven cloth, the social, cultural, religious, and familial connections of Asheville and Charleston continually intertwined to make up the "fabric" of the Ravenscroft story. William Patton was the first cousin of James W. Patton, the previously mentioned owner of the Eagle Hotel in Asheville, but even more important to our story is the fact that they were also brothers-in-law, having both married Kerr sisters, the daughters of Andrew Kerr of Charleston. William married Elizabeth Kerr in 1816 and settled in Charleston. James married Elizabeth's sister Henrietta around 1840, following the death of his first wife, Clara Walton Patton. That brings us back to the Patton family and their continuing connection to our story.

In 1831, James Patton Sr. bought "Warm Springs," a hotel and resort north of Asheville along the French Broad River. The area is now called Hot Springs. There he built a large brick hotel with 13 columns, representing the original 13 original states. The new hotel, managed by his sons John and James W., catered to the visitors who had not built permanent summer residences but needed the rest, relaxation and healthy atmosphere of the mountains. By the late 1830s James Patton's eldest son, James W. Patton, was managing his father's enterprises as well as establishing his own. Visiting Methodist circuit preacher Francis Asbury once, after lodging at Patton's home, described James Patton Sr. as "how rich, how plain, how humble and how kind!"[8]

At the age of 83, James Patton penned an autobiography of his long and adventurous life. In his writing, intended for his family, he recounted the story of how he, a penniless immigrant, through frugality and hard work, became wealthy. But he was quick to remind his family that much of his success was divinely ordained and that those who are rich have a responsibility to use their wealth for good, since, as he writes, "We are informed by divine authority, that we are nothing more than stewards, and are bound to account for the talents put into our hands. The rich man, who lives only for himself, does not deserve the respect and esteem of his fellow-man."[9]

In 1846 James passed away, leaving James W. and another son, John, as executors of his will. Although James Sr. was kind and generous, upon writing his will he was given either bad counsel or likely no counsel, as he left a confusing and conflicting will. The conflicting document resulted in a long and drawn-out legal battle between his executors and their younger brother Thomas T. Patton. Contrary to his strong warning to his family in his autobiography: "Let me advise you to live in a peaceable and friendly manner with each other. Never encourage family quarrels, but strive against them. If any difference should take place among you, suffer it not to come to the knowledge of the public, if you can avoid it."[10]

In the August term of 1856, the case reached the North Carolina State Supreme Court. Some historical records say that Thomas T. Patton was disinherited by his father, but the case was a bit more complicated, and the facts are confusing. The executors brought the case to the court, as they were anxious to have "the whole estate finally settled, so that they might be discharged of the trust imposed by their testator's [father's] will."[11] According to the testimony, James Sr.'s will, written in 1835 (he didn't die until 1846), stated, "Believing that it would promote the interest of all my family, I concluded, upon the 24th of September, 1827, to commit to my son James the entire management of the estate. I estimated my personal property to be of the value of forty five thousand dollars, and determined that he should pay out of it such legacies as I might bequeath to his brothers and sisters." Later in that same will he further states, "In compliance with my original intention, and to enable him (James) to pay the several legacies herein mentioned, and to perform faithfully the many important trusts which will devolve upon him, I give to him all my personal estate, not herein before specifically bequeathed, with the exception of the house-hold and kitchen furniture, stock, crops and farming utensils, at my farm on the Swannanoa which I give to my son Thomas." But then he conflictingly states, "Of the legacy to my daughter Anne, (Mrs. Anne E. Smith,) I direct that two thousand dollars shall be paid by my four sons, (James W., John E., Thomas T. and Benjamin,) in equal proportions-$500 each-out of the legacies to them given." If the will itself was not confusing enough, in 1832, James W. (in his father's lifetime) sold his father's farm to Thomas for $2,244,50, acting as his father's agent, but apparently without his father's knowledge.

The court determined that Thomas was exempt from paying his $500 share to his sister, since he was given no monetary legacy through the will. It further stated that Thomas was entitled to be reimbursed the $2,244.50 (with interest from the date of his father's death) that he had paid for the farm, which had actually been willed to him prior to his purchasing it.

This may be the reason that in the 1850 census "T. T. Patton" is listed as living with Joseph R. Osborne, farmer. Perhaps Thomas was living with Osborne while the fate of the

Swannanoa farm was being resolved. Nonetheless, this brings us to the next major player in the early history of Ravenscroft.

Joseph Roland Osborne, the ninth of ten children born to Jonathan and Martha Roland Osborne of Haywood County, was born in 1812. Little is known of his early background, but by the 1840s Joseph was living in Asheville and actively buying and selling land.[12] In his history of western North Carolina, historian John Preston Arthur writes, "Just north of Aston street was the brick store of Patton & Osborne, and later Patton & Summey."[13] So between farming, land speculation, and store-keeping Osborne, like his fellow merchant/entrepreneurial friends, William and James W. Patton, was able to amass a healthy fortune.

This 1870s view from Court Square (Pack Square) looking down South Main Street (Biltmore Avenue) in Asheville, shows the "Patton & Summey" (formerly Patton & Osborne) store on the left. This photograph, originally taken by Rufus Morgan in the 1870s, was publised by W.T. Robertson as "Stereoscopic Views of Southern Scenery," "Asheville, Main Street looking South." Robertson, a photographer in Ahseville, acquired Morgan's stereoscopic negatives in 1876 (image B366-5 from the North Carolina Collection, Pack Memorial Library, Asheville).

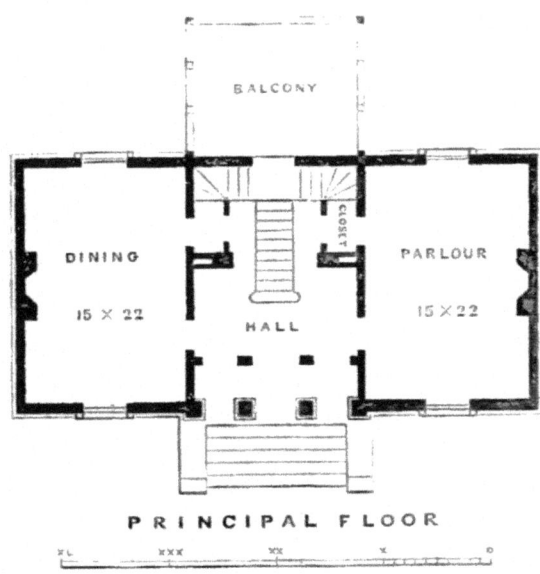

Design IX for a "Cottage in the Italian or Tuscan Style" from *Cottage Residences: or, A Series of Designs for Rural Cottages and Their Gardens and Grounds, Adapted to North America*, first published by A.J. Dawning in 1842.

The 1850 Slave Schedule shows that Osborne owned 26 slaves (14 males and 12 females), aged 1 to 75 years old.[14] By 1860 he had become so wealthy that instead of being listed as a "farmer" (as in 1850), his occupation in the 1860 census was listed as "Gentleman."

In February 1845 he purchased 73 acres from his brothers, John and Ephraim Osborne, in what is now downtown Asheville. His brothers had together previously purchased the land in 1840. The large tract of rural land was only a few blocks west and south of the town's center square. Osborne quickly began selling off some of his land, perhaps to help finance the building of his mansion. The first "Lots 2 & 3" were jointly sold to James W. Patton and the builder Ephraim Clayton. Joseph continued to sell the lots closest to the city limits but retained a large parcel just southwest of Asheville's Methodist Church.

At the time, Joseph was a single man in his early thirties with apparently a good deal of accumulated wealth, for sometime between 1845 and 1850 he decided to build a fashionable new "villa" for himself. Osborne, no doubt influenced by the "Charleston culture" of Flat Rock and also by his association with William Patton of Charleston, chose to build in A. J. Downing's popular and romantic picturesque style. He may also have been influenced by reading the local farming publications of his day: "The values and models espoused by Downing and his successors gained wide exposure in national agricultural journals and found their way into the North Carolina press. Such progressive periodicals as the Farmers Journal, the Arator, and the Carolina Cultivator ran plates and texts from Downing's books."[15]

Osborne, or his builder, chose Design IX, "A Cottage in the Italian or Tuscan Style," from Downing's 1842 publication *Cottage Residences* for the floor plan and massing of his new mansion. The house, with its three-story center tower section and two-story flanking wings, closely followed Downing's Design IX[16]; however, instead of using the "Italian or Tuscan style," Osborne's mansion was built in the Greek revival style. This is not surprising as most local builders were already familiar with the Greek revival style in which they had been building for over a decade and a half.

Design IX, unlike most of Downing's designs, is surprisingly symmetrical in its plan and massing. This is even more astounding given that Design IX was designed and submitted by Philadelphia architect John Notman, who was noted for his asymmetrical Italianate designs. In fact, Prospect House in Princeton, New Jersey, designed by Notman, is an asymmetrical version of Design IX, with its offset tower.

Though Osborne's use of Downing's Design IX was perhaps the first in the state, there were later incidences in North Carolina of local builders adapting that particular design. Three examples are the 1855 Jacob Holt house in Warrenton; the 1856 "Dunleith" for Judge Robert P. Dick by Samuel Sloan[17] or W. S. Andrews, in Greensboro; and the later George Nissen House in Lewisville near Winton-Salem in 1876.

Although Downing "urged his readers not to hire a 'country carpenter or mason' who too often altered the concept of buildings as he proceeded,"[18] Joseph Osborne probably had no access to an architect in Asheville in the 1840s; thus, it is generally accepted that Osborne selected master builder Ephraim Clayton and master brick-mason George Wesley Shackleford to build his new mansion (villa). Clayton and Shackleford were most certainly the builders, as they are shown to have had other dealings with Osborne around that time.[19]

The use of Clayton and Shackleford as builders is the reason that Ravenscroft's design became a unique blend of Downing's picturesque with the prevalent Greek revival style of its time and place. Just as Downing warned, Ravenscroft's builders "altered the concept" of an asymmetrical picturesque cottage to that of a more formal symmetrical Greek revival mansion, in keeping with the neoclassical plantation homes being built in the antebellum South at that time.

Ephraim Clayton, a carpenter and builder from a prominent pioneering family in the area, developed a large contracting business that was among the most important in western North Carolina and also extended into neighboring states. His works included many of the most stylish and substantial buildings of the time in a region still dominated by simple, traditional building. Clayton was also associated with Charleston architect Edward C. Jones on two projects built for Charleston clients in North Carolina. In 1853 Jones provided the vestry of St. John-In-the-Wilderness Episcopal Church in Flat Rock with an Italianate design for enlarging their church and Clayton was awarded the contract. In 1857 Jones also designed a Gothic revival-style brick building for Calvary Episcopal Church in Fletcher, another summer resort for Charlestonians, and Clayton won the $6,000 contract. Jones and Clayton may also have collaborated on some of the many summer houses erected or remodeled in picturesque styles for Charleston families in Flat Rock and other summer resorts. Clayton often worked with brick mason George Wesley Shackleford, for whom Clayton named one of his sons.[20]

Born in Tennessee, Shackleford (also spelled Shackelford) moved to Buncombe County before 1850. By that year he had $1,000 invested in a brick manufacturing establishment in Asheville in which seven employees produced 300,000 bricks a year valued at $3,000. Working with Clayton, he was involved in constructing many of the substantial brick buildings in the city and beyond, of which only a few have been identified.[21]

Clayton and Shackleford's collaboration resulted in the use of red-brick bearing walls (probably laid up by Shackleford) and finely detailed wood windows, lintels, trim, columns and interior casings by carpenter Clayton. The use of brick with classical wood trim is reminiscent of Clayton and Shackleford's later institutional work, such as the Polk County Courthouse, built in 1853–1859, and the Mars Hill College Building, Mars Hill, North Carolina, of 1856.

The Greek revival detailing of Osborne's mansion was not unlike those of contemporary buildings then being constructed in the community. The Greek revival multi-storied portico with its boxed columns was used on a number of local buildings, including James Patton's Eagle Hotel; another hotel on the west side of N. Main Street later called the "Carolina House"; a residence on Charlotte Street that was later known as the Hawley House; the Nicholas Woofin house; and the Dickson/Johnston residence on the corner of Church Street and Patton Avenue, just a few blocks up the street from the Osborne mansion.

Just as Osborne chose the "plans" for his new house from Downing's book, so also did his builders use contemporary "pattern books" to execute the building and ornamentation on his mansion. This was standard practice, notes architectural historian Catherine Bishir, for antebellum houses as they "adhered to standard forms and plans and attained a classical demeanor from columned porches, broad moldings and pilastered mantels and entrances. These elements were often drawn from popular architectural books by American architects, including Asher Benjamin and Minard Lafever. Especially popular in North Carolina was Asher Benjamin's Practical House Carpenter (1830) with its plain, bold decorative motifs and clearly explained Grecian orders geared to the provincial builder."[22]

Evidence confirms that builder Ephraim Clayton, a carpenter-turned-contractor, used

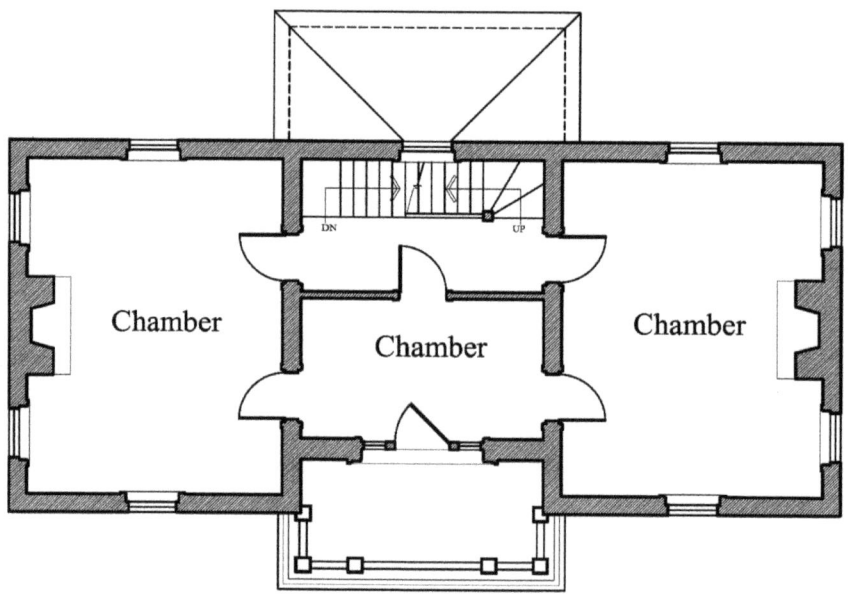

SECOND FLOOR PLAN

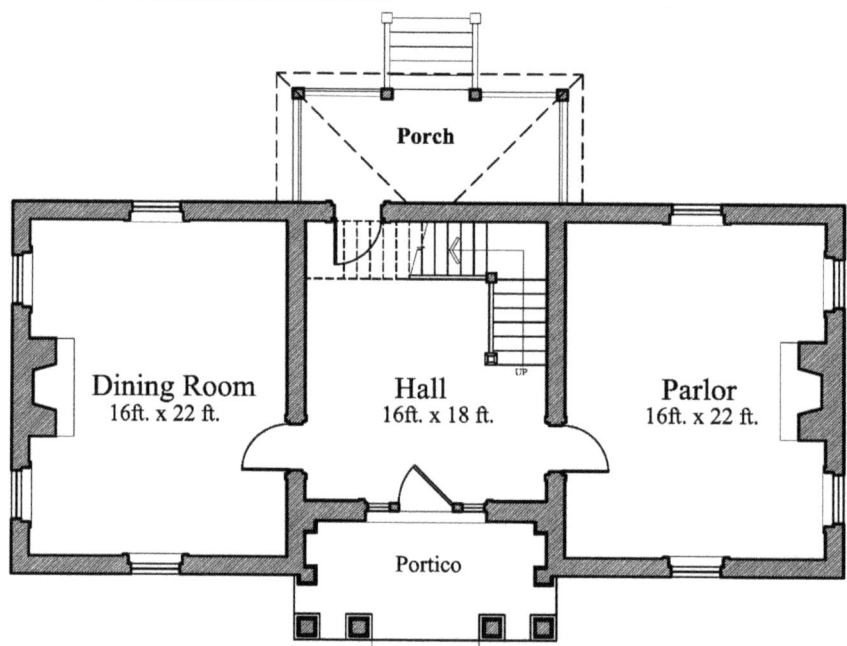

FIRST FLOOR PLAN

Joseph R. Osborne Mansion
-circa 1850

Floor plans for Joseph Osborne's mansion show that its designer/builder closely followed "Design IX" from A.J. Dawning's *Cottage Residences* (plans drawn by the author).

numerous "builder's manuals" for his patterns for Ravenscroft's doors, windows, interior and exterior trim details, and fireplace mantels. And, in fact, careful investigation of Ravenscroft's details and a study of the nineteenth-century pattern books confirm that both Benjamin's and Lafever's books were consulted.

Ravenscroft's front entrance is in a typical Greek revival style, with its two-paneled door with flanking sidelights separated by scaled-down Doric antae columns. The whole is framed by larger-scaled Doric antae columns and full entablature. The design of the entrance (especially the column capitals) no doubt was taken from Lafever's *The Beauties of Modern Architecture* (1835), Plates 2, 3, and 4. One difference is that on Ravenscroft's entrance the inner columns next to the door do not extend to the top architrave, but stop at the middle architrave, separating the top of the door and its transom. Although Lafever's plates were probably used for the entrance, similar Grecian-style Doric capitals, with their odd double band of square fillet-bands, were also detailed by Asher Benjamin in Plates 10 and 13 of his 1833 book, *The Practice of Architecture*.

The same style of column was used for the front portico. Although Clayton was known to have his own millwork business, he apparently was not comfortable making round columns—thus the use of square columns, usually reserved for antae columns. In his defense, perhaps he used square columns to make the portico look more like Downing's plate, which

The Dr. John Dickson/Billy Johnston house was formerly located at the corner of Church Street and Patton Avenue (site of Dhrumor Building). The Greek revival boxed columns that faced Church Street were similar to those on the Osborne mansion, which was just a few blocks away (image #B409-X from the North Carolina Collection, Pack Memorial Library, Asheville).

shows square columns. All the columns have simple six-inch-high bases. The front rows of portico columns now sit on brick pedestals that were added sometime after 1978.

The crowning entablature is the same on the tower and flanking wings. It is a simplified version of a Grecian Doric order entablature illustrated by Benjamin in Plate VI of his 1830 book, *The Architect or Practical House Carpenter*. Interestingly, though true to the Grecian Doric order, the end triglyphs were on the corner (instead of centered over the column, as is the Roman Doric), but the mutules were only above the triglyphs and not the metopes, which is more like the Roman Doric. Comparing Ravenscroft's entablature to the pattern books reveals that not only did it match Benjamin's plates, but Benjamin also gave an explanation for the apparent dilemma. In his explanation of Plate VI, Benjamin states, "The mutules over the metopes have been left off in further imitation of the Romans; and, where simplicity only is desired, it is believed that object is obtained with one over every triglyph."[23] The height of Ravenscroft's entablature measures approximately 24"–25", which is twice the 12" width (1 diameter) of the portico columns. This further matches Benjamin's plate, which, he says, "is two diameters in height."[24] The builder of Ravenscroft also, perhaps for the sake of simplicity, used conic-shaped guttae under the triglyphs instead of the pyramidal-shaped ones shown in Benjamin's plate. This is to the builder's credit, as the conic-shaped guttae are more in keeping with the Greek order.

The interior door and window trim, true to the classical canon of "hierarchy," is more elaborate on the principal public floor and simpler on the upper private floors. Again we see the influence of the pattern books, as the first-floor interior window and door trim is similar to ones illustrated by Benjamin and Lafever. It appears that the trim is most closely derived from Plate 43, figure A of Asher Benjamin's *The Practice of Architecture*, except that Ravenscroft never had interior shutters. The floral-carved corner blocks shown in figure A of Benjamin's plate most closely match those used at Ravenscroft.

Joseph Osborne lived in his beautiful mansion for less than a decade before selling it to William Patton of Charleston in 1854.[25] Shortly thereafter Osborne married and moved to Loudon County, Tennessee.[26]

Joseph Roland Osborne, the builder of Ravenscroft, circa 1850–1860 (courtesy Marshall Ramsey Jones, Birmingham, Alabama).

Into this milieu of early nineteenth-century Asheville came the missionaries. The Methodist circuit-riding preachers such as Francis Asbury were probably the first to enter the mountains, soon to be followed by the Baptists, Presbyterians and Lutherans. The Episcopalians, who are more pertinent to our story, were one of the last denominations to send missionaries to the region. By 1840 Asheville already had established Methodist, Presbyterian and Baptist churches, but no Episcopal church.

There was no official Episcopal denomination in North Carolina until April 24, 1817, "when nine men met in Convention to form the Protestant Episcopal Church in North Carolina."[27] As a new diocese, with no presiding bishop, they asked the Right Reverend Richard Channing Moore, bishop of Virginia, to provide visiting oversight along with his duties in Virginia.

Bishop Moore was only able to visit the North Carolina denomination two or three times a year, which essentially left the fledgling diocese without any real leadership. Finally, at the 1823 Annual Convention, the diocese, consisting of about 400 communicants in 23 congregations,[28] managed to select and duly call their first bishop, the Rev. John Stark Ravenscroft, a clergyman and assistant to Bishop Moore in Virginia.

Ravenscroft (for whom the subject of this book was named) was born in 1772 at Blandford, Prince George County, Virginia. Before he was one year old his parents moved the family back to northern England and then to Scotland. Ravenscroft returned to Virginia at the age of sixteen to attend William and Mary College. He left college before attaining a degree, married Anne Spottswood Burwell in 1792, and bought a plantation in Lunuenburg County. After years of riotous living, at the age of 38, Ravenscroft began reading his Bible and was soon converted to faith in Jesus Christ. Soon thereafter he felt called to the ministry and presented himself to Bishop Moore for "holy orders." On May 6, 1817, he was ordained a priest in the Episcopal Church of Virginia.[29]

Most of the early work of the Episcopal Church in North Carolina was in the eastern regions of the state, and in fact Ravenscroft rarely visited the western mountain regions. Apparently he did visit Asheville at least once (in 1828) and held a service or two in the courthouse, though he essentially ignored western North Carolina. In his address at the 1825 General Convention he reported, "In the western section of the Diocess, the prospect is very discouraging, though not without hope."[30]

The only Episcopal church anywhere near Asheville during Bishop Ravenscroft's era was the small wooden chapel erected by the Baring family for the summer "Charlestonians" in Flat Rock, but even that church was built privately and not part of any diocese.

The Rev. Levi Silliman Ives, upon the death Bishop Ravenscroft in 1830, became the second bishop of North Carolina in 1831. Having a heart for missions and for spreading the Gospel of Jesus Christ and the work of the church, he made the western regions his priority. In 1842, Bishop Ives visited "Wataga Valley" in Watauga County, North Carolina, upon the recommendation of a botanist friend from New York. He named the area "Valle Crucis" (Valley of the Cross) for the shape made by the junction of three streams. He saw the immediate need for a mission and training school and, after another visit to the area, he sent the Rev. Henry H. Prout to begin the work. In his address to the 1844 Convention, Bishop Ives reported, "The section of country where it is situated is beautiful and striking, far beyond my powers of description; while the inhabitants cannot be overmatched in spiritual destitution by the inhabitants of any other known land. A portion of them had not, before the arrival of our brother, heard for seven years, even an uncertain sound of the Gospel. And they are now willing to be taught — many of them eager to be taught — the way of salvation by Christ!"[31]

The "Valle Crucis Mission" was fully operational by the next year's Convention in May of 1845. The bishop gave a full report in his annual address to the Convention: The past year has been one of struggle with our Missionary work.... Encouraged by a few zealous individuals and impelled by the afflicting necessities of our confiding and kind-hearted mountaineers, your Bishop, in accordance with the views he expressed the last year, has made a strenuous effort to establish a Missionary family and school in Valle Crucis near the head of Watauga River, Ashe County. In company with a worthy Presbyter, he has purchased a farm in that place, consisting of sufficient land to sustain the largest Missionary establishment, 100 acres of which are under improvement. One half of this farm is secured by deed of trust forever to the support of the Mission: while the avails of the other half are substantially applied to the same object. When purchased, the farm had upon it a small grist mill and tannery. We have since erected a saw mill, a log kitchen and dining room, a log dwelling house containing four rooms, and a framed building, 60 by about 20 feet, affording two rooms for teachers in each end, with a large school room in the centre on the ground floor, and over it a dormitory for boys. This latter building, though not completed, is to be ready to be occupied about the middle of June. The farm is partially stocked, and is being put in good order under the direction of a skilful young farmer[32] from the State of New York.... I feel encouraged to hope that, before my return from Valle Crucis in the ensuing Autumn all the essential parts of the establishment will be completed. We shall then, by God's blessing, be prepared to proceed slowly and quietly upon the following plan, increasing our operations as the Church shall give us means: 1. To extend the message and means of salvation for some thirty or forty miles in every direction, to a fearfully destitute population. 2. To give instruction in the rudiments of knowledge to poor children at and in the immediate neighborhood of the establishment, on any terms easy to their respective parents. 3. To receive into the establishment and educate a limited number of young persons, selected from the mountain region, on condition that, for a certain period after their education, they shall act, under our direction, as teachers and catechists in the most needy mountain settlements. 4. To train poor boys of pious dispositions and promising parts, with a view to the holy Ministry, or to subordinate stations in the Church. 5. To give Theological instruction to candidates for Holy Orders. 6. In connection with the above, and as a means thereto, to conduct a Classical and Agricultural School — receiving its support from the farm — where boys may be thoroughly prepared for College or for any of the employments or professions of life, at a moderate expense, under the best influence, and remote from the ordinary temptations either to idleness or to vice. 7. To prepare and keep up a model farm, as a guide to agriculture and an incentive to industry among the surrounding population. At the head of this establishment I propose, God willing, to pass a considerable portion of every Summer. For its constant and efficient maintenance, I have already engaged the services of four or five of the best furnished and most devoted of our young Clergymen, who, for the love of God and souls, are willing to enter upon these self-sacrificing labours for a bare support. These, by a judicious arrangement of their duties as Classical and Theological instructors, and by aid from the candidates for Orders in the Classical department, will be able, without hindrance, to carry forward the great objects of the Mission.[33]

The Classical and Theological School, the foundation of the mission, opened in 1845 "with thirty boys, the number increasing to fifty during the summer."[34] Earlier that year, the bishop had appointed the Rev. Henry Thurston, former rector of St. Bartholomew's Church, Pittsboro, to be the rector of the school and to oversee the construction. The bishop, after having spent much of the summer of 1845 on site and having expended much of his energies on the mission, made the following report to the 1846 Convention: "Our establishment in Valle Crucis is, under all the circumstances, advancing more prosperously than could well have been expected. Notwithstanding a Summer of extraordinary drought, subjecting us to much inconvenience from want of lumber, and a Winter of exampled severity, putting us to unusual expense in tending and protecting our stock, yet, under favor of a kind Providence, the interests of the establishment have not been materially affected. The family of some 40 souls has enjoyed remarkable health, except in a case or two of constitutional delicacy, where, on the whole, no injury has been sustained. The Classical School is in successful operation, and in short, to use the language of the Rector, the prospects of the establishment were never higher. [...] For the past year, an average number of about 28 pupils have been in the Classical and Agricultural school, nine of whom have received gratuitous board and instruction. The number of Candidates for Holy Orders, and of young men designed for the sacred offices, connected with the school, is now seven."[35]

However, when the bishop arrived the next summer (1846) he was immediately "distressed to find ... the self-denying Rector of the School, prostrated with inflammatory fever, contracted on his way from the Convention."[36] After a few days the Rev. Thurston seemed to be improving, so the bishop left him temporarily to officiate at a church consecration in Charlotte, but the rector's condition had not improved, and the bishop, while on his way back, at a place called New River, "received the sad and stunning intelligence of his death."[37] Bishop Ives stayed three months to provide some temporary leadership and help to the mission and especially the school. He soon appointed Jarvis Buxton, one of the candidates for Holy Orders, to replace Thurston as manager of the school.

The bishop's grand experiment was short-lived as, unfortunately for himself, the mission, and the diocese, in 1847 he quietly established (in conjunction with the mission) a monastic order called "The Society of the Holy Cross." He first asked Jarvis Buxton to be the "superior" in charge of the Order. But Buxton declined the offer and instead accepted a missionary post as rector of the fledging work at Rutherfordton, North Carolina.

Soon word of the bishop's monastic society and his "Catholic-leanings" began to surface. Finally, in 1852, the resultant turmoil came to the fore with the bishop requesting a six-month leave of absence. He and his family left for Europe in September, and then in December he sent his letter of resignation, along with news that he had taken vows to the Roman Catholic Church.[38] Without the bishop's leadership, and because of the controversy of the monastic affiliation, the Valle Crucis school and mission ceased soon after the bishop's resignation.

The Valle Crucis ministry is important to the Ravenscroft story for two reasons: first, this "ministry model," consisting of a classical school for general education of the neighborhood boys, a "training school" for training those seeking "Holy orders" to be ordained as Episcopal lay leaders and priests, and a "mission" from which outlying churches could be established and maintained, would be used two decades later as the model for the ministry at Ravenscroft; second, these events forged a connection with Jarvis Buxton, the person who would be a key player in the history of Ravenscroft.

Two

Reading, 'Riting and Rectors: *1850–1864*

Jarvis Barry Buxton Jr. was born on February 20, 1820, near Washington, North Carolina. Soon after his birth Buxton's father, the Rev. Jarvis Barry Buxton, Sr., moved his family to Fayetteville, North Carolina, to take up the position of rector of St. John's Church.

After Buxton's primary education, he was sent to school in Flushing, Long Island, where he studied under Doctor Muhlenberg, founder of St. Luke's Hospital in New York City. He was prepared for college and, returning to North Carolina for his collegiate course, entered the State University at Chapel Hill. He graduated in 1839 and then, proposing to enter the ministry, became a student at the General Theological Seminary in New York, where he graduated in 1842.[1] Shortly thereafter, he began his training for Holy Orders under the tutelage of Bishop Ives at the bishop's new diocesan school at Valle Crucis; following his appointment as head of the classical school, he was posted to Rutherfordton.

On the "Ninth Sunday after Trinity" (August 1, 1847) twenty-seven-year-old Jarvis Buxton, along with William West Skiles, was ordained a deacon in the Episcopal Church of North Carolina by Bishop Ives at the Valle Crucis mission. Deacon Buxton immediately moved to Rutherfordton to take up his new charge. Little did he know at the time that he was embarking on a lifetime ministry (over 50 years) to the people of western North Carolina.

In his report to the 1848 Convention less than a year later, Deacon Buxton reports that the small congregation of seven at the Rutherfordton church have begun meeting for public worship in various places such as the courthouse and female academy, but that they have already contracted to have a church building constructed.[2] And in the same report, he also tells the Convention that he has begun working in Asheville as well. He reports, "I have ministered at this place in connection with my charge at Rutherford[ton]. The friends of the Church have obtained the use of the large upper room in the new brick Academy, and fitted the room up handsomely with seats and a lectern."[3]

On January 6, 1848, Deacon Buxton married Anna Nash Cameron in Fayetteville. The young couple immediately returned to western North Carolina. Buxton was ordained as a "priest" by Bishop Ives on June 17, 1849, at Rutherfordton.

Buxton's presence in Asheville was upon the request of three women (one of them being Henrietta Kerr Patton) who were Episcopalians living in Asheville without a place of worship. Again the story weaves back to the Patton family. Henrietta was the second wife of James W. Patton. Interestingly, the Pattons were hard-core Presbyterians — in fact, James

W.'s father, James Sr., was even buried beneath the Presbyterian church in Asheville. But upon his marriage to Henrietta, James W. Patton became an Episcopalian and, being a wealthy entrepreneur, soon donated land for the fledging congregation of four communicants.

The congregation at Asheville, by the 1849 Convention, could report, "The plan of a Church Building, in the Pointed Style, has been ordered from Mr. Frank Wills, Architect, and finished, though not yet received."[4] Construction began on the new building in late 1849 or early 1850, and was completed just before the Convention of May 1851, as Buxton reported to the 1851 convention: "The building is now ready, on a site given by a member of the congregation: cost (which has been paid,) $1325. A Bell is on the way to us from Meneely's Foundry — weight 224 lbs. A handsome silver Service has been presented by one who desired to be unnamed. Also, we have received from a Lady of St. Michael's, Charleston, a Surplice, and a fair white linen cloth for Communion times."[5] Also, the church was completed enough to show in Sarony & Major's 1851 "View of Asheville."

Trinity Episcopal Church was built by Ephraim Clayton on land donated by Patton, just south of the Presbyterian Church and east of Joseph Osborne's mansion. Like its neighbors (Osborne's house, and the Presbyterian and Methodist churches), the new church faced east toward S. Main Street (now Biltmore Avenue). As the church in Asheville began to materialize, the Rev. Buxton decided to relocate from Rutherfordton to Asheville, although St. John's Church at Rutherfordton had 18 communicants compared to only 6 communicants at Trinity. He had a valid and godly motive, as he reported to the 1851 Convention: "I now

"View of Asheville N.C. and the Mountains from the Summer House." This lithograph by Sarony & Major (117 Fulton St, New York City), was originally published by James M. Edney, 1851. Ravenscroft sits prominently outside of town on the left-hand side of the photograph. Trinity Episcopal is shown just to the lower right of Ravenscroft (image # L721-XX from the North Carolina Collection, Pack Memorial Library, Asheville).

officiate in this Parish [Rutherfordton] one-third of the Sundays in the year, my residence being in Asheville, 41 miles distant. It is highly desirable for a Minister to be resident here, who might easily open other points for Missionary labor within this large County."[6] Having a heart for mission work, Buxton realized that Asheville, with its access to the Buncombe Turnpike and its well-stocked supply stores, would make an excellent base for mission work to the surrounding mountainous areas. In hindsight, we can see that Asheville did indeed become the hub of Episcopal mission work in the western Carolina region.

On December 3, 1851, the Rev. Buxton purchased nine acres near the southern limits of Asheville from Charles Moore,[7] upon which he built a small picturesque cottage for his growing family. The site was just southwest of the new Trinity Episcopal Church and bordered on Joseph Osborne's property to the north. Little did he know how strategic his home would be for the events of the following fifty years. The snug Gothic-style cottage faced south and perched atop a small hill, later called "Buxton Hill."

Meanwhile, Bishop Ives was preoccupied with his personal problems, which resulted the following year in his leave of absence and resignation in December of 1852. Following Bishop Ives' resignation the diocese promptly elected (in June 1853) the Rev. Thomas Atkinson, rector of St. Peter's Church, Baltimore, as his successor.

The Rev. Buxton could have settled for the easy life as the priest of a growing city parish, with his nine-acre farm within walking distance of his church, but instead he had the heart of a missionary and felt that he was called to spread the Gospel of Jesus Christ to the remote areas. So, early on he began reaching out to nearby areas from his base at Asheville, as well as preaching to his church body about the need for more workers to help reach their remote mountain neighbors with the Gospel of Jesus Christ.

The Rev. Buxton's heart for mission work and for the people of this region is revealed in his report to the 1853 Convention: "Beside my Parochial ministration in Asheville, I have visited during the year the villages of Marion, Waynesville, and Burnsville, where good congregations attended upon our Services. I have also, as Presbyter, visited Rutherfordton four times to administer the Holy Communion. [...] In this region of country, the cause of Christ — one with His Church — suffers sadly for the want of more Ministers. The harvest seems ripe enough, but the laborers are few. While we pray the Lord of the harvest to send

The Rev. Jarvis B. Buxton — portrait from *Biographical History of North Carolina from Colonial Times to the Present*, by Samuel A. Ashe, 1916 (North Carolina Collection, Pack Memorial Library, Asheville).

forth more laborers into His vineyard, and to stir up the spirit of the few who are already working therein, it cannot be forgotten that prayer implies the use of all proper means within our power, and until some approved system be devised for training up Missionaries in our midst, I am persuaded that nothing of moment, as compared with what might and ought to be done, will ever be achieved among the mass of the people in these Western parts."[8] The following year, the missionary priest ended his report with the repeated clarion call: "The Church, in these parts, loudly calls for more men for the work of the Ministry; and until this want be supplied, the few scattered laborers can do little more than bear their testimony in the wilderness."[9]

Bishop Atkinson had only been in office for about six months when the diocese had its Annual Convention in May of 1854. At the Convention, held at St. James' Church in Wilmington, the subject of the need for a diocesan boys' school came to the fore. The second resolution on the matter emphatically stated "That this Convention considers the want of such an institution for boys to be one of pressing and crying emergency."[10]

The Church had been diligent in establishing parochial schools, which were local schools that students who lived nearby could attend during the day while returning to their homes in the evening. However, in many rural areas of North Carolina the low numbers of students within proximity to a central school prohibited many children from attending any local parochial school. Therefore, while still recognizing and supporting the continued establishment of parochial schools, the 1854 Convention body further concluded, "But, as in some places Parochial Schools cannot be maintained, and to many families, from their isolated position, they would not be accessible if they could be, and as in the Diocese of North Carolina there is not a school for boys, inviting them from a distance, and making thorough provision for their education, in which they can be taught according to 'the form of sound words,' which we have received from our fathers, and which we consider ourselves bound to transmit in all its fullness to our children."[11] The Convention took action on this matter by appointing a committee of the bishop and three laymen to select a rector and location for the school. They further authorized the three laymen to raise and collect funds for this purpose.

The committee consisting of Bishop Atkinson, Henry Loudon, Thomas Hill of Pittsborough, and George Mordecai of Raleigh "determined to locate the School at Pittsborough, where some two thousand dollars in money and a handsome lot had been offered."[12] However, their search for a suitable rector for the school proved to be difficult, as all their proposed candidates for the position "on various grounds, declined to serve."[13] So the bishop took action and made a reluctant but ultimately momentous decision "to offer the post to the Rev. Jarvis Buxton of Asheville, whose services, likely to be of great value to the School, were at the same time greatly needed in his own Parish and the contiguous part of the Diocese."[14]

The Rev. Buxton, feeling duty-bound, quickly accepted his new post but, as the bishop reported, "When, however, he understood that no buildings belonged as yet to the School, he considered that this would be a formidable obstacle to its success, and his Parishioners showing the greatest reluctance to be separated from him, and making the Diocese some liberal offers in case the School were established at Asheville, he proposed to resign the post offered him at Pittsborough, and to endeavor to establish a Diocesan School at Asheville. Under the circumstances I thought it best, as did the other Trustees, to consent to this, and the rather because, remote as Asheville and Pittsborough are from each other, the success of a School at one place would not impede the prosperity of a similar institution at the other. Mr. Buxton, therefore, is now engaged, with my entire approbation, in seeking aid for the establishment of a Diocesan School at Asheville."[15]

The bishop's 1855 report mentioned "some liberal offers" from Buxton's "Parishioners." Though not enumerated, perhaps the bishop was referring to the Joseph Osborne property of 13-plus acres with its large brick mansion. As mentioned in the previous chapter, Osborne had sold his property to William Patton on January 14, 1854. Interestingly, and perhaps providentially, William Patton was one of four (including his cousin James W. Patton) lay delegates from Trinity Church to the 1854 Convention, where the matter of the establishment of a diocesan school was brought forth.

Although a resident of Charleston, William Patton owned a good deal of property in and around Asheville and spent much of the year as a local resident and communicant at Trinity Episcopal Church. Whether it was Patton's or the Rev. Buxton's idea to use the property for the new school, it was nonetheless a perfect property for such an institution, as it was large enough to develop into a "campus," was located near Trinity Church and the Rev. Buxton's residence, and included a substantial brick structure.

On July 11, 1855, William Patton officially deeded the property to the Rev. Buxton, the appointed representative of the diocese. Though deeded directly to Buxton, the provisions of the deed stated that the property was conveyed "*In Special* Trust ... that he [Buxton] will hold and appropriate the same as a site upon which to erect & keep up a classical and theological boarding school, and when he shall have been reimbursed all expenditures made by himself personally and indemnified against all personal liabilities incurred in its purchase and improvements, he shall convey the same to the Trustees of the Episcopal Church of the Diocese of North Carolina."[16] It was a generous offer, as Patton sold the property to Buxton for $4,000, substantially less than the $5,500 he had paid for the property just the year before.

Although all the needed funds were not yet raised, Buxton began immediately to make the necessary improvements to convert the residence into a school. He had the builder team of Clayton and Shackleford erect a three-story L-shaped addition to the west and north sides of Osborne's mansion.[17] The new addition included a large "common room," headmaster's study, and passage hall on the first floor and a large dormitory, staff bedroom and passage hall on the second floor. The west portion of the addition also included a daylight basement, which perhaps was used as the school kitchen. A frame house was also erected behind the main building as a tenant house.[18]

All improvements were completed by the Convention held in May of 1856, where the Rev. Buxton reported, "On account of the burning up of the materials which had been prepared for the New Building, and the severity of the Winter, which prevented the plastering, we have just been enabled to complete and occupy the Buildings intended for a Diocesan School. The whole property, as improved, is cheaply valued at $8000. There is an insurance of $3000 upon the brick building. The doors of the Institution are now open for the admission of pupils. As soon as the number of pupils warrant, no pains or expense will be spared to procure the services of an able and efficient Lay-teacher. Our aim is, not only to furnish facilities of study to older youth who may have the Ministry directly in view, but also to take and educate the boys of the Church, under the method of the Prayer Book, and in all Christian culture."[19]

In a letter[20] written after the 1856 Convention, the Rev. Buxton states that during the

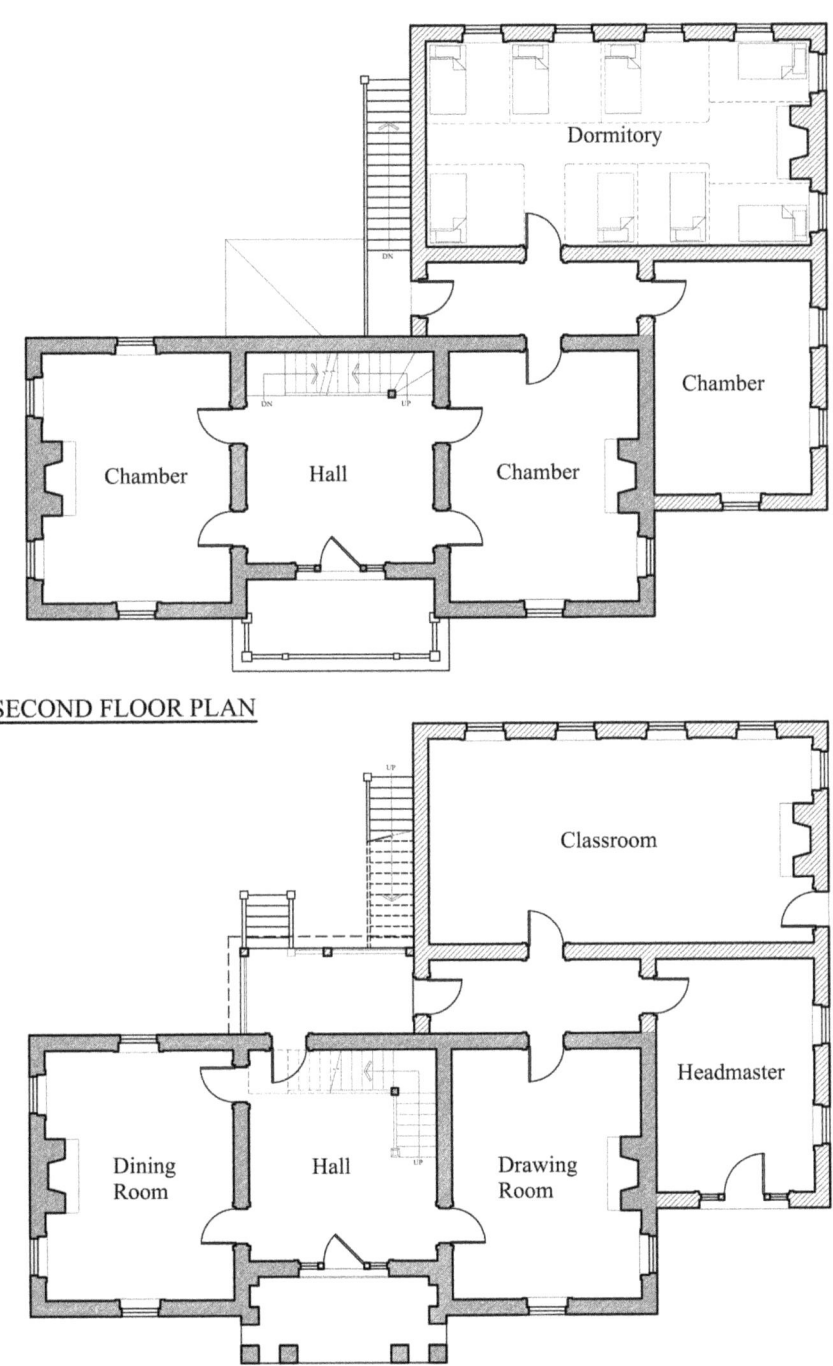

SECOND FLOOR PLAN

FIRST FLOOR PLAN

Ravenscroft Classical & Theological School

In 1855 the Rev. Buxton added a two-story addition (upper right) to the northwest corner of the Osborne mansion. The addition included a dormitory, classroom and headmaster's study to accommodate the new "Ravenscroft Classical and Theological School" (plans drawn by the author).

Convention when he had "the occasion to make a statement before the friends of the Church concerning the Church School at Asheville," the following subscriptions were made on the spot:

Mr. Thompson	$100.00
The Rev. Mr. Cheshire	$100.00
Josiah Collins, Esq.	$125.00
Mr. Wm. Eaton	$50.00
Vestry of Edenton	$200.00 or more
The Rev. Mr. Hines	$100.00
The Rev. Mr. Burison	$100.00
The Rev. Mr. Buxton	$100.00

Buxton further reported that the total costs for the purchase of the property and its retrofitting for use as a school came to $6,900, but that most of the costs (except for $1,500 remaining) had already been paid through small donations, which, as he said, had been "laboriously collected by myself" on a recent two-month tour.

Bishop Atkinson was pleased with not only the progress of the building of the new school but also his choice of headmaster, Jarvis Buxton. In his address to the 1856 Convention, the bishop praised Buxton and spoke of his endorsement for the school:

> While speaking of Asheville and Mr. Buxton, I must take the opportunity of earnestly recommending to the members of the Church throughout the Diocese, to do what they can to promote the interests of the school he has recently established there. He has in a self sacrificing spirit, added this new and onerous class of duties to his previous parochial engagements, not for profit, nor any personal end, but to advance the cause of sound learning and true religion generally in the Diocese, and especially in that Western section of it, where these high interests especially need aid and furtherance. He is esteemed by those who best know him, to be extremely well-fitted for the headship of such an Institution, and the locality chosen for it is one of the most healthy and beautiful in our entire country. Assured as I am that the Church must do her part in the great work of Christian education, or that she will be derelict in duty and cursed with barrenness, I hail with pleasure every such effort as this, and earnestly hope that there will very soon be another of the same character set on foot in a more central part of the Diocese.[21]

And so the Rev. Buxton, along with his duties as rector of Trinity Church and roving missionary to the surrounding regions, became the first headmaster of the new "Ravenscroft School."[22]

During the ensuing year, the Rev. Buxton continued his "onerous class of duties," with the added responsibility of trying to raise the funds to pay off the indebtedness incurred in opening the new school. He gave a full report to the Convention in 1857:

> I have endeavored during the past year to pay off entirely the liabilities of the Church School at this place, by the help of contributions from abroad. But my efforts thus far have only been partially successful. Since the needed improvements made during the past year, consisting mainly of tenant's house, with cistern and well, nothing farther seems wanted on the premises for the convenience and uses of the purposes to which they were designed.
>
> The total liabilities, therefore, up to date, are as follows:
>
> | | |
> |---|---|
> | $1009 00 | balance due on improvements. |
> | 800 00 | note given for Lot, on interest. |
> | 82 50 | interest on above note, and cost of insurance. |
> | $1891 50 | |

To meet this sum, in part, the Rector of Edenton and his Assistant, they assure me, still hold their Parish bound for the $200 pledged at the last Convention, notwithstanding their generous contribution during the year of $503. 63, being their refunded subscriptions to an Episcopal Residence at Raleigh. There was also pledged another hundred dollars, payable at this Convention. To pay the remaining $1591.50, we look to the liberality of friends, whenever it may suit their convenience to help us; but I shall make no farther direct appeals for aid after this statement. All contributions received will be faithfully appropriated as heretofore. Upon the payment of the above indebtedness the Diocese will become possessed of property, available, if not immediately, yet in no long time, and to a remarkable degree, for Educational and Missionary purposes.[23]

The "Ravenscroft Classical and Theological School" officially opened its doors in 1856. The school, because of its dual purpose as a classical and theological school, admitted two classes of boys. Younger boys, ages 15–18, were admitted as classical scholars and were taught the basic subjects of reading, writing and arithmetic, as well as the rudimentary doctrines of the Church. Older boys, who usually were in their early to mid-twenties, were admitted with the aim of pursuing Holy Orders.

One of the school's first students was Girard William Phelps, who in 1856, at the age of twenty-four, enrolled as a potential candidate for Holy Orders. If not for Phelps, who kept a detailed diary/journal[24] during his years (1856–1859) as a student at Ravenscroft, we would have very little record of the early years of the school. But as it is, Phelps' recordings give us a good insight into what life was like as a student at Ravenscroft, and they also reveal some of the social structures surrounding the school and the community at the time.

Girard William Phelps was born to Jeremiah and Deborah Fortune Phelps on July 14, 1832, in Washington County, North Carolina. Girard was 17 years of age when, in 1849, his father passed away, leaving him as the only surviving male in the small family of four (mother, two sisters and Girard). In the 1850 census, Girard, at the age of 18, was listed as a "laborer," but fortunately their neighbor and friend, Josiah Collins, III, soon came to the aid of the struggling family. Collins was a prominent and wealthy planter who owned "Somerset Place" at Lake Phelps near Creswell, in Washington County, North Carolina. "Somerset Place," which was (and still is) located just south of the Albemarle Sound, was one of the largest plantations in the South, and was home to over three hundred slaves.

Josiah Collins was a prominent leader of both St. David's, Creswell, North Carolina and St. Luke's Episcopal Church,[25] Washington County (near Roper), as well as an active leader in the Episcopal Diocese of North Carolina. Collins was a delegate to the 1855 and 1856 Conventions, where the Rev. Jarvis Buxton presented his reports on the new diocesan school that was being established in Asheville. In fact, Collins was one of a handful of delegates who gave an "on the spot" donation toward the establishment of the school following the Rev. Buxton's appeal in 1856. Sometime after his return home from the Convention in 1856, Collins decided to sponsor Girard Phelps as a student at the new school. Whether Phelps appealed to Collins for help or whether Josiah Collins singled him out for aid is something we may never know. However, since Phelps was already in his twenties, more than likely he had expressed an interest in pursuing the ministry. Nonetheless, Josiah Collins decided to become Girard's benefactor, sponsor, and, ultimately, fatherly advisor.

Girard Phelps arrived in Asheville in the summer of 1856. Since he received his journal as a Christmas present in December of 1856, after his first year at Ravenscroft, Phelps recorded his first year's experiences in a summarial essay titled "The First Twelve months in Asheville" near the beginning of his journal. "After traveling through a broad expanse of country, he came to A.[sheville]," wrote Girard in the third person, "where he met a very kind reception from Mrs. Ship and Mrs. Buxton."[26] Mrs. Buxton, who acted as matron for the school, was the wife of the headmaster, the Rev. Jarvis Buxton. "Mrs. Ship" was Mrs. Buxton's sister, Catherine LaFayette Cameron Shipp, who was married to Judge William Marcus Shipp and lived in nearby Hendersonville. The ironic reality of having an Episcopal school in western North Carolina in the 1850s was that there were very few Episcopal churches in the western half of the state, and so most of the students came from families in the eastern part of the state. Girard's "broad expanse of country" was just that, as Asheville was over three hundred and fifty miles from his home in Washington, North Carolina — a long, eight-day[27] journey by horse and buggy or stagecoach.

The Rev. and Mrs. Buxton, along with their six children, lived at Ravenscroft with the students. From Girard's descriptions, it seems that the Buxtons occupied the second- and third-floor bedrooms in the front part of the school/house, and then shared the first-floor parlor and dining room with the students (or at least the older students). The first-floor north addition room, with its Greek revival entry, was no doubt the headmaster's study and reception room leading into the rear hall, which connected to the main house and the large "schoolroom" addition to the rear of the house. The large room on the second floor above the schoolroom and the smaller second-floor room above the headmaster's study no doubt functioned as dormitory rooms for the students. Girard described his room as "very large and poorly furnished, the only furniture was several couches, a small table and mirror."[28] The "couches" may have been small beds. Phelps described the dormitory rooms and adjacent passage hall as being accessed by "steps that went down upon the outside."

The older students who were preparing for, or had hopes of pursuing, Holy Orders were tutored by the Rev. Buxton and taught separately from the younger boys. Girard often mentions various subjects that he had to study, including algebra, Greek, Latin, geometry and philosophy. "Up at four and shortly afterward at my Latin and then follow all my lessons in succession,"[29] Girard entered into his journal on July 27, 1857. Some time later he wrote, "Study on with the same untiring perseverance, rising early that I may be able to pursue my duties. One day my Latin is hard, the next my Greek, another my geometry and so it changes successively through the week, by that means I am able to get all my lessons."[30] He also often refers to his "recitations," which he would give to the Rev. Buxton after studying his lessons on a specific subject.

Surviving correspondence between Josiah Collins and the Rev. Buxton shows that Girard's tuition at Ravenscroft was $120 for a six-month term, paid in advance before each term. Indications are that this included room and board as well. Apparently the students' food came from their garden. Whether it was a communal garden, or whether each student had his own, we don't know, but Girard often recorded such entries as this: "Writing at half past four. Have great deal to do today, must write mother, dig my potatoes, sow my turnips and many other things too tedious to mention."[31]

Social interaction with the community was encouraged for the students, especially for the older students who were pursuing the ministry. "I am glad to see that you have begun to visit some of the families at Asheville, under the guidance of Mr. Buxton," wrote Josiah Collins to his protégé Girard, "this may be made a great source of improvement to you, for a Clergyman to be truly useful [he] should know something of men as well as books."[32]

The list of families from whom Girard received frequent and varied invitations included many of Asheville's most prominent citizens: Aston, Ballard, Chapman, Corpening, Chunn, Hildebrand, Johnston, Patton, Roberts and Shackleford, and Woodfin. "That evening by an invitation from Mrs. Lester [Leicester] Chapman, I took tea with her," records Girard one autumn day, "spent the evening very pleasantly. There were some ladies there. The two young Miss Murdocks and Miss Car where [sic] my favorites however."[33] On a later occasion he recorded, "In the evening I went to Chapmans, spent about an hour there conversing on various topics then returned home."[34]

James W. Patton, who was a member of one of Asheville's earliest and most prominent families, and one of the founders of Trinity Church, would often invite the boys to his home for dinner and conversation. "I am going to Mr. Pattons tonight and I think that I shall have a pleasant time,"[35] wrote Girard after a busy week of study and prayer. James Patton, whose family had been in the mercantile and hotel business for many years, occasionally used his experience to encourage the students. Girard recorded that one evening during a social visit with the Pattons, "Mr. James Patton gave me a sum which is as follows: 'What will be the cost of eighteen yards of callica at eighteen per yard?' I readily solved the question."[36]

Besides Girard Phelps, we only have a handful of names of some of the other students at Ravenscroft during those early days. Girard often mentioned the names of other students, but usually only by their last names, such as Leonard, Forbes, Douglass, Mott and Wm. Gordon. However, he did often mention his friend and fellow student, Maurice Vaughan. Maurice Hamilton Vaughan, who was from Elizabeth City (near Girard's home), was four years older than Girard, and so he finished his schooling earlier than Girard and was ordained a deacon in 1859, while Girard was still a student at Ravenscroft. Both Vaughan and Phelps later served as Confederate Army chaplains during the Civil War. Vaughan served with the 3rd North Carolina Regiment, and Girard served with the 17th.[37]

We have no names of any of the younger students, as Girard only occasionally mentions their presence at the school, and when he does he always refers to them en masse as "the boys." "Mr. B. had the boys up to night for certain misdemeanors, but they are very angry," wrote Girard one Friday evening, "but they can't help themselves."[38] In December of 1857, Girard recorded the events of the last day of the term. From his entry, we get a good sense of the excitement that "the boys" experienced just before Christmas break:

> This is the last school day of this year, and the boys are running and playing and talking of many fine things which they will have when they reach their several homes. They appear to be very glad that the time has at last come round that they can rest from study and freed from the irksome task of lessons. It is amusing to see them hurrying [sic] their books and clothes into their trunks, and running up and down stairs, one minute in the school room the next up stairs or at the wood pile laughing and shouting and talking of what they are going to do when they reach home.[39]

But the next morning, the stagecoach arrived earlier than anyone anticipated, and it was left up to Girard to help the boys on their way. Girard chronicled their sudden departure:

> The stage came for the boys about 3 o'clock. They had not long been in bed and only just fallen to sleep. I heard the stage and roused them from their quiet slumbers — they quickly dressed and rushed from the room leaving [me] quite alone. I hastened down to bid them a pleasant trip, and hope them a safe return. They being gone I returned to the room which appeared lonely

indeed not even the wind, which at other times made the shutters to rattle moved around the lonely room, nor was the stillness broken by the chirping of a single cricket. I soon dropped to sleep amid this silent place and slep[t] soundly for sometime and when I woke it was time [to] rise up for [day] had come and the darkness had fled.[40]

When school resumed, after the Christmas break, on January 15, 1858, apparently only a few of "the boys" returned. Girard simply noted, "The school began with three boys."[41]

But "boys will be boys," as they say. The following Christmas, a year later, the scene was not so joyous. Girard recorded the disappointing affair:

> At the end of the session, Mr. [Nicholas] Woodfin gave a party to Mr. Buxton's students. They hailed invitations with much pleasure, not as they considered the party of much importance, but as it was the conclusion of the session. Only three of us went to the party, the others spent the evening somewheres in town as they liked best. For they were more inclined to their own way than to that of another person. Dissipation was their delight. They had not been absent [home for break] when Mr. Buxton heard about their long concealed evil habits. He wrote two or three letters to them in consequence of the matter and telling them that they could not return to his school.[42]

During those first few years of the Ravenscroft School, the Rev. Buxton was the sole headmaster and instructor. But he was constantly looking for a replacement headmaster, so that he could devote more time to his missionary efforts. In the spring of 1858, Buxton reported to the Convention, "I have not been able this year, from being disappointed in procuring a proper Assistant Teacher, to give that attention to calls outside of the Parish of Asheville, which I desire to do."[43] Remaining ever hopeful, Buxton further reported that "arrangements doubtless will be made in regard to Ravenscroft School, the next session, which will leave me free and ready for Missionary calls."[44] However, no replacement headmaster was found for "the next session," and the Rev. Buxton remained as the school's headmaster and instructor until 1861.

Two years after the school opened, the Rev. Buxton informed the delegates of the 1858 Convention that "the Institution is not yet out of debt — but the debt is due to those who will extend all required indulgence."[45] He appealed to the delegation for the necessary funds to pay off the indebtedness. However, I can't find any further report as to whether the delegates responded to his appeal, and in fact, no further published reports of any kind pertaining to the school were submitted for the subsequent two years (1859 and 1860).

Unfortunately for the Ravenscroft School, it had only been in operation for a few years when the national civil unrest exploded into the Civil War. The year 1861 was a momentous year for the school, the church, and the state. Following on the heels of Virginia, North Carolina joined its fellow Southern states in seceding from the Union on May 20, 1861. The Episcopal Church of North Carolina's Annual Convention had been scheduled for May 10, to be held in the coastal town of New Bern. However, Bishop Atkinson, using his granted authority, promptly moved the Convention to be held in July at Morganton, on the western side of the state, well away from the coast, which was the center of the emerging conflict.

It is not surprising that the bishop's address to the 1861 Convention dealt mostly with the predicament of the Episcopal churches in the seceded states, and in particular the North Carolina Diocese. The bishop recognized that North Carolina was now a "Confederate State" and under new civil authority, and he asked for prayers for the new leaders. However, the bishop argued that the change in civil authority certainly brought about a change in church authority, but in what form? He advised, "It is clearly wise, and even necessary, that the Protestant Episcopal Church in the United States shall be greatly modified; perhaps it may be necessary that it should cease to exist as one Church."[46] He went on to exhort the Convention that the one thing that was not advisable was that each state diocese should remain independent of each other. For as the bishop warned, "Its results must be to deprive our Bishops and Delegates of their rights to seats in the General Convention, in the Board of Missions, and in the Board of Trustees of the General Seminary [of the Protestant Episcopal Church in the United States]."[47] The bishop went on to make the compelling argument that though a modification in the church might be necessary, a complete dissolution of and from the Protestant Episcopal Church of the United States was not necessary or right. And though the "Confederate States of America" was now considered a "foreign country" to the United States of America, the Protestant Episcopal Church in the United States should not confine its authority by political bounds. He further stated, "And if she may rightfully have, as she actually has, Bishops and other Ministers and congregations out of the United States, it is difficult to conceive why they might not be arranged in the form of Dioceses, if that form should be more convenient than the present one, as indeed it must be if our Missions shall go on to prosper."[48]

The bishop concluded his argument as follows: "While, then, I see insuperable objections to the acceptance of the theory that the secession of the State does, without any act of the Church, produce a disruption of the Church, I see no plausible arguments to incline me to accept it. At the same time some very important changes are necessary in our relations with the Northern Dioceses, and it may be best to form an entirely new Ecclesiastical system."[49] He then urged the Convention to pray for, and to elect delegates to attend, the upcoming meeting of "the Bishops and Delegates of all the Dioceses within the seceded States."[50] That meeting was indeed held at Columbia, South Carolina, in November of 1861, with Bishop Atkinson and a full delegation from North Carolina attending. At that meeting a constitution forming the Protestant Episcopal Church in the Confederate States of America was adopted. The Diocese of North Carolina ratified the constitution in May of 1862 and thus joined the new church.

The 1861 Convention journal reveals that an additional event occurred that year which impacted the Ravenscroft School on a local level: the Rev. Buxton, who had held the headmastership since the school's opening in 1856 along with his missionary and pastoral duties, was encouraged by the appointment of the Rev. Lucien Holmes as the new headmaster of the school.

The school struggled on for the next few years, but finally had to close its doors in 1864. Though there is no published reason given for the closing of the school, sources reveal that, along with the lack of men and boys, who were away fighting as soldiers, the devastated Southern economy made it difficult, if not impossible, to find families who could afford to pay for schooling. Also, the state of affairs in this region made it unsafe for people to be away from the security of their homes as, although only one minor battle was fought in this region, the mountains of western North Carolina were notorious for hiding numerous bands of Yankee "marauders" who used the turmoil of the war to mask their criminal acts of violence against unsuspecting civilians. One such recorded account is that of Capt. Thomas Walton Patton, son of James W. Patton, regarding an incident that occurred upon his return home from the war. After spending the night at Alexander Robertson's house, "Struan," in

Fletcher, North Carolina, Patton set out for Asheville the next morning. He recounts, "At daylight the next morning, after a breakfast of corn bread and milk, all that this once wealthy gentleman had to offer, he was speeded on his way, Mr. Robertson walking some distance with him to guide him through the woods to escape the lawless bands of pillagers from the Federal army, which were infesting the roads. When Mr. Robertson returned it was to see lying on the road side the dead body of his son-in-law, Capt. Allen, a gallant soldier, but now surrendered and paroled. He had been shot down without provocation, by the very men from whom Capt. Patton had escaped by Mr. Robertson's thoughtful care."[51]

We are fortunate to have Girard Phelps's diaries that give us a glimpse into the workings of the Ravenscroft Classical and Theological School, as there are very few remaining published records of that phase of the Ravenscroft School. The handsome addition to Joseph Osborne's house and Phelps' diary is all that remains of that period. The closing of the Ravenscroft Classical and Theological School in 1864 signaled an impending change in the institution.

Three

Post-War: Postulants and Priests: *1865–1883*

The Civil War and its post-war era of "reconstruction" would bring about a reorganization of the Ravenscroft institution to meet the needs of a "New South." But the winds of change for Ravenscroft School were adrift even before its closing in 1864.

The 1863 Convention of the Protestant Episcopal Church of North Carolina was the first to be held as a body of the newly formed Protestant Episcopal Church in the Confederate States of America. Consequently, we see that the word "Convention" was changed to "Council" and that instead of being the "Forty-Seventh Annual Convention," it was called the "First Annual Council." More important to our story, however, is Bishop Atkinson's address to the council, in which he implores the church body to recognize "the necessity of making provision for the training of young men for the Ministry."[1] He further explains the current situation: "A large part of our present body of Clergy came to us originally from the North, and we have none more useful, more respected, and whom we could less afford to lose than these. But that supply must now be expected to cease. Clergymen from a country now hostile to us will not desire to come to us, nor would they be cordially received should they come. We at the South, then, must train our own Clergy. But for this we need Theological Schools."[2]

Along with telling the church body of the need for a Southern Episcopal seminary to replace the General Seminary in New York as the place of training for new clergy, the bishop immediately presents his solution to the dilemma: "And we have already a great advantage in its establishment, in possessing a beautiful and extensive building with ten or twelve acres of land in the town of Asheville, in one of the most healthy and delightful regions of country on this continent, which property had been bestowed on the Diocese by contributions solicited thereto mainly by the Rev. Mr. Buxton, who had long cherished the earnest desire to establish in that part of the State a Diocesan School of Classical and Theological learning. The sum of $2800 or $2900 was, however, still due on this property, and I was about making an effort to raise it, and anxiously meditating on the whole subject, when unexpectedly, and I believe Providentially, I received a letter from Dr. Cheshire, informing me that Mrs. Martha Clark, of Trinity Church, Scotland Neck, a devout and liberal Christian lady, had placed in his hands $2000 for religious education in this Diocese. Through him, I suggested this object to her, which she entirely approved, and I have thereby had it in my power to release the property at Asheville to a great extent from debt, and as soon as means are provided for sustaining such a School, it can be immediately set in motion."[3]

As usual the bishop's address was referred to the "Committee on the State of the Church," but the part of the address concerning the matter of a theological school was specifically referred to a sub-committee of five members appointed by the chairman. The sub-committee's final resolutions to the council confirmed the need for such a school, implored the rectors to bring it to the attention of their respective congregations, and authorized the bishop "to adopt such measures as he may deem most expedient for accomplishing the said object, And among them the appointment of an agent for soliciting contributions from the members of the Church in this Diocese."[4]

The months following the 1863 Council were ones of mere survival for the Episcopal Church in North Carolina. Thus, the matter of the establishment of a theological seminary was barely mentioned at the 1864 Council, and in fact the bishop reported that because of the civil unrest and state of the economy, he "had not thought it best to urge contributions to this object."[5] He did, however, assign the Rev. Watson to circulate among the parishes to deliver sermons on the subject, with the aim of soliciting funds for its establishment. Surprisingly, for the state of affairs, the bishop was able to report that five thousand dollars had been raised for the proposed seminary. By the latter years of the Civil War the subject of a theological college became of little importance and, in fact, not only was there no mention of it at the 1865 Council, but there was not even any parochial report that year from the Rev. Buxton, Trinity Church or Ravenscroft.

However, in 1866, just one year after the ending of hostilities and the reunification of the Southern Episcopal Churches with the Protestant Episcopal Church in the United States, the subject of a theological school at Asheville was again presented at the Annual Convention. In fact, following a lengthy report on the state of the diocesan missions, the Rev. Jarvis Buxton, part of the three-member committee, presented the following motion: "Whereas, It is highly important for the interests of the Church in this Diocese, at this time in particular, that preparation be making, in order to use with effect and without delay, the Church property at Asheville for the purposes of a Theological Seminary, in connection with an Associated Mission; therefore. Resolved, That an agent be sent abroad by the Standing Committee, in the absence of the Bishop, to solicit funds for carrying these purposes into effect, with the aid, if possible, of the General Domestic Committee, and that he be commended by this Convention to the Christian attentions and charities of the members and Ministers of this Church."[6] the Rev. Buxton was duly appointed by the Convention to be their agent to solicit funds for the Theological School and Associated Mission (the same school that was originally presented by Bishop Atkinson at the 1863 Council).

The call for Ravenscroft to be reorganized as an "associate mission" and "Theological School" was reminiscent of the diocese's previous attempts at Valle Crucis twenty years earlier. For those readers unfamiliar with Episcopalian terminology, an "Associate Mission" is the name of a house of clergy and/or laity living under a common rule but with no formal vows, subject to Episcopal oversight for evangelization and for educational and charitable enterprises.[7]

In 1863, Bishop Atkinson had advocated for a theological school in the South (specifically to be located at Asheville) to replace the General Seminary in the North, which, because of the war, was inaccessible to the Southern dioceses. However, after the war and the return to peace, the bishop still felt the urgent need for Southern theological schools. In particular, he advocated for a school at Asheville that would be of lower academic quality in order to train local men from the surrounding mountain regions to bring the Gospel of Jesus Christ to their fellow mountain people.

The Rev. Jarvis Buxton was very excited about the prospect of opening an associate mission. He had been doing missionary work in the area for over a decade and a half, and knew that the need for additional laborers was great. On the strength of the success of the newly established mission at Beaverdam, north of Asheville, the Rev. Buxton, in his report to the 1867 Convention, revealed his determination to make the proposed associate mission a reality:

> This Mission affords a specimen of what could be done within this vicinity, and throughout Buncombe County and adjoining Counties, by the aid of an Associated Mission at this point. The time has come for enlargement, or else the work of the Gospel in the Church must continue to languish on within old narrow parochial limits. Laborers must be had to evangelize the people in the country, as well as in towns and villages, by regular, systematic, combined work. This seems now to be the pressing want of the Church, with fields white for harvesting spreading out so broadly and invitingly all around her. Firmly persuaded of the necessity of meeting this want by special effort, I have devoted myself, according to a plan of mine own, to carrying out the errand, imposed upon me by the Standing Committee under resolution of the last Convention, of collecting funds abroad for setting in immediate operation our Missionary College at Asheville: not forgetting, but rather strengthened and sustained by the thought, that issues are from God, who yet requireth the use of reasonable means, as well as constant prayer, in acknowledgment of His all disposing sovereignty.[8]

The Ravenscroft building, now with its dual status as theological school and associate mission, needed some necessary improvements in 1868 for it to house not only a school, boarding students, and teaching staff but also numerous adult male missionaries. Also in 1868, the Rev. Buxton reported that he had raised $948.80 as an agent to solicit funds for Ravenscroft and that, with those funds, he had purchased the "Leicester High School Building" with five acres for $350, which was the balance due on the building, but, as Buxton reported, "the building and land are worth $1,500."[9] There is no further mention of this purchase after this date, and because he mentioned it in the report of funds that he had solicited, perhaps he planned to use this property as an investment to resell in order to raise additional funds for Ravenscroft.

In 1868 the Rev. Lucien Holmes, who had formerly been principal of the Ravenscroft Classical & Theological School until its closure in 1864, was hired to assist with the teaching at the newly formed theological/training school. Within the year a director was found for the new Ravenscroft Associate Mission and Theological School. The Rev. George T. Wilmer was hired as its first head, coming from Alabama, where he had been rector at Christ Church in Mobile. His father and half-brother were also Episcopal ministers. Bishop Atkinson felt that the Rev. Wilmer was highly qualified for this new and important position, as the bishop elaborated to the 1869 Convention: "It is a very important one. The mountain region of this State with a large population is as truly missionary ground as any in the United States. The people deeply need religious instruction and moral training. They deeply need consequently, the Gospel, the Church and the Ministry. That Ministry must be supplied from themselves if the body of the people is ever to be reached, and we must consequently be prepared to instruct candidates for orders, coming from among this very people."[10]

Wilmer also gave a report to the 1869 Convention, in which he told his audience that "one student has commenced the study of Divinity"[11] since he began his duties as head of

This published photo from the 1870s shows the Ravenscroft School after it had been reorganized as the Ravenscroft Associate Mission and Training School. Notice the Greek-revival side-lighted entrance door on the 1855 addition (on right side of photo). This is the only known photograph that shows this additional entrance, which may have served as the students' entrance. The original entrance to the mansion (under the portico on the left), was most likely retained as an entrance to the residential section of the school. This photograph was published as a stereoview by Taylor & Jones, "Land of the Sky, Beauties of WNC & NE GA, Class D, #80," labeled "Ravenscroft Episcopal Seminary" (image #B287-5 from the North Carolina Collection, Pack Memorial Library, Asheville).

the theological school. Further in his report, he reminded them that his duties included much more than just heading up the theological school, and that "it is designed to connect a Parish School with the Seminary. The proposed missionary operations will be outside the limits of Asheville. The prospect is encouraging. Already the efficient zeal of the Rev. Mr. Buxton and his congregation have established several missionary stations hereafter to be included in this mission."[12]

Wilmer's report reveals an inherent difficulty (unacknowledged by Wilmer) that would plague all who would hold his position in the future. That is, the expectation that one man could be the administrator and instructor of a theological school while simultaneously directing an associate mission as a missionary in charge of numerous mission stations in outlying areas to which he would have to travel for days on end. And yet people also expected Wilmer to run a parochial school on top of everything else. Fortunately for Wilmer (and subsequent directors), the idea of a parochial school soon fell by the wayside as the monumentality of the position unfolded over the next few years.

However, Wilmer did not stay long enough to feel the burden of the position, as he resigned by the end of 1869 to accept a professorship at William and Mary College in Williamsburg, Virginia. He was quick to accept the position, no doubt because he and his father had both previously been rectors at Bruton Parish Church and he consequently had strong family ties to that region.

Wilmer's vacancy was filled by the Rev. Francis J. Murdoch, but not until June of 1870. Murdoch, a local man who had been trained by the Rev. Buxton, had been a recent candidate for Holy Orders and had just been ordained as a priest at the 1870 Convention in May. Murdoch was born and raised in Asheville[13] and had attended Col. Stephen Lee's military academy prior to attending the South Carolina Military Academy at Columbia and Charleston. After the Civil War, he was called by God to the ministry and commenced his theological training under the tutelage of the Rev. Buxton in 1868. By 1870 he was serving as the deacon/pastor at St. John's Episcopal Church in Gaston County, North Carolina, when he was asked to be the new head of Ravenscroft.[14]

Interestingly, the Rev. Murdoch's report to the 1871 Convention was titled "Asheville Mission," and in it he gave a report of the services held at his various mission stations,[15] but there was no mention of the theological school. In fact, in the "List of Clergy" at the start of the journal, the Rev. Murdoch's description merely said, "Missionary in Buncombe, Haywood and Rutherford Counties. P. O., Asheville."

The only mention of the theological school at the 1871 Convention is in the bishop's report, where he reports on his fund-raising efforts for the school:

> During the year I have received from various friends in the City of Baltimore, and mainly from the congregation of Grace Church, or persons formerly connected with it, contributions toward the maintenance of the school and associated mission at Asheville. During the year 1868 I had received for the same object, from some of the liberal members of the Church in the City of New York, contributed through the Rev. D. Everhart, the sum of $750, and this winter I have received from I. H. Swift, Esq., ten shares of the stock of the Iron Mountain R. R. Company, to be used for the same object, in addition to ten shares which he had previously given me in aid of the Episcopal Fund of this Diocese. From the donations thus made I have been enabled to assist in the training of several young men for the ministry, and the maintenance of the Asheville Mission; and have also done something towards the beginning of the endowment of the Theological School, having invested for that purpose $750, and having also the ten shares of stock to which I have referred contributed for the same purpose. The object is one of such paramount importance in its influence upon the diffusion of Christian truth, in a very large and very neglected part of this Diocese, that I cannot but earnestly invoke the aid and cooperation of all who love Christ and His Church, whether living in the Diocese or out of it, in establishing on a permanent basis a school in which young men shall be taught, so that they may authoritatively teach others, the very truth of God as this Church has received the same.[16]

Obviously, the theological school was still in a fledgling state in 1871. The Rev. Murdoch's service at Ravenscroft was short-lived, as he became ill late in 1871 and by 1872 was "compelled to forsake his missionary labors in Buncombe and the adjoining Counties."[17] An interesting side note to the story of the Ravenscroft Associate Mission and Training School is that after the Rev. Murdoch regained his strength, he was sent to Salisbury, North Carolina, to be the rector of St. Luke's Episcopal Church. Murdoch, who had been trained at Ravenscroft, soon began to replicate in Rowan County the mission work that he had learned and performed at Ravenscroft. Not only did the Rev. Murdoch remain at St. Luke's for 37 years, but he was also responsible for training countless new ministers and founding a number of mission churches, as well as being instrumental in establishing local textile mills, which became the backbone of North Carolina's industry for the subsequent century.[18]

The work at Ravenscroft was only momentarily interrupted by Murdoch's departure, as it was reported that "the Rev. Dr. D. H. Buel, D. D. will take his place at Asheville, together with the care of the Training School."[19] The speed with which Murdoch's vacancy was filled was probably due to the fact that Dr. Buel was the son-in-law of Bishop Atkinson.

David Hillhouse Buel was born in Troy, New York, on May 26, 1817. He was educated at Bristol College, Bristol, Pennsylvania, prior to attending the General Theological Seminary, graduating in 1842. The Rev. D. Hillhouse Buel was ordained as a priest on September 24, 1843, at St. Paul's Church, Baltimore, by Bishop Whittingham, having been presented as a candidate for the priesthood by the Rev. Theodore B. Lyman (then rector of St. John's Church, Hagerstown, Maryland). He first served as a pastor and church planter for many years at churches at Westminster, Sykesville, and Cumberland in Maryland.

In 1849, while serving as rector of Emmanuel Episcopal Church in Cumberland, he convinced its congregation to build a new church. The church at first had obtained a design from architect Frank Wills of the New York Ecclesiological Society, but later decided to hire noted Philadelphia architect John Notman to design a larger church. Notman's design was accepted and the cornerstone laid on Ascension Day, May 17, 1849.[20] An interesting side note is that Notman was also the originator of the design of Ravenscroft, and Frank Wills was the designer of Trinity Episcopal Church, in the parish that maintained Ravenscroft, and all three buildings were built in the late 1840s.

Dr. Buel also displayed profound bravery as the rector at Emmanuel Church when he hired Samuel Denson, a runaway slave, as the church janitor and then aided him in helping countless slaves escape through the Underground Railroad. The runaways would follow the canal to Cumberland and, while under the cover of the high brush, wait for a signal from the church. Samuel Denson, a free black who had escaped to Maryland from Mississippi, rang the church bell twice when the coast was clear. The runaways would come up the hill to a gate that led to a maze of tunnels under the church. After resting and receiving food and instructions, the runaways were taken through the tunnels that exited to the other side of the rectory, which was across the road, from which point it was only a five-mile walk to the Mason–Dixon Line and freedom.[21]

Buel later served as the priest at St. Paul's, Burlington, Vermont, and finally at Christ Church, Cooperstown, New York, prior to his appointment to Ravenscroft in August of 1872. At age 55, he seemed perhaps rather old to begin a new position that would require much difficult travel to remote mountain stations. Dr. Buel, however, was the perfect man for the job, as he had much experience both as a parish priest and as a church planter, having previously founded and maintained numerous mission churches. Also, he knew much grief and sorrow in his life, having only one of his four children survive into adulthood. The loss of his third child (age 16) occurred in 1876, only four years after moving to Asheville. Through these life experiences, he had to rely on God's strength, which gave him the necessary stamina to endure hardships. Not only was this stamina necessary for the rigorous mission work he would have to undertake, but his life experiences were also good examples of God's faithfulness that could be passed along to the young men he would be training for the ministry. To his credit, Buel would end up having the longest tenure of any director of the Ravenscroft institutions.

Dr. Buel got right to work and was able to give a full report to the 1873 Convention:

> The charge of the Diocesan Training School and Associate Mission at Asheville was entered upon by the present incumbent on the 1st of September last and he has been officiating at the foregoing places since that time giving to Calvary, Leicester, Glencoe and Waynesville each one Sunday in the month, and when a fifth Sunday occurred, giving that to St. John's, Rutherfordton. He has also lately visited Brevard, in Transylvania County, spending a Sunday there. He officiates also at a station on the French Broad, four miles, from Asheville on the same Sunday with the visit to Glencoe.[22] This widespread work extending over five large and mountainous counties — and that in connection with regular instruction of young men who are studying for the ministry is obviously too large for one clergyman, and urgently demands the services of several additional missionaries. Two young men were found in the Training School,[23] and these have been pursuing their studies faithfully, and aiding in the Missionary work. In the coming autumn we hope for an increase in the number of students.[24]

A portrait of the Rev. Dr. David Hillhouse Buel, principal of the Ravenscroft Associate Mission and Training School. The original portrait hangs in Emmanuel Parish of the Episcopal Church in Cumberland, Maryland, where Dr. Buel had previously served as rector (1847–57) (courtesy the Emmanuel Parish of the Episcopal Church in Cumberland, Maryland).

Meanwhile, the North Carolina Diocese was showing "growing pains." In the previously mentioned address to the 1871 Diocesan Convention, Bishop Atkinson not only called for "the necessity of increased Episcopal services in this diocese"[25] but he further emphasized "that necessity becomes greater from year to year, as the field enlarges continually and my own strength wanes."[26] The call for "increased Episcopal services" actually started in 1866, upon the request of the bishop, whose failing health motivated him to seek an assistant. At the 1868 North Carolina Convention, it took the form of two options: either a division of the diocese or the appointment of an assistant bishop. Both options were complicated issues, as the rules and laws of the Constitution of the Protestant Episcopal Church of America, specifically Canon 13, had restrictions and requirements for either option. The option of dividing the diocese was quickly determined to be out of the question at the time, as a division would not allow for the required minimum number of parishes to form a diocese, and they could not meet the "self-supporting" requirement. Though the 1871 General Convention amended the Canon and relaxed the rules for division of dioceses, it remained an impossible option, and the matter would take the diocese another decade to resolve.

Because no division of the diocese was possible under the existing constitution of the National Church, the next expedient seemed to be the appointment of an assistant bishop.[27] But Canon 13, Article 5, only allowed for one assistant bishop (per diocese) in the case that the presiding bishop was permanently infirmed and could not carry out his duties. The canon was specific in disallowing any suffragan bishops. A suffragan bishop was an assistant bishop who would have administrative duties but no jurisdictional authority. In laymen's terms, a suffragan bishop would be subordinate to the presiding bishop. By allowing an assistant bishop only in the case of permanent infirmity, the assistant bishop essentially would not be an assistant, but would really be functioning as the acting bishop, with the same authority as the presiding bishop. In the case of Bishop Atkinson, he was able to perform some of his duties, but due to failing health he was unable to cover all of the parishes in his diocese because of the extent of the area, especially in the western regions of the state. At the 1871 Diocesan Convention, delegates from the North Carolina Diocese were instructed to go to the General Convention and push for revision of the canon to allow for suffragan bishops. Interestingly, "the General Convention of 1871 showed no disposition to authorize the election of suffragan bishops but did ratify the amendment of 1868 relaxing the rule for the division of dioceses. It also made easier the election of assistant bishops by amending Canon 13 to allow the election of an assistant bishop when by reason of the extent of the diocese the diocesan was unable to discharge his Episcopal duties."[28] Bishop Atkinson acted immediately, and at the next General Convention of 1872, he pushed for the election of an assistant bishop for his diocese; after obtaining a consensus from the other dioceses, he opened the way for the North Carolina Diocesan Convention of 1873 to elect (from 15 nominations) its first assistant bishop, the Rev. Theodore Benedict Lyman. The Rev. Lyman was born in Brighton, Massachusetts, in 1817, and graduated from Hamilton College, Clinton, New York, in 1837 and from the General Theological Seminary in New York City in 1840 (just two years before the Rev. Buel). Upon graduation from the seminary he was ordained a deacon at Christ Church, Baltimore, and raised to the priesthood fifteen months later at Hagerstown, Maryland. He served as rector of St. John's Church in Hagerstown from 1841 to 1850. While rector at St. John's he married (in 1845) a wealthy young woman, Anna Margaret Albert, of Baltimore. In 1850, the Rev. Lyman accepted the call to the pastorate of Trinity Church in Pittsburgh, Pennsylvania, and remained there until 1860, at which time he resigned to spend some time in Europe. Though he only planned to spend two years in Europe, the intervening Civil War and his wife's wealth led to his remaining there for ten years, during which time he was active in church work in various European countries. He returned to the United States in 1870 and accepted a call to a church in San Francisco, which is where he was laboring when he received the news of his election as assistant bishop of North Carolina.[29]

Though he was 58 years old, Assistant Bishop Lyman was vigorous and energetic and soon became the "legs and feet" of the ailing Bishop Atkinson, traveling from one end of the diocese to the other on visitation duties. He soon "acquired a wide circle of acquaintances in North Carolina and achieved a position of great respect and popularity both among Episcopalians and among members of other churches."[30]

Despite the wrangling in the diocese during the 1870s and early 1880s, life at the Ravenscroft Associate Mission and Training School, under the direction of Dr. Buel, continued at a slow but steady pace. For most of those years there were only two students each year, studying for deacon's orders or priest's orders (except for 1876, when there were four students). These seem like small numbers, especially considering that the school was advertised in nation-wide magazines such as *The Churchman*. It is from one of those advertisements, from 1877, that we learn that the school term ran from October 1 through July 31, with a "short recess at Christmas and Easter." We also learn that the tuition/board was $15/month, which was steep, especially considering the diocese was trying to attract young men from the working classes. At $150/term it was expensive, considering that the average yearly income for a family in 1877 was around $700.[31]

It must be remembered that Ravenscroft at this time was not only a school but also a mission, all being maintained by one man — the Rev. Buel, who was responsible for at least seven mission stations and churches covering a broad area of six counties. These included Calvary Church, Henderson County; St. John's Church, Rutherfordton, Rutherford County; Glencoe, Buncombe County; St. Paul's in the Valley, Brevard, Transylvania County; Waynesville, Haywood County; and, beginning in 1880, Webster, Jackson County. To add to his already overwhelming responsibilities, the published reports often refer to Dr. Buel's assisting the Rev. Buxton (in whose parish Ravenscroft was located) at either Trinity Church or one of the mission churches under Buxton's charge.[32] The students would help Dr. Buel with services and duties at the mission stations, thereby relieving him of some of the burden, but also gaining the much-needed practical experience to go along with their theological studies.

In the June 1875 issue of *The Spirit of Missions*, a periodical of the Episcopal Board of Missions, the Rev. Dr. Buel published a nine-page article titled "Work in North Carolina." "I have thought it might interest Churchmen, and give them a more vivid and complete picture of this Mission field and its wants and capabilities, to hear from one who has been at work in it for more than two years, some results of his personal observation and experience,"[33] wrote Dr. Buel at the start of the article. Buel went on to tell of his duties as head of the Ravenscroft Associate Mission and Training School: "I have during this period been teaching a few young men who are seeking the Ministry, and at the same time (so great is the spiritual destitution and the lack of laborers) have had to do Missionary work at seven churches and stations, lying in all directions from Asheville and at distances from it varying from ten to forty miles."[34] He further lamented that "my duties in the Training School have constantly demanded so much of my time, that I could usually devote to my Mission stations only three days in the week, Saturday, Sunday and Monday. Still with this amount of Missionary labor, only those stations lying in five counties could be visited once in a month, or even quarterly."[35]

In the summer of 1876 Bishop Lyman made his annual tour of the western parishes. In his address to the 1877 Convention, which included (as always) an annotated itinerary of his parish visits for the previous year, Bishop Lyman inserted an acknowledgment of the difficulty of Dr. Buel's task. On August 13, 1876, after a brief entry recording that "at Waynesville, I preached, confirmed two persons, and administered the Holy Communion," and "In the evening Dr. Buel preached," Bishop Lyman made the following astute observation:

> The whole of that part of this great State which lies west and southwest of Asheville, is as strictly missionary ground for our Church as any part of the United States, and is at the same time a most attractive field of labor. Its climate is most healthy and invigorating, its scenery, often beautiful, is still more frequently grand, even to sublimity; its hills teem with valuable minerals, and its fat valleys produce abundantly grain and grass. Yet in all this attractive country, there is no clergyman of our Church between Asheville and Murphy, a hundred and twenty miles apart from each other as these two places are. Dr. Buel, indeed, extends his services to points thirty and forty miles from Asheville ; but what can any one man do in such a vast area of territory?[36]

As 1880 dawned, two events would greatly affect the Ravenscroft Associate Mission and Training School. The first was the arrival of the railroad in 1880, and the second was the death of Bishop Atkinson in 1881.

Prior to 1880 one could only get to Asheville by traversing the rugged mountain roads by horseback, stagecoach, or horse-drawn buggy, making traveling to Asheville long and arduous. Even though Asheville had been known for decades for its temperate and healthful climate (since the Pattons built the Warm Springs resort in the 1830s), the difficulty of travel had greatly limited the number of visitors. When the railroad was finally able to traverse the rugged slopes to deliver passengers directly to downtown Asheville, the face of the city changed quickly and dramatically. Not only did the number of visitors increase substantially, but the social class of the visitors changed as well. Now, instead of just wealthy Southerners coming for day or week-long visits, the railroad brought the wealthiest of both the South and the North to the city for long "seasons" of the year. Many of the new visitors would maintain second homes here, and many (like George Vanderbilt) would even decide to move to Asheville permanently, bringing their wealth and influence with them. By the end of the 1880s Asheville's population would boom from 2,500 in 1880 to over 12,000, with 100,000 visitors annually, by 1890. Ravenscroft would benefit over the next decade by increased students and increased attention and involvement from interested wealthy men and their families.

The event that had the greatest effect on Ravenscroft during this period, however, was the death of Bishop Atkinson on January 4, 1881. Although Bishop Atkinson had been in ailing health for many years prior to his demise, having delegated most of his authority and duties to Assistant Bishop Lyman, Ravenscroft was always foremost in his heart and mind. This was evident upon the reading of his will, as he left a number of provisions concerning the Ravenscroft Associate Mission and Training School, which he had not only originally instituted but also retained control of for all these years. The particulars included bequeathing his 1,000-volume library along with a $500 endowment for the Training School.

The diocese was quick to take up the cause. On the third day of the 1881 Diocesan Convention, held in Raleigh just five months later, the Rev. Buxton, as chairman of the Committee of Minutes, presented a report on the death of the beloved bishop. The Rev. Buxton concluded his report with two resolutions:

> **Whereas** our revered and beloved Bishop, in bequeathing his theological library of one thousand volumes to the Ravenscroft Institution at Asheville, together with $500 to its endowment fund, manifested how closely that Institution lay at his heart, and how important he deemed it to the future welfare of the Diocese; Therefore:

Resolved 1. As a lasting memorial of our regard and affection, that a professorship of the value of $15,000 be founded in the Ravenscroft Institution at Asheville, to be styled "The Bishop Atkinson Professorship of the Evidences of Christianity and of Christian Doctrine," and that it be commended to the offerings of the Church in this and other Dioceses.

Resolved 2. That a page in the Journal of the Convention be devoted in honor of his memory.[37]

The matter was further brought up in the "Report of the Committee on the State of the Church" presented by R. S. Bronson:

> With what shall this Diocese identify the name of her lamented Bishop? What work in his Diocese during his life touched more closely his warmest interest than that Institution which, bearing the great name of Ravenscroft, may worthily be blended with that of Atkinson, as a grateful Diocese there establishes in some theological professorship a permanent memorial of a life so richly gifted and so freely spent for others?[38]

The Convention quickly formed the "Committee on the Bishop Atkinson Professorship," which subsequently met and reported before the end of the Convention. The committee, whose task was to determine the best means for raising the funds for the new professorship, recommended that the amount to be raised should be increased from $15,000 to $20,000. True to fashion with committee politics, it decided and recommended to the Convention that "the best mode of accomplishing this object will be the appointment of the Committee, who shall appeal in behalf of the object to the whole Diocese, and to the Church throughout our land, and shall make use of any means they deem best for obtaining the endowment."[39] So the committee decided to elect another committee. This new committee consisted of the bishop, two clergy and two laymen — a model of cooperative church politics.

Perhaps the most important effect of the death of Bishop Atkinson, and the subsequent renewed interest in the work of the Ravenscroft Associate Mission and Training School, was the impetus for a renewed vision for the Rev. Buel, who had labored alone for many years. In his report, which he called a "meager one" (though it was the longest he had ever given at a Convention), he made a startling confession:

> The wide-spread and growing missionary work connected with Ravenscroft, a work which the Bishops have felt compelled, by the want of other labourers, to lay wholly upon the Principal of Ravenscroft, necessarily prevents the successful prosecution of the important work of theological instruction. Indeed, the Principal, feeling as he did, the weight of this great mission work, and how it utterly prevented the requisite devotion of time and effort to the Training School, has for several years, not encouraged the many applications from candidates that have been coming to him.[40]

Buel quickly followed this confession with evidence of a renewed commitment to the work:

> But the work of the Training School was very near the heart of Bishop Atkinson. He founded Ravenscroft Mission and Training School, and he showed his undying devotion to it by bequeathing to it his very valuable theological library of more than 1,000 volumes, and also $500 in money towards its endowment fund. Another like sum came about the same time, from the Bishop's dear friend and helper, Mrs. Lewis Thompson, of Bertie County. Now what so fit tribute to the memory of our Bishop can the Diocese make as to undertake at once the building up and the firm establishment of this Diocesan Training School which lay so near his heart?
>
> Arrangements have already been made to re-inforce the institution by the valuable services of

another and a most competent theological teacher. Our new year will open on the first of October with at least two Clergymen, engaged in the work of the Training School, and with provision for the constant care and instruction of a goodly number of theological students."[41]

By the next Convention (1882), the committee charged with raising funds for the Bishop Atkinson Professorship had not even met once. Although they did meet again at the Convention and decided to urge that donations be made toward the fund, nothing much came of it and the diocese soon lost interest in the matter. However, the Rev. Buel, with renewed vigor, continued on with the ministry at Ravenscroft and was happy to report that year that he had three students studying for "holy ministry" and also "that a lady of Baltimore, a devoted and dear friend of our late Bishop, has founded at Ravenscroft a scholarship to be called the Bishop Atkinson Scholarship, and one of the present students is enjoying the benefit of it. The Library bequeathed to the school by the Bishop is now arranged in a substantial and handsome case, which is to bear on its face the title, 'The Bishop Atkinson Library.' Ravenscroft now has an admirable library of more than twelve hundred volumes."[42]

In 1883 the first "Asheville City Directory" was published, listing the names, addresses and occupations of it citizens. It is from this, and subsequent city directories, that we see that the staff at Ravenscroft included more than just the Rev. Dr. Buel and the other white instructors — a staff of servants, mostly African Americans, was required to keep the school clean, drive and care for the horses and wagons, do general housekeeping, and do the cooking and serving of meals. The 1883 directory shows only two "domestics," Isaac Dickson and his wife Delia. Those familiar with Asheville history will recognize the name of Isaac Dickson, who became one its leading African American citizens.

Isaac Dickson was born a slave in June of 1839 in Shelby, North Carolina. His mother was a slave, owned by a Dutch plantation owner who was also the father of Isaac. Following his emancipation in 1868 he moved to Morganton, North Carolina, and then in 1870 he moved to Asheville.[43] It's not known exactly when he began working for the Rev. Buel, perhaps even as early as 1872, but by 1876, he had accumulated enough income to purchase land and begin a small grocery and livery business in Asheville's African American community. Interestingly, the land was sold to him by Thomas W. Patton, and it had previously been the site of slave cabins on the plantation of James W. Patton, Thomas' father. Dickson accumulated and developed so much land that the community was soon called "Dickson Town."

There was a frame building behind Ravenscroft that may have been used to house some later servant staff, but the Dicksons probably lived in Ravenscroft house with the Buels. Isaac was the butler while Delia, no doubt, was in charge of housekeeping and meals. Isaac Dickson was proud of his work, as his obituary years later (1919) noted that "for many years after coming here [he] was the butler to the late Dr. Buel."[44] Dr. David H. Buel, who had been active before the Civil War in aiding the efforts of the Underground Railroad, was a friend to the Dicksons. Buel practiced what he believed, that the saving and transforming message of the Gospel of Jesus Christ was to all who believe, regardless of their skin color. Evidently the Dicksons greatly admired him, as they named one of their sons, who was born in 1877 while they were in service to Dr. Buel, "David Buel Dickson."

By 1883 the winds of change were beginning to blow. Three important topics were broached at the 1883 Diocesan Convention, with all of them coming to the fore at the 1884 Convention. These three topics, which would greatly affect the future of Ravenscroft, were the reawakening of the possible division of the diocese, the question of ownership of the Ravenscroft property, and the need for more parochial schools in the diocese. Though the question of the division of the diocese had been heatedly debated back in the 1870s, the election of the assistant bishop, along with Bishop Atkinson's failing health, seemed to have drawn the Convention's attention away from the subject. However, in 1883, the matter arose at the Convention in a furious way. Bishop Lyman was strongly opposed to a division, as he maintained that though the diocese was large in territory, it was small in numbers and weak in sustainability. He adroitly argued in his address to the 1883 Convention, "But it is said that no man, even if blessed with the most vigorous health, can possibly discharge the Episcopal duties which are so imperatively needed, in so widely extended a territory. On the contrary, I believe there is no Diocese which has been more thoroughly visited than this. Nearly every Parish and Missionary Station has been reached since our last Convention, and more than twenty have been visited twice, while those that remain will receive a visit within the next few weeks.... Now, if North Carolina is divided, nothing can be plainer than that we shall have two very weak and feeble Dioceses."[45]

Despite the bishop's advice, the Convention convinced him to consent if the Convention voted favorably for the division. And so after approving the revised division line to follow the western boundaries of Hereford, Bertie, Martin, Pitt, Greene, Wayne, Sampson, Cumberland, and Roberson counties, the bishop gave his canonical consent on May 26, 1883. The eastern diocese was appropriately called the "Diocese of East Carolina," with the western diocese retaining the name of the "Diocese of North Carolina."[46]

Two additional topics also surfaced at the 1883 Convention. The topic of the ownership of the Ravenscroft property was precipitated by the approved division of the diocese. The Rev. Joseph B. Cheshire Jr. offered a motion to select a committee of three to "consider the rightful ownership" of the Ravenscroft property. The motion passed, with the bishop appointing the committee of the Rev. Joseph Cheshire, Mr. Richard H. Smith and Col. A. W. Atkinson. The other topic was that of the need for a diocesan parochial school for young men, which it had a more subdued introduction. In the report (at the 1883 Convention) from the "Committee on the State of the Church," after commending St. Mary's Girls School, committee chairman R. S. Bronson put forth the question, "But where is the school of the same grade for our boys? Is no duty owing to them?"[47] However, no further consideration was addressed at the Convention.

Despite the political disputes at the diocesan level, the work of Ravenscroft was going strong. Author James Brawley records, "When Bishop Lyman visited the western part of the Diocese he found three new churches were being erected in the counties of Haywood, Jackson, and Macon. He laid the cornerstone of St. Phillip's Church at Brevard, visited St. Mary's at Micadale, which was subsequently consecrated on 17 May 1891; and held services in the partly constructed church at Cullowhee, which was consecrated on 2 August 1892. All these churches were erected under the guidance of the Reverend Mr. Buel [and young men from the Ravenscroft Training School] who received assistance not only from the diocesan Missionary fund but also from churchmen in the North."[48]

The Episcopal Church of North Carolina emerged from the Civil War in a weakened condition, but in the post-war years it was strengthened and began to grow again. By 1883 it could boast that from only 2,453 communicants in 1866, it had doubled in size to 5,889 communicants.[49] This growth was in large part due to the missionary efforts of Bishop Atkinson and the establishment of the Ravenscroft Associate Mission and Training School in Asheville. But the events of the 1883 Convention signaled an impending change for both the diocese and the Ravenscroft institution.

Four

Redirection: Rectors and Ravenscroft High: *1884–1897*

By 1884, less than five years after the first load of passengers arrived by train at the depot in the village of Best, just a mile or two south of Asheville's center square, there were signs of what was to come. Across the street from James Patton's 1814 Eagle Hotel, the block-long Swannanoa Hotel opened in 1880, and soon more hotels were to follow, such as the Kenilworth Inn, Berkley Hotel, Glenrock Hotel, and the largest of all, the sprawling Battery Park Hotel (developed by wealthy Northerner Col. Frank Coxe), which opened in 1886. In the ensuing decade Asheville's scenic beauty and healthful climate, aided by the railroad, would be the catalyst for rapid and substantial growth. Soon the small mountain town would become a city and grow to be the third-largest city in the state. The Ravenscroft Associate Mission and Training School, situated in the midst of these rapid changes, would find itself undergoing drastic changes during this period as well, from influences within and outside of the institution. The Rev. Dr. D. H. Buel had been the principal in charge at Ravenscroft since he first arrived in Asheville in 1872. In 1884, at almost 70 years of age, he found himself in the midst of controversy and impending change in his ministry. The controversy was not of his making, but was a result of the generosity of the late Bishop Atkinson, who had recently passed away and bequeathed his 1,000-volume library, a $500 endowment, and various funds to the trustees of the Diocese of North Carolina for the work of the Ravenscroft Associate Mission and Training School. The controversy was complicated by the recent division of the diocese, which occurred shortly after the reading of the bishop's will. These concurrent events brought up the question of who owned and controlled the Ravenscroft property and institutions. At the 1883 Convention the Rev. Joseph B. Cheshire offered a motion "that a committee of three be appointed to consider the rightful ownership the Ravenscroft University [property]."[1] The motion was approved and Bishop Lyman appointed the Rev. Cheshire, Mr. Richard H. Smith, and Col. J. W. Atkinson as the "Committee on the Ravenscroft Property." Later, during the Convention, the committee met and submitted the following resolution: "That a Committee of three, one of whom shall be from the proposed new Diocese, be appointed to inquire into the title to the property and funds of the Institution, known as the Ravenscroft Associate Mission and Training School, and the trusts upon which said property and funds are held, and that they report to the next Convention of this Diocese, and of the proposed new Diocese — what action, if any, is necessary to be taken in regard thereto."[2] In a comical twist, the resolution was approved and the same "committee of three" that offered the resolution was asked to continue as the new committee of three.

Meanwhile, the Rev. Buel was happy to report that "the work of the school has been going on well" and that five students were studying at Ravenscroft, including a former student, the Rev. George H. Bell, who was now pursuing priest's orders. The Rev. Bell was also acting as a diocesan missionary, helping Buel with the mission work of the associate mission.[3]

Although the 1883 Convention hinted at the impending changes coming to Ravenscroft, the 1884 Convention would be the real impetus to change. The 1884 Convention journal reveals that Ravenscroft was the hot topic that year. On the second day of the Convention the "Committee on the Ravenscroft Property" presented their three-and-a-half-page report titled "REPORT OF THE COMMITTEE ON THE PROPERTY AND FUND OF THE RAVENSCROFT ASSOCIATE MISSION AND TRAINING SCHOOL AT ASHEVILLE, N.C." The lengthy report was followed by a two-page "Minority Report."

The first part of the report included a summary of the items that the committee determined constituted the "property and funds of this Institution." The four items were the following:

1. The Real Estate in the town of Asheville, being about thirteen acres, with the buildings and improvements thereon, now occupied and used for the purpose of The Ravenscroft Associate Mission and Training School.
2. The Endowment Fund, proper, amounting to the sum of $7,086.00 in invested securities.
3. The Hix Fund, amounting to the sum of $3,758.00 in invested securities, and also of some land in Detroit and in Canada, of not much present value.
4. A Theological Library of some 1,500 volumes, mostly given by Bishop Atkinson in his will, valued at $8,000.00.[4]

The report went on to elaborate on the first two items, not only on what each item specifically included, but also on how each was obtained and, most importantly, what relationship each now had as a result of the disposition of the late bishop's will and the recent division of the diocese. The matter was a complicated one and made even more so by the differing opinions and subjective nature of the interpretation of the facts.

Concerning the first item, the property, the committee report explained how the property was sold to the Rev. Buxton in 1854 by William Patton, by deed of trust for the special purpose "upon which to erect and keep up a Classical and Theological school." It further reported that when the Rev. Buxton had been reimbursed for all his incurred expenses, he was to deed the property to the trustees of the diocese (which he did in 1863 and 1868).

The second item, "The Hix Fund," was a bit more complex. "Of this Bishop Atkinson says in his will: 'I hold certain property under the will of the late Miss Hix,[5] of Detroit, Michigan to be used in my Diocese for the benefit of the mountain region, and still more particularly for the Counties of Watauga and Mitchell, [...] this property I hereby give and bequeath my right, title and interest in, to the Trustees of the Diocese of North Carolina, to be used for the purpose above mentioned, and especially for the benefit of the Training School at Asheville, until that shall be otherwise endowed.'"[6] Apparently Miss Hix had stipulated in her will that if the "said mission" was ever disbanded the monies could be used for any other church or mission that the diocese successors "may establish within the Diocese of North Carolina." The committee reported that as the said mission had disbanded, Bishop

Atkinson, who was holding the property in trust, "seems to have had full power to appropriate the fund to the Ravenscroft Associate Mission and Training School, as he had done in his last will and testament."[7] The committee supported the bishop's actions in regard to the appropriation of the Hix Fund to Ravenscroft.

The committee also went on to settle the question of the property and funds in regard to the division of the diocese. They concluded, "It is, therefore, clear that none of the above property and funds are in the strict sense of the words Diocesan property. The Diocese, indeed, holds the property, but holds it only for the purpose of effectuating the trusts created by the several instruments conveying the property namely, to maintain the school at Asheville. No part of the property, either real or personal, can be taken by the Diocese for any other purpose. Therefore, it seems to your Committee that the division of the Diocese necessitated no action with regard to the property and funds of The Ravenscroft Associate Mission and Training School."[8]

The controversy hinged on what was to follow. The middle of the third page contained this divisive sentence: "But by the death of Bishop Atkinson, a very important change has been made in the relationship between this Institution and the Church in the Diocese, as represented in her Convention of Bishop, Clergy and Laity."[9] This statement was directly followed by a recounting of how the Ravenscroft School was founded, with an explanation of how the death of Bishop Atkinson had changed the relationship. The report explained that although Ravenscroft had always been administered by the bishops (Ives and Atkinson), by bequeathing the funds and endowment to the diocese, Bishop Atkinson's will had now given the administration of Ravenscroft to the trustees of the diocese. This meant that the oversight of Ravenscroft was now to be administered through the Convention and its authorized committees. The report was concluded with the following resolution:

> **Resolved.** That this Convention accept the trust imposed upon it, by the last will and testament of its late revered Bishop, the Rt. the Rev. Thomas Atkinson, D. D, LL. D., in the bequest of property for the support of the Ravenscroft Associate Mission and Training School; and that it will take such further action as may be necessary for the due administration of the same.[10]

The above report was signed by only two committee members, the Rev. Joseph B. Cheshire and Richard H. Smith. In an unprecedented turn of events, the third member of the committee, Col. John Wilder Atkinson, requested that his "Minority Report" be immediately presented:

> The undersigned unites in the above Report so far as concerns the relation of facts contained therein, but desires to express his dissent from the conclusion stated in the latter part thereof, from the paragraph beginning, "But by the death of Bishop Atkinson a very important change." & c.
> It is admitted, as beyond question, that Bishop Atkinson had a right to administer, and did administer the affairs of the Training School at Asheville, without the intervention of the Convention of the Diocese. It may well be assumed, he did this because he deemed it best, in the interest of this Institution,— the success of which he had greatly at heart,— that its affairs should be under the control of the Episcopal Head of the Diocese, rather than administered by any committee, however judiciously selected. And, as matter of fact, the undersigned knows that such was his opinion.
> It is confidently believed that Bishop Atkinson, by his will, intended to confer upon his successor the same power and authority with reference to this property, he, himself, used and exer-

cised, without dispute. Without undertaking, at this time, to discuss the legal effect of his will, which, it is claimed, creates an "important change" in the relation of this property to the Diocese of North Carolina, the undersigned would remind the Convention that the Church in this Diocese should regard the Church law and custom, and this has been to have this Diocesan School administered by the Bishop of the Diocese.

A portion of this property, to-wit: the Real Estate has always been vested in the Trustees of the Diocese, and yet the Bishop controlled the uses of it. Again, there is a great amount of Church property — churches, schools, parsonages, &c., — the title to which is in the Trustees, yet no one ever supposed it would be right or proper for the Convention to interpose and manage these Trusts by a committee. This has always been left to the Bishop and the local authorities, which act under his direction.

In conclusion, the undersigned holds firmly to the opinion that there is nothing to indicate any purpose on the part of Bishop Atkinson to change the administration of the affairs of this Training School from the mode it had heretofore been administered by him as Bishop of the Diocese; and would therefore respectfully recommend the adoption of the following resolution:

Resolved. That the Committee on the Training School at Asheville be discharged from further consideration of the matters submitted to them.[11]

The Convention immediately postponed for a recess. When it reconvened at 4:00 P.M., the Rev. Buel offered the minority resolution as a substitute for the majority resolution. Obviously, Buel, a veteran priest, knew that to have Ravenscroft administered by the Convention could potentially be a bureaucratic nightmare and so could be detrimental to the growth of the mission and school; however, Buel lost the vote. H. A. London quickly made a motion that the majority resolution be referred to a committee "of three legal gentlemen," to be appointed by the bishop. London's vote was also lost. Forthwith the majority resolution was voted on and adopted. The matter was concluded with a final resolution from R. H. Battle:

Resolved. That it be referred to a Committee of (3) three, to enquire into the title to the fund known as the "Hix Fund," with direction to ascertain who, under the law, has control or management of the same, and any other matter of importance in respect to said Fund, and report to the next Annual Convention.[12]

But the indefatigable Dr. Buel was not deterred by diocesan politics from carrying on with the work at Ravenscroft. In fact, he was elated to report to the same Convention of 1884 that construction had begun on St. John's Church at Webster in Jackson County and that construction was also well underway on St. David's Church in nearby Cullowhee. He was especially excited that the bishop had transferred the Rev. George Bell, Asheville native and training school graduate, to assist with duties at the mission. Buel also reported that three students were at the training school and that he was very delighted, as it seemed that the need for an assistant teacher would "soon be admirably supplied."[13]

Bishop Lyman was very pleased with the mission work and happily reported to the Convention that "the whole Mission field in Haywood, Jackson and Macon Counties offers much encouragement, and we have good hope that three Churches will be completed in that district during the present year. Dr. Buel has been able to secure considerable assistance at the North, during the past season, to help him in church building."[14] It seems that much of the financial support for building these mission churches came from donors in the Northern states from contacts that Dr. Buel had cultivated from his previous charges in the North. The Rev. Buel was no doubt feeling a bit of relief as 1884 progressed and 1885 dawned, for he now had two assistants. Not only had the Rev. George Bell come to help, but also the

Rev. Thomas Atkinson Jr.[15] grandson of the late bishop, was appointed specifically to be an instructor at the training school. However, as is often the case in church work, Atkinson served "double duty" by also assisting in the mission work, holding services at nearby mission stations. At this time the Ravenscroft Associate Mission included seven mission stations: "Grace Church in the Mountains," Waynesville, Haywood County, with two "outlying stations" ("Micadale" and "Fork of the Pigeon" [Pigeon River]); "St. Paul's in the Valley" and "St. Phillip's Church," Brevard, Transylvania County; and the church at Webster, Jackson County, with outlying stations at "Love's School House" and "Cullowhee Valley." In addition to the established mission stations, a "new work" was developing at Alexander, ten miles west of Asheville, with services being held at a local union meeting house "at the request of F. Randolph Curtis, of New York."[16]

Bishop Lyman visited the missionary work in the mountains during the summer of 1884. His address to the following year's convention offers a glimpse into the life and rugged conditions that faced Dr. Buel and the men serving at the Ravenscroft Associate Mission on a daily basis:

> We left the following morning for Webster, and hoped to reach Cullowhee that evening, where I had an appointment for Sunday. We found the road in a very bad condition, and when about five miles from Charleston [a village in Swain County, North Carolina] met with an accident to the carriage, which occasioned us considerable delay. With the assistance of some young men who were passing, we endeavored to remedy the break, as far as possible, and then got on very comfortably for some miles; but when passing over a spur of the mountains, we came upon a sideling, rocky bed, and the carriage turned completely over into a deep hollow on the right side of the road. The horses very providentially stopped at once, or we might have received serious injuries. Dr. Buel escaped unhurt, but I was stunned by the fall, and received severe bruises and a heavy strain. By the help of strangers who were passing, we soon got our carriage back on the road, and finding that it had received no considerable injuries, we soon started on again. We were unable to find any shop where repairs could be had, and consequently we made but very slow progress. We did not reach Webster until 8 P.M., so that we were about twelve hours making the twenty miles. We secured another vehicle at once, so that we might be ready for an early start the next morning, as we were most anxious, on no account, to miss the appointment for that day.[17]

We also have from the bishop's address, besides a chronicle of the many services held and people confirmed, a description of the mission churches that had been or were in the process of being built, as a result of the work of Ravenscroft Associate Mission. Here are two examples:

> Monday, August 25th, I spent visiting several families in the neighborhood and inspecting the neat brick Church in course of erection there, the walls of which were nearly raised. The site is a very beautiful one, near the base of a mountain spur, and overlooking the lovely Cullowhee Valley.[18]
>
> At 4 P.M. [Wednesday, August 27] held service in the new Church at Mica Dale, when Dr. Buel read Evening Prayer, and I preached. The Church was only so far completed that we were able to hold service in it, but we hope soon to have it entirely finished. We have there a very interesting and encouraging field, and like Cullowhee, we need, at once, a school in connection with the Church. A neat wing has been constructed as part of the Church building, to be used for that purpose.[19]

Providentially, the Diocesan Convention of 1885 was convened at Trinity Episcopal Church in Asheville on Wednesday, May 27. The Rev. Jarvis Buxton had made the motion at the previous year's Convention to meet in Asheville in 1885. It was a logical place, as Trinity Church had just erected a new and enlarged building, but, more importantly, the Rev. Buxton wanted the Convention to see first-hand the work of the Ravenscroft Associate Mission and Training School, which was directly across the street from the church. This location was strategic, as the dispute over the mission and school, which had been going on for a number of years (ever since Bishop Atkinson's death), would come to a climax and final resolution at the 1885 Convention.

The bishop would begin each year's Convention with his yearly "address," which often would contain topics the bishop proposed for the diocese to consider. Not surprisingly, Bishop Lyman ended his 1885 address on the first day of the Convention with the following charge:

> And there is yet another matter to which I desire to call the attention of the Convention, which is very closely related with this whole Missionary work. I refer to the "Ravenscroft Associate Mission and Training School." I am gratified to be able to state that during the past year arrangements have been made whereby the services of an additional and well qualified Clergyman have been secured for this work, and thus much greater efficiency has been given to both its departments. In my address to our last Convention, I expressed the wish that some aid might be given me, in the general oversight and direction of this institution, and I would now specifically propose that this Convention shall appoint a Board of Fellows, upon the nomination of the Bishop, to act with him in the general guidance of the work. And I would suggest that this Board consist of three Clergymen, of which the Principal of the school shall always be one, and two Laymen. And to give greater stability to this management, those thus chosen should continue in office until, by the action of a future Convention, a change should be thought desirable. I think I clearly see ways in which this institution may be made a powerful agency for good in the Diocese, and I am most anxious that every reasonable means should be employed to secure such a result.[20]

On the following morning, the first motion was that of Mr. R. H. Smith, who resolved "that the part of the Bishop's Address in reference to the Ravenscroft Associate Mission and Training School, be referred to a Committee of three (3) Clergymen and two (2) Laymen, and that they report by eleven o'clock Friday morning."[21] A committee was quickly appointed by the bishop, including the Rev. Jarvis Buxton, D.D., the Rev. B. S. Bronson and the Rev. W. R. Wetmore, and Messrs. R. H. Smith and H. C. Jones.

Immediately on the heels of the morning's first motion was the report of the "Special Committee on the Hicks[22] Fund," presented by C. M. Busbee. Following a reiteration of the facts of the matter, the report ended with the following summation:

> Your Committee are of opinion that the Fund so realized vested in the Trustees of the Diocese under Bishop Atkinson's will, in trust primarily for the benefit of the Ravenscroft Associate Mission and Training School; and that it is the duty of the Church in the Diocese to see that the wishes of Miss Hicks,[23] as set forth in the codicil to her will, are respected and, as far as possible, carried out; and that any payments that have been made since Bishop Atkinson's death, or which may hereafter be made on account of the fund not realized in his life-time, should be held by the said Trustees on the same trusts.

The report was referred to the "same committee."

Honoring the request to "report by eleven o'clock Friday morning," the Rev. Jarvis Buxton "presented the report of the Special Committee appointed to consider that portion of the Bishop's address in reference to Ravenscroft Training School at Asheville, and moved the adoption of the accompanying resolutions":

Whereas, The Diocesan Convention of 1884 did accept the trust imposed upon it by the last will and testament of the Rt. the Rev. Thomas Atkinson, late Bishop of the Diocese, in the bequest of certain property for the support of the Ravenscroft Associate Mission and Training School and decided that it would take such further action as might be necessary for the administration of the same:

Resolved 1. That the Convention proceed to the election by ballot of a Board of Fellows, consisting of six members, three of whom shall be Clergymen and three Laymen, who shall hold office for the term of three years, and until their successors are elected,—of which Board the Bishop of the Diocese shall be Chairman ex officio, and all vacancies in the Board shall be filled by the Convention.

Resolved 2. The said Board of Fellows, at their first meeting shall make all needful rules and by-laws for the management of said Institution.

Resolved 3. In case of a vacancy occurring in any of the offices of the Institution, the vacancy shall be filled by the Board of Fellows on nomination by the Bishop, at such time and in such manner as may be provided by the by-laws.

Resolved 4. That the Trustees of the Diocese are instructed to pay over, on the order of the Bishop, all appropriations made by the Board out of the annual income arising from the trust funds invested for the support of said Institution.

Resolved 5. That the Board of Fellows shall submit to the Convention an annual report of the work of the Institution, and its annual expenditures. In regard, also, to the report on the Hicks Fund, which was referred to the Committee, it is herewith returned, subject to the order of the Convention.[24]

Each resolution was considered separately by the Convention. Resolution 1 prompted the most discussion and was eventually changed to read:

Resolved 1. That the Board of Fellows shall be composed of seven members of whom the Principal of the School shall be a member, ex-officio, and the remaining six members shall be chosen by the Convention by ballot, and shall consist of three Clergymen and three Laymen, one Clergyman and one Layman for six years, one Clergyman and one Layman for four years, and one Clergyman and one Layman for two years, and their successors when elected shall be elected for the full term of six years, of which Board the Bishop of the Diocese shall be Chairman ex officio, and all vacancies in the Board shall be filled by the Convention.[25]

The new resolution had two good changes: first, the number of board members was increased to seven to include the principal of the school; second, the initial graduated terms for the board members were brilliant, as they would provide continuity rather than having to elect an entire new board every six years.

True to Convention procedural practices, a committee was appointed to nominate potential board members. The nominating committee included the Bishop of the Diocese; the Rev. A. S. Smith, D.D.; Mr. R. H. Smith; W. R. Wetmore; H. K. Nash; and H. C. Jones. Later that evening, Mr. R. H. Smith, for the committee, reported the following nominations for "The Board of Fellows of the Ravenscroft Associate Mission and Training School":

> For Six Years—the Rev. Jarvis Buxton, D.D., and Mr. R. H. Smith.
> For Four Years—the Rev. W. R. Wetmore and Mr. R. H. Battle.
> For Two Years—the Rev. W. S. Bynum and Mr. H. C. Jones.[26]

The new "Board of Fellows of the Ravenscroft Property" had an initial meeting at the end of the Convention. The official published report says that they met on the "20th day of May, 1885." But that was a typographical error, as the "20th" would have been before the Convention. They met on May 30, the last day of the Convention, as the board members were already in Asheville for the Convention. At that first meeting the new board determined the official yearly meeting would be the fourth Wednesday in July, to be held in the Library of the Ravenscroft "Institution."[27]

The first regular meeting of the Board of Fellows of Ravenscroft was held as planned on Wednesday, July 22, 1885. The first order of the day was the election of Dr. D. H. Buel as secretary and Mr. Richard H. Smith as treasurer. The board then took on the weighty task of adopting rules and bylaws. Although many of the bylaws were probably incidental organizational and procedural rules, the board issued one monumental bylaw titled STATUTE 1, which stated, "There shall be two departments of this Institution. One the Training School for the Ministry, and the other a High School for Classical and Academic Education."[28]

There is no indication of whose idea it was to reinstitute the classical school, but it is probably not too far off the mark to suggest that it may have been the Rev. Buxton, who had been the first headmaster of Ravenscroft in 1855. Also, because of the attention brought to the property deeds (after the death of Bishop Atkinson) over the last few years, the board felt it incumbent on them to meet the stipulations of William Patton's deed of 1854, which had conveyed the property "in Special Trust" to be used for a "Classical and Theological School." Nonetheless, the statute had the full sanction of Bishop Lyman, as he was appointed along with two other board members to a committee whose task was to "make all necessary arrangements for opening the Classical and Academical School."[29] The committee planned to open the new high school on October 1, 1885, but no suitable principal could be found.

Despite the unsuccessful attempt to open the new high school, the Associate Mission and Training School was still going strong. In fact, it was reported at the following Convention that "It has been a year of constant and faithful study. The young men now studying at Ravenscroft give excellent promise of usefulness, and we are encouraged to believe that with the prayers and the cordial aid of the people of the Diocese in sending us Candidates and helping to support them, this training school will grow in usefulness and greatly aid in supplying our mission fields with well equipped and earnest laborers."[30]

The board met for a third time in a specially called meeting on May 12, 1886, in order to compose their report and proposals to be presented to the upcoming 1886 Convention, which was only two weeks away. This was a brilliant move, as the board perhaps realized that if they waited until July to meet, any actions or proposals they enacted would have to wait for almost a whole year to be approved by the next Convention in 1887. They essentially admitted to this fact in their report to the 1886 Convention as they presented their resolutions:

> **Be it Resolved**, That it is the sense of this Board that the following action should be taken at its next regular meeting in July, and that this plan be communicated to the Convention with a view of securing its approbation and the necessary assistance:
>
> **1st.** That at a cost of not more than fifteen hundred dollars ($1,500.00) a brick residence be erected near the main building for the Principal of the Theological Department, with proper rooms for recitations, and for Library, out of any funds procurable. The original Ravenscroft Building to be altered and enlarged for the purposes of the classical school for boys.
>
> **2d.** When completed the aforesaid building shall be placed in charge of the Head Master of the Classical Department of this school.

3d. The Ravenscroft Associate Mission and Training School for the Ministry shall be under the direction of the Principal of that Department.

4th. Proper buildings for the accommodation of Professors and their families shall be erected on the ample Ravenscroft ground as means shall be available.

On the third day of the 1886 Convention, the Rev. J. B. Cheshire made a motion "that the order of the day be postponed to enable the Report of the Board of Fellows of Ravenscroft [shown above] to be made."[31] However, without any discussion, the report was immediately "laid upon the table to be called up at some subsequent time." Later on during the Convention, Col. W. H. S. Burgwyn made the motion that "the report from the Board of Fellows of the Ravenscroft Property be made the order of the day at 4 P.M."[32] "The order for the hour being called [4 P.M.], the Convention took up the consideration of the report of the Board of Fellows of the Ravenscroft Property. The question was discussed at length by the Rev. W. S. Bynum, the Rev. Dr. Buel and the Rev. Dr. Buxton until the hour for the special order, when the Convention proceeded to the election of a Treasurer."[33] But it was not until the fourth day of the Convention that the report was finally accepted and approved, with the following resolution:

> **Resolved.** That the report of the Board of Fellows of the Ravenscroft property be approved, and that they proceed to take such measures as may be practicable for carrying out the measures therein proposed, and to secure the faithful execution of the trusts committed to them, including those expressed in the deed for the Ravenscroft property.

This was the green light that the board needed to move ahead with their plans. Note that the report was not only accepted, but the Convention also gave them the leniency "to take such measures as may be practicable" instead of specifying exactly what measures to take. However, the Board of Fellows would later find that this ambiguity would open the way for subjective criticisms of the "measures" that they would take toward establishing the high school and relocating the training school. But let me not get ahead of the story!

The Board of Fellows wasted no time in implementing their plans. At their July 1886 meeting, just two months after the Convention, the board took affirmative action toward the measures approved by the Convention. Two committees were formed: one to procure the cost and plan for erecting a new building, and a second committee to "put in operation the Classical Department of the Institution" and secure a headmaster.[34] The second committee "corresponded with various persons, and advertised in the church papers for a Head Master, offering a salary of $1,000 for one year to be guaranteed by individuals."[35]

The first committee took two substantial actions during the year. They had some necessary repairs made to the Ravenscroft building and they had erected, for $250, a "single story brick building arranged for an academy"[36] (elsewhere in the report it is called a "School House"). This building was to be the classroom building for the new high school, with the original Ravenscroft building being used to house the library, headmaster's study, staff and dormitory space for the boarding students.

As would be the case for the next few years, as the diocese and Board of Fellows worked toward their goals of expanding the ministry, Dr. Buel continued his day-to-day mission work, as well as the instruction of students at the training school. He was happy to report to the 1886 Convention that he had had seven students (postulants) during the year, of which three[37] had "passed the canonical literary examination and first examination for the priesthood."[38] With those three moving on to their practical training in other parishes, four students remained at the school.

Apparently the dilemma of what to do with the training school (theological department) was not resolved, and hence it became an issue at the 1887 Convention. The Report of the Board of Fellows to the 1887 Convention was over 4 pages long. The lengthy report included a chronicle of the actions instituted by the board since the 1886 Convention, a report of the work of the training school, and a treasurer's report of the Ravenscroft funds and expenditures. The report concluded with a number of resolutions, the first being one of clarification:

> **Be it resolved**, That the Board of Fellows be styled The Board of Fellows of Ravenscroft; that the Institution be styled Ravenscroft; that the Training School for the ministry be styled Ravenscroft Training School and Mission; and that the Boys' School be styled Ravenscroft High School for Boys.

But it was the last resolution that brought a substantial amount of subsequent discussion:

> **Resolved**, That the Board of Fellows, having ascertained that the sum of $1,500 is quite inadequate to the erection of a building for the Training School on the Ravenscroft property, request the Convention to release them from the limitation of $1,500, and allow the Board to erect a suitable building at the least possible cost with such funds as they can procure.

The Rev. W. R. Wetmore, the newly elected treasurer of the Board of Fellows who presented the report, immediately amended the report by stating, "While presenting the report of the Board of Fellows I feel constrained to say that I do not approve of the last resolution offered above."[39] Wetmore argued that the training school was small and should "be content, for the present, with a humble but comfortable frame cottage" and that they should immediately vacate the Ravenscroft building and turn the building over to the high school. He further recommended that instead of simply releasing the board from the $1,500 limitation for a "suitable building" for the theological training school, the Convention should limit the board to the "erection of a cottage that shall not cost over $2,000."[40]

The report was immediately referred to a "Special Committee," which was to report back to the Convention at 4:00 P.M. that day. At the appointed time, the Rev. B. S. Bronson, head of the "Special Committee," presented a lengthy (longer than the Board of Fellows') and critical report. The gist of the report was that the committee felt that the board's report created a lot of "uncertainty" and that the Board of Fellows had not done enough toward their commission to establish a "Classical School" at Ravenscroft, and that those measures they had taken were wrong measures. It is surprising that the board did not resign en masse upon facing such harsh criticisms of all they had accomplished.

First, the Special Committee complained that the Board of Fellows seemed not to understand the various funds (endowment fund, Hicks Fund, and Bishop Atkinson Scholarship) available to them, and who had control of the disbursement of each. Perhaps this matter was one of semantics and misinterpretation of the board's report.

Furthermore, the part of the Committee's report that was particularly scathing and unjust was the following critical statement:

> It does not appear that the $250 spent for the School House have proved of any use in accomplishing the purposes of the trust for which the property was given, and the inquiry might naturally arise whether it was not at least prematurely expended. Your Committee would suggest to

FOUR. Redirection: Rectors and Ravenscroft High

the Convention that the two Departments of the Classical and Theological Boarding School, or Training School, can only be conducted successfully as they are conducted economically. Your Committee has no such love for financial statements, as well as too high an appreciation of the laborious, self-sacrificing Missionary labors of the Superintendent of the Theological Department and of his coadjutors, to enter into any calculation of the expense of maintaining a student in the Theological Department, especially at this epoch of its history — before the inauguration of its sister Department. Yet the time must inevitably come ere long when this inquiry will arise and create investigation on the part of the Convention in the management of its sacred trust.[41]

Although the committee acknowledged their respect for the Rev. Buel and "his coadjutors," the report certainly had a condescending and "holier-than-thou" tone. And if it was anything else, it was certainly unjust, as anyone who was acquainted with the Ravenscroft property would have acknowledged. Although the dormitory wing, added to Ravenscroft before the Civil War, had a relatively large "Common Room" on its first floor, the building had no sizeable rooms capable of handling more than a dozen students. The "School House" that the Board of Fellows had erected not only provided the necessary space but also was modestly and economically built, having simple brick walls and roof lines devoid of any frivolous ornamental trim. No building could have been built more economically (except perhaps for a frame building, which of course would not have survived the abuse of boarding school boys).

The final point of contention for the Special Committee was the matter of the theological department. They first criticized the board for acting on the establishment of the classical school without at the same time acting on the relocation of the theological department, as the committee felt that the intention of the Convention of 1886 was that both actions "should move concurrently."[42]

While the committee stated the obvious ("It is evident that no action has been taken by the Board" and "So far as the information of your Committee goes, the Classical Department cannot be started at present without thrusting out of doors the Theological Department"[43]), it also rejected the board's resolution asking for a release from the "limitation of $1,500, for the erection of a brick building for the Theological Department, and granting the power to the Board of erecting a suitable building at the least possible cost."[44] And yet in a seemingly contradictory statement the Committee further proclaimed, "Yet, your Committee feels that this Convention should, with a very impatient spirit, brook any delay under its sacred trust in the inauguration of a Classical Department in the Classical and Theological Boarding School. This part of her trust this Convention has long suffered to be in abeyance."[45] The committee concluded their report with a final resolution:

> That it is the settled sense of the Convention that a High School for Boys should be established by the Board of Fellows at Ravenscroft at the earliest possible moment, and that the sum of $2,000 be borrowed for the improvement and necessary addition to the present building, and that the erection of a separate building for the Theological Department be postponed for the present.

Surprisingly, the resolution passed, despite containing the two hallmarks for which the committee had criticized the report of the Board of Fellows. It did not promote the intention of the 1886 Convention that the establishment of both departments "should move concurrently," and in fact, by postponing any action on erecting a separate building for the theological department, it in essence impeded the Convention's intentions. Also, although the committee

The Ravenscroft Associate and Training School campus (soon to become the home of the Ravenscroft High School for Boys) is pictured in this photograph from February 1887. The original Ravenscroft building is pictured at right center. The front and cross gables of the school's new classroom/chapel building are shown at the extreme left side, just above the hip roof in the foreground. The site of the chapel is now occupied by the Graybar Co. at the southwest corner of Hilliard and Church. This photograph was taken from an upper balcony on the rear of the Swannanoa Hotel (on the southwest corner of Biltmore Avenue and Aston Street), just prior to the construction of Shoenberger hall (photograph from the author's collection).

had chided the board for the "indefiniteness" of one of the board's resolutions, the committee's resolution was totally indefinite about the fate of the theological department It did not say if it should continue "for the present," and if so, where it was to be relocated. The Rev. Buel and the Board of Fellows of Ravenscroft had every reason to be discouraged after the 1887 Convention, as now the theological school was homeless and the board's credibility seemed to be under severe scrutiny. However, they showed no signs of discouragement and immediately got to work carrying out the intentions of the Convention. The board borrowed $2,000 from the funds bequeathed by Bishop Atkinson for the benefit of the training school, pledging to pay back the funds as soon as possible and also cover the 8 percent interest on the loan. $1,307 of the funds was used to buy furniture and fittings for the main building and school house. The remaining $692 was given to the general fund to help defray the year's expenses.[46]

The year 1887, which started out to be a disappointing year, proved to be very beneficial for the ministry because of two providential occurrences, the first being the fact that a suitable headmaster was finally found to run the high school. After corresponding with a number of candidates and advertising in the church newspapers, offering a salary of $1,000, the board hired H. A. Prince to be the first headmaster of the Ravenscroft High School for Boys.[47]

Henry Axtell Prince was born at Geneva, New York, in 1861. After receiving his B.A. degree from Hobart College (an Episcopal college located in Geneva) in 1882, Prince took a position as a master at St. Paul's School in Concord, New Hampshire. In 1883 he moved to Southboro, Massachusetts, to take a position at St. Mark's School. While at St. Mark's he also began pursuing his M.A. degree, which he obtained from Hobart in 1885. Prince was teaching at St. Mark's when he accepted the position at Ravenscroft.[48]

Ravenscroft High School for Boys officially opened on Wednesday, October 5, 1887, with Mr. Prince as headmaster and Mr. Haywood Parker as second master. Mr. Parker, a native of Halifax County, North Carolina, was trained at Bingham School[49] and obtained his B.A. degree from the University of North Carolina, graduating in 1887. Under the tutelage of these two qualified men, the board reported, "There have six Boarders and nine Day Scholars. These have been in four forms,[50] the course being directed to prepare boys for our Universities or for the various pursuits of business."[51] A "Miss Kedie" is reported to have been hired as matron. The matron not only provided a motherly influence for the boys, but, more importantly, was also in charge of household duties such as meals, cleaning, dormitory care, and supervising the servants.

The Board of Fellows set the school fees as follows:

For Boarding Scholars, including tuition in all the branches taught,
Board. Washing. Fuel and Lights, per annum $300
Day Scholars in Latin, Greek and all English Branches$ 90
Day Scholars in English only $75
(but the fee for ALL Day Scholars was soon changed to a uniform–$80)[52]

Although the board went to great lengths to economize the school's expenses and even made a thorough analysis of actual costs after the first year, they found they were in a deficit; yet they were criticized for having high fees. Nonetheless, they continued on, knowing that admission of a few more scholars would cover the deficit.

After the 1887 Diocesan Convention, the Board of Fellows of Ravenscroft were in a huge dilemma, as the Convention had not only ordered that the new high school should immediately take over the building then occupied by the training school, but they had also given no instructions or guidance as to what should be done with the training school, and had even resolved to postpone the erection of a separate building.

The second providential occurrence of 1887 completely solved this major problem. The unfolding of this is a story in itself and best told by Bishop Lyman, who was God's instrument in solving this dilemma. About a month after the 1887 Convention, Bishop Lyman was visiting Baltimore on June 5 when he succumbed to an attack of fatigue and was ordered by his physician to cease his duties for the summer and spend time resting and regaining his strength. The bishop decided to go to New York to the home of a dear friend, and it was from there that the story begins, as the bishop recounts:

The next day, Monday, June 6th, I went on to New York and spent a few days very quietly at the house of my old and highly esteemed friend, Mr. John H. Shoenberger, formerly of Pittsburgh. At the time I was in great anxiety in regard to the future of our Theological Training School at Asheville, the great value of which I deeply felt, and which my predecessor Bishop Atkinson had labored so earnestly to build up and sustain. The importance of this work and the need of a suitable building for carrying it on, I urged upon Mr. Shoenberger, and my heart was much gladdened by his cordial agreement to erect the needed building for us at the cost of $8,000. This pledge lifted a heavy weight from my mind, and had much to do with my later improvement. The whole amount has been paid, and a substantial brick building is now nearly completed on the grounds of Ravenscroft, and is to be known as "Shoenberger Hall."

As the work proceeded, which we aimed to do in the most thorough and substantial manner, we found that the estimated cost was considerably below what would be necessary to complete the building in conformity with the details of the architect. After careful examination the contractor found that the work could not be finished in a satisfactory way without the additional sum of $3,000. Upon making known to our kind benefactor the exact state of the case, he very kindly and generously sent me a further check for the amount thus needed, so that now in a very few weeks the building will be entirely completed, and will be found one of the best constructed edifices in the city of Asheville. In all its appointments it is everything which we could desire, and we are thus fully equipped, so far as this building is concerned, for the training up of a succession of faithful ministers to aid in the extension of the Church.[53]

John H. Shoenberger, born in 1809, was the son of Dr. Peter Shoenberger, the "Iron King." Andrew Carnegie once commented, "Peter was to the iron industry what I later would become to the steel industry." John Shoenberger and his brother George inherited the lucrative iron businesses of their father, which included coke works, iron furnaces and rolling mills. After being part owner in a number of corporations, John went on to form his own business, John H. Shoenberger & Co. He was also, for a number of years, president of the Exchange National Bank of Pittsburgh. He had moved from Pittsburgh to New York City in 1880.[54] Bishop Lyman had known Shoenberger for over thirty years, having been rector of Trinity Episcopal Church (1850–1860), where Shoenberger was an active parishioner and deacon.

Construction on the new hall was well underway when the bishop visited Asheville in the spring of 1888. Bishop Lyman made the following subsequent report: "On Monday morning, April 30th, I took the train to Asheville. Upon my arrival, I drove at once to the new Theological building, to be known as Shoenberger Hall, and which I had not seen since they were making excavations for its foundation. I was much gratified to find so noble a building, already under roof and requiring only a few weeks to complete it. It is a most admirable and imposing structure, solidly built, and finished in the most satisfactory manner. It promises to prove a great blessing to the Diocese for many generations to come."[55]

Having vacated the Ravenscroft building in October of 1887, Dr. Buel and his four students then at the training school had to board in town while Shoenberger Hall was being completed. It was finished in late 1888 and first opened "after the Christmas recess."[56] The two-story brick building was built by a local contractor, Milton Harding,[57] and included rooms for the training school classes, a library, and a residential section for the principal's family. The new hall was located just a few hundred feet southeast of the Ravenscroft High School. It is a strong possibility that Shoenberger Hall was also designed by Milton Harding. Harding was listed in the 1890 Asheville City Directory as "architect," and was living at 93 Bailey Street, just one street west of Ravenscroft.

Meanwhile, the high school, after just one year, found itself without a headmaster. Mr. Prince, upon the recommendation of his physician, resigned his position at the end of the term (Spring 1888) due to health problems. The Board of Fellows began looking for a replacement immediately. Being unable to find a suitable replacement before the opening of the school in the fall of 1888, they asked Second Master Haywood Parker to be the principal for the coming year. The board also, upon Parker's recommendation, hired Mr. L. P. McGhee as his assistant.[58] Although under Parker's leadership the school had nineteen students (six of them being boarders), the Board of Fellows continued to look for a new principal. Perhaps the board felt that Parker was too young and inexperienced to be the long-term principal, or perhaps being a graduate of the University of North Carolina was not presti-

FOUR. *Redirection: Rectors and Ravenscroft High* 59

gious enough to give the school name recognition. However, Parker did have one supporter who thought that he should be given the position. Thomas Walton Patton, son of Trinity Episcopal Church founders James W. and Henrietta Patton, had been newly elected to the Board of Fellows. At the 1889 Convention, Patton, being the board's treasurer, submitted his Treasurer's Report, in which he added his endorsement for Parker:

> I beg leave to express my high admiration of the faithful manner in which Mr. H. Parker, Head Master, and Mr. L. P. McGhee, Assistant, have performed their duties, and my regret that the Board may lose the services of the former. So far as I have been able to learn, Mr. Parker has given satisfaction to the patrons of the school, and by close attention to every detail, has conducted it at much less loss to the Convention than was done last year. If the Board can secure his services for another year, I fully believe he can make his department self supporting.[59]

Nonetheless, the board decided to look elsewhere for the school's new principal.[60] The following was reported to the 1889 Convention: "The Board received yesterday two names highly recommended for the headmastership by the Rev. Dr. Henry A. Coit, of St. Paul's school, and one of these also recommended by Mr. Prince. The Board has instructed its committee to offer the position at once to this gentleman."[61] (Dr. Coit's St. Paul's School in Concord, New Hampshire, was one of the first and most highly esteemed boarding schools in the country at the time.)

The "gentleman" the Board offered the position to was Mr. Ronald MacDonald, the son of the popular and widely acclaimed British author, George MacDonald. Ronald was an 1885 graduate of Oxford and was serving as a teacher at Hill School in Pottstown, Pennsylvania. He originally came to America to teach as a single man in 1887. In 1888 he returned to England for the summer and married his fiancée, Louise Virenda Blandy, an artist who had been trained by John Ruskin. Ronald and his new wife returned to Hill School in the fall of 1888, where he resumed his teaching, until being contacted by the Board of Fellows in the spring of 1889.

Ronald, after a visit to Asheville and meeting with the board, accepted the board's proposal. On July 30, 1889, Asheville's *Daily Citizen* ran a small front-page article announcing MacDonald's appointment. The board's enthusiasm was evident as they ended the article with resounding hopefulness: "We believe that the school under the headship of Mr. Mac-Donald, aided as he will be, by competent assistants, will afford the very highest educational advantages and must prove an assured success."[62]

However, as later reported, "Mr. MacDonald was obliged to be absent several weeks last summer in England and could not reach Asheville until very near the time of the opening of the school."[63] The MacDonalds had gone back home to England to show off their new daughter Ozella, who had been born in Pottstown in May of 1889. Ronald's late arrival delayed the opening of the term and also resulted in fewer students than had been anticipated.

The new term began with sixteen students, three of them being boarding students. The board had also, with Ronald's approval, hired an assistant master, Mr. D. W. Bissell, a recent graduate (Class of 1889) of Yale University. Dwight Walter Bissell was born in Ahmednagar, India, to missionary parents, but returned to the United States when he was 9 years old. One former student described Bissell as "small and dapper,"[64] and from a photo of him one can see that this was an apt description. Coincidentally, Bissell had two classmates who had ties to Asheville. At the same time that Bissell was working at Ravenscroft, his fellow classmate from Yale, Gifford Pinchot (Class of 1889), was working nearby at Biltmore, the large estate then being built by millionaire George Vanderbilt. Pinchot was instrumental in developing a forestry management program on the estate, the first of its kind in the United States. Pinchot went on to not only be famous in the forestry industry, but was also a two-time governor of Pennsylvania. The other classmate, who had even a closer connection to Asheville, was Hillhouse Buel (Class of 1889), the son and only surviving child of Dr. D. H. Buel of Ravenscroft. There is no record as to this being a "coincidence" or whether this connection contributed to Bissell obtaining his position.

Miss Ramseur was hired as the new matron, replacing Miss Kedie, who had been hired in 1887. But after only a few months she resigned because of ill health and was replaced by a "Miss Gibbs of Charleston."[65] Very little is known about these women except that Miss Ramseur was probably one of two daughters of Mr. H. M. Ramseur, a civil engineer listed in the 1890 Asheville City Directory. This is a good possibility, as it is known that Ramseur's son, Vernon, was a student at Ravenscroft during that time.

Headmaster MacDonald had held the position for only a few months when he discovered that, besides running a school, he also had to deal with diocesan politics. In an effort to defray expenses, "the Board at its annual meeting [July 1889] authorized the Bishop to lease the school buildings and property to Mr. MacDonald for five years, the school to continue as a school of the Church and to be under the due supervision of the Bishop."[66] MacDonald's efficient management of the school was apparent after only a few months, so "accordingly, in the month of January [1890] the Bishop, with the hearty concurrence of the Executive Committee, made such a lease to Mr. MacDonald for the term of five years, he paying all expenses and receiving all the income."[67]

Beginning at the 1889 Convention, in another effort to economize on expenses, the decision was made to begin subdividing some of the Ravenscroft property into lots in order to raise necessary cash. By the 1890 Convention, not only was the diocese considering selling off portions of the property, but they also were considering relocating the high school off property to a location outside of town. This subject was first broached by Bishop Lyman in his address to the 1890 Convention:

> During my stay in Asheville last summer I became fully convinced that the interest of the school would be greatly advanced by its removal some few miles out of Asheville, and on a road which would secure easy access to the city. One great reason for this change is found in the fact that the grounds now occupied have only a small surface that is comparatively level, while a much larger area is needed for such athletic sports as it is so desirable to encourage. Another reason is that our present building is only the adaptation of a private residence for school purposes. What we need is a larger building, and one erected expressly for the required object, with all the conveniences and appliances which are so very desirable. The greatly increased value of our present property, which lies in quite a central part of the city, would command for it so good a price that with the proceeds of its sale we can secure just what we need for the school. I beg to call the attention of the Convention to this matter, and I hope the Board of Fellows may receive authority to sell a portion of the property, reserving, of course, a liberal tract as the permanent domain of our Theological Training School.[68]

True to Convention procedure, on the following day the bishop formed a committee to address the issue. The appointed members were the Rev. Dr. Buxton, the Rev. M. M. Marshall, D.D., the Rev. Gilbert Higgs, W. L. London, and C. E. Johnson.[69]

On the third day of the Convention, the Rev. Buxton presented the committee's findings and resolution, which essentially asked that the relocation of the high school be left up to the discretion of the Board of Fellows of Ravenscroft. The matter was immediately voted to be tabled until the next Convention, but later that day, Col. W. H. S. Burgwyn presented a motion to have the matter "taken up and reconsidered."[70] His motion was followed by a request that Ronald MacDonald address the Convention. Though not recorded, his address resulted in a passed resolution to add him to the committee.

Meanwhile, the Rev. Buel was continuing his mission and training work at Shoenberger Hall with four candidates, one of whom, he was happy to report, had already been ordained a deacon and was now officiating at Grace Church in Morganton.[71] Mr. C. L. Hoffman had been ordained a deacon the previous fall and was now pursuing priest's orders at Ravenscroft while concurrently serving at Morganton. Buel was also encouraged by the news that the Rev. W. S. Barrows would be joining the mission as his assistant beginning in the fall.

Headmaster Ronald MacDonald no doubt rushed home from the Convention, which had been 300 miles away in Tarboro, North Carolina, as his dear wife Louise had been in ill health for some time and was becoming increasingly frail. By mid–June, within a month of the end of the Convention, Louise was gravely ill. Ronald sent word back to England to have Louise's younger sister come to help. Winnie Blandy[72] arrived in early July 1890 and Ronald wrote to his mother (whom he affectionately called "Mammy") that Winnie "is just exactly what we need — always plucky, happy & opinionated & enthusiastic."[73] But Ronald also sadly wrote in the same letter that Louise "has seemed less well — has been downright hysterical over her meals, crying over every mouthful, & begging always off, &generally carrying on."[74] The letter reveals what does not show in any published reports: the inner struggles of Ronald MacDonald, Headmaster. He confessed to his mother that "my temper is sometimes abominable. I never openly lose it in official relations — with boys, master, or servants, but they have all tried me, & housekeeper & parents have nearly driven me wild &constant attendance on Louise & keeping indoors has driven me sometimes to my wits end. God helps me through all these troubles wonderfully, but I sometimes think that if I should lose Louise, I should never do any more good work."[75]

By the following month it was apparent that Ronald's wife was dying, so his family decided to send his sister Lilia from England to provide some additional help. Sadly, Louise Virenda MacDonald passed away on August 27, 1890, just a few days before Lilia arrived. The funeral was held the next day at Trinity Episcopal Church, with the Rev. Buxton officiating. Her body was laid to rest in the city's newly established Riverside Cemetery. Only a one-paragraph notice[76] was published in the local newspaper.

There is no mention of Ronald's loss in the Convention journals, or any other published church records. Ronald's wife died just weeks before he was to reopen the high school for a new scholastic year. In addition, he had a baby daughter (barely a year old) to care for, as well as managing the school and household. A lesser man would have resigned instantly, but Ronald immediately got to work preparing for the school's opening. Fortunately, his sister Lilia had arrived from England and decided to stay on and give whatever assistance she could.

Lilia MacDonald was a keen observer and an avid letter writer. Her letters provide many first-hand accounts of life at Ravenscroft. The school opened near the end of September, and on September 21, 1890, Lilia wrote: "All the boarders are not arrived — only 5 at present — two are very small & one is very tall. Fresh day boys[77] seem to come every day—Boys are taught so badly at the public (i.e. board & high) schools here and parents are beginning to find it out—and @ the Military Academy[78] they are so badly fed that they say it is a scramble to see who will get the food first."[79] A few weeks later she sent an update: "Of the eight boarders, two are gentleman & have the best heads—two are tiny boys (one of them always in angry tears)—two are brothers from a very proper & Y.M.C.A. family whose Mom-ma w(ouldn't) like them to play cards & who have brought bicycles."[80]

One of Lilia MacDonald's letters[81] was written on a discarded report card, which revealed that the subjects taught at Ravenscroft High were quite rigorous and comprehensive. The subjects (which were printed on the right-hand side on the card) included Latin, Greek, algebra, arithmetic, English literature, English grammar, history, geography, sacred study, composition, reading, declaration, spelling, and writing. The boys were also graded on the following character traits: punctuality, industry and decorum.

Lilia gives us a glimpse into the human emotion and dedication of her brother, Headmaster MacDonald: "He is smoking before the fire at this moment & says, 'Oh dear, I'm so tired of teaching little boys!'"[82] But then Lilia goes on to comment, "But no one else does it so much to his mind—It is beautiful to see the time he will spend in making a tiny chap get a grasp of Latin declensions—He thinks it so important."[83]

In one of her letters, Lilia MacDonald remarked that "in a small school, the headmaster has a considerable influence that is very hard to find—& hard to get in undermasters—especially in this country."[84] But she felt that Ronald had been fortunate to find Mr. Bissell as an assistant master (undermaster). "Bissell," observed Lilia, "has a very pleasant influence—his constant good-temper, is a great thing, & he is quite at home on the playground."[85]

The headmaster and masters of Ravenscroft High often had to deal with difficult parents of difficult boys. Lilia writes of one such altercation: "Poor Mr. Bissel has just come in bothered by an irate father. He & R [Ronald] had very strong reasons to suspect the boy of forging notes of excuse from his father. (They have been expelled from three schools before). So Mr. Bissell called to make sure,—& it was a mistake!—& the father furious. Mr. Bissell told him they w'd. not have suspected him if he hadn't been caught cheating badly—"all boys cheat" says the aggrieved father.—R says he will make it all straight with him.—R. has a wonderful way of bringing parents to reason."[86]

Discipline was maintained by the headmaster and his assistants, but sometimes it was difficult to know what was the right means of administering it. On one occasion, several students had seen two of their fellow students "pelt a countryman in a cart, ask the price of turnips etc. & cut his face with a stone."[87] When the observers were reluctant to give the culprits' names, Headmaster MacDonald suggested that if he were one of them, he would give the culprits a "whipping," but, he warned, "no black eyes or broken noses—just with sticks." However, the boys decided to handle the situation in a more formal manner. The next morning, when Headmaster MacDonald came into the schoolroom, he found a student-led court-martial already in session! Lilia MacDonald describes the scene:

Bush[88] in R's chair as judge—Wilson[89] chief jury man, (such a dear fellow) others of the jury, witnesses, officers of the court who had arrested the prisoners, McBee and Millard.[90] ... The only slip was that the jury in their righteous indignation gave judgement before the judge cd. get it out! But he repeated it with emphasis so no harm was done, & the culprits were being led off to execution when R[onald] suggested that the school was sanctuary so the poor wretches

FOUR. Redirection: Rectors and Ravenscroft High   63

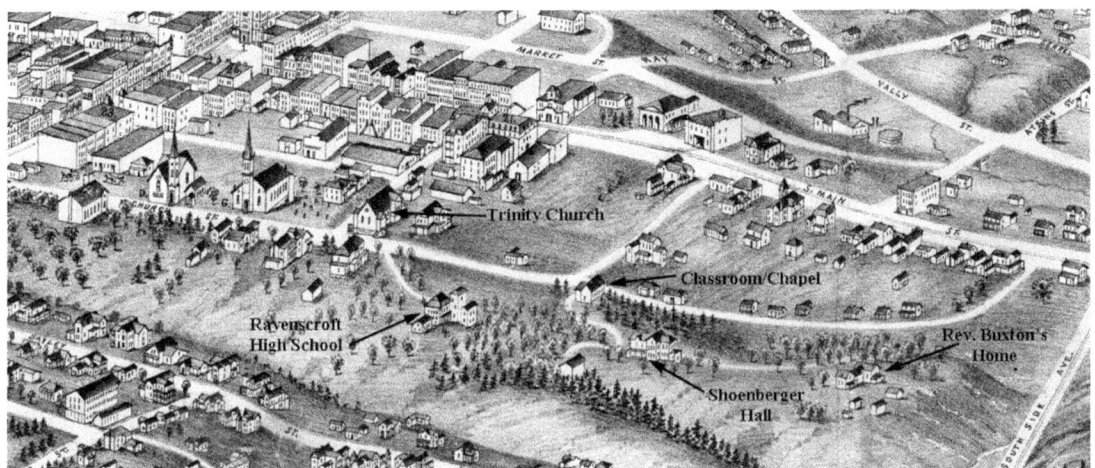

This 1891 "Bird's-Eye View of Asheville" clearly shows the entire Ravenscroft campus, including Ravenscroft High School for Boys, Shoenberger Hall, the classroom/chapel building, as well as Trinity Episcopal Church and the Rev. Buxton's home — from the 1891 "Bird's-eye view of the city of Asheville, North Carolina." Burleigh Lithographing Establishment, Madison, Wisconsin (G3904. A8A3 1891.R8, Library of Congress Geography and Map Division, Washington, D.C.).

had to march out of themselves to receive their stripes — the most guilty went out with firmness, the other had a serendipitous shove. R. was much pleased with the tone of the whole proceedings. One of them had got wind of what was in store, & escaped & was half down Main (ie. High) St. when the officers arrested him.[91]

The letters also show that it was not "all work and no play" for the students at Ravenscroft. On one occasion the boys wanted to show their appreciation to Headmaster MacDonald by surprising him with a bonfire and fireworks display in the front yard to celebrate "Guy Fawkes Day"—a British holiday, celebrated on November 5, in which an effigy of Guy Fawkes is burned on a bonfire. The surprise was directed by Mr. Bissell, and the ruse was aided by a general pandemonium about the town resulting from it being an election day. Lilia MacDonald writes of the eventful occasion:

The fireworks last night were a great success — the boys managed to slip out without his [Ronald's] finding out, in spite of the open door — When the bonfire was good they raised a cry (an English shout seems beyond their powers) & they blew a whistle — a sort of cat call. — W.[92] & I professed great agitation, & R[onald] dashed out perfectly furious — he thought the Democrat or Republican mob had got into the garden. "Get out of that," he bawled ... & he hurled himself like mad down the path into the mob of his own boys — by the time we joined him he was in fits of laughter, & as jolly as another boy himself.[93]

Another incident occurred during the 1890 Thanksgiving holiday, when the boys and masters decided to have a bit of fun: "Last Friday being Thanksgiving time, 16 boys went out riding with Ronald & Mr. Parker & Mr. Bissell. Such a cavalcade! It was charming to see them all preparing.— They made it a paper chase, & this little Cocke [Phillip C. Cocke] was sent first as hare, with a bag of papers as big as himself before him on his saddle."[94]

Of course, every boarding school has its share of pranks. Lilia tells of one:

There was some alterations in the stoves at the end of the last term that left for a day or two a hole in the flooring of the dormitory so that a string cd. Be let down into the common room —

one night; we heard a great clatter & when r. rushed into the common room to see, there was a most absurd ghost head, made by Eugene, the wag, of the turnip-head order — It had been put there for our edification, & a lot of chains tied together, and pulled by a string from the dormitory when the boys were safe in the bed to attract our attention.[95]

Just as Dr. Buel had required the assistance of servants when Ravenscroft was used as a training school, servants were also needed when it functioned as a high school. In fact, even more servants were needed, as the number of staff and students living in the house were much greater. Dr. Buel only had his small family and two or three students at a time, whereas the high school on average had 8–10 boarding students, plus another dozen "day-scholars," as well as two or three masters.

Lilia MacDonald often wrote home about the servants, all of whom were African American. Though she was surprised and perplexed because they did not behave the same as the highly trained British servants to whom she was accustomed, she shows that the servants were treated not just as employees, but as members of the Ravenscroft family. One such encounter illustrates this. She writes to her mother that she had just shown the "big-head Dundee photo" of her father, George MacDonald, to their coachman, Ben, "who finds that he 'favours' us, indeed so much so that another photo of Father that he made bold to look at 't other day struck him by the likeness — quite the same nose and brow as mind — 'and a noble face it is, is he living ma'am?'"[96] Lilia affectionately responds, "I think Ben a very nice man & did so before this verdict — He has been awfully nice to Ronald ever since Ronald rowed him as he says he never rowed anyone, for beating — I think — his wife[97] when he was drunk — That was long before I came, & B[en] has had only one outbreak since. He is a coachman, but does odd jobs about the house at times — At present R[onald] is much more comfortable & we are well served."[98] Lilia also mentions two other servants: "Nuckolds,[99] the man, is a very nice fellow (& good looking, but goes @ rags!!! tattered & torn in every detail, when not dressed out) & Dolly, the hugely tall house parlor maid, is a really good servant."[100]

The men at the training school, next door at Shoenberger Hall, often lent their experienced advice to the new headmaster and instructors at the high school. Headmaster Ronald, after lamenting that "no one would believe that four boys went in one term without some common & unsatisfactory reason," was advised by "Mr. Burroughs [Barrows], a nice clergyman here, who prepares the Theological students ... 'You may be sure it is a result of yr. doing yr. duty — & that such things will happen as long as you do it.'"[101] Mr. Barrows "had before given R[onald] a very depressing description of the subordinate condition of the American father to his sons."

Dr. Buel often gave his kind and fatherly encouragement to the men of the high school. In January 1891, Headmaster MacDonald sought Buel's advice after a run-in with a father (a Mr. Wainwright) of one of the boys, who had become angry because Ronald did not include "Sunday School teaching" at the school. MacDonald's sister happily reported, "R. was very much pleased to find old Mr. Buel [he was 74 years old], who was a theological light here, quite of his opinion too on the subject — He went to tell him @ the Wainwright affair, & Mr. Buel quite approved his mode of teaching the Bible."[102]

Lilia's description of Dr. Buel, "who *was* a theological light here," is quite revealing. The Rev. W. S. Barrows had originally been appointed to work at the training school as an assistant to Dr. Buel, but had recently been assuming the bulk of the work, as Dr. Buel was in increasingly declining health. But the final blow came less than two weeks later when tragedy struck at Shoenberger Hall. On February 5, 1891, Dr. Buel's wife of 34 years suddenly passed away. The shock, compounded by his increasing health problems, completely incapacitated Dr. Buel.

Dr. Buel's loss impacted the entire Ravenscroft institution. Mrs. Buel's funeral was held at Trinity Church. The whole school attended—"boys too," wrote Lilia MacDonald. The Rev. Buxton[103] officiated alongside the new rector of Trinity, the Rev. Neely DuBose. Lilia reported, "The service was very nicely given, & old Dr. Buxton read the lesson magnificently— He had a very impressive port &delivery, &is an ecclesiastic all over."[104]

But it was a very sad situation for Dr. Buel, as he was too feeble to accompany his wife's body to her burial in New York State; Mrs. Buel's body had to be shipped north on a train to be met by one of her brothers. Ronald, a pallbearer, had to help carry the body down to the depot for transport and wait while the coffin was properly packaged and loaded on to the train. Lilia describes the sad state of affairs: "R. felt it most unseemly, as the coffin was placed on a truck on the platform, just like any other piece of luggage.... It was enclosed in an ordinary packing case & at the corner was nailed a card of directions combining a tombstone inscription and a luggage label setting forth the names, wife of,-daughter of- and then where she was bound for— beyond N. York a little bit."[105]

The death of Mrs. Buel and the incapacitation of Dr. Buel were of the utmost concern to both the bishop and the diocese at the 1891 Convention, which was held just a few months later. In his address at the start of the Convention, Bishop Lyman tells of the sad state of affairs when he visited Asheville the previous November:

> It gave me much concern to find the health of the Rev. Dr. Buel so greatly impaired that he was wholly unable to go on with his duties in connection with our Theological Training-school and the mission fields so long under his charge. I endeavored to make such arrangements as might enable the Rev. Mr. Barrows, who had been appointed by me to be associated with Dr. Buel, to go on with the work. Not long after that time the unexpected death of Mrs. Buel, who had been such an invaluable helper and support to her husband, came with stunning effect upon him, and he has ever since been entirely disabled and disqualified for any work.[106]

The bishop follows with a surprising statement:

> But while this great trouble came upon me in connection with our Theological Training-school I was, on the other hand, much cheered and encouraged by the increasing prosperity of Ravenscroft High-school for boys. Under the wise, able and judicious management of Mr. MacDonald there has been a constant advance, and now the school has won for itself a very high reputation, and has secured the warmest confidence on the part of those whose sons have been enjoying its privileges. I feel quite sure that no more thorough and admirable school has ever been established in our State, and now its triumphant success seems fully assured. Parents may, indeed, consider it a high privilege to have their sons surrounded by influences so salutary and elevating, and where the training of mind, body and spirit are alike so constantly regarded. The school will need no further commendation to secure all the pupils who, under our present arrangements, can possibly be accommodated.[107]

This is surprising because, although he sings high praises of MacDonald and his work at the high school, the bishop makes no reference to Ronald's loss, which also occurred since the last Convention. There is no mention at all of Louise MacDonald's death in the Convention records. Perhaps this was because MacDonald was able to continue to carry on with his work at Ravenscroft High School.

Dr. Buel's difficulties also brought to the fore another matter, which had not been dealt with in the past. Apparently, although Mr. Shoenberger had increased his donation from $8,000 to $11,000 to cover the costs of building Shoenberger Hall, the final cost of construction was several thousand dollars more. Buel, who was put in charge of supervising the construction, had paid the additional cost (over $2,500) from his own money. Although a motion was made[108] at the 1891 Convention to reimburse Dr. Buel, the matter would not be settled for a few more years. The Rev. W. S. Barrows, Buel's assistant, took over the responsibilities of the mission and training school. Barrows' reports to the Convention that year tell of the faithful and tireless service that Dr. Buel had given over the years. Reporting on St. Mary's Church at Micadale, Barrows says, "This Mission was established ten years ago through Dr. Buel's efforts, and owes its excellent buildings to him."[109] In his report on Grace Church in the Mountains, Waynesville, Barrows kindly remarks, "Dr. Buel, to whom the Church in Waynesville owes almost everything, has not been able to come out since September."[110] But Barrows gives his greatest tribute to Dr. Buel in his report on St. David's

This circa 1891 photograph of headmaster Ronald MacDonald and the faculty and students of the Ravenscroft High School was published in the July 11, 1954 issue of the *Asheville Citizen Times*, with the following caption: "Ravenscroft High School was one of Asheville's leading educational institutions in earlier days. In this photo, which belongs to George Colt, some of the students are pictured with the headmaster, Ronald MacDonald, whose English training set the educational pattern for the institution. Identification of the boys shown reveals many who were later to become community leaders. From L to R: Front row, Hamilton Bigelow, P. C. Cocke, Walter Hatch Lee, V. E. McBee Jr. Arnold W. VanderHorst, Preston Patton, McRee Hatch and C. C. Millard. Second row, Mynot Davis, Walton Cheeseborough, Charles E. Jones, J. C. Burrage, H. R. Millard, Ronald MacDonald, Vernon Ramseur and Winthrop Campbell. Back row, Eugene Holt, Silvio Von Ruck, Huntington Wilson, L. A. Burrage, Tom Bush, J. E. Cheeseborough, James A. Gwyn, Prof. Parker, Prof. D. W. Bissell, James Hyman, Walter Erdman and Erwin Holt." (This photograph is from a photocopy made by the author in the late 1990s from the original newspaper clipping, since discarded, in the archive files of the newspaper office. George Colt, who owned the original photo, was a retired commercial artist who had worked for the *Asheville Citizen-Times* for many years).

Mission, Cullowhee: "As an instance of 'patient continuance in well doing,' it may be interesting to note that Dr. Buel, who has continued in charge ever since he began this work, more than eighteen years ago, before the day of railroads, was long accustomed during the greater part of the year, to drive once a month regularly from Asheville, more than sixty miles away."[111]

The committee appointed to look into the relocation of the high school made no report to the Convention in 1891, and that fact was duly noted. After a number of years of "no report" at the Conventions, the matter was dropped.

The work of both departments continued on: the training school under the direction of the Rev. Barrows, and the high school with Headmaster MacDonald and his two assistants, D. W. Bissell and Phillip S. Parker. Despite the interruption and slowdown at the training school, the next few years were banner years for the Ravenscroft High School for Boys.

Phillip Stanley Parker joined the staff at Ravenscroft immediately upon graduation from Harvard in 1890. Parker was well liked by Headmaster MacDonald. In fact, shortly after Parker's arrival, MacDonald commented in a letter to his father, George MacDonald, "I have a new master, who is a gentleman, thank God."[112] Lilia MacDonald also wrote of Parker, "He is an extremely nice young fellow — comes of Boston & Phila. people and will manage the boys well."[113] He remained a year or so and then returned to Harvard for a graduate degree, and eventually became a successful lawyer in Boston.

We have two existing artifacts from life at Ravenscroft High School for Boys during this period. The first artifact is a photograph of the staff and boys of the school, the only known one of its kind. The photo was published in 1954 in the *Asheville Citizen–Times* and was listed as belonging to George Colt, a retired newspaper man. But the photo, from other evidences, was made fifty years earlier, in 1891 or 1892. As the caption so aptly says, "Identification of the boys shown reveals many who were later to become community leaders." One such boy, Walter Hatch Lee, did not survive long enough to become a community leader, but he did become a gallant and distinguished hero of the Philippine–American War. Lee was the son of James Hardy and Sara Hatch Lee of Glencoe, North Carolina, a small hamlet just a few miles west of Asheville. It was reported that Lee entered Ravenscroft at 10 years of age. After graduating from Ravenscroft in 1893, Lee transferred to Bingham Military School and then to West Point, where he graduated as an officer in 1901. Unfortunately, Lieutenant Walter Hatch Lee took part in a dangerous expedition in the Philippines and was killed on June 10, 1901.[114] "Battery Lee" at Fort Flagler, Washington, was named in honor of this valiant Ravenscroft boy.

Walter Hatch Lee, as a young man, had kept a few scrapbooks of newspaper articles and memorabilia. The second surviving artifact of life at Ravenscroft High School is from one of Lee's scrapbooks, now housed at the University of Chapel Hill. Along with a clip of a newspaper article about the event, there is a published program of the results from a "Field Day" held on the small athletic field in front of Ravenscroft School on Tuesday, June 18, 1891. Although the newspaper called it a "Field Day," the program called it a "Handicap Athletic Meeting." The events included numerous running and jumping events, such as the broad jump, 100-yard run, hurdles, three-legged race, sack race, and even a "Lubricated Pork Chase."

Another boy in the photo from 1891 is Huntington Wilson, whose full name was Francis Mairs Huntington Wilson. Wilson went on to become a U.S. diplomat and served as assistant secretary of state under presidents William Howard Taft and Woodrow Wilson. In his 1945 book, *Memoirs of an Ex-Diplomat*, Wilson wrote of his experience as a student at Ravenscroft. Since it is not long and is the only known published account from a student of the school, I quote the passage in its entirety:

> Then, when I was thirteen, my restless father took us to Asheville, North Carolina, and turned to quail-shooting and trout fishing. I was sent as a boarder to the Ravenscroft School. There were about fourteen boarding pupils in a dormitory with cubicles curtained off. All were Southerners but me and the first night, after the lights were out, there began a low menacing chorus of "Hard times for the Yankees." I got all my shoes up on the bed and awaited the attack, but nothing really happened.
>
> In addition to us boarders, there were about two dozen day-scholars, and at recess the next day I had a successful fisticuff and was thereafter admitted to a small group who ruled the roost, especially among the boarding pupils. We carried large green slats from window shutters with Sic Semper Tyrannis carved on them. The meanest thing we did was to make smaller boys warm the seats of the outdoor privies on cold winter mornings, for our comfort. Arnoldus Vander Horst, of Charleston [who is also in the 1891 photo], was the ring leader in the initial Yankee-baiting and also the head of our little group.
>
> The school was run by Ronald Macdonald, a handsome man, the son of George Macdonald, the English novelist, assisted by one of his sisters[115] and by another Englishwoman[116]; and there was another master, small and dapper, named Bissell. We were well fed and often had those fruit pies in a deep dish with a cup buried at the bottom for some reason. The headmaster was crazy about riding and dressed well for the part; but he held himself so rigidly that he often took a spill. Everyone rode horseback down there at that time. In fact, at wet seasons it was the only way to get about. Wagons would sink up to the hubs in the clay soup that some of the roads became.
>
> After one term as a boarder, I became a desultory day-scholar for a second term.

Two other instructors came during MacDonald's tenure a "Mr. Bonnele" (Bonnell?) and "Mr. Waite," whose names are mentioned in one of the MacDonald family letters from 1892.[117] We know little of "Mr. Bonnele," but the latter "Mr. Waite" was Herbert Waite, who joined the Ravenscroft staff immediately upon graduation from Amherst College in 1892. Herbert Harold Waite spent two years teaching at Ravenscroft High School before moving on to graduate school at the University of Michigan, Department of Medicine, where he received his M.D. in 1896. Waite became a noted professor of bacteriology and pathology at the University of Nebraska from 1903 to 1931.

The professors and Headmaster MacDonald all lived in the Ravenscroft building, together with the boarding students, who resided in the dormitory section of the house. The MacDonald family letters often speak of the professors and staff eating meals together and having nightly card games of whist. Lilia MacDonald in one of her letters gives us a sense of their playful camaraderie: "The whist players are expressing themselves with great freedom. 'I hate Parker worse than death,' says Mr. Bissell in his quiet way — 'You will find Bissell, that more can be done with some natures by kindness than by severity,' says R[onald] with the eternal pipe in his mouth."[118]

With such qualified assistants, it is no wonder that the high school's name and recognition grew steadily during MacDonald's tenure. Bishop Lyman proudly sang its praises at the 1893 Convention: "Let me also especially commend that most noble Diocesan School which we have established at Asheville. I mean the Ravenscroft High School for boys. Under the very wise management of Mr. Ronald MacDonald, we have now one of the most valuable

FOUR. Redirection: Rectors and Ravenscroft High

Advertisement for Ravenscroft High School for Boys, published in an 1891 issue of *The Forum*, a late-nineteenth century periodical (collection of the author).

institutions for Christian training and sound learning which has ever been inaugurated in our State."[119]

Though the Rev. Barrows carried on the work at the training school and mission after Dr. Buel was unable to do so, he was never given the title of "principal," not even after the death of Dr. Buel, which occurred on January 13, 1893, in Baltimore, where he had moved to be near his son in his last days. Bishop Lyman gave a wonderful eulogy of Dr. Buel in his address to the 1893 Convention:

For about twenty years he had been actively engaged in missionary work in the western part of the Diocese, while engaged also in instructing young men for the ministry, as Principal of the "Ravenscroft Mission and Training School," at Asheville. He led a very self-sacrificing and laborious life, never sparing himself, but making almost every week a long and fatiguing journey to his several Missions, and carefully keeping his appointments, even in the most severe and inclement weather. Sincerely devoted to his work, and thoroughly conscientious in the discharge of his duties, he ever set an example worthy of all imitation.[120]

Those were probably the last public words of endorsement that Bishop Lyman gave for the school, as he passed away a few months later on December 13. Bishop Lyman had been concerned about his failing health and had implored the 1893 Convention to elect an assistant bishop. The Convention decided to reconvene on June 27 at Raleigh in a special conference for that purpose. After a grueling two days of balloting, the Rev. Joseph Blount Cheshire won the vote on the thirty-ninth ballot.[121] Then, after serving as assistant bishop for only five months, the Rev. Cheshire became the fifth bishop of the Episcopal Diocese of North Carolina on December 13, 1893.

Joseph Blount Cheshire Jr. was born the son of the Reverend Joseph Blount Cheshire, Sr. (rector of Calvary Church, Tarboro, North Carolina) and Mary Toole Parker on March 27, 1850. After earning his B.A. degree from Trinity College in Hartford, Connecticut, Blount took a position as a Greek and Latin instructor at St. Clement's Hall in Ellicott City, Maryland. In 1871, he moved back to North Carolina and began his study of law under the tutelage of two prominent lawyers, William Ruffin and Judge George Howard. Upon obtaining his license to practice law in 1872, he moved to Baltimore to begin his practice in partnership with a college friend. That only lasted for little more than a year, at which time he moved back to North Carolina and got a job with a law firm in Tarboro.

Cheshire became restless as a lawyer and began to feel the call of God to the ministry. In 1876, he began theological studies under the tutelage of his father. Two years later, he was ordained a deacon and began his internship as a rector at the Chapel of the Cross at the University of North Carolina at Chapel Hill. His heart for mission work was evident early in his ministry, as he was responsible for organizing the mission of St. Phillip's at Durham, North Carolina, while still a "novice" rector at Chapel Hill.

In 1880 Cheshire was ordained a priest, and the following year he was called to be the rector of St. Peter's Church in Charlotte. While at St. Peter's, Cheshire continued in his zeal for mission work, establishing at least five other churches in the surrounding area.[122] He served at St. Peter's for twelve years until his election as bishop in 1893.[123]

Cheshire had been the bishop for less than six months before he had to preside at his first Convention in May of 1894. In his address to the Convention he reported that he had visited Asheville in February and attended and officiated at a number of events while there.

Two of these events are noteworthy. First, he attended a meeting of the Board of Fellows of Ravenscroft on Thursday, February 15, in the library of Shoenberger Hall. At that meeting the Board of Fellows offered to the headmaster of the Ravenscroft High School "to continue ... The lease of the property free of rent for another term of five years, on condition of his keeping the building in repair and paying for the insurance on the same."[124] Later in the Convention the board also reported that "the Rev. W. S. Barrows, S.T.B., Instructor in the Training School for the Ministry, has had the direction of the Theological Students, and at the same time he and the Rev. Samuel Rhodes have been conducting in an acceptable manner the work of the Associate Mission."[125] It was further reported that the Rev. Barrows would soon be leaving the diocese.

The second major event that the new bishop attended during his visit to Asheville in February was the laying of the cornerstone for St. Matthias Church. Originally started around 1872 as a Sunday school for "colored people" by General J. G. Martin and others from Trinity Church, it was first called "Trinity Chapel." Isaac Dickson, the former butler to Dr. Buel and now a prominent leader of the African American community, was a longtime member of St. Matthias. The new brick church was replacing the original wood-framed structure, which sat adjacent to the newly erected brick church. Bishop Cheshire decided to change the name of the church from "Trinity Chapel" to "St. Matthias," as he felt it was "very undesirable to call so many of our churches by the same name."[126]

Unfortunately, 1894 proved to be a very difficult year for both the associate mission/training school and the high school. Contrary to the glowing reports at the Convention that year, both institutions were headed for major upheavals, which ultimately would change the nature of their operations and set them on the course to their eventual demise. The Rev. Barrows' resignation from the directorship of the Associate Mission and Training School, following so soon after the death of the Rev. Buel, was of great concern to the bishop. At the July meeting of the Ravenscroft Board of Fellows, the bishop announced the appointment of the Rev. Alfred H. Stubbs as "Warden of Shoenberger Hall."[127] Though it sounded like a new position, essentially it entailed the same responsibilities previously carried out by the Rev. Buel. They included administering the training school and coordinating the work and ministry of the Ravenscroft Associate Mission, with its various mission stations and churches.

The Rev. Alfred Houghton Stubbs was born on August 22, 1841, to the Rev. Alfred and Emelia Stebbins Houghton Stubbs in New Brunswick, New Jersey. The Rev. Stubbs, after obtaining his B.A. degree from Rutgers in 1861, continued on at the same institution and obtained his M.A. degree in 1864. That same year he enrolled at the General Theological Seminary in New York to begin training for the ministry. He was ordained a priest in 1865 by Bishop Odenheimer. After serving in parishes in Orange, New Jersey, and Windham, Connecticut, the Rev. Stubbs took a position as rector of Trinity Episcopal Church in Davenport, Iowa. It was there that he married Ella V. Hunt Weiser on April 25, 1867. Two years later he moved to a pastorate in Otsego County, Mississippi, and then on to Mechanicsville, New York, in 1871 before settling in North Carolina in 1881. After a few months at Wadesboro, North Carolina, Stubbs took a more permanent position as rector of St. Barnabas's Church, where he was serving when appointed as Warden of the Ravenscroft Associate Mission in 1894.[128]

Bishop Cheshire appointed deacons Samuel Rhoades, William F. Rice, and the Rev.

Frederick F. Wey to be the Rev. Stubbs' assistants at the associate mission. The Rev. Wey served and lived at Waynesville. Two other priests who had previously been trained at Ravenscroft Training School were already serving mission churches in western North Carolina — the Rev. John Deal at Macon County, Cashiers, and Highlands and the Rev. Milnor Jones at charges in Haywood, Jackson, Swain and Cherokee counties.

Although the associate mission work continued under the Rev. Stubbs, the work of the training school had come to a halt. An economic crisis had forced Bishop Cheshire to take drastic measures. He explained the situation to the 1895 Convention:

> I last July nominated to the Board of Fellows the Rev. Alfred H. Stubbs, who was thereupon elected Warden. But I find that, from causes useless to enumerate in this place, the endowment of this institution, which a few years ago yielded a thousand dollars annual revenue for the support of the work, now yields practically nothing. I have had the use of part of the building known as Shoenberger Hall, and for an income only what I could get out of the scanty appropriations of our Diocesan and Domestic Boards.[129] ... Ravenscroft Associate Mission has already been spoken of. It is at present without any students, there being no means at my command for

This contemporary photograph shows Shoenberger hall shortly after its construction in 1888. The Samuel Kepler family, who leased a portion of the building in 1894, are shown on the front lawn. They are as follows: (*right to left*): Samuel Kepler, son Thomas Kepler and Thomas' daughters (Martha holding her father's hand and Mary in the nurse's arms); Mrs. Mary Wooldridge Kepler and two unidentified young ladies (image #C762–8 from the North Carolina Collection, Pack Memorial Library, Asheville).

their support.... As the Warden of Ravenscroft and his only associate,[130] who lodged in Shoenberger Hall, occupied only a small portion of the building, and as the defective construction and poor materials used already demanded repairs, I thought it wise to acquiesce in the judgment of the local Fellows, and to rent the hall as a private residence, reserving the library and sufficient accommodation for the Warden and his Deacon associate. By this means needed repairs have been made in the building, and it has been connected with the city water and sewage systems.[131]

Shoenberger Hall was rented to "Mrs. Kepler of Trinity Parish" for eight months for the sum of $240, of which $200 was paid up front to cover the costs of the needed repairs.[132] Martha C. Wooldridge Kepler was the wife of grocer and local businessman Samuel R. Kepler. Interestingly, a photo of Shoenberger Hall was taken during those months, with the Kepler family standing on the front lawn.

Shoenberger Hall was not the only place of change in 1894. The Ravenscroft High School for Boys was floundering as well, despite the glowing reports. At the 1894 Convention in May, the Board of Fellows of Ravenscroft "respectfully" reported, "The School for Boys, under the management of Mr. Ronald MacDonald, as Head Master, has won for itself an excellent reputation. We have offered to continue to Mr. Ronald MacDonald the lease of the property free of rent for another term of five years, on condition of his keeping the building in repair and paying for the insurance on the same."[133] The minutes from the "Journal of the Board of Fellows of Ravenscroft," however, reveal that the offer to continue the lease came at the request of MacDonald. The minutes from the February 14, 1894, meeting report:

> The Sec. next read a communication from Mr. Ronald McDonald [sic] in which he asked for a renewal of the lease on Ravenscroft School on the same terms as before & further asked for the entire use and control of Shoenberger Hall for which he agreed to give preparatory education & board to not more than four (4) young men or boys, certified by the Bishop to be in preparation for Holy Orders, at one half the usual school rates, viz.— one hundred fifty dollars ($150.00) pr. annum & to lodge them in Schoenberger [sic] Hall.[134]

A committee was formed to communicate with MacDonald about his request, but apparently the matter was not settled even as late as July, just two months before the beginning of the fall term. MacDonald was present at the July 11, 1894, meeting of the Board of Fellows and the minutes report:

> Mr. Ronald MacDonald was next called before the Board, & tho' as yet no lease had been presented to him for signature, he agreed to abide by the conditions presented by the comt. to the meeting in Winston [North Carolina]. A communication from Mr. McDonald [sic], offering to lay water pipes from nearest point on Church St. to Ravenscroft School & Schoenberger [sic] Hall, if the Board would furnish the water pipes, cost of 500 ft. of one inch pipe, & 700 ft. of ¾ inch pipe, not to excede [sic] $53.00 was favorably considered, & Capt. Patton [Thomas Walton Patton] was appointed to act in the matter with Mr. McDonald [sic] & have the pipes laid if it could be done for $53.00.[135]

Despite MacDonald's plans to not only continue his lease but also expand his school by offering "preparatory education" for the young men at the training school at the opening of the new scholastic year in September, MacDonald suddenly resigned his post and returned to England. One later report described MacDonald as "abandoning it suddenly."[136] Most people, even those in the inner circle of Ravenscroft, knew little of the personal agonies and travails that MacDonald had endured during his headmastership. Most men would have given up years earlier, but MacDonald persevered after the death of his beloved wife (in 1890) and worked out his five-year agreement, and had even made plans to expand his sphere of influence. So why did he seemingly "abandon it suddenly" in the fall of 1894? We must remember that MacDonald was not being paid a "salary." Instead, his agreement stipulated that he lease the buildings (free of charge) from the diocese and that he receive "all the monies" from the tuition and boarding fees, and keep up the repairs and insurance on the buildings. But of course, out of "all the monies" he not only had to pay for the building upkeep and insurance, he also had to pay the salaries of the staff—assistant masters and servants (housekeepers, cooks and stablemen)—as well as buy all supplies and food for the boys and staff. It is a wonder that any "monies" were left over for his salary.

An early hint of his financial difficulties was revealed in a letter MacDonald wrote to his sister Winifred in 1892: "In the last few days, indeed, I have succeeded in screwing some very important oof [money] out of my people, which is interesting, perhaps. It is the hardest up place & time I ever knew. Everybody says everybody else won't pay. I however, have managed to tide over my difficulties."[137] When the school term was about to begin in the fall of 1894, Ronald realized that not enough students had enrolled to make it fiscally viable. A report published a few years later sheds light on this by stating that MacDonald had "undertook (with the approval of the Diocesan Convention) to run the school as a private educational enterprise; but, not meeting with patronage sufficient to justify its continuance, he finally gave up the undertaking."[138]

Although this was a sign of things to come, this was not the final demise of the school. The Board of Fellows scrambled to find a last-minute replacement. An emergency meeting of the Board of Fellows met on October 8, a month after the school term was to have begun, to "consider the applications of Messers Valentine & Wight for the Head Mastership of Ravenscroft School made vacant by the resignation of Mr. Ronald McDonald [sic]."[139] The board chose "Mr. J. H. Toynbee. Wight"[140] as the new headmaster, offering him a one-year term on the same conditions that MacDonald was given (rent-free, but paying for insurance and repairs). The new headmaster's full name was Thomas Henry Toynbee Wight, although he mostly went by "Toynbee Wight."

Wight was born in London to Thomas Henry and Annie Wight in 1871. Toynbee's father was a master mariner at sea with the British Merchant Marine and was often away from the family. He died at sea in 1881, leaving Annie to care for their four children, including 9-year-old Toynbee.[141] In 1887, at the age of 16, Toynbee Wight began his studies at St. Chad's College Denstone in Staffordshire, England. He graduated in 1890 with a distinction in chemistry, geology, and natural philosophy. In 1891 he was hired as a master at St. Chad's.[142] Shortly thereafter he married and moved to America.

The report of the Board of Fellows to the 1895 Convention stated, "Ravenscroft School is very small, but we consider Mr. Wight in every way competent to make a good school, provided he receives a proper patronage."[143] The bishop also informed the Convention that the school had "carried on with some success as a day-school since Mr. MacDonald's departure last fall."[144] However, the Committee on the State of the Church was not so encouraging when it reported, "The Ravenscroft Training School is somewhat disappointing in the work done for the boys and young men of the Diocese. Your Committee would recommend that some kind of change be made and some efficient and commendable scheme started for a suitable training school for boys, and that this need be urgently pressed upon the authorities whose province it is to take action in this matter."[145]

A change was indeed imminent, not just for the school but also for the entire diocese. The year before (1894) Bishop Cheshire, after being "on the job" for just over one year, came to the same realization as his predecessors — that travel to the vast western section of the state was not only difficult but also very time-consuming. But yet it was also the region that needed the most attention. Therefore, at the 1894 Diocesan Convention he urged that a delegation be appointed to solicit the General Convention of the Church to consider separating the western region from the Diocese of North Carolina as a missionary jurisdiction, with the eventual election of its own bishop. Hence, even as the State of the Church Committee was recommending a change, the wheels were already in motion to effect one.

After a bit of a struggle, the General Convention and House of Bishops agreed to the separation. And so just months after the committee's report the first Convention of the new Missionary District of Asheville was held on November 12–13, 1895, at Trinity Church in Asheville, with Bishop Cheshire presiding. The new missionary district consisted of the entire western section of the state west of the dividing line that ran along the eastern boundaries of the counties of Allegheny, Wilkes, Alexander, Catawba, Lincoln and Gaston. The new district included eight parishes, thirteen organized missions, and thirty-five unorganized missions, all administered by only sixteen priests and six ordained deacons.[146]

With the separation came a few sticky issues, such as the financial support of the new district and the election and support of a new bishop (this issue would take a few more years to be resolved). But the stickiest and most controversial issue was the ownership and administration of diocesan property within the new district. This greatly impacted both the Ravenscroft Associate Mission/Training School and Ravenscroft High School, as the Ravenscroft property was the largest diocesan property in the district.

The issue was complicated even more by Bishop Cheshire's proposed solution. He presented his recommendations to the Diocesan Convention of 1896. Although lengthy, I present his entire argument as a reference for further discussion:

> The Diocese owns a very valuable property in the city of Asheville, commonly known as the Ravenscroft property. As misapprehension exists in the minds of many persons as to our diocesan interest in this property, and as some have supposed that we have no power to dispose of it, I may state for the information of the Convention that I had looked carefully into this matter, and had taken the advice of eminent lawyers upon the chief points involved long before the present state of things had been anticipated, and with reference to entirely different questions. The facts of the case are substantially as follows:
>
> Very soon after Bishop Atkinson's consecration a movement was made in the Convention for the establishment of a Diocesan School for Boys. It was determined to establish it at Pittsboro [sic], and the Rev. Jarvis Buxton was chosen principal of the school. The people of Asheville, unwilling to give up Mr. Buxton, proposed that the school should be established in Asheville, and offered to aid the enterprise upon this condition. This was done, and a subscription (alleged to have amounted to thirteen or fourteen hundred dollars) was made in Asheville towards the purchase of lands, etc. The property in question, about thirteen acres, was bought and conveyed to the Trustees of the Diocese. The Asheville subscribers, however, stipulated that if the property should cease to be used for a school it should be sold, and their money refunded to them, incorporating this condition in the deed, and providing that the amounts to be thus repaid should be ascertained by a list of the names of the subscribers, with the sums severally given, which list was to be recorded along with the deed. I am advised by those learned in the law that

the effect of this stipulation is to make the deed a mortgage upon the property to that extent, and that upon the happening of the specified contingency the Diocese would be liable to the extent of the value of the property for the sums so recorded, and for no others; and that, subject to this encumbrance, the Diocese owns the property in fee-simple. To conclude this part of the subject, it should be added that no list of names and amounts was recorded, as provided in the deed, so that there is no legal claim against the property on this account, and it is probably impossible at this time to ascertain with any exactness the names of the contributors or the sums subscribed. If I am correctly informed, this disposes of any legal claim under the deed, and clears the title to the property. But in my judgment the Diocese should hold itself ready to repay the amounts subscribed to any parties, whose claim should be established, and who should require it, in case the property should cease to be used as a school.

Upon the property thus acquired the Diocese has spent considerable sums of money in improvements. This money was raised in all parts of the Diocese and in other Dioceses. My father obtained from one of his parishioners a single gift of two thousand dollars, mentioned by Bishop Atkinson in his address of 1863. The money raised in other places was given unconditionally to the Church, with no stipulation for repayment, as in the case of the Asheville subscriptions. This property, therefore, belongs to the Diocese of North Carolina, to be used for the work of the Church in such manner as this Convention may choose to order: such, at least, is my understanding of its legal and equitable status.

This, however, is, in my judgment, subject to a very important qualification or limitation. A friend of Bishop Lyman supplied the funds with which he had erected upon this property the building known as Shoenberger Hall as a permanent home for the Ravenscroft Associate Mission and Training School. Though there has been no action by this Convention or by the Board of Fellows of Ravenscroft, declaring this a local institution, yet I cannot help feeling that both Bishop Atkinson and Bishop Lyman intended it to be a permanent institution for the special benefit of that mountain section which has now become the Jurisdiction of Asheville, and I think we should respect that intention and carry out the purpose of our departed Bishops. The same considerations apply with even greater force to the endowment left by Bishop Atkinson for the support of this institution. In my judgment it should go with Shoenberger Hall to the Missionary Jurisdiction of Asheville. The Hix Fund, being the bequest of a lady specially interested in the Watauga and Linville section, and intended primarily, by an express direction of her will, for missions in that locality, should, it seems to me, go to the Trustees of the Jurisdiction for missionary work under the direction of the Bishop.

I therefore recommend to this Convention that it direct the Trustees of the Diocese to convey to the Trustees of the Missionary Jurisdiction of Asheville the building known as Shoenberger Hall, with the land whereon it stands, and a sufficient quantity of land adjacent thereto for the convenient use and occupation thereof for all its intended purposes, and that they further convey and assign to the same Trustees the securities and other property in their hands constituting what are known as the Ravenscroft Endowment Fund and the Hix Fund, subject to the same trusts under which they are now held by the Trustees of this Diocese.

I further recommend that all legislation by this Convention creating the Board of Fellows of Ravenscroft Associate Mission and Training School be rescinded and the said Board of Fellows abolished. In this event the Convention should appoint some committee to have control of the Ravenscroft School proper, with the land adjoining, to make such disposition thereof as the Convention may direct. It would seem proper also that Bishop Ravenscroft's robes and books, heretofore deposited in this institution by the order of the Convention, should be returned, with any other articles of a like character, being the property of the Diocese.[147]

Thus, Bishop Cheshire was recommending that the Ravenscroft Associate Mission and Training School, Shoenberger Hall, the Ravenscroft Endowment, and the Hix Fund be declared "local institutions" and conveyed to the new missionary district, but that the original Ravenscroft School (Joseph Osborne's mansion) be retained by the North Carolina

FOUR. *Redirection: Rectors and Ravenscroft High* 77

Diocese as their property to be maintained or disposed of as seen fit. This proposal, in essence, would have split up the property and possibly put an immediate end to the Ravenscroft High School.

As the bishop had hoped, a delegation from the missionary district was present at the convention, and so the matter was soon taken up. A special committee was elected, consisting of the bishop and Edward Benedict, H. C. Jones, Chas. E. Johnson and Paul B. Means. The committee's resolutions, which matched the bishop's recommendations, were readily approved.[148] This, of course, left the Ravenscroft High School property to be discussed. But shortly after their first proposal the committee's chairman, H. C. Jones, further proposed "that all legislation heretofore passed by the Convention of this Diocese creating and regulating the Board of Fellows of Ravenscroft be, and the same is hereby repealed, and the Trustees of the Diocese are hereby authorized to lease or otherwise use and employ the property until the next meeting of the Convention."[149] By rescinding the legislation appointing a Board of Fellows and authorizing the lease of the property, the diocese was claiming their ownership of the property. Amazingly, that resolution was adopted as well, despite the fact that there was some dissent, especially from the delegation from the missionary district.

The missionary district held their Convention a few months later, where they elected

This photograph of the ragtag Ravenscroft High School football team circa 1891–95 was recently found in the archives of the Diocesan offices "Lindsey & Brown" (courtesy of the Episcopal Diocese of Western North Carolina, Asheville).

a Board of Fellows of Shoenberger Hall and Ravenscroft Associate Mission and Training School. This replaced the former Board of Fellows of Ravenscroft, which had administered the associate mission, training school and the high school. Meanwhile, Warden A. H. Stubbs carried on the work of the mission and training school, reporting that with the help of Deacon William F. Rice, in addition to instructing two deacons, examining five candidates for Holy Orders, and preaching sermons at various places, he administered the work of the fourteen missions under his care.[150]

Mr. Toynbee Wight continued to operate the Ravenscroft High School for Boys during this period, despite the diocesan wrangling over the property. Although he operated as a day-school during his first year (1894–1895), Wight made attempts to recruit boarding students, as evidenced by an advertisement found in a national periodical called *The Nation*.[151] The eye-catching title in capital letters claims, "IF YOU WANT YOUR SON WELL TAUGHT, WHY NOT SEND HIM TO RAVENSCROFT?" The advertisement goes on to tell of the "three departments" of the school: "*Preparatory* (for young and backward boys)"; "*High School* (prepares for Soph. Class at any University in U.S.*"; and "*Special Courses* in Philosophy and Science for all who are prepared to take them." The ad also states that the "teaching staff represents the culture of one English and two American universities," which, interestingly, was the same mix as when Ronald MacDonald was headmaster.

At the July 3, 1895, regular meeting of the Board of Fellows, Mr. Wight was approved to be the headmaster again for the 1895–1896 scholastic year. However, just a few months after the start of the new term Headmaster Wight handed in his resignation, to be effective January 1, 1896, halfway through the school year. Not surprisingly, another emergency meeting of the Board of Fellows was called on November 14, 1895, and a committee was appointed "to confer with Mr. Wight, and if possible to persuade him to reconsider the matter."[152] The committee was unsuccessful, as Mr. Wight was vacating his position as headmaster to pursue a degree in medicine at Harvard.[153] At a later meeting, the board hired "Messers Valentine" to take over on February 1, 1896, under the same conditions as the previous headmasters. "Messers Valentine" included not only Frank Valentine, who was previously a candidate for the position with Wight, but also his son, Thomas Valentine, who was hired as assistant principal.

Prof. Frank Valentine was born near Birmingham, in England, in 1841, and graduated from Cambridge University, from which institution he held an M.A. degree. When quite a young man, he went to Australia to assume charge of a school, and was married there a short time later. He returned to his native land after living in Australia for about ten years, and taught in private schools in England until 1883, when he came to North Carolina and settled among the English families who were living at Bowman's Bluff in Henderson County.[154] Another historian writes, "Mr. Frank Valentine, who came to America in this colony, was educated at Cambridge, England, graduated with highest honor, holding several degrees.[155] He went from Bowman's Bluff to Asheville, and later moved to Hendersonville, where he spent his remaining days. He was known as one of the finest educators in Western North Carolina."[156] Valentine lived in the Ravenscroft House along with his wife Anna, sons Thomas and Basil, and daughters Lily and Elizabeth.

Those opposed to the action taken by the 1896 Convention to retain a portion of the Ravenscroft property for the Diocese of North Carolina continued their diligent fight to have the entire Ravenscroft property turned over to the Missionary Jurisdiction of Asheville.

Their efforts even went as far as threatening the diocese with a "friendly lawsuit" to settle the matter. These efforts were led by former headmaster Haywood Parker, who had remained in Asheville and married the daughter of former Board of Fellows chairman Thomas Walton Patton. Not only was Parker a staunch supporter of Ravenscroft and married into a prominent Episcopalian family, but he was also a skilled lawyer. The protesters met with the bishop and other delegates of the Diocese of North Carolina and presented their case. In an almost miraculous way, they were successful in changing the mind of the bishop, and in an unprecedented act at the next Convention of the Diocese of North Carolina in 1897, the bishop reversed his previous decision and convinced the Convention to do likewise. In his address to the 1897 Convention the bishop told how his change of mind came about:

> There is another very important matter connected with our last year's proceedings, which it is my duty to notice. In my address to the Convention of 1896, while urging the Convention to convey to the Jurisdiction of Asheville so much of the property in Asheville as should be amply sufficient for all the needs and purposes of the Ravenscroft Associate Mission and Training School, I recommended that the remaining portion should be disposed of for Diocesan purposes. The action taken last year seemed to be based upon this my recommendation. Though the Clergy and Laity of the Jurisdiction seemed disposed to acquiesce in the action of our Convention, yet there were some who thought that we had acted under an erroneous view of the merits of the case. Accordingly Commissioners were appointed on the part of the Jurisdiction for the purpose of presenting their views to the Diocese of North Carolina. I have myself had full Conference with these Commissioners, and I am obliged to say that I have become thoroughly satisfied that I was wrong in my position last year, and that I now think we should convey the whole of the Ravenscroft property to the Jurisdiction of Asheville. The consideration which has forced me to this change of conviction on this subject is this: In 1883 the question was raised, whether this property should be divided in the interest of the newly created Diocese of East Carolina. This Convention adopted a report in 1884 which asserted that the Ravenscroft property was held for a purely local purpose and, therefore, should not be divided with East Carolina. In this report, so far as the point now under consideration was concerned, the Diocese of East Carolina concurred, and that Diocese made no claim to any part of the property. After this we cannot now maintain, as I argued last year, that this is general Diocesan property, part of which we may retain for Diocesan purposes. I hope I may be pardoned for adding in my own behalf, since it happens that I myself wrote the report of 1884, that this point of the local character of the property being generally acquiesced in occasioned no discussion, whereas other parts of the report gave rise to much heated debate. The consequence was that this particular point, which has now become crucial, had entirely escaped my memory. When it was pointed out to me by one of the Lay Commissioners on the part of the Jurisdiction of Asheville, I at once recognized and admitted its decisive, and even conclusive, force as bearing upon the matter now in question.[157]

It seems that the matter was much simpler than the bishop had thought. The Diocesan Convention immediately acquiesced to the bishop's request by forming a committee, making a resolution, and adopting the resolution, thereby transferring "the whole of the Ravenscroft property" to the Trustees of the Missionary Jurisdiction of Asheville.

Although the thirty years from the close of the Civil War to the dawn of the twentieth century were ones of great trials and transitions for the Ravenscroft School, they were also its most productive years in teaching and training men and boys to be contributing members of society.

FIVE

Buxton Hill, Bishops and Boarding Houses: *1898–1950*

As the twentieth century dawned, the newly formed Episcopal Missionary District of Asheville was now positioned for growth. In 1897, the Diocese of North Carolina, from which the new district had been separated out, had approved the transfer of the whole of the Ravenscroft property and funds to the new district. And also to the district's benefit, proceedings were underway to elect their own presiding bishop.

Although Bishop Cheshire, from his home in Raleigh, was acting as the presiding bishop over the new jurisdiction, the district badly needed a local bishop. The 1897 Convention of the new Missionary Jurisdiction of Asheville expressed its regrets that the House of Bishops of the General Convention "has for so long a time refused to elect a Bishop for the Jurisdiction."[1] Although the district had met all the qualifications for requesting their own bishop, the Board of Missions was impeding their request, as the board, from which the new bishop's financial support would come, was in financial difficulty. However, the needed funds were finally raised, and on October 22, 1898, at the General Convention held in Washington, D.C., the House of Bishops elected the Rev. Junius Moore Horner as the first bishop of the newly established Missionary Jurisdiction of Asheville.[2]

Junius Moore Horner was born on July 7, 1859, to James Hunter and Sophronia Moore Horner of Oxford, North Carolina, where James Horner had founded the Horner School in 1851. Following his education at his father's school, Horner attended the University of Virginia for one year (1879–1880), before transferring to John Hopkins University, where he graduated in 1895 with a B.A. degree. Later he enrolled at the General Theological Seminary in New York, graduating in 1890. In 1891 he was ordained as a priest by Bishop Theodore Lyman and began his ministry as a missionary to churches in Leaksville and Reidsville, North Carolina. In 1892, following the death of his father, Horner took over as principal of the Horner School. On December 14, 1892, he married Eva Harker of Augusta, Georgia. Horner served as principal until his election as bishop in 1898.[3]

The newly elected Bishop Junius M. Horner was consecrated by Bishop Cheshire in an elaborate ceremony at Trinity Episcopal Church in Asheville on December 28, 1898. On January 1, 1899, Horner officially took office in his new residence at Shoenberger Hall. The bishop and his family were to share Shoenberger Hall with the Rev. A. H. Stubbs and the Ravenscroft Associate Mission for many years.[4]

The trustees of the district reported at their 1898 Convention that the Ravenscroft Fund contained $8,610.51, with $8,000 of the fund "in good solvent securities" and $610.51

as cash on hand. The Hicks Fund was reported to have $4,800 in securities and assets. Besides these two monetary funds, it was reported that the Ravenscroft Property "consists of 13½ acres of land in Asheville, North Carolina, upon which are two large brick residences." The report went on state that "the title to this property is now in us, encumbered with the conditions of the old deeds."[5]

When the property was originally deeded to the Rev. Jarvis Buxton in 1854 from William Patton, specific provisions were written into the deed. The provisions of the deed stated that the property was conveyed "*In Special* Trust ... that he [Buxton] will hold and appropriate the same as a site upon which to erect & keep up a classical and theological boarding school, and when he shall have been reimbursed all expenditures made by himself personally and indemnified against all personal liabilities incurred in its purchase and improvements, he shall convey the same to the Trustees of the Episcopal Church of the Diocese of North Carolina." These provisions were met in 1865 and 1868 when Buxton conveyed the deeds to the diocese. But the deed also had the provision that "in case the purposes of the said shall be abandoned, or the trusts herein violated the contributors to the fund with which the same has been purchased, as shown by a list-signed by the said Buxton and attested by John Baxter ... shall be entitled to the several sums so contributed by them, and for its payment it is expressly agreed that a lien is hereby declared attached to the property herein conveyed."[6]

In other words, the district owned a large and valuable property, but they could do nothing with it except use it for a "classical and theological school"; otherwise, they would be breaking the "special trust" in the deed and have to yield to its provision to pay back the original investors. Why was this considered such an encumbrance? Were not the Ravenscroft Associate Mission and the Ravenscroft High School for Boys being successfully operated on the property? In a "Historical Sketch" read and published for the first Convention of the new district in 1895, the author writes, "In our disappointment at Ravenscroft's not reaching that success we desired for it, we have doubtless unconsciously overlooked the actual good the institution has done.... Then quite a number of ministers have received their theological training, either in whole or in part, at the training school. Fifteen of these have been counted up by one familiar with the school."[7] Obviously the trustees felt that the training school was not being successful and had plans to use Shoenberger Hall for other purposes, and the high school was floundering as well. Also, plans had been bantered back and forth for a number of years regarding possibly subdividing and/or selling off part of the property to raise funds. But with the special provisions in the deed, this made any of the options impossible, or at best very difficult. The provision was also an encumbrance because, as soon became apparent, no "list of contributors" had been made, thereby complicating the fulfilling of the provision if the special trust were to be broken. It is no wonder that in 1898 the trustees reported that they "have begun legal proceedings to clear if possible the title to this property, so that it can be used as seems best for the good of the Church."[8]

By the 1899 District Convention, the trustees were happy to report that legal proceedings to clear the title had begun. They reported that "by order of the court all persons claiming a lien on said land for the amounts contributed toward the purchase money by reason of the clause in the deed conveying said land to Jarvis Buxton were to prove their claims before the Clerk of the Superior Court of Buncombe County on or before July 1st 1899, or be forever barred from setting up such a claim. This order was published for six weeks, and only two claims for $50 each have been proved. As soon as these are paid, the final decree can be gotten. This will put the title in such a shape that the Trustees can sell free from encumbrances."[9] The report went on to claim that "the trustees, however, are not in favor of selling any part of the Ravenscroft land." They felt that because they paid no taxes on the land, it would be better to hold on to it and let it increase in value. Also, the trustees wanted to free the title so they could use the property for other purposes. In fact, on the confidence of the outcome of their legal proceedings, the report went on to tell of various actions the trustees had already taken in improving, reusing and even constructing new buildings on the property. The clear title would allow the trustees to utilize the property for additional income-generating uses.

The first project reported was that the Trustees "had thoroughly renovated and repaired the old Ravenscroft House, which was in a very dilapidated and neglected condition and rapidly going to ruin. The repairs and additions cost about $3,000. We now have a good house of sixteen rooms, which is rented for $500 a year."[10] This may be when the small two-story brick addition was constructed on the southwest rear corner of the house and dormitory. The new addition may have contained a new stairway to improve the circulation in the dormitory and rear portion of the house. The house was leased to Mr. Frank Valentine, headmaster of the Ravenscroft High School. Apparently Mr. Valentine's arrangement was the same as that of the previous headmasters in that he took in all the monies from tuition and board of the students and then used that for all the supplies and staff salaries as well as his own (the only difference being that he now had to pay $500 a year in rent).

The report also told of another building project undertaken by the trustees: "The walls of the little chapel building which was likewise in a very dilapidated and neglected condition, were utilized, as by some additions a very neat brick cottage of nine rooms was built at a cost of $1700. This is now occupied by a teacher, Mr. Valentine who pays $300 rental. By an arrangement with the Trustees, Mr. Valentine was allowed to pay the first year's rent by the board and tuition of a candidate for orders."[11] The chapel building had been built in 1887 when the school was divided into two departments, the associate mission/training school and the high school. It was mainly used as the classroom building for the high school. Perhaps after the trustees turned it into a residence, Mr. Valentine had to use the first-floor common room in the dormitory section of the old Ravenscroft House as the classroom space for the high school. He may also have used some of the other rooms in the house for classrooms as well, to make up for the loss of the chapel/classroom building.

In addition, the trustees reported that "some needed repairs and desired changes were made to Shoenberger Hall, which costs about $700. It was then rented to the Bishop and Mr. Stubbs for $500 a year, of which $380 is to be paid in cash and the balance, $120, by tuition of candidates for holy orders."[12]

The trustees' improvements in 1899 also included the building of a "cottage for a gentleman who obligated to take it for five years at $275 a year. This was done at a cost of about $2200."[13] The building of this cottage was also reported in the May 8, 1899, edition of the *Asheville Daily Citizen*: "J. A. Tennent is building a 10-room frame cottage for the Missionary Jurisdiction of Asheville on the Ravenscroft grounds, Church Street."[14]

The trustees ended their 1899 report by recommending that all the Ravenscroft securities of the Ravenscroft Fund be sold and the money be used to pay off any indebtedness "and in erecting cottages on the Ravenscroft grounds."[15] It appears, in looking at the 1912 published "Bird's Eye View of Asheville," that only one additional cottage was subsequently constructed at what is now 89 Church Street. This cottage was built in 1902, at which time the trustees reported that "in addition to Shoenberger Hall, there are now four dwelling houses on the Ravenscroft property, the annual rent from which amounts to $1315.00."[16] The four houses were Ravenscroft House, the refurbished classroom/chapel, and the two above-mentioned cottages.

Mr. Frank Valentine continued to lease the old Ravenscroft House and operate the Ravenscroft High School for Boys for the next couple of years. The 1899–1900 and the 1900–1901 Asheville City Directories show the Ravenscroft High School at 95 Church Street (old Ravenscroft house). But in 1901, Frank Valentine and his family moved back to Henderson County for Valentine to assume his new job as one of four faculty members hired to teach in the first public school established in Henderson County.[17] Thomas Valentine, Frank's son and assistant master at Ravenscroft, also left at this time to pursue post-graduate studies, and was later hired to teach in the Hendersonville High School in 1919.[18] The 1902 city directory contains no mention of the school and the house is shown to be leased as a boarding house, thus quietly ending two decades of the Ravenscroft High for Boys.

So, what led to the school's final demise? The short answer is "lack of sufficient patronage." But there were certainly other contributing factors as well. For instance, the school had difficulty keeping headmasters and/or teachers for more than a few years. Ronald MacDonald had the longest run, and that was only for five years. It may have been, as is often the case with church schools, that the salaries were low and so one only lasted a few years until a higher-paying position would become available elsewhere. These positions attracted newly graduated undergraduates who soon moved on to seek further education or loftier career pursuits.

The "lack of sufficient patronage" was often cited in the reports and frequently blamed on the high costs of tuition. However, it seems that an inherent cause of the school's "lack of patronage" may have been its location. Asheville is on the extreme western side of the state, and even after the railroad arrived in 1880, the fact remained that it was still a great distance away from the higher populated cities in the eastern and Piedmont regions of the state, and therefore parents were no doubt reluctant to send their young boys so far away to school. Very few boys whose parents lived a long distance away were sent on the train to boarding school. Many of the boys who were from those distant areas, or even outside the state, had parents who were financially well-off and either lived in Asheville seasonally (at which time their boys would attend Ravenscroft) or were retired or seeking respite from health issues and had moved permanently or semi-permanently to Asheville.

However, the major cause of the school's lack of sufficient patronage and the cause of its final demise were one and the same: the rising popularity of the free public school system at the end the late nineteenth century. In 1891, Headmaster Ronald MacDonald had recognized the impending dilemma. His sister Lilia, in a letter to her mother, wrote, "R's opinion & experience is quite adverse to belief in the success of an Englishman out here as schoolmaster. Free public schools have lowered the price of education all over the country."[19]

In the mid-nineteenth century public education movements began to sweep across the country. The movement in North Carolina was interrupted by the Civil War, but was taken up again following the adoption of the new state constitution in 1868, which provided that "the General Assembly at its first session under this Constitution shall provide by taxation and otherwise, for a general and uniform system of public schools, wherein tuition shall be free of charge to all the children of the State between the ages of six and twenty-one years."[20] Further state legislation was later passed allowing local municipalities to levy taxes to establish their own public school systems. Asheville had lagged behind other cities, as local wealthy citizens felt that there were adequate educational opportunities in the city for those who could afford them, but finally "a tax for the purpose of organizing and maintaining a municipal school system"[21] was passed in Asheville in July 1887. Local African American businessman (and former butler to Dr. Buel at Ravenscroft) Isaac Dickson is credited with casting the deciding vote. He immediately became the first African American in North Carolina to serve on a board of education.

By 1897 Asheville had built four large schools and had over 1,500 students receiving free education. Ravenscroft High School, with its high tuition and fees, could not compete and so it closed permanently in 1901.

Tourism in Asheville, by the turn of the century, was quickly becoming the region's main source of income. In 1899 the railroad published a tiny booklet appropriately titled "A Nutshell Guide to Asheville." This was soon followed by yearly tourist guides, giving tourists information on where to board, what to see, and what to do in Asheville. It is no wonder that, following the closing of the Ravenscroft High School in 1901, the old Ravenscroft house began its long career as a boarding house. Little did anyone suspect at the time that it would serve as a boarding house for longer than it had served as a school. Interestingly, the first person to lease the house and operate it as a boarding house was Martha C. Kepler. Martha and her husband Samuel (a local grocer) had previously leased Shoenberger Hall in 1894. The Keplers simply named their establishment "The Ravenscroft." They operated the boarding house for three years until the death of Samuel Kepler in November of 1905. At that time the second-time widowed Martha moved to live with her son in the newly built Montford suburb of Asheville.[22]

The operation of "The Ravenscroft" was not interrupted, as Mr. William E. Tyack quickly assumed the lease and management in 1906. He ran the boarding house until it changed hands in 1912, at which time Mrs. Ridgely Penniman assumed its management. Mrs. Penniman was Margaret Campbell Allison Penniman, the widow of William Ridgely Penniman Jr. Mr. Penniman, who died in 1900, was the co-owner, along with his brothers, of Penniman & Company, a hardware store established on Pack Square by William Ridgely Penniman, Sr. Mrs. Penniman had previously been the proprietor of the "Elbermar," a boarding house in Oakland Heights on Victoria Road. Although she only operated Ravenscroft for one year, a wonderful full-page advertisement survives from that year. The advertisement touts Ravenscroft's amenities as "centrally located, modern improvements, new management, splendid view, and large lawn."

The trustees of the Missionary Jurisdiction of Asheville, even after the clearing of the title to the Ravenscroft property in 1899, had for many years been adamant that "no part of the land be sold, but that it be held and improved."[23] But in 1910, after the donation of 26 acres of land (on Biltmore Avenue) to the district from John A. Roebling and his wife, the trustees changed their position and decided that selling its properties would put them in a better position toward becoming "self-supporting." Thus, the Convention of 1910 directed that the trustees "sell or convey in fee simple all or any part or parts of the property given by Mr. John A. Roebling, or of the Ravenscroft property, except Shoenberger Hall and the ground immediately connected therewith upon such terms and conditions as they deem best."[24]

So the trustees hired Chauncey Beadle of Biltmore Nursery to plot out a new subdivision to be called, of course, "Ravenscroft." Beadle's plan divided the property into four quadrants containing a total of 31 parcels. The quadrants were divided by two new cross-shaped streets, one of which was "Ravenscroft Road," which ran south from and parallel to Church Street, intersected about midway by an east-west street called Shoenberger Place. Shoenberger Place came off of Church Street along the north boundary of the property of the old classroom/chapel building. The largest parcels surrounded Shoenberger Hall and Ravenscroft House. The remaining parcels were divided in such a way that the two existing cottages and the old classroom-turned-residence each had their own lot.

The first portion of the Ravenscroft property to sell was lot 27, a one-acre parcel surrounding the old Ravenscroft house. On July 6, 1911,[25] the trustees sold the lot and Ravenscroft to Roger Lamsom Jr. a wealthy "capitalist"[26] who had recently moved his family to Asheville, and who was a boarder at Ravenscroft. Lamson was an Episcopalian and, no doubt, attended services at Trinity Church, where he may have heard of the district's desire to sell. It is unclear if he intended to actually manage the boarding house himself, but less than a year later, on March 15, 1912, Lamson signed an agreement to lease the house, "including the two cottages and grounds situated on the west side of Church Street," to Mrs. Nellie Hyman for a term of three years at $1,299 per year, to be paid in monthly installments. For his part, Lamson agreed to "improve the front entrance in a satisfactory manner and replace closet on second floor landing with a service sink."[27]

Mrs. Hyman changed the name of Ravenscroft to Belvedere, the name she had used previously at a similar boarding house she had managed at 57 Spruce Street. Hyman then bought "Lot #28" adjacent to the south side of Ravenscroft in October of 1912 and built a small bungalow to serve as her residence. She managed the Belvedere for the next three years, as per her agreement, despite the unfortunate death of Roger Lamson in 1914. It was probably during this period that the two-story frame wing was added to the south side of the building to house additional bathrooms and a kitchen.

After the trustees of the Missionary District sold the first lot (#27) to Roger Lamson in 1911, there was no further activity until 1913. By the 1914 Convention the trustees were able to announce that in the previous year they had sold six additional lots.[28] Lot 23 was sold in 1916, and then in 1919 the trustees sold off the two cottage properties on lots #2 and #5, and were happy to report that they had "disposed of all the houses owned, and held by the Trustees for rent, and also of all the good lots in the Ravenscroft lands."[29]

In 1917, a series of new managers of the Belvedere began with Leon and Kathryn St. John. The St. Johns signed a lease agreement with a local realtor, W. K. Howe, who was managing the property for the Lamson estate. It was an odd arrangement, as the St. Johns were to pay W. K. Howe $25 a week in rent, in return for allowing Mr. Howe twelve months of free "board and lodging." In addition, they agreed that after providing for Howe's lodging and after paying an accumulation of $1,200 in rent, "the said furniture, and fixtures herein described shall become the property of the said Lessees." The list of furniture included beds, mattresses, and other household furnishings and even "one Mason and Hamlin Piano."[30]

A full-page advertisement in the 1918 Asheville City Directory has a photo of the house showing the recently added front porch and two-story frame addition built onto the south

This full-page advertisement for the "Belvedere" was published in the 1918 Asheville City Directory (Volume XVII). The photograph shows the recently added front porch and two-story frame addition constructed on the southwest corner of the original house (http://www.archive.org/details/ashevillenorthca1918pied).

corner of the house. The ad claims that the Belvedere's "interior is modern, home-like and attractive" and that it has steam heat and private baths. But the most enticing line is that "the table is under the proprietor's direct care," indicating they served good meals.

In 1919, while the Belvedere continued to be managed by the St. Johns, Roger Lamson's widow, Mabel Nelson Lamson, who was living in New York, sold the property to Mr. E. H. Luckett. The property was sold for ten dollars, as Mr. Luckett assumed the $4,000 mortgage still owed on the property. E. H. Luckett was a realtor and prolific buyer and seller of properties. A search of the Buncombe County records shows that he had over 450 property transactions from 1919 to 1939.

The St. Johns managed the boarding house until 1921, when a new manager, Mrs. B. P. Edwards, took over.

During the 1920s and early 1930s the Belvedere had a succession of proprietors. From 1925–1926 it was managed by a Mrs. Anna Christian, who changed the name back to "Ravenscroft." Later, in 1931, Lena N. Buckner assumed management and advertised as the "Belvedere Apartments." In 1938 she changed the name to "The Buckner Home," which also included a few adjacent cottages (the city directory has 29–37 Ravenscroft Drive as its address). The Buckner Home lasted only two years. Subsequently, in 1941 and 1942 Mayme Martin, as the new proprietor, changed the name to "The Biltmore Inn."

Finally, some stability was restored when, in 1943, W. H. Nollman and his wife Nellie purchased the old Ravenscroft boarding house and opened it as the "Chateau Nollman" (actually, for the first five years, 1944–1949, it appeared in the city directories as "Chateau Nollwood"). W. H. and Nellie Nollman operated Chateau Nollman for the next two decades, until 1966, when they sold it to Walter Deal, a former lodger. Deal owned Asheville Acceptance Corporation, which he moved into the old Ravenscroft house in 1967.

Meanwhile, during the first half of the twentieth century, while Ravenscroft was being used as a boarding house and in the hands of successive owners and managers, Shoenberger Hall remained in the hands of the Missionary District of Asheville. It continued to be the home of Bishop Junius Horner and his family, even after the missionary district became the Western North Carolina Diocese in 1922. It also continued to be the home of the Ravenscroft Associate Mission, under the direction of the Rev. A. H. Stubbs, although it was no longer used as a training school. The Rev. Stubbs continued to reside at Shoenberger Hall, in a separate apartment, until his death in 1924.

As the stock market crashed and the country dropped into the Great Depression, Bishop Horner began to deteriorate. On April 5, 1933, at the age of seventy-three, Bishop Junius Horner died after suffering through a long and painful illness.[31]

A new bishop, Robert Emmet Gribben, was soon elected and duly consecrated on January 25, 1934, at St. Paul's in Winston-Salem, North Carolina. A few months later, on the first day of the Annual Convention of the Western North Carolina Diocese, a motion was considered to sell Shoenberger Hall and use the monies to purchase a more suitable residence for the new bishop. A committee was formed to look into the matter, but after a year, as no buyer was found, the diocese decided to keep Shoenberger Hall as the bishop's home. The home was subsequently renovated and the Gribbens installed in their new residence. The Gribben family eventually moved out of Shoenberger Hall in 1947, following the resignation of Bishop Gribben, who resigned his post due to ill health.

Just south of Shoenberger Hall, though not technically on missionary district land,

This circa 1912 photograph shows the north and east elevations of the old Buxton home at the end of Church Street. Shortly after the death of the Rev. Jarvis Buxton, his daughter, Mary R. Buxton, opened the old Buxton home as a boarding house named "Buxton Place." "The North State Fitting School" operated in another section of the same house. This private school, which was run by John Munsey Roberts and his wife Margaret Elizabeth Hines Roberts, was later made famous by its famed pupil, author Thomas Wolfe. The house and hill were demolished in the 1920s (image #F741–5 from the North Carolina Collection, Pack Memorial Library, Asheville).

was Buxton Place, the former home of the Rev. Jarvis Buxton, founder of the Ravenscroft schools. The Rev. Buxton's daughter, Mary R. Buxton, had inherited the home following the death of her father in 1902. Mary, not surprisingly, opened a portion of her home as a boarding house named "Buxton Place." The other portion of the home was leased to the "North State Fitting School." The school was privately owned and operated by John Munsey Roberts and his wife, Margaret Elizabeth Hines Roberts. The award-winning hometown author Thomas Wolfe was not only one of the first students of the school (1912–1916), but he also immortalized the school and the nearby Shoenberger Hall in his 1929 novel, *Look Homeward Angel*, when he wrote, "Mr. Leonard had leased an old pre-war house, set on a hill wooded by magnificent trees. It faced west and south, looking toward Biltburn, and abruptly down on South End, and the negro flats that stretched to the depot."[32] In the novel he often describes walking up Church Street and passing "Bishop Raper's House," a fictionalized description of Shoenberger Hall, which was right next door to the Roberts' school. One of Tom's fellow classmates, Junius Horner Jr., the bishop's son, was the fictionalized character Justin Raper in the novel.

Unfortunately, the North State Fitting School and Buxton Place did not survive the real-estate frenzy of 1920s Asheville. In 1926, the "Buxton Hill Investment Company"[33] was organized to develop the "Buxton Hill Subdivision" on the former site of the Rev. Buxton's property. Not only was the house demolished, but the entire hill was also removed and lowered about 20 feet, leaving a cliff-faced dirt bank along the south property of Shoenberger Hall. The ugly, unsafe bank remains to this day.

The first half of the twentieth century was a difficult time for Ravenscroft. Not only did its various institutions cease to exist, but its buildings and property were also sold out of the Episcopal Church and poised for uncertain, and even potentially devastating, futures.

Six

Postscript: Peril or Preservation? *1951–2010*

By the second half of the twentieth century, the buildings of the now defunct Ravenscroft institution were being swallowed up by the encroaching urban fabric of downtown Asheville. Adding to their peril were the devastating effects of suburban sprawl, the abandonment of downtown retail establishments, and the misguided proponents of "urban renewal."

In 1951, shortly after the death of Bishop Robert Gribben, the Episcopal Diocese of Western North Carolina sold Shoenberger Hall, the final vestige of property from the former Ravenscroft property, to Mrs. Laura Lee Horner for $18,500.[1] Mrs. Horner was married to Junius Horner Jr., son of Bishop Junius Horner, a former resident of Shoenberger Hall.

A few weeks later the *Asheville Citizen–Times* ran an article about the sale: "*Ownership of Schoenberger Hall Passes from Episcopal Diocese.*" After giving details of the sale, the article provided a history of the Ravenscroft institution, followed by a description of the fate of the valuable contents of the house. The several portraits, including one of Bishop Atkinson, were moved to the new bishop's residence on Macon Avenue. The books of the Shoenberger Hall diocesan library, which at one time numbered 10,000 volumes, were divided up. Some of the most valuable books, "including Latin folios," had previously been sold to Duke University, and many of the remaining books were transferred to a parish house of the local parish of the Church of the Redeemer, and the "left over books" were sold to the "Biltmore Book Mart."

The new owners lived in the residence section of the building and Mrs. Horner turned the front section into a retail establishment, which she operated as the "Woman's Exchange Gift Shop and Gay-Nineties Tea Room" from 1952 until its closure in 1957. In 1958 Horner began leasing the hall to Helen S. Donald, an artist, who used it as her studio and residence. A fellow renter, John L. Boswell, resided in another section of the house in 1960 and 1961. Then, in 1964, J. Thurston Henry leased the hall as his residence and business, "Henry's Frame Shop." Many current Ashevillians still remember Thurston Henry's establishment, as it remained in that location for almost a decade. From photos of the period, it is evident that little was altered in the building at this time. All the lovely architectural moldings, doors, hardware, fireplace mantels, and even the stained glass windows were kept intact.

As the 1970s dawned, it was becoming apparent that downtown Asheville was becoming a ghost town, especially for retail businesses. The city was still burdened with municipal debt from the late 1920s and could barely maintain, let alone update, its infrastructure.

Added to that was the growing national movement to relocate retail businesses out of the downtown areas and into the suburbs in centralized malls. The Westgate Shopping Center opened as a "strip-mall" in 1955 just west of downtown Asheville, across the French Broad River. But the final blow to Asheville's downtown retail business sector came in 1971, when three of Asheville's largest retailers (Belk, Bon Marche, and Sears) fled the downtown area to become the anchor stores in the new Asheville Mall, which was built two and a half miles southeast of the city.

It is not surprising that by 1976 Mrs. Horner, who had since remarried and was now Mrs. Fowler, was looking to sell Shoenberger Hall. Mr. Richard Whittington, a local printer who serviced many of the downtown offices and businesses, decided to buy the property for his printing firm, Groves Printing. However, it quickly came to the attention of local preservationists and historians that Whittington was merely interested in the two acres of land that came with the property, and not the house (Shoenberger Hall).

In 1976, Asheville's preservation movement was still young and, in fact, the newly formed Preservation Society of Asheville–Buncombe County held their first meeting in May, but did not receive their official charter until October of that year. However, even in their fledgling state, after being informed of Mr. Whittington's proposed plans, members of the society, along with officials from the North Carolina State Historic Preservation Office, approached Whittington to try to persuade him to consider alternatives to demolition. (Although the North Carolina State Preservation office had surveyed and photographed Shoenberger Hall in 1974, it had not been nominated for National Register status.)

John Kinney, staff architect working for the North Carolina State Historic Preservation Office, along with Preservation Society members Mike Cox and Betty Betts, met with Whittington in December of 1976 and suggested that the building was a good candidate for "adaptive re-use" and talked with him "at some length about technologies to accomplish this."[2] Mr. Kinney also suggested that a 5,000–10,000-square-foot addition could be added to the building to house the largest and heaviest printing equipment, leaving the wood-framed floors of the existing structure for the lighter loads. The Preservation Society promised to help Whittington measure the building and analyze the suitability of housing his process.

Throughout the following year (1977), while Whittington was busy having a feasibility study done on the building, members of the Preservation Society frantically hunted for alternative downtown sites that could be used for his business. But alas, no alternative site could be found and the feasibility study concluded that it would be cheaper to demolish Shoenberger Hall and build a new building.

Finally, the decision was made and reported in a March 25, 1978, article in the *Asheville Citizen–Times*. The article's title said it all: "Schoenberger Hall: Efforts To Save It Are Unsuccessful."[3] The article quotes Robert Orr, the president of the Preservation Society: "He went the extra mile for a private investor," Orr said. "If everyone were as cooperative as Dick, it would be a lot easier. But it just hasn't worked out." That may have been a diplomatic statement, for, no doubt, most people probably felt more like Preservation Society member Betty Lawrence, who at the end of the article is quoted as saying, "We just sit and shake our heads at it when we think about it!" A bulldozer shortly appeared and the building was demolished. Mike Cox, an architect who was then vice-president of the Preservation Society, managed to save the date stone, but not before the workers had started to smash it to pieces. Fortunately, it was salvageable and now hangs above Cox's fireplace. Whittington replaced Shoenberger Hall with a one-story manufactured steel building. Ironically, it has now been abandoned.

Meanwhile, the old 1840s Ravenscroft building was also in jeopardy. Although it had been successfully operated as the "Chateau Nollman" apartments for almost thirty years, by the late 1960s it was evident that its days were numbered as well. The era of boarding houses was well past its prime of the 1920s, 1930s and 1940s. On August 19, 1966, W. H. and Nellie Nollman sold the old house at 29 Ravenscroft Drive to Walter Deal of the Asheville Acceptance Corporation. Mr. Deal had been a former boarder at Chateau Nollman, but was now a successful businessman in the auto-dealing industry. The Asheville City Directory shows the building being occupied by the Asheville Acceptance Corporation for just one year; however, in most subsequent years it is said to be occupied by the "Chateau Apartments." The apartments were apparently owned by Deal, who then hired a succession of property managers. Deal first hired the Nollmans back as managers, for the first few years, but then Nettie Hartley was hired as the manager from 1970 to 1974. In 1975, Cardelia Wilson briefly became the manager but was soon replaced by William A. Rayfield.

But by the late 1970s, after going through a succession of managers, Deal decided to close down his business and sell the building. The tired old building was vacant and badly in need of attention in 1978 when David Black happened to walk by and noticed that the building was starting to be dismantled. Black had been hired the previous fall by the North Carolina State Historic Preservation Office to conduct a survey and National Register nomination for downtown Asheville. "I remember a stack of doors that an old carpenter was taking out," recalls Black. "He was breaking the cast-iron hinges, since they had no pins he could remove. That really got me." Black immediately contacted Jim Gray, director of the Western Office of the North Carolina State Historic Preservation Office, as well as the Preservation Society of Asheville–Buncombe County.

Following on the heels of the loss of Shoenberger Hall, the Preservation Society was quick to respond to the threat of the potential loss of another historic downtown building. They were now in a better position than they had been in 1976, as they were more organized and experienced. Also to their advantage was the ready aid of the Raleigh-based North Carolina State Historic Preservation Office, which had recently opened a "western office" in Asheville. Together, in addition to continuing negotiations with Mr. Deal, the two organizations quickly began working on nominating Ravenscroft to the National Register of Historic Places. After a tedious process of photographing, measuring, documenting, and researching the history and significance of the building, the nomination was submitted in October 1978, with final approval being granted in December.

Experience had already proved that a listing on the National Register provided little actual protection from potential alteration or demolition of an endangered property, so local preservationists enlisted the aid of Preservation North Carolina, the state's only private nonprofit historic preservation organization, founded in 1939. Working through PNC's Endangered Properties Program (with the help of their revolving fund called the Historic Preservation Fund of North Carolina), Preservation North Carolina bought a six-month purchase option for $5,000, with an option to renew annually for an additional $5,000. This was a mutually beneficial solution for all — for the Deals, as they now had the benefit of PNC's expertise in marketing historic properties and finding a potential buyer, and for the preservationists, as this allowed PNC the opportunity to write protective and perpetual

SIX. *Postscript: Peril or Preservation*

covenants into the deed. "The decision to option it for $5,000 (money at risk!) was made at one of the first board meetings with me as the young, inexperienced Executive Director. I remember much angst and gnashing of teeth," recalls J. Myrick Howard, who was then (and still is) the executive director of PNC.[4]

Fortunately, buyers were quickly found and on September 7, 1979, Asheville Acceptance Corporation officially sold Ravenscroft to the Historic Preservation Fund of North Carolina, who in turn (on the same day) sold the property to Dr. and Mrs. Stuart Davis Tauber. The Taubers had made an offer to buy the property the previous May, but it took a few months to have the protective covenants drawn up to include in the new deed. The covenants, which numbered a dozen, included such items as the following: the Taubers agreed to restore the building within 36 months or else the seller (HPFNC) would have the option of purchasing back the property; the new owners agreed to make no alteration, addition or removal not included in the restoration agreement without the permission of the seller; the owners also agreed that the "general public shall have access to view the interior of the restored historic structure" at the convenience of the owners; the seller (HPFNC) was granted first option to buy the building if/when the new owners wished to sell the property; when the property was resold, the North Carolina Division of State Archives had to be notified; the Historic Preservation Fund of North Carolina would administer the covenants; and, finally, the covenants had to be written into any and all subsequent deeds for this property.

Dr. and Mrs. Tauber hosted a celebratory champagne reception in the lobby of Raven-

The restored Ravenscroft building stands today at 29 Ravenscroft Drive both as a reminder of its glory days as a boys school, as well serving as an example of the benefit of preserving the historic fabric of downtown Asheville (photograph by Joe Franklin).

scroft following the completion of the property transfer. "We are happy to be a part of giving new life to a fine old building and by doing so state our faith in the plans and purposes set forth by the downtown Revitalization Commission,"[5] Tauber reported in a contemporary newspaper article.

The Taubers, under the guidance of the local preservationists and the PNC guidelines, hired architects William Moore and Donald Luke to design and coordinate the restoration. Moore and Luke had the large early twentieth-century porch removed and also restored the original projecting columned portico. A poorly built frame addition at the rear of the building was demolished, while the early twentieth-century two-story addition on the southwest corner was retained (although the wood siding and shingles were replaced by a coating of "pebbledash" stucco). A new three-story pedimented rear stair tower and elevator addition was added for increased accessibility and improved circulation to all the areas of the building. Also, the exterior grade level at the rear was lowered in order to better utilize the ground-floor areas. The south driveway was removed and parking areas were designed for the north and west sides of the property. In accordance with the covenants of the deeds, all the original trim, doors, windows and fireplace mantels were restored to their former luster.

Not only were the Taubers and the local preservationists excited and pleased with the restoration of such a historic and beautiful building, but Asheville city officials were also proud of the restoration. They publicly expressed their satisfaction with an official ordinance (#1213) on May 15, 1981,[6] declaring Ravenscroft a designated local historic property and ordering a sign declaring such to be erected on the property.

The restored Ravenscroft both functioned as the offices of Dr. Tauber's medical practice and featured numerous other office suites leased to various professionals. Although the building has since passed on to new owners,[7] it still retains the same configuration today, with numerous professionals filling the various suites.

Dr. Tauber, who recently passed away, was being prophetic when he proclaimed, "Historic buildings preserve the character and charm of a city's past and represent an important focus in the future of the city of Asheville."[8] Today Asheville boasts almost fifty designated local landmarks, fourteen National Register Historic Districts, and four local designated historic districts. In addition, any building in a historic district slated for renovation, restoration or removal is put under the scrutiny of, and must obtain approval from, numerous historic and preservation authorities such as the Preservation Society of Asheville–Buncombe County, the Western Office of the State Historic Preservation Office, and the city's own Historic Resources Commission.

Ravenscroft, though now listed on the National Register of Historic Places as a "significant example of Greek Revival Architecture," was and is more than just a building. It is a symbol of what can be achieved through cooperation and diligent advocacy to save and maintain the historic fabric of our cities and towns. But it is also a reminder to us of those men and women of the Ravenscroft schools who invested their lives in work that not only improved the conditions of life for the people of the western Carolina mountains but also influenced the lives of countless men and boys for the good, many of whom went on to become prominent local, state and national leaders.

Seven

Ravenscroft Boys: Biographical Notes of Notable Alumni

On the exterior north wall of the dormitory of Ravenscroft are etched the names of former students. Though their etchings today would be deemed "defacing of public property," I am glad that they took the time for such mischief. It was from this wall, along with the 1891 photo (and names mentioned in the MacDonald family letters), that I retrieved the names of former students. You will see from the list (which is not exhaustive) that Ravenscroft High School produced students who became prominent local, state and national leaders. Some went on to be businessmen, college professors, clergymen, missionaries, statesmen, and even a foreign diplomat!

Samuel Westray Battle Jr. (1883–1905) was born to Dr. Samuel Westray and Alice Maude Belknap Battle at Salem, North Carolina. Dr. Battle moved the family to Asheville in 1885 upon his retirement from the U.S. Navy. Dr. Battle was quite familiar with Ravenscroft, as he was Headmaster MacDonald's wife's attending physician in 1890. After his education at Ravenscroft, Samuel Jr., following in his father's footsteps, was commissioned as a midshipman, fourth class, at the U.S. Naval Academy on August 29, 1902. Sadly, Samuel died of a heart attack in 1905 while at the Academy.[1]

Hamilton Storrs Bigelow (1880–1901) was the son of Allen Gilman Bigelow and Genevieve Dayton (Boyce) Bigelow in Buffalo, New York. Major Allen Bigelow, Hamilton's father, died in Asheville in 1891 while visiting a relative. Hamilton went on to Phillips Exeter Academy and then to Harvard, where he was to graduate in 1904. But sadly Hamilton Storrs Bigelow tragically died on June 11, 1901, from injuries as a result of being run over by a fire engine. The June 12, 1901, edition of the *New York Times* reported that a crowd of students had gathered around watching a fire that had broken out in one of the campus buildings. Bigelow was struck by a passing chemical engine whose "wheels passed over Bigelow's body, crushing his lower chest."

Alvah Lowell Burrage (1883–1919) was born to Hamilton and Mary Davis Burrage at Lowell, Massachusetts. He shows in the 1891 picture but is incorrectly labeled as "L. A. Burrage." Following Ravenscroft, Alvah attended Tufts College (now University), graduating in 1906, with a degree in civil engineering. Immediately upon graduation, he married Louise B. Eames and settled in Reading, Massachusetts, and set up practice as an engineer. Burrage and his wife had four children: Ruth, Richard, Edward B. and Elizabeth.[2]

John Otis Burrage (1876–1950) was born to Hamilton and Mary Davis Burrage at Lowell, Massachusetts. He shows in the 1891 picture but is incorrectly labeled as "J. C. Burrage." Following Ravenscroft, John attended Tufts College (now University), graduating in 1900, with a degree in civil engineering. Burrage moved to San Francisco, California, and married Elizabeth Allen. John Burrage and his wife had two daughters: Mary Frances and Katherine Allen.[3]

Thomas Frederic Bush (1875–1940) was born to the Rev. Franklin Leonard and Mary Walker Bush at Southborough, Massachusetts. Thomas' family moved to North Carolina in 1878, when his father was installed as rector of St. James' Church in Lenoir. The family was living in Pittsborough when Thomas attended Ravenscroft. The 1900 census shows Bush living in St. Louis, Missouri, working as a cotton broker. By 1910, he was still single, but had moved to Waco, Texas. His mother Mary and sister Gertrude were living with him at the time. By 1920, he had married Adelaide Burnett, a widow with two children. Bush had a lucrative career as a cotton broker until his death on July 3, 1940. Following his death, his estate gave a large donation to the University of Texas. The Thomas Frederic Bush Scholarship Fund was established by the Board of Regents of the University of Texas System on September 29, 1941, for the benefit of the Office of Student Financial Services.

James Winthrop Campbell (1876–1924) was born in Providence, Rhode Island, to James M. and Phebe Babcock Campbell. Just before 1890, the family moved to Asheville, where James's father opened a real estate business on the southwest corner of Patton and Biltmore Avenues. Following Ravenscroft, Campbell went on to Brown University, where he graduated in 1899 with a B.A. in philosophy. Campbell never married and lived mostly in Providence, except for a brief time after college, when he lived in Mercedes, Texas. In 1909 Campbell obtained a patent for an improvement to the nozzles of sprinklers.[4] He died in 1924 in Houston and is buried in Providence. Interestingly, Campbell's death certificate lists his occupation as "capitalist."[5]

Phillip Charles Cocke (1879–1949) was born to William J. Cocke Jr. and Maria Johnston Cocke. Headmaster Ronald MacDonald's sister Lilia, in a letter to her sister, wrote of "a tiny little boy — his name is Philip Cocke — and he is a regular little game un — his pugnacity at football is intensely satisfactory to Ronald, & he rides a huge horse on wh. he looks like the little button atop, & has a splendid seat."[6]

Following his schooling at Ravenscroft, Cocke attended Wofford College and then obtained a law degree from the University of North Carolina. He was a Democratic Party worker; judge of city police court (1909); special judge of the superior court; reading clerk in the North Carolina state senate (1923); and a county lawyer and judge. Always called "Judge," he was known as an impromptu speaker and orator for local occasions and celebrations and a writer of feature stories.[7] Being a local "celebrity," he was well known and allegedly the model for "Judge Rumford Bland" in Thomas Wolfe's novels.

SEVEN. Ravenscroft Boys: Biographical Notes

Judge P. C. Cocke (left) and an unidentified woman are shown in this 1937 photograph with famed author Thomas Wolfe. Cocke was visiting Wolfe, who had a summer lease on a small cabin in Oteen, North Carolina, from Max Whitson, a local newspaper publisher (William B. Wilson Collection, Houghton Library, Harvard University).

Joseph Edmond Cheesborough (1874–1959) was born to Louisa Patton and John Cheesborough in their "Springvale" home on the banks of the Swannanoa in Asheville. Joseph never married and lived at "Springvale" with his maiden sisters, Mary and Septima, and made his living as a farmer.

James Walton Cheesborough (1876–1967) was born to Louisa Patton and John Cheesborough in their "Springvale" home on the banks of the Swannanoa in Asheville. He was the brother of Joseph E. Cheesborough, who also attended Ravenscroft High School. Following Ravenscroft, James attended Union College in Schenectady, New York, and New York Law School. In 1901 he was recommended to the U.S. Bureau of Insular Affairs to go to the Philippines as a member of an expedition to organize schools to teach English to island inhabitants. He worked in the Philippines in that capacity for seven years, whereupon he returned to Asheville and was admitted to the North Carolina bar in 1909. He first was a lawyer with Judge Harvey Merrimon and his son, J. Gibbon Merrimon. Later James was associated with the firm of Harkins and Van Winkle. In 1918, he married Annie Roach Campbell in Charleston, South Carolina. Also that same year, Cheesborough was appointed chief claims adjuster for T. H. Martin & Co. of Kansas City, operating from Wilmington, North Carolina. In 1953 he returned to Asheville and opened up a law office, though remaining with T.H. Martin. He retired from T. H. Martin as an adjuster for the Gulf States in 1959. James and Annie had one son, Walton W. Cheesborough.

John D. Croft (1871–1937) was born to Daniel and Martha Smith Croft in Beverly Manor, Augusta, Virginia. Lilia MacDonald, a visitor to Ravenscroft in December 1890, writes of the boys leaving for Christmas break: "Croft was off to Virginia early today."[8] Following Ravenscroft, he became a teacher in Virginia, but by 1900, Croft had moved to Asheville, had married Callie (Caledonia) Coady, and was living in nearby Leicester. He retired from 38 years of teaching in 1927 and went into the dairy business until his death on September 26, 1937, at the age of 66.

Minot Davis (1879–1952) was born in Lawrence, Massachusetts, to Edwin Pascal and Harriet Folsom Davis. According to the recollections[9] of Minot's sister Margaret (called "Aunt Grits"), the Davis family moved to Asheville around 1884[10] and bought 100 acres on the Swannanoa River just one mile east of the Biltmore bridge near "Rossi's Creek,"[11] with an existing house called "Tanglewild." Minot's mother passed away in 1887, leaving his father to care for five children. In 1890 Edwin Davis built a new shingled house for the family just northeast of "Tanglewild" and named it "Crowhurst." Minot attended Ravenscroft that same year, after which he was sent to two Northern schools. He went on to attend Harvard University, but had to quit in 1899 due to a severe bout of pneumonia. Interestingly, although I knew from a period photo that Minot attended Ravenscroft, his biographical "notes" published in the Harvard reports[12] only list the Northern schools (Powder Point and Brown & Nichols). But "Aunt Grits" solved the mystery by recalling that in between the two schools, "one year of a small private school in Asheville was tried with rather poor results." Obviously that "small private school" was Ravenscroft.

After leaving Harvard Minot moved west and began a career as a lumberman and surveyor. After numerous jobs, in 1910, he was hired by Weyerhaeuser Timber Co. in

Tacoma, Washington, for whom he subsequently worked for 37 years. He married Nelsie Bennett in Tacoma in 1912. They had three children: Nelson, Edwin, and Virginia. Minot Davis died in 1952 at the age of 72.

Frederick Erdman (1874–1969) was born to the Rev. William J. and Henrietta Rosenbury Erdman in Fort Wayne, Indiana, where his father had a pastorate at the time. Frederick's father was a prominent pastor, Bible teacher and conference speaker, and was noted for following D. L. Moody as the pastor of Moody Church in Chicago. The family moved to Asheville in 1888, perhaps for some rest and relaxation, or possibly to spend some time with their relatives, Mr. and Mrs. Henry T. Collins.[13] Frederick and his brother Walter were enrolled at Ravenscroft in the early 1890s. Lilia MacDonald often mentioned "Fred Erdman" in her letters home to her family. Erdman was an avid photographer as a boy and took many photos around the school. Lilia once wrote to her mother, "Ronald sends his love to you and the photograph Fred Erdman took the other day."[14] In 1890, at the age of sixteen, while a student at Ravenscroft, Fred severely strained his back. His condition worsened over the next few years and he had to drop out of school. In 1902 the family moved to Philadelphia to find help for him. None of the doctors seemed to be able help him, so after a lengthy time of prayer in 1909, Fred felt impelled to apply "cold" to his back, instead of heat as the doctors were prescribing. His condition began to improve. After much further experimentation, he developed therapy techniques that not only helped him but assisted others as well. Erdman went on to be a self-taught alternative medicine physician and a pioneer in the field, forming the Frederick Erdman Association in 1930. Shortly after moving to Philadelphia, Fred married Mary Hickok, formerly of Asheville. Fred had met Mary while he was living in Asheville, where Mary was the principal of the Normal & Collegiate Institute, a girls' boarding school run by the Presbyterian Mission Board.[15]

George L. Erdman (1871–1908) was born to the Rev. William J. and Henrietta Rosenbury Erdman in Fort Wayne, Indiana. George's father was a prominent pastor, Bible teacher and conference speaker, and was noted for following D. L. Moody as the pastor of Moody Church in Chicago. Following his schooling at Ravenscroft, George enrolled at Princeton Seminary in 1889, graduating in 1893. Due to failing health he moved to California, Arizona and other parts west shortly after graduation from Princeton. In 1900, he moved to Asheville to live with his aunt and uncle.[16] There George joined his first cousin, George R. Collins, in the Balfour Granite Co. and the Catawba Gold Company. Unfortunately, after an illness of only a few weeks, he passed away in 1908 at the age of 37. George was the brother of Frederick and Walter Erdman, both of whom were Ravenscroft graduates.

Walter Collins Erdman (1877–1948) was born to the Rev. William J. and Henrietta Rosenbury Erdman in Fort Wayne, Indiana, where his father had a pastorate. Walter's father was a prominent pastor, Bible teacher and conference speaker, and was noted for following D. L. Moody as the pastor of Moody Church in Chicago. Walter attended Ravenscroft High School with his older brothers George and Frederick. Walter went on to Princeton Seminary in 1899, graduating with honors in 1902. Immediately upon graduation, Walter took a position (from 1902 to 1904) as assistant pastor at First Presbyterian Church in Germantown, Pennsylvania, under Senior Pastor the Rev. Charles

R. Erdman (his older brother). Following this pastorate, he joined the Home Department of the Foreign Mission Board of the Presbyterian Church as a promoter of missions in Sunday schools. Then, in 1906, Walter and his family moved to Korea as missionaries at Taiku.

Charles E. Folsom (1881–1937) was born to Paris Hill and Eleanor Lowry Folsom in Washington, DC, where Paris Hill was serving in the civil service in the auditor's office and as an agent to the Indians. The Folsom family moved to Asheville for health reasons in 1887 and bought a farm named "Maple Springs"[17] four miles east of Biltmore along the Swannanoa River and just three miles east of "Tanglewild," the home of the Paris' sister Harriet and her husband Edwin Pascal Davis. Charles was the youngest of seven children, but the only one to attend Ravenscroft. He was the first cousin of Minot Davis, who is in the 1891 photo. Although Charles is not in the photo, we know he attended the school, as Lilia MacDonald often mentions "little Folsom" in her letters. "Charley," as they called him, was only 9 years old when he started at Ravenscroft, and since he was a "boarder," he was under the matronly care of Lilia. On December 18, 1890, Lilia wrote that at 2 A.M. in the morning she had "settled little C. Folsom down — who is sleeping in my room with sore throat & fever symptoms."

Following Ravenscroft, Folsom became a civil engineer, first going into a brief partnership in 1908 with Ralph Adelbert Carrier (brother of Albert Heath Carrier) in the firm of "Carrier & Folsom, Architects and Surveyors," and then with Charles E. Waddell & Co. While with Waddell, Charles was "resident engineer" (1910–1912) on the building of a hydroelectric plant on the French Broad River, 25 miles northwest of Asheville, for the North Carolina Electrical Power Company.[18] In 1912 he married Cornelia Covington Bass in Hopkinsville, Kentucky. They had their first child, Wendell, in 1914, and Dudley in 1916. Then, in 1917, Charles Jr. was born while the family was living at "Dam #2" on the Wilson Dam in Florence, Alabama. Charles was serving as an engineer on the building of "Wilson Dam," a huge hydroelectric dam commissioned during World War I by President Woodrow Wilson. Sadly, Cornelia died in October 1918, leaving Charles a widower with three small children. He remarried in 1928 in Florence, Alabama, to Cera Lee of Mississippi. Folsom is buried between his sons Charles Jr. and Dudley in Hopkinsville, Kentucky.

James Alfred Gwyn (1876–1965) was born to James M. and Amelia Harper Foster Gwyn at "Springdale," the family home at Cruso (Haywood County), North Carolina. Following his education at Ravenscroft High School he went on to get a degree from the University of North Carolina in 1896. After college, Gwyn was an instructor at Bingham School in Asheville before moving to New Jersey and embarking on a distinguished career in management with the Arlington/DuPont de Nemours Company. He married twice, first to Merle L'Armoreaux in 1921, and then to Bessie Lee Page in 1939. He was also an editor of the Cyclopedia of Law and Procedure, (1901).

James McRae Hatch (1878–1925) was born to Walter N. and Margaret McRae Hatch in Asheville, North Carolina. He obtained the rank of first lieutenant in Company C, Second Infantry, and then resigned his post in 1906. He subsequently married Nell Gross and went to work as a bookkeeper in the offices of the Jones-Cable Lumber Offices in Gadsden County, Florida. While in Florida he became ill and was moved to Thomasville, Georgia for an operation. He died in surgery at Thomasville on June 20, 1925.[19]

Edward Isaac Holmes Jr. (1883–1916) was born in Asheville to Edward Isaac and Jane Cheesborough Holmes. Edward Sr. was in business with John Cheesborough as a manufacturer of smoking tobacco, with a shop at 45 Church Street in Asheville. Following Ravenscroft, Edward Jr. became a traveling salesman based in Asheville. In 1910 he married Annie Martin of Philadelphia. A son, Edward III, was born in 1911 but he died as an infant in 1912. Sadly, Holmes died just four years later of tuberculosis. His spouse later remarried and lived until 1962.

Erwin Allen Holt (1873–1961) was born in Alamance County, North Carolina, to Lawrence Shackleford and Margaret Locke Erwin. He was the brother of Eugene Holt, another Ravenscroft student. His grandfather, Edwin M. Holt, was founder of the first cotton mill in Alamance County, its operations starting on Big Alamance Creek in 1837 (its manufacture of "Alamance Plaids" became nationally famous). Erwin first married Mary Warren Davis in 1903. Mary passed away in 1942, and Holt subsequently married Laura Ballard Magill in 1944. He worked in the family business of Lawrence S. Holt & Sons.

Eugene Holt (1875–1948) was born in Alamance County, North Carolina, to Lawrence Shackleford and Margaret Locke Erwin. He was the brother of Erwin Holt, another Ravenscroft student. His grandfather, Edwin M. Holt, was founder of the first cotton mill in Alamance County, its operations starting on Big Alamance Creek in 1837 (its manufacture of "Alamance Plaids" became nationally famous). Eugene became vice-president of Atlantic Bank & Trust Co. in Greensboro, North Carolina.

James P. Hyman (1873–1946) was born to John Durante and Ellen Patton Hyman in Hendersonville, North Carolina. James' father had been a lawyer in partnership with William Love in Hendersonville, and previous to that had been editor of the Asheville newspaper, *The Spectator*. For many years the Hymans lived in a stone house on Patton Street in the section of Hendersonville now known as "Hyman Heights."[20] John D. died shortly after James' birth. James' mother, Ellen Patton Hyman, having written her will in 1887, died shortly thereafter, leaving James a $500 legacy. James' older brother, Victor L. Hyman, was mayor of Hendersonville in 1889, about the time that James was attending Ravenscroft High School. I can find nothing much about James except that his World War I draft card, which listed his address as Bakersfield, California, listed his occupation as "miner," and his employer as "Works for self." James Patton Hyman died in Inyo County, California, in 1946.[21]

Charles Earl Johnson Jones (1876–1951) was born to William Westwood and Bertie Johnson Jones in Raleigh, North Carolina. In 1879 W. W. Jones moved the family to Asheville and opened the law firm of Jones & Ashford in partnership with George Ashford. Following his education at Ravenscroft, Charles Jones obtained his law degree from the University of North Carolina at Chapel Hill, graduating in 1898. The Honorable Charles E. Jones was in the Department of Justice in Washington, DC, for many years, and also had a law practice in partnership with his father ("Jones & Jones").

Walter Hatch Lee (1878–1901) was the son of James Hardy and Sara Hatch Lee of Glencoe, North Carolina, a small hamlet just a few miles west of Asheville. After graduating from Ravenscroft, Lee transferred to Bingham Military School in 1893 and then on to West Point, where he graduated as an officer in 1901. But unfortunately, Lieutenant Walter Hatch Lee took part in a dangerous expedition in the Philippines and was killed on June 10, 1901.[22] "Battery Lee" at Fort Flagler, Washington, was named in honor of this valiant Ravenscroft boy.

Richard Henry Lowndes (1879–1967) was born on Cat Island, Charleston, South Carolina, to Richard Ion and Alice Izard Middleton Lowndes. The Lowndes family were Charleston planters who "summered" in nearby Flat Rock, North Carolina. Lowndes' father built a house at Flat Rock in 1885. The "Lowndes House" is still extant and part of the property of the Flat Rock Playhouse. Following his education at Ravenscroft (1892–1894), Richard Henry attended the College of St. James, Hagerstown, Maryland, for one year, then attended and graduated from Porter Military Academy three years later. After one year at Wofford College, Spartanburg, South Carolina, Lowndes entered Georgia Tech in 1899, graduating first in his class in 1903, with a B.S. in mechanical engineering. Immediately upon graduation, he began a long career as a mechanical drawing professor at his alma mater. He was affectionately called Professor "Pud" Lowndes.

Vardry Echols McBee Jr. (1879–1910) was born in Charlotte, North Carolina, the only son of Vardry Echols and Rosa Brooks McBee. Following his education at Ravenscroft, he attended Virginia Military Institute, from which he graduated in 1899. He immediately went to work as a civil engineer with the Seaboard Air Line Railway, which had been founded by his father. He became prominent, as he was responsible for the design and construction of many extensions of the railroad into parts of the South, such as Columbia, South Carolina; Birmingham, Alabama; and Florida. Unfortunately, while working on an extension along the west coast of Florida, after an illness of two weeks, he succumbed to an attack of paralysis and suddenly died on June 20, 1910, at the age of 30.[23]

Charlton C. Millard (1877–1948) was born to Dr. David and Josephine E. Millard of Asheville. He became a prominent local business man in Asheville, forming a partnership in the livery business with W. H. Lassiter. In 1907 he married Grace Lipscomb of Kansa City, Missouri. Millard and his brother were among a group of Asheville citizens who bought the former lands of the Swannanoa County Club and developed it into "Proximity Park," one of Asheville's first "suburb" communities. Subsequently, C. C. Millard became one of Asheville's largest property owners. "David Millard Junior High," a well-known former city school, was named for his father, David Millard.[24]

Herbert R. Millard (1875–1933) was born to Dr. David and Josephine E. Millard of Asheville NC, and was the brother of C.C. Millard. He attended and graduated from the University of Tennessee following his education at Ravenscroft. In 1924, Millard married Katherine Erwin. Herbert became a prominent local businessman in Asheville, owning and operating the "City Baggage Co." and later becoming a partner in the firm of "Millard & Stikeleather" with J. G. Stikeleather. A life-long resident of Asheville, Millard was a member of First Baptist Church.[25]

Preston Fidelia Patton III (1878–1967) was born to Preston F. Patton Jr. and his wife, Annie Eliza Farmer Patton, in Hoopers Creek Twp., Henderson County, North Carolina. Following his education at Ravenscroft, Patton attended the North Carolina College of Agriculture & Mechanic Arts (now North Carolina State University), graduating in 1898. He married Sadie M. Smathers in 1913. Preston and Sadie became leading citizens of Hendersonville. Preston was vice-president at First Bank & Trust for many years, and was instrumental in building the road (old US 25) from Hendersonville, North Carolina, to Spartanburg, South Carolina, acting as "county road supervisor." Patton's wife Sadie was a noted historian, authoring *The Story of Henderson County*, *Sketches of Polk County History* and *Ghost Stories and Legends of the Mountains*, among numerous articles and short stories.

Vernon Badham Ramseur (1878–1963) was born to Harvey M. and Mary Badham Ramseur of Lincolnton, North Carolina. Harvey M. Ramseur, "civil engineer" (with the Western North Carolina Railroad), his wife, and four of his six children were residents of Asheville in 1890, according to the city directory. Vernon's uncle, Stephen Dodson Ramseur, was an acclaimed Civil War hero. Sometime following his education at Ravenscroft, Ramseur moved to California and got a position with the San Francisco Y.M.C.A. as an "assistant physical" officer.[26] His World War I draft card shows that at the same time he was working for Metropolitan Life Insurance Company, probably as a salesman. By 1942, Ramseur had moved to New York City and was working for the firm of "Pierce & Hedrick," one of the pioneering "fund-raising" firms in America. This is not surprising, as most employees of Pierce & Hedrick were hired from within the ranks of the Y.M.C.A.[27] He married Fannie Francis Barker Lynch (1875–1937) sometime before 1918. They had no children of their own, excepting two children from Fannie's first marriage. The couple are both buried in the Ramseur family plot at Oakdale Cemetery in Birmingham, Alabama.

Harry W. Redwood (1874–1947) was born in Statesville, North Carolina, to Henry and Susan Taylor Redwood. He moved to Asheville with his parents in 1881. Following his education at Ravenscroft, he attended the University of Virginia, where he was an accomplished athlete. After leaving college he was in business in Baltimore for a few years before returning home to Asheville to join his father's clothing and dry goods firm, H. Redwood & Co. He was a member of Trinity Episcopal Church and even, at one time, played for the Asheville baseball team (Tourists) in its "non-professional" days. Redwood passed away in 1947 after a long illness — in fact, his obituary stated that he "died in a local hospital where he had been a patient since 1933."[28]

William Morris Redwood (1872–1955) was born in Statesville, North Carolina, to Henry and Susan Taylor Redwood. He moved to Asheville with his parents in 1881. After he attended Ravenscroft, William went on to the University of Virginia, Richmond. He began his business career with the First National Bank of Richmond immediately upon graduation from college. Soon thereafter, he moved to Baltimore, Maryland, where he organized the banking and brokerage firm of Heywood and Redwood. After the Baltimore fire of 1904, he moved back to Asheville and joined his father's mercantile business, H. Redwood & Co. In 1905 he married Nina Boykin of Baltimore. He served as manager in his father's firm until they were bought out by

Gilmer's Chain Stores. He served as manager with Gilmer's for a few years before going into banking as the executive director of First National Bank and Trust Company, Asheville. In 1926, he built a new colonial-revival house, designed by Charles N. Parker, at 20 Cedar Cliff Lane in the newly established Biltmore Forest. When he died at age 82, his funeral service was held at Trinity Episcopal Church, and in addition to the six pallbearers, 47 honorary pallbearers were named. Among the names were notable locals such as the Rev. Rufus Morgan, Judge Junius Adams, George A. Ashford, and Charles Waddell.[29]

Eugene Colton Sawyer (1871–1966) was born to James Pinckney and Nancy Colton Sawyer, and was the grandson of Isaac B. Sawyer, Asheville's first mayor. Shortly upon graduation from Ravenscroft, Eugene opened a bicycle business in downtown Asheville in 1890. By 1900 he began selling automobiles, the first of which he sold to George W. Vanderbilt for use on the Biltmore estate. However, Sawyer lost out on the deal, as one of his employees, Raymond Lemons, left his employ to become Vanderbilt's new chauffeur. In 1928 Sawyer opened the Sawyer Motor Co. on Coxe Avenue and became one of Asheville's most noted businessmen. The Sawyer Motor Co. building has recently been converted to luxury condominiums.[30]

Arnoldus VanderHorst V (1878–1943) was born to Arnoldus IV and Adele Allston VanderHorst on their large plantation on Kiawah Island off the coast of Charleston, South Carolina. Arnoldus' father died in 1881 after being shot while on a hunting expedition.[31] Arnoldus shows in the 1891 photo and is mentioned in Huntington Wilson's memoirs. Following Ravenscroft, he moved back to the family plantation and eventually became a lawyer in Charleston. He never married and died of natural causes at the age of 65. Kiawah Island was sold out of the family following Arnoldus' death in 1943.[32]

Silvio Von Ruck (1876–1918) was born in Kent, Ohio, to Dr. Karl and Delia Moore Von Ruck. He moved to Asheville with his parents in 1883, at the age of thirteen. His father came to Asheville to open the Winyah Sanitarium for tuberculin treatment. Following his education at Ravenscroft, Silvio received an extensive medical education, first at the University of Michigan at Ann Arbor, and then post-graduate work at universities in Vienna and Berlin. He became a noted pulmonary physician and in 1912 returned to Asheville to assume the leadership of Winyah Sanitarium and Von Ruck Research Laboratory. He was in New York City in 1918 on professional business when he contracted pneumonia. He died on April 7, within a week of being stricken, at the age of 42.[33] Tragically, his 15-year-old daughter, Silvia, contracted the same illness and died 7 days after her father.

Eric Ross Wainwright (1881–1966) was born to Englishman the Rev. Richard Wainwright and his second wife, Emily Ross, at Truro, Nova Scotia, Canada, where the Rev. Wainwright was serving as an Episcopal priest. Emily Ross died in February of 1881, less than a month after Eric's birth. Within the year, the Rev. Wainwright moved the family to Honolulu, Hawaii, to serve as a missionary, and there, in October of 1881, he married his third wife, Henrietta. In 1885, the family moved to Bowman's Bluff in Henderson County, North Carolina, near Asheville, where the Rev. Wainwright became rector of Gethsemane Church.[34] Lilia MacDonald wrote about this boy, "Eric is the cry baby — who invites them all to tease him by his belligerent threats & aspect, & collapses and cries directly he is touched. — His parents are English parsons, one of them is a stepmother who idolizes him & wishes him to learn an extra collect on Sundays & a verse of a hymn as a corrective to his evil temper."[35] Eric went on to graduate from the University of the South at Sewanee, Tennessee, in 1897. He married Frances Mabel Ross at Lunenburg, Nova Scotia, on September 19, 1906. By 1910, the couple was living in Asheville, with two sons, Richard and Ralph, and Eric was employed as a bookkeeper at the English Lumber Co. The 1920 census shows that Eric and his family, which now also included son John and daughter Nina, were living in Norfolk, Virginia. At some point they moved to the west coast of Canada, where Eric died at Vancouver in 1966 at the age of 85 years.

William Way (1876–1974) was born at Asheville on December 18, 1876, to Charles Burr and Martha Julia (Howell) Way. He was educated at Asheville High School and Ravenscroft High School. He attended General Theological Seminary (1901) and the Harvard Summer School of Theology (1907–09–10). In 1901, he was ordained a priest at Grace Episcopal Church, New York City.[36] In 1902, Way was called to be the rector of Grace Church in Charleston, where he remained until his retirement in 1946 at the age of 70. He married Marie Wagener of Charleston, South Carolina, on January 12, 1904; they had only one son, William Jr. The Rev. William Way died at the age of 98 in 1974. (He was probably the longest surviving Ravenscroft alumnus!)

Francis Mairs Huntington Wilson (1875–1946) was born in Chicago to Benjamin Mairs and Francis Huntington Wilson. Wilson's parents moved to Asheville in the early 1890s and sent him to Ravenscroft for his high school education. After two years at Ravenscroft, Huntington was sent to Hill School in Pottstown, Pennsylvania. He then obtained his B.A. degree from Yale in 1897. Immediately upon graduation, he joined the foreign service and became first secretary and charge d'affairs for the American Legation in Japan. Wilson returned from Japan in 1906 to take a position as third assistant secretary of state under President Theodore Roosevelt's administration. Roosevelt subsequently assigned Wilson to various additional foreign missions as U.S. envoy to Turkey and then Argentina. In 1909, Mr. Wilson became assistant secretary of state under President William Howard Taft. While Assistant Secretary of State, Wilson was responsible for designing and implementing a reorganizational plan for the State Department. He held his post until March 19, 1913, just after the election of President Woodrow Wilson, where upon Francis Wilson resigned his post and retired from civil service in opposition to President Wilson's foreign policies. Wilson went on to become a newspaper editor, among other jobs. But in 1935, he largely devoted his life to writing books and articles advocating American-British cooperation in foreign affairs. In 1945 he wrote of his life experiences in *Memoirs of an Ex-Diplomat*, in which some of the life experiences Wilson records are those of his years as a student at Ravenscroft School.[37]

Eight

Histories of Ravenscroft Associate Mission Churches

The Rev. James B. Sill's 1955 book, *Historical Sketches of Churches in the Diocese of Western North Carolina Episcopal Church*, served as the inspiration for these sketches. Some of the following churches are mentioned in Sill's book, but a number of these mission churches were long forgotten by 1955. I have given special attention to these forgotten churches, as little record of their existence now remains.

The Ravenscroft Associate Mission and Training School was established in 1868 in the Ravenscroft building at Asheville, as a reorganization of the former classical and theological school. However, the majority of mission work to the outlying counties did not begin until after 1872, when Dr. David Hillhouse Buel became principal of the training school. In 1888, the Associate Mission and Training School moved out of the Ravenscroft building to its new home, Shoenberger Hall. The Rev. W. S. Barrows replaced Dr. Buel in 1891, followed by the Rev. A. H. Stubbs, who was appointed "Warden of Ravenscroft" in 1894. The training school, whose students also aided in the mission work, ceased to function in the late 1890s, and had limited success overall, having only about 15–20 graduates in its 30-year span. However, the Ravenscroft Associate Mission remained in operation until shortly after the formation of the Western Carolina Diocese in 1922. The Ravenscroft Associate Mission was responsible for establishing and maintaining numerous Episcopal congregations in seven counties in western North Carolina during its fifty-plus years of operation.

In the June 1875 issue of *The Spirit of Missions*, a periodical of the Episcopal Board of Missions, the Rev. Dr. Buel published a nine-page article titled "Work in North Carolina": "I have thought it might interest Churchmen, and give them a more vivid and complete picture of this Mission field and its wants and capabilities, to hear from one who has been at work in it for more than two years, some results of his personal observation and experience."[1] Later in the article, in an attempt to give his readers a vivid picture of "this great Mission field," Buel took his readers on a "Missionary tour" by describing in detail the tour he had made in the fall of 1874 with Bishop Lyman to visit the numerous mission stations in the mountains of western North Carolina. The descriptions of the mission stations in Buel's article were essential to unlocking the histories of some of the earlier stations, especially those of Leicester and Glencoe.

When selecting the churches to include in these sketches, I found that it was not easy to decide as there are a number of churches that had indirect connections to Ravenscroft but were not ever under the direct supervision of the associate mission. For instance, the

Rev. E. A. Osborne, while rector of Calvary Episcopal Church in Fletcher, North Carolina (which was then an official mission station of Ravenscroft Associate Mission), reported during the early 1880s that he also held "missionary services" at Boiling Springs, Arden, Smoky Hollow, Mill Pond, Pinner's Cove and Bat Cave. Of these, Pinner's Cove and Bat Cave are the only ones that became actual churches, but I chose to include only Pinner's Cove in these sketches, because it is the only church ever reported as a Ravenscroft Associate Mission station. It is doubly difficult to choose given that Pinner's Cove (Mt. Calvary) is no longer in existence and yet Bat Cave (Church of the Transfiguration) remains an active and growing congregation.

A study of the mission work of Ravenscroft is also a study of life in the mountains during the late nineteenth and early twentieth centuries. Some familiar place names appear, but we also see a number of old place names that are unrecognizable to us today, such as Bull Creek, Forks of the Pigeon, Glencoe, Owenby, Rockwood, Smith's Mill Creek, Micadale, Candlersville, Silver Springs, Warm Springs, and Bowman's Bluff.

Buncombe County

ACTON MISSION/ST. PAUL'S — ACTON AREA, WEST ASHEVILLE

The Rev. James H. Postell, a former Methodist minister, joined the Ravenscroft Associate Mission and Training School in 1883, and immediately began ministering at various mission stations while pursuing his theological studies at Ravenscroft as well.

The Rev. Postell filed a parochial report in 1885 for a mission station called "Norman Stevens' House," where he had been ministering since the year before (1884). "At this point," reported Postell, "we are making an effort to build a Church, and would do so by the coming Fall if we could receive some help from our friends abroad."[2] In the same report he noted that there were four communicants and "eighteen or twenty Sunday School scholars," whom he claimed he "could control if we only had the books."[3]

Samuel Norman Stevens II was born in Charleston, South Carolina, to Samuel Norman and Mary Smith Tennant Stevens in 1833. Samuel Norman Stevens I, a cotton factor in partnership with John and William Ravenel in Charleston, built the family home at 20 South Battery Street in 1843.[4] Samuel N. Stevens II inherited the house upon the death of his father in 1848. But in 1859, he sold the property and moved his young family (wife Martha Buist and daughter Mary Tennent) to the mountains of North Carolina. Stevens bought 220 acres southeast of "Harkins" in the Lower Hominy Valley in Buncombe County. This area was near the present-day Sand Hill School Road, west of Asheville. Stevens not only set up a large plantation farm but also began a flour-milling operation.[5]

One can understand that Mr. Stevens probably had a substantial-sized home in which to host a church congregation. By 1884, Stevens and his wife had produced eleven more children, giving them a total of twelve children — enough to start their own congregation!

In 1887, the small group of communicants that had been meeting at Mr. Stevens' house moved to the nearby Sand Hill Academy. In fact, the Rev. Postell's parochial report for that year was labeled "Sand Hill Academy." This was an old academy building at Sand Hill, west of Asheville. The "Sand Hill Academy" was a private school started by Charles Moore in the early 1800s, and by 1887, the original academy building had been replaced by a two-classroom brick building located at what is now the intersection of Sand Hill Road and Sand Hill School Road.[6] The Rev. Postell reported to the Convention that year, "This appointment is hopeful. The congregations are good and very attentive, and we hope and pray for the prosperity of the Church."[7]

The next year, 1888, the Rev. Postell submitted the following report of his work at "St. Paul's Mission": "I have been preaching at this point for over four years, and the opposition from without has been very bitter, but thank God, we are more in favor with the people, and feel that the Church will succeed here with proper care and prudence."[8] "St. Paul's Mission" was now the official name given to the church, which had heretofore been designated only by its places of meeting ("Norman Stevens House" and "Sand Hill Academy").

The Rev. Postell's report of 1888 included some additional good news: "Our people have bought a Church at this point for five hundred dollars, worth one thousand. We will have to put to the building Vestibule, Belfry and Vestry, which will cost considerable. The people have been taxed in this respect to their utmost capacity. After they get their church fixed as desired, we feel we will be able to do more for missions."[9]

The congregation had bought the former "Loricks View Baptist Church" property, which included a brick building, with a seating capacity of 125, situated on a two-acre plot.[10] The Baptists had bought the property just five years earlier from Thomas J. Candler and his wife for fifty dollars.[11] The substantial increased sale price from fifty dollars to five hundred dollars in such a short time span indicates that the brick building was no doubt built by the Baptists, resulting in the increased property value. The property was just fifty feet west of the current Smokey Park Highway overpass on the southwest side of Montevista Road near the intersection of Acton Circle. The property was either part of or adjacent to the site of the defunct Candler College, a Methodist institution of the mid–1800s.

A large portion of the funds for the buying, building and refurbishing of these mission churches came from interested donors from outside the region, many funds even coming from moneyed people in the Northern states. In 1889, the Rev. Postell's report to the Convention was more appeal than report: "This chapel is situated in the Hominy Valley, seven miles west of Sulphur Springs. The church was bought by the Church for five hundred dollars; we have title for two acres of land in church lot. We need a vestibule and belfry, chancel and vestry-room; we need a rectory to be built on the lot, and Parish school-room, all of which will cost fifteen hundred dollars, but will be satisfied with the chapel being remodeled and the rectory- built, which will cost one thousand dollars and make St. Paul's a grand success. Brothers, help us!"[12]

Little mention is made of St. Paul's over the next few years, until 1893, where a report shows that the church consisted of only four families, down substantially from the twelve families reported in 1888, and that services were held twice a month. The Rev. Postell again made an appeal to his fellow churchmen to help with this struggling mission: "This Chapel has no Sunday-school for the want of teachers. There are about thirty scholars who could be reached very easily if we had teachers. If we had on the lot a Parish school-room we could procure the teachers, and the Chapel would soon be a success. This has been the misfortune of my work; if I had school-rooms on each Chapel lot we would look for almost immediate fruit as the result of this plan. Will not some liberal-minded person or persons help us in this matter?"[13]

By 1895, the Rev. A. H. Stubbs, the newly appointed warden of Ravenscroft, was listed as the "Minister-in-Charge" of St. Paul's, with the Rev. Postell and Samuel Rhoades listed as "Deacons." Besides giving a few statistics, including that the church still only had four families, the Rev. Stubbs also submitted a short one-sentence statement: "This church is a brick building, in bad repair inside, and destitute of necessary furniture."[14] This report is also the first time that the location of St. Paul's is listed as "Acton." Henceforth, the church was known as "St. Paul's–Acton."

The Rev. Stubbs kept a diary of his mission work (for over 30 years), and it is from his dairy that we have a record of some of the families associated with St. Paul's. According to Stubbs' diary, he often would often dine with "the Harkins" after the services, and on many occasions he would stay overnight and return to Asheville on Monday morning. Thomas Jefferson Harkins and his wife Margaret Candler Harkins lived next door to the church, and were strong supporters of St. Paul's. Margaret's brother, Thomas J. Candler, was the original owner of the St. Paul's property and it was he and his wife who had sold the original lot to the Loricks View church in 1883.

Besides delivering the litany and preaching, the Rev. Stubbs would preside over baptisms and confirmations. But on July 5, 1895, the Rev. Stubbs records that he, the Rev. Postell (a priest studying at the training school), and Bishop Cheshire (who was on his summer western visitation) all officiated at a service at St. Paul's. The bishop gave the sermon and also confirmed Mary Angeline Osborne and Charles Jefferson Osborne.[15]

This small mission church did not thrive; in fact, by 1904 it was listed as having only one family and one communicant. By 1918, St. Paul's–Acton was on the list of "Missions Where No Services Have Been Held."[16] The mission had been abandoned for several years and the building was rapidly decaying, and so in 1920, the trustees of the Missionary District of Asheville sold "the old church building and lot at Acton for $300."[17]

ALEXANDER'S MISSION — ALEXANDER, NORTHWEST ASHEVILLE

The Buncombe Turnpike opened in 1828 to provide a direct route for the mountain farmers (drovers) of Tennessee and North Carolina to transport their goods and livestock to markets in the South. The route of the new turnpike followed along the French Broad River for many miles, snaking from the western shore to the eastern shore and back again numerous times. One of the major crossings was ten miles north (downstream) of Asheville at a place that came to be known as "Alexander's."

There were numerous stands established along the route where the drovers could corral and feed their animals while they obtained rest and nourishment for themselves. James Mitchell Alexander, who had operated a saddling business in downtown Asheville since 1816, and who had been one of the contractors of the turnpike, decided to capitalize on the new venture by purchasing land along the route and establishing a stand. Alexander, an entrepreneur, had bought his land at one of the locations where the turnpike crossed the French Broad. On the eastern shore he built a hotel (Alexander's Hotel) and stables, and established a mercantile business.[18] He also operated a ferry to provide transport across the river. Not surprisingly, a small village soon grew up around the hotel. The village was called "Alexander's," or sometimes "French Broad."

The Alexanders were Methodists, but apparently other members of the growing community were of different religious persuasions, and so at some point in time the various denominations banded together and built a shared chapel. The chapel, named Trinity Union Chapel (also called "French Broad Union Chapel"), was built on the western shore, across the river from the hotel.

By 1884, Alexander's Hotel was under the management of Brigadier General Robert Brank Vance, the brother of famed North Carolina Governor Zebulon B. Vance. General Vance, a former six-term U.S. Congressman,[19] had purchased the hotel from James Mitchell Alexander's sons, who had earlier assumed the operation of the hotel from their father.

In 1875, Assistant Bishop Theodore B. Lyman, who was filling in for the ailing Bishop Atkinson, reported that, due to an accident during his travels to Tennessee, he had to spend a few days at Alexander's Hotel, where "on Sunday I conducted the service and preached in the parlor of the hotel."[20] But the work of the Episcopal Church at Alexander's did not begin until 1885. Interestingly, the first attempt to establish an Episcopal church at Alexander's was through the efforts of Bishop Atkinson's grandson and namesake, the Rev. Thomas Atkinson, who in 1885 was serving as an instructor and missionary at the Ravenscroft Associate Mission and Training School in Asheville. The Rev. Atkinson reported to Diocesan Convention in May of that year, "Since the beginning of the present month, at the request of Mr. F. Randolph Curtis, of New York, now living in North Carolina, I have held two services in a union meeting house at Alexander, a station on the W. N. C. R. R., about ten miles west of Asheville. These were, with one exception, the first Church services ever held at this place, and they have met with a most encouraging reception, the congregations on both occasions being large, attentive and devout, and apparently much impressed by the service. It is hoped that these services can be kept up on one Sunday of each month, as Mr. Curtis is doing all in his power to give the Church a good start in this place where she has hitherto been entirely unknown, by providing liberal supplies of Prayer Books and Hymnals, training the people in the music and responses, and in short, leaving nothing undone in order to make the services intelligible and attractive."[21]

Francis Randolph Curtis was born in New York City to William Edmond and Mary Ann Scovill Curtis on October 11, 1858.[22] Curtis attended Trinity College in Hartford, Connecticut, where he obtained an undergraduate degree in English in 1880[23] and then completed an M.A. degree in June of 1883.[24] However, he must have decided before graduation to settle in Asheville, as records show that in November of 1882[25] he purchased the first parcel of land to establish a farming operation, which by 1883 would encompass five hundred acres of land.[26]

Mr. Curtis' land was on the western shore of the river just above (and west of) the railroad depot. The farm was in the area of the present-day Curtis-Parker Road, off of Fletcher Mountain Road. A survey[27] of Curtis' lands (made after his death) shows that on either side of a large barn, he maintained extensive orchards. The survey also shows a church, located just south of his estate. This, I believe, was Trinity Union Chapel, which was located on the property that is now the cemetery of the French Broad Baptist Church on Curtis Miles Road in Alexander. The cemetery (and site of the former

Trinity Union Chapel) is directly across from the intersection of Curtis Miles Road and Haney Road.

The Rev. J. H. Postell, another Ravenscroft missionary, was the person who filed the 1885 parochial report for the new work at Alexander under the title "Trinity Union Chapel." Postell reported that the congregation had only one communicant, but yet had twenty families attending the services. "This is a new appointment," writes the Rev. Postell, "and much interest is manifested by the people. They are orderly and respectful, and the congregations are steadily improving. This appointment is located in a neighborhood of good lands, and the people are becoming concerned about the education of their children."[28]

Oddly, there is no mention of this mission in the Convention journals from 1886 until the end of the nineteenth century. However, we do find mention of the mission, beginning in 1898, in diary entries written by the Rev. A. H. Stubbs, who had become warden of Ravenscroft in 1894. Although the Rev. Stubbs could have assigned one of the Ravenscroft missionaries under his charge as the "priest-in-charge" at Alexander's, it seems that he assumed the primary leadership of the mission. Beginning in 1899, he occasionally identifies the mission at Alexander's as "St. Mark's Mission," although he records that they continued to meet in the Union Chapel.

F. Randolph Curtis died in 1892, so we see in the Rev. Stubbs' diary entries the names of other parishioners. Stubbs writes of his visit to the mission on October 15, 1898: "Went down to Alexander's. Found Miss Lee to be at Asheville having obtained a position there. Called on Mrs. Plato Lee and then went to Buncombe House [Alexander Hotel]."[29] "Mrs. Plato Lee" was Eugenia Lee, the wife of Dr. Plato Herman Lee, a young physician who had recently graduated with a medical degree from the University of Tennessee.[30] Plato and his wife, in 1898, had only been married about six years and at that time had three young children.[31] I suspect that "Miss Lee" was Plato's older sister Elizabeth.[32] The Rev. Stubbs also mentions a "Miss Coxe" in one of his entries.[33] Mary Vance Coxe, a young divorcee, was the daughter of Gen. Robert Brank Vance. Mary and her daughter Hattie lived at the Alexander Hotel with her brother James N. Vance, who was the hotel's manager.[34]

"Gen'l. Robert B. Vance dies at 11:30 A.M.— was present at his death," the Rev. A. H. Stubbs enters in his diary on November 28, 1899. "Mrs. Vance sent for me on account of financial tribulation, and because she could not appeal to the Methodists."[35] Although the Vance family were Methodists, apparently their daughter Mary's work with St. Mark's, and the frequent visits of the Rev. Stubbs, resulted in Mrs. Vance's respect and affection for Stubbs' ministry.

The Rev. Stubbs often made remarks in his diary of numerous impediments to reaching the chapel. The first impediment was getting a key to the chapel from Miss Coxe or Miss Lee. Although he would try to write or telegraph ahead of time, often he would arrive to find that nobody was home who had a key. But perhaps the biggest impediment that the Rev. Stubbs encountered was the logistical problem of getting to the chapel. The Union Chapel was difficult to reach, especially in inclement weather. The Alexander Hotel and Gen. Vance's house were on the eastern shore of the French Broad, but some of the parishioners, the railroad depot, and the chapel were on the western shore, with the only connection being a timber bridge. After one visit, the Rev. Stubbs records, "Railroad has almost cut this building off,"[36] and after a subsequent visit just a few months later, he records, "We were cut off from the meeting house by high water and the timber on the bridge."[37] And in February of 1903, the Rev. Stubbs writes, "Chapel closed on account of small pox. Service at Hotel."[38]

By 1904, St. Mark's had dwindled to just two communicants and two families. The record shows that one of those two members was still able to conduct a Sunday school with forty-seven pupils.[39]

This photograph by W. T. Robertson, circa 1880s, shows the "timber bridge at Alexanders." The Rev. Stubbs often mentioned this bridge over the French Broad River, in his diary entries. The bridge, which was often flooded, was a vital link to the Alexander community that straddled both shores of the river (photograph collection MS222.002F, photo "D"—from the North Carolina Collection, Pack Memorial Library, Asheville).

The last record of St. Mark's at Alexander is in the 1914 Convention Journal. And even there it is merely a name on a list of unorganized missions maintained by the Ravenscroft Associate Mission. It seems the final blow came with the terrible flood of 1916. The front page of July 16 edition of the *Asheville Citizen* reported, "The French Broad river at Alexander swept away all of the village on the west side of the stream except the Southern Railway station. The post office, a store and two dwelling houses went down in the swirling currents."[40]

BEAVER DAM CHAPEL/GRACE EPISCOPAL — GRACE STATION, ASHEVILLE

Grace Episcopal Church, originally known as the "Beaver Dam Mission," was not only the first mission church established in Asheville, but it also predated the Ravenscroft Associate Mission and Training School by about one year. The Rev. Jarvis Buxton, rector of Trinity Church in Asheville, submitted a lengthy report of the new mission at Beaver Dam to the 1867 Convention: "Within the last few months a promising field for a Mission Sunday School and services has been opened on Beaver Dam, three miles from town."[41] The new mission was in the Beaverdam Valley, which runs between Elk Mountain and Sunset Mountain and follows the Beaverdam Creek, which flows mostly east to west across the modern-day thoroughfare of Merrimon Avenue, three miles north of present-day downtown Asheville. Beaverdam is referred to as one word today.

The Rev. Buxton also reported that through the contributions of the new congregation and the members of his congregation at Trinity Church, enough money was given to erect a building on a donated site. The lot for the new church building (a log structure) was given by Professor John Kimberly from his surrounding farmlands. Prof. Kimberly and his family had moved to Asheville the previous year following the closing of the University of North Carolina at Chapel Hill, where he had been teaching. The Civil War had taken its toll on the university. The loss of numerous professors and students who were either killed or severely wounded, combined with the lack of funds (both state-allocated funds and individual funds for families to pay for tuition and school fees), caused the closing of the university in 1866.[42]

John Kimberly was born on September 1, 1817, to David and Elizabeth Ferris Kimberly of Brooklyn, New York. He graduated from New York University with an A.B. degree in 1837, and soon thereafter accepted a position at Buckhorn Academy in Murfreesboro, North Carolina. While teaching at Buckhorn, Kimberly met and married Caroline A. Capehart of Murfreesboro in 1840. The young couple was married for only eight years before Caroline's passing in 1848. They had four children, with only two surviving to adulthood — Elizabeth Ferris and Emily Southall. Kimberly then pursued his master's degree, graduating from Harvard's Lawrence Scientific College at Cambridge in 1854. In 1857, Kimberly accepted the position of professor of chemistry at the University of North Carolina at Chapel Hill. The following year (1858), he married his second wife, Elizabeth "Bettie" Meredith Maney, of Nashville, Tennessee. In the summer of 1865, foreseeing the potential closing of the university, and at the urging of Governor David Swain, Kimberly bought a 600-acre farm in Asheville. It was to that farm that he came in 1866.[43]

Members of the Rev. Buxton's congregation at Trinity Church volunteered to help the new mission get started. "Five or six young persons, out of the Asheville congregation," reported the Rev. Buxton, "have volunteered their services as [Sunday school] teachers."[44] Prayer books and furniture were donated as well. One interesting donation was that of a "service-desk which was first used in Asheville nearly 20 years ago, before the building of the Church."[45] Mr. Francis Murdoch, a member of Trinity preparing for Holy Orders, acted as the mission's first lay reader. Murdoch was soon joined by Gen. James G. Martin and Thomas W. Patton of Trinity Church, who also functioned as lay readers at Beaverdam Chapel.

The first official record of the numbers of persons worshipping at Beaverdam was in 1868. The Rev. Buxton then reported that there were seven communicants, and that he had baptized 22 persons (6 adults and 16 children) and confirmed ten children.[46]

For the next two decades, the Rev. Buxton and volunteers from his congregation, and men from the newly formed Ravenscroft Associate Mission and Training School, kept the fledgling mission alive. Although they would occasionally gain and lose a communicant here and there, the number remained around seven or eight during that period. However, after the coming of the railroad in 1880, Asheville began to grow rapidly. Being hemmed in on the south and west by the Swannanoa and French Broad Rivers, and on the east by the Beaucatcher and Sunset Mountains, the natural direction for the city to grow was northward, toward the Beaver Dam area. The increased population of Asheville also brought an increased congregation to Beaver Dam Chapel.

In 1886, the Rev. Buxton reported, "I have visited the three chapels in the country belonging to this Parish monthly. The Sunday Schools connected with them are flourishing." He reported that between the three missions, they had ninety pupils attending their Sunday schools that year.[47] The Kimberly family no doubt added to the increased number of pupils at the Beaver Dam Sunday School. In 1867, when the mission first began, John and Elizabeth Kimberly had only two small children, but by 1880 they had added five more children, for a total of seven.[48] Between 1886 and 1887, Beaver Dam Chapel added eleven new communicants, for a total of eighteen,[49] a substantial increase from the four communicants reported in 1883. Perhaps this is the reason that Ravenscroft-trained missionary priest William F. Rice was assigned to be the priest-in-charge in October of 1886. William Francis Rice, a native of nearby Riceville, had recently been ordained as a deacon, and was assigned to the charges of Beaver Dam Chapel and Trinity Chapel, Haw Creek.

The community surrounding the Beaver Dam Chapel changed its name to "Grace," opening the "Grace" post office in 1889. The chapel maintained the name "Beaver Dam" until 1895, when it began to show up in the reports as "Grace Mission" or "Grace Church."

Grace Mission was growing so rapidly that when Bishop Theodore Lyman visited the mission in the summer of 1891, he "made an address to the congregation on the importance of securing a Parsonage as speedily as possible for the accommodation of the Missionary [W. F. Rice], whose residence is many miles away."[50] The congregation heeded the bishop's advice, and within a year they built a "comfortable parsonage of six rooms, each 16 × 16."[51] The new parsonage, which cost $1,200, was constructed on a one-acre lot adjacent to the chapel, which had been conveyed to mission by the Kimberly heirs (Prof. John Kimberly had passed away in 1882). The Rev. Rice also reported that "much credit is due Mr. P. M. Kimberly, who was in sole charge of and gave much time to the building operations."[52] Actually, "P. M. Kimberly" was thirty-year-old "T. M." (Thomas Maney) Kimberly, who was the eldest son of Prof. Kimberly.

EIGHT. *The Churches — Buncombe — GRACE EPISCOPAL* 115

The following year, 1893, it was reported that in addition to receiving "a new Communion service, altar linen, a Bible, lectern, prayer-desk and Bishop's chair," the mission had also dug a thirty-six-foot-deep well, built a small barn and well-house, and made many improvements to the grounds around the chapel and parsonage.[53]

Much of Asheville's increased population in the 1880s and 1890s was made up of wealthy northerners, many of whom moved there for health reasons, in order to take advantage of Asheville's notable temperate climate. However, many also had a social conscience, and sought to use their wealth for the betterment of those less fortunate mountain people living nearby. One such family was Mrs. Charles T. Chester and her daughter, Susan, who moved to Asheville in the early 1890s and became members of Grace Church. Mrs. Chester was the widow of Charles Thomas Chester, an inventor and manufacturer of telegraphic instruments in New York City.[54] But most notable was her daughter Susan Chester Lyman, who not only was an active communicant of the chapel but also was noted for her charitable and social work among the local people.

Susan Guion Chester was born to Charles T. and Lucretia Roberts Chester (of New Bern, North Carolina) in Englewood, New Jersey, in 1867, and graduated from Vassar College in 1888.[55] While at Vassar she became involved with group of collegiate women headed by Episcopalian Vida Scudder, which in 1890 formed into the "College Settlements Association." The "college settlement" movement began in the late 1880s as a Christian

Grace Episcopal Chapel, circa 1890s. This frame church replaced the original log structure, but predated the 1906 stone church. The house at right is probably the rectory (image P-4326/6, in the David E. Whisnant papers #4326, Southern Historical Collection, Wilson Library, University of North Carolina at Chapel Hill).

social reform movement in America, inspired by the work of John Ruskin and Octavia Hill in nineteenth-century England. "*The idea of this work*," said Vida Scudder in an 1893 *New York Times* article, "is to have a group of college educated women live in a house in the very locality of the people who are to be reached, becoming a part of their social life and learning all that is possible of the civic life of the neighborhood. Certain definite forms of work are carried on by these young women. Some of them have charge of circulating literature among the people who are to be reached. Others do what they can to stimulate savings among them. Others pay particular attention to their social condition. They cooperate with existing educational and charitable agencies."[56]

The first "settlement houses" were established in poor urban neighborhoods in New York, Philadelphia, and Boston. But after visiting (or moving to) Asheville in the early 1890s, Susan Chester hit upon a novel idea — why couldn't settlement houses be established in poor rural neighborhoods, such as those she saw in the mountains of Southern Appalachia? So in 1894 she and her mother bought a five-acre parcel in the Beaverdam Creek area, near Grace Church, and began building a large log building to be the center of her "Log Cabin Settlement."

As she was building the settlement, Chester began a promotion campaign to raise funds from her Northern friends. In a lengthy address to a convention of Episcopal Churchwomen in Philadelphia in 1893, Susan explained not only the premise for her new work but, more importantly, the relationship it would have to the church body: "The relation of the settlement to the Church is twofold; It may prepare the way for the missionary, by overcoming the prejudices against innovations, so deeply rooted in the mind of the sturdy mountaineer, or it may work with an already established church. [*sic*] A few miles from Asheville is one of our small mission chapels near which it is my hope to establish a settlement which will

Susan Chester Lyman's Log Cabin Settlement House was designed by noted architect Richard Sharp Smith. The settlement house was located in the Beaverdam valley, near Grace Episcopal Chapel (image P- 4326/3–4 in the David E. Whisnant papers #4326, Southern Historical Collection, Wilson Library, University of North Carolina at Chapel Hill).

illustrate the second relation. The deacon-in-charge [William Francis Rice], a native mountaineer, has won his way to the hearts of the people near, by his earnestness and true kindliness. With a library, kindergarten, cooking school, sewing classes, clubs, a simple lecture course, and other attendant circumstances, working hand in hand with the Church and Sunday-school, the results would be far-reaching and the influence incalculable."[57]

The Log Cabin Settlement opened its doors in September of 1894. Its main aims were to "cooperate with a mission chapel [Grace Church] and a district school in the neighborhood, to revive the weaving industry, and to provide a good library for the community."[58] It also maintained an active women's club, girls' club, and women's auxiliary. Eventually, the settlement became famous for its woven coverlets, which were first sold by Chester to friends in the North, but were later marketed through the "Asheville Exchange for Women's Work," which maintained a shop in Pack Square in downtown Asheville.[59]

The Rev. A. H. Stubbs became warden of the Ravenscroft Associate Mission and Training School in 1894. He assumed the direct oversight of all the chapels and churches affiliated with the mission, including Grace Church, although Mr. William F. Rice continued on as the deacon-in-charge. By that time, Grace Church had 39 communicants, with an average of over sixty persons attending services.[60] Also that year, the Rev. Rice reported that Grace had received various financial gifts, and that the church was "particularly under obligations to Mr. George W. Pack, of Asheville, for $50, and Mr. John Nicholas Brown, of Providence, R. I., for $100."[61]

In 1895, the Rev. Rice reported that "the building of St. Titus' Chapel, Upper Beaver Dam, only three miles from Grace, has caused the removal of nineteen communicants from Grace Church."[62] However, with the addition of new communicants throughout the year, the church could still boast 23 communicants and almost fifty attendees.

In 1898, Susan Chester, who, along with her work at the Log Cabin Settlement, had become an active lay leader of Grace Church, married her fellow parishioner and neighbor, Mr. A. Hunt Lyman.[63] Alonzo Hunt Lyman was a wealthy banker, who, along with his brother, Charles, had moved to Asheville in 1888 for health reasons.[64] After moving to Asheville, Mr. Lyman became interested in buying and selling land and investments. In fact, it was he and his brother who sold the original five-acre parcel to Susan Chester in 1894 for her Log Cabin Settlement.[65]

As the turn of the century approached, Grace Church, though still under the auspices of the Ravenscroft Associate Mission, was in desperate need of a new building to replace its dilapidated wooden chapel. Even as far back as 1891, Deacon Rice had reported, "The Mission at Beaver Dam is in a flourishing condition. The Sunday school is always large, and great interest is always manifested in the services. A new chapel is much needed at this place."[66] So finally, in 1905, under the leadership of the Rev. W. F. Rice, the church asked local immigrant architect Richard Sharp Smith to design a new building for the growing congregation. The British-born Smith designed a picturesque English-Gothic stone chapel, reminiscent of the country chapels in his homeland. Assisting the Rev. Rice were several active church leaders, such as Mrs. Susan Chester Lyman, William S. Cornell, and members of the Kimberly family (Thomas Maney Kimberly, Miss Mary Kimberly, Miss Rebecca Kimberly, and Miss Fannie Kimberly).

For the first two decades of the twentieth century, Grace Church remained under the jurisdiction of the Ravenscroft Associate Mission, headed by the Rev. A. H. Stubbs. However, the Rev. Rice soon left to be the priest-in-charge at St. James in Black Mountain, North Carolina. Rice was replaced at Grace Church by another Ravenscroft priest, the Rev. Walter S. Cain.

Today Grace Episcopal Church remains a growing and vibrant congregation, still worshiping in the quaint 1905 stone chapel that sits atop the hill on the west side of Merrimon Avenue, near the intersection of the present-day Beaverdam Road

Beaver Dam Mission/St. Titus'—Beaverdam area, Asheville

St. Titus, often referred to as "Upper Beaver Dam," was established many years after Grace Episcopal and was located further north along the Beaverdam Road northeast of Asheville. Beaverdam is referred to as one word today.

The first mention of this mission was in 1887, when the Rev. William F. Rice, then minister-in-charge at Beaver Dam Chapel (Grace), reported, "I also hold service at a small chapel three miles from this place and have good attendance."[67] A year later he reported that, in addition to his other duties, he also held services at "a School House near Beaver Dam Chapel."[68] I suspect this may be the same school house (further up the Beaverdam Valley along Beaverdam Creek) mentioned by historian John Preston Arthur in his book, *Western North Carolina: A History*: "Bishop Asbury records the fact that in September, 1806, he and Moses Lawrence lost their way in Buncombe County when within a mile of Killion's on Beaver Dam creek, and spent the night in a school house, without a fire. The floor of this school room was of dirt, on which Moses slept, while the Bishop had a 'bed wherever I could find a bench.'"[69] But in his 1893 parochial report, the Rev. Rice notes that "since last report, the Mission at Upper Beaver Dam has purchased and paid for an organ and an excellent lot of over an acre in extent, upon which we hope soon to build a Chapel."[70]

The Buncombe County Register of Deeds shows that in 1893, James Madison Herren and his wife Hannah sold a one-acre lot to the diocese for a new chapel. According to the deed, the property was "along the waters of Beaver Dam Creek," adjacent to the lands of J. Henry Palmer and Joseph Stradley. John Henry Palmer was the son-in-law of James and Hannah Herren, having married their daughter, Leui Alice Herren, in 1880. The other adjacent property owner was Joseph Stradley, the brother of Hannah Stradley Herren and the son of the Rev. Thomas Stradley, the first Baptist minister to come to western North Carolina.

The new chapel, named "St. Titus," was built on a one-acre lot off of Old Herren Cove Road, now called Pinecroft Road, just north of Beaverdam Road. The lot is now part of the property of George T. Henderson Jr. at 31 Beaver Valley Road. The entrance to the property from Pinecroft was closed in the 1960s.

The Rev. A. H. Stubbs, warden of Ravenscroft, filed a parochial report for "Beaver Dam, St. Titus' Chapel" in 1895, in which he noted that "the exterior of St. Titus' Chapel has been completed; the interior is not completed. Four pieces of memorial chancel furniture were presented by Mrs. Gordon Dexter, of Boston, Mass."[71] In that same year, Stubbs noted at the end of his parochial report on Grace Chapel that "the building of St. Titus' Chapel, Upper Beaver Dam, only three miles from Grace, has caused the removal of nineteen communicants from Grace Church."[72] That's interesting because St. Titus' Chapel was reported that year to have "20 communicants," which means all but one of its communicants transferred from Grace. At the time it was reported that 40 people (communicants and non-communicants) were worshiping in the new chapel, which was built to seat 125 people.

The Rev. William Francis Rice was the "priest-in-charge" at Grace, and so would most often be the one to provide ministerial services to St. Titus'. According to Frank David Roberson, the grandson of the Rev. Rice. Services at St. Titus were in the afternoon, not on Sunday mornings. Roberson never attended St. Titus, but his mother, Willie Marietta Rice Roberson, related to him her recollections of helping her father, the Rev.

This is the only remaining image of St. Titus' Chapel in Upper Beaverdam. This photograph was taken of the church after it had been closed and remodeled into a residence; it shows the chancel (east) end of the church. Notice the gothic pointed arch on the gable vent. The church entrance vestibule was on the opposite (west) end of the church (courtesy of George Henderson Jr. and Rex Redmon).

Rice, with the services at the chapel. Mrs. Roberson stated that she and her father, after the Sunday morning service at Grace, would take the horse and buggy out to St. Titus'. They would arrive before the scheduled service time, and while the Rev. Rice swept the floor and dusted the pews, Willie would prepare the altar and prayer rail and distribute the hymnbooks.[73]

Records show that Prof. Frank Valentine performed the duties of "lay reader" at St. Titus' for a number of years (1897–1901). Prof. Valentine was a British ex-patriot who had been a member of the British colony at Bowman's Bluff in Henderson County, but in 1896 he had moved to Asheville to be the headmaster at the Ravenscroft High School for Boys. Valentine was one of eight lay readers and three missionary priests who comprised the Ravenscroft Associate Mission staff in 1899.[74]

Just a few years into the turn of the century the attendance declined severely at St. Titus', and in 1904 the church was closed and the remaining members transferred to Grace Church. The property was sold out of the diocese to the Buncombe County Board of Education in 1905.[75] The property was used as a public school[76] until the property was sold to Charles B. Scarborough in 1920.[77] It eventually was sold to George T. Henderson, Sr., father of the current owner. Converted to a residence and used by the Henderson family for many years, the chapel eventually became derelict, and was torn down by George T. Henderson Jr. in the early 2000s.

BLACK MOUNTAIN MISSION/ST. JAMES — BLACK MOUNTAIN

Black Mountain station was the first stop on the Western North Carolina Railroad line after traversing up the mountain through the many switchbacks and tunnels from the station of Old Fort at the foot of the mountain. The extreme grade and rugged mountainous terrain were finally conquered in 1879, when Major James W. Wilson, chief engineer and contractor for the Western North Carolina Railroad, announced the completion of the new line up the mountain. Hotels and boarding houses soon grew up around the station to cater to the many travelers and visitors who began flocking to the mountains.

Around the turn of the twentieth century, Black Mountain also became the hub for denominational summer conference and retreat centers. The Presbyterians built "Montreat" in 1897, the Y.M.C.A. established "Blue Ridge Assembly" in 1906, and the Baptists built "Ridgecrest" in 1907. These conference centers brought many seasonal visitors to Black Mountain, and soon the town became a major tourist center for western North Carolina.

Not surprisingly, then, author James B. Sill records that St. James at Black Mountain was begun in 1907, when "Major Wilson, a devout Presbyterian living near Black Mountain, invited the Rev. A. DeRossett Mears (of St. John's Church, Marion) to hold services at his home, for the benefit of some Episcopalian neighbors and guests."[78] However, Sill was unaware that a previous foundation had been laid, as early as 1890, for the establishment of an Episcopal church in Black Mountain. The Rev. James Harvey Postell, a former Methodist minister, was ordained as an Episcopal deacon in 1883, after receiving training at the Ravenscroft Associate Mission and Training School in Asheville. Following his ordination, the Rev. Postell assumed ministerial leadership over a number of Ravenscroft Associate Mission stations and chapels. In 1890, the Rev. Postell submitted a parochial report for "Black Mountain Station," where he reportedly had a small congregation of twelve, with five of them being regular communicant members. He also reported that the small congregation had two Sunday school teachers with twenty-five "scholars."[79] But interestingly, there were no further reports, after 1890, of any congregation at Black Mountain until the Rev. Mears was invited to hold services in 1907.

The Rev. Mears continued to hold services at Black Mountain in the Methodist church, and aided the fledging congregation in raising enough funds to purchase property to begin building their own church building. In November of 1908, the congregation purchased property on Vance Avenue from the Black Mountain Hotel Company. The property was part of a subdivision surveyed for the Black Mountain Hotel Company in 1904, and consisted of lots 2, 3, 6 and 7 of Block 7.[80]

In 1910, the Rev. Mears left the district, and the Rev. F. M. Osborne of Charlotte, who was vacationing at Black Mountain for the summer, held services at Black Mountain Inn, where he was staying. Also during that time, the Rev. Osborne called a meeting of the congregation at the home of "Miss Dissosway," where he aided them in organizing as a permanent mission. The cornerstone for the new church building on Vance Avenue was laid on July 25, 1912.[81]

After the departure of the Rev. Mears, the new mission went under the general oversight of the bishop until around 1915, at which time the bishop transferred the oversight to the Ravenscroft Associate Mission, under the leadership of the Rev. A. H. Stubbs. The Rev. Stubbs assigned veteran missionary priest the Rev. William Francis Rice to be the "priest-in-charge," requiring Rice to commute from his home in nearby Riceville. The Rev. Rice, who had been serving as a missionary priest since the mid–1880s, was at this time nearing the end of his long ministry to the churches of western North Carolina.

In April of 1917, under the Rev. Rice's leadership, St. James' congregation purchased a triangular lot adjoining the church lot on the west,[82] for the purpose of building a rectory. At the request of the congregation of St. James, the trustees of the diocese voted to mortgage the new lot for a sum not to exceed $1,500, and used the proceeds to finance the construction of the new rectory.[83] Rice also helped the fledgling congregation to complete their church building, holding the first official service in the (almost) completed church on September 23, 1917.

Having aided the new mission in completing their church building and erecting a new rectory, Rice decided to retire in 1918 under the newly established diocesan pension fund. The general oversight of St. James continued under the Rev. A. H. Stubbs, warden of the Ravenscroft Associate Mission, but the Rev. Cortez Cody, another Ravenscroft priest, was appointed to replace Rice as minister-in-charge. St. James at that time was also governed by the lay leadership of James R. Many, as warden; Jacob S. Wahab, as secretary; and Robert E. Currier, as treasurer.

St. James continued under the Ravenscroft Associate Mission until 1923, when the Rev. George Sutherland was appointed to be the priest-in-charge. The small congregation struggled for many years as a mission church, not obtaining the status of a self-supporting parish until 1956. In 1994, St. James' church sold the property on Vance Avenue and moved to a new location on State Street. Today, St. James is a vibrant and growing congregation.

Candler's Mission/St. Clement's — Candler

Mr. William Gaston Candler, for whom the town of Candler was named, was the prime motivator behind the establishment of an Episcopal mission church in the Upper Hominy Valley, southwest of Asheville. An 1883–1884 listing of land owners shows that, at that time, W. G. Candler was the largest landholder in the area, owning over 1,250 acres.[84] He also was a lawyer and a businessman, owning a grocery store and a grist mill–sawmill.[85]

The first account of the start of mission work at Candler (which in the church records was first called "Candler's" or "Candlerville") was in 1885. The Rev. George H. Bell, the minister-in-charge of the new work, made the following report: "I have held services irregularly at this place for a little more than a year. There is good prospect for a rapid and healthy growth for the church. A church building is needed here. A beautiful site has been secured for that purpose."[86] Bell was a native from the Haw Creek region east of Asheville, and had been trained by the Rev. Buxton and the Rev. Dr. D. H. Buel in the beginning years of the Ravenscroft Training School (early 1870s). Bell was now a missionary in Watauga County, but was soon to be reappointed as a missioner with the Ravenscroft Associate Mission.

The fledgling church at Candler, during those early years, was meeting in the home of W. G. Candler. On Bishop Lyman's 1884 visit to the western regions, he visited the new work and reported that on "Monday, September 1st, I continued my journey on to Asheville, and on the way stopped at the house of Mr. Wm. G. Candler, where I was met by the Rev. Mr. Bell, who read Evening Prayer, and I preached, and confirmed two persons, making also an address on the subject of confirmation."[87]

The Rev. J. H. Postell, another Ravenscroft missionary, served the Candler church in 1886 as temporary substitute for the Rev. Bell, who had extended duties elsewhere that year. Postell reported not only that the congregation now included 28 families but also that he thought "the prospect good for the success of the church."[88]

It is not surprising, then, in light of the rapid growth of the congregation, that in 1887 the Rev. George Bell was ecstatic to report, "The Mission at this place is in a flourishing condition. The attendance is better than it was a year ago and is increasing. By aid kindly given me from various places I have been able to secure house and land formerly owned and used by the Methodists. We are having the building repaired and altered in some respects, and will make it a comfortable and churchly structure."[89] Elsewhere, Bell reported that he had raised the money himself.[90] The diocese purchased the 1.5-acre lot and church building in January of 1887 from Dr. W. W. Clark,[91] who had only bought it a few months earlier at auction, from the Montmorenci Methodist Church. The Montmorenci congregation had outgrown their church, and had decided to buy new land, about half a mile west, and build a new church, so they auctioned off their property. According to Montmorenci's church history, Dr. Clark had purchased the property to convert to his residence, "but due to pressure from the Episcopalians, who were striving to establish a church in that area, he sold the property to them."[92] According to the recollections of a former church member, the Episcopalians purchased "a gray, wooden-framed building" with "one large room and a large porch with white pillars that rested against the church."[93]

All the repairs and alterations were completed by the autumn, chiefly, as reported by the Rev. Bell, through the diligence of Mr. W. G. Candler, who "contributed not only weeks of his time towards the remodeling and general repairs needed but was by far the largest donor towards defraying all the expenses connected with it."[94] Bishop Lyman came to consecrate the new church on September 23, 1887. The bishop happily reported to the next Convention that "at 11 o'clock I consecrated the building which had been purchased and fitted up for our services, under the name of St. Clement's Church. The request to consecrate was read by the Rev. Geo. H. Bell, and the sentence of consecration by the Rev. Dr. Buel. The sermon was preached by me, and I also confirmed one person. I organized St. Clement's Mission in accordance with the provisions of the Canon, and appointed the regular officers. The Rev. Mr. Bell holds services statedly at this Mission, which is a very encouraging one."[95]

Over the next few years, St. Clement's began to increase in attendance and ministry, mainly through Mr. Candler, who served as a lay leader of the congregation. The Rev. Bell, the minister-in-charge, was only able to officiate on one Sunday of each month, as he had at least four other charges. In 1893, the Rev. Bell reported that the church now had 48 attendees and that "attendance on services better than it ever has been. The Church is well filled every service. Miss M. L. Hoyt is doing a noble work in that community."[96] Miss Hoyt's Sunday school included "42 scholars."[97] "Miss Hoyt" was actually Miss Marie Louise Brush, the stepdaughter of Capt. John Keais Hoyt. The Hoyt family had moved to the Hominy Valley in 1883, where Capt. Hoyt built the family home, "Engadine," in 1885.

The Rev. A. H. Stubbs assumed the position of "warden of Ravenscroft" in 1894, which included the oversight of the various mission stations of the Ravenscroft Associate Mission. He also took over the charge of St. Clement's, sharing it at various times over the next few years with fellow missioners G. H. Bell, Samuel Rhoades and William F. Rice. However, the bulk of the leadership of St. Clement's continued to rest on the shoulders of Mr. William G. Candler and his wife, who by 1904 were named the "Committee of the Mission."[98]

The journal reports give very few names of the parishioners of St. Clement's. But the Rev. Stubbs, who kept comprehensive diaries and notes, occasionally mentions a few names.

In 1902, he reports on July 20, after officiating at a service at St. Clement's at 10:00 A.M., that at 3:00 P.M. that afternoon, he baptized Katie Buxton Ogden Brewton, a recent widow, and her two sons, Cecil and William Allen, at her residence in Candler. William Allen, who was then less than a year old, grew up to be a beloved physician in the community, and the first physician in Buncombe County to enter the armed forces during World War II.[99]

As is often the case when a church is founded by one person or family, St. Clement's began to decline as Mr. Candler began to age. In 1914, W. G. Candler celebrated his eightieth birthday, and the church was reported to have dwindled to only two families, making up a congregation of only five persons.[100] The church closed shortly thereafter, and in 1915 the property was sold to Dr. A. P. Willis, who turned it into a residence. The diocese retained a forty-foot square parcel of the property, which had become the church cemetery.[101] Dr. Willis' residence is still extant on the former church property at the intersection of Queen Road and Candler Town Road, just off of the Pisgah Highway, near Candler, North Carolina.

CHUNN'S COVE MISSION/ST. LUKE'S — CHUNN'S COVE, ASHEVILLE

Chunn's Cove is a small, two-mile long cove, northeast of downtown Asheville, running north along Ross' Creek between Sunset/Town Mountain on the west and Piney/Cisco Mountain on the east. St. Luke's Church, located near the entrance to the cove, is one of the later churches founded by the Ravenscroft Associate Mission, having been established in the early 1890s.

The story has been told that the Rev. Jarvis Buxton of Trinity Church, Asheville, held the first Episcopal service at Chunn's Cove in 1858 at the home of Hosea Lindsey. And it has been further told that those services continued on through the Civil War years and possibly even for a few decades.[102] However, I can find no record in the Convention journals of any services at Chunn's Cove being held before the 1890s. Throughout the 1850s and 1860s the Rev. Buxton would include reports of the three chapels that were ministries of Trinity Church, which were Haw Creek, W. Asheville (St. Andrew's), and Leicester. For a few years in the 1860s, the Rev. Buxton reported ministering at a mission station at "Reems Creek" where there was one communicant. The only record I could find that could possibly include Chunn's Cove was the Rev. Buxton's 1872 report, where he recorded that he had "during the year, visited and officiated at other stations in the country, not belonging to this Parish, where there are in all nine communicants, not elsewhere reported."

The first official report of any Episcopal work in Chunn's Cove comes from 1893. The Rev. William F. Rice, a local priest who was a missionary with the Ravenscroft Associate Mission and Training School, Asheville, made the following report to the 1893 Convention: "CHUNN'S COVE MISSION, BUNCOMBE COUNTY.— This is a new Mission, started in a field not occupied by any religious body. A lot for the Chapel is offered to us as a gift, and the whole outlook is very encouraging."[103] The Rev. Rice does say in his report that "this is a new mission," and thus, combined with the lack of any earlier records, we can conclude that ongoing work at Chunn's Cove did not begin until this time. The lot mentioned in Rice's report was a half-acre parcel on Chunn's Cove Road, donated by a former slave, Mr. Matthew Baxter, and his wife Jane.

The first services at Chunn's Cove were held in the home of Mr. and Mrs. William T. Owen, and at times "under a weeping willow tree in Mrs. Metz's yard,"[104] until construction of the new church was completed. The congregation raised a portion of the funds for the new building, and through a loan from the "Church Building Fund Commission of New York" they were able to complete sufficient construction to hold their first service in the building on July 17, 1894. The church is said to have been designed by Mr. E. J. Armstrong, one of its founding members. The church was finally completed and consecrated as "St. Luke's" by Bishop Joseph B. Cheshire on July 9, 1898.[105]

Mr. William T. Owen, the church's first lay reader and primary founding member, was born in England and immigrated to America in 1870.[106] In 1872, Mr. Owen purchased a 22-acre farm from Col. Stephen Lee and his wife, Sarah Rosanne Patton Lee.[107] Owen started the church's first Sunday school in his home, and as early as 1894, the records show that this small congregation of only six communicants had seven Sunday school teachers teaching fifty "scholars." They were able to accomplish this huge task through the help of the "Faithful Endeavor Society" of Trinity Church, Asheville.[108]

From its beginning, the fledgling church was provided with ministerial services through the Ravenscroft Associate Mission. The Rev. William Rice, mentioned earlier, was the church's first "deacon-in-charge." Mr. Rice, who had begun his theological training at Ravenscroft in 1876, had been ordained as a deacon in 1886. At the start of the Chunn's Cove mission, Rice was also serving the church at Beaverdam (Grace) and pursuing his theological studies at Ravenscroft toward his ordination.[109] Deacon Rice was supervised by the Rev. A. H. Stubbs, who had been appointed warden of the Ravenscroft Associate Mission and Training School in 1894. Mr. Samuel Rhoades, a deacon studying at Ravenscroft, also assisted Mr. Rice during the first few years of work at Chunn's Cove.

The Rev. Rice remained in charge of St. Luke's until 1915, when the church was then put under the care of the Rev. George H. Bell, another local priest who was part of the Ravenscroft Associate Mission. St. Luke's continued under the care of the Ravenscroft Mission until the early 1920s, at which time it was put under the control of the newly formed Missionary Jurisdiction of Asheville.

St. Luke's remained a mission church for many years, only becoming a self-supporting congregation in the 1960s. But St. Luke's remains today on its original site and is a growing and active congregation.

Glencoe Mission — near Bent Creek, southwest of Asheville

The village of Glencoe, southwest of Asheville, is now a place of the past. "Glencoe," now part of the Pisgah National Forest, was located just off of today's Rt. 191 in the Bent Creek area of Buncombe County, near the present-day North Carolina Arboretum.

In the 1870s, photographer Rufus Morgan, passing through the area, captured a photo of "Glencoe Mill."[110] This is one of the few known photographic records of Glencoe. Although the Glencoe area had been settled earlier, most of its history really began in 1866, when Colonel Lewis Melvin Hatch moved into the area and set up "Glencoe Mills." Wilson Boyd, an early settler to the area, had set up his gristmill-sawmill and blacksmith operation on Boyd's Branch in 1820. When Colonel Hatch bought out Wilson Boyd around 1866, he "immediately rebuilt and expanded the whole enterprise,"[111] relates William Nesbitt in his

History of Early Settlement and Land Use on the Bent Creek Experimental Forest. "Colonel Hatch first moved the dam farther down the stream from its original location [*sic*] so that the present lake site could be used for cultivation purposes; he then constructed new building space for tenants, a combined school and church building, store and a large building for a combined mill and workshop, his new mill-and-shop was equipped with a grist mill, an up-and-down head saw for cutting large dimension stock, several re-saws for cutting special products, dry-kiln, planing machine, turning lathe and other equipment needed for wagon building and furniture construction. In addition to his regular work of sawing, milling, and blacksmith work, he built wagons, tables, chairs, beds, and anything else demanded. A portion of the manufactured products was sold in the community, with the remainder going to the South Carolina, Georgia and Asheville markets. It has been related that Hatch kept three wagon-teams busy hauling his articles to market and bringing supplies back for the store. For power, Hatch used a 'flutter-wheel' for his sawmill and a 'breast-wheel' for his grist mill and furniture shop."[112]

The work of the Ravenscroft Associate Mission at Glencoe not only predates the establishment of the "Glencoe" post office in 1873, but it is also heavily tied to the Hatch family. In 1871, the Rev. Francis J. Murdoch, a native of Asheville and product of the Ravenscroft Training School, who was then the principal of the Ravenscroft Associate Mission and Training School, submitted his first report on the "Glencoe Mission, Buncombe County": "Several communicants (included in Mr. Buxton's report) reside at this point. A Sunday School has been opened, and I hold services once a month." Then, following the listing of the statistics of the mission, which included the news that the Sunday school had twenty-five scholars with four teachers, he encouragingly reported, "The prospect of the Church at this point is very bright. The untiring labors of the ladies who teach the Sunday School will, with God's blessing, soon be rewarded with a goodly harvest."

The Rev. Dr. David H. Buel, who became principal of the Ravenscroft Associate Mission in 1872, in an article for *The Spirit of Missions*, published in June of 1875 by the Board of Missions of the Episcopal Church, gives us the best surviving description of the work at Glencoe. Due to its rarity and brevity, I quote Buel's entire account:

> Returning from the valley of the French Broad, we spent a Sunday at Glencoe, eleven miles distant from Asheville. Here again there is one refined Christian family, which before the war was wealthy but is now sorely impoverished. Five years ago they were all Presbyterians. Now, three young ladies[113] of that house are devoted communicants of the Church, and all the family take a warm interest in her Services. These young ladies, when they came into the Church four years ago, went to work like true Deaconesses among the people all around them within a circuit of four or five miles; and they have worked so earnestly and judiciously, that they have gathered a noble Sunday-school which is doing great good, and a large congregation attends my ministrations there on one Sunday of each month. There is a goodly number of communicants, and at every annual visit of the Bishop there is an addition to this number. One of these young ladies[114] teaches a day-school, and in every possible way that cultivated intelligence and Christian sympathy and admirable tact can suggest, this one Christian family is working to build up the Church and to elevate the community in which they live. We have to worship in the upper room of a barn, but the good taste of these ladies has rendered it Churchly in appearance; and with the aid of an excellent cabinet organ, sent anonymously to Glencoe by a friend in New York, on which one of the young ladies plays, and through her training of the congregation in the music of the Church, our Services there are always beautiful, and they are very hearty. There are unusual facilities for work both in stone and wood at Glencoe, so that a very nice church

can be built there for $1,000, and it will be whenever the good Lord, through some of His loving children, shall send us that sum for the purpose.[115]

It seems that the mainstay of the church at Glencoe was the large Sunday school taught by the Hatch sisters, as the number of adult communicants for 1875 was reported as only "10," but yet the Sunday school was reported to have "80 scholars." These numbers remained steady for the next five or six years. However, the church at Glencoe was not to survive for very long.

The last parochial report for Glencoe was submitted to the Diocesan Convention in

Col. Lewis M. Hatch's dam and mill at Glencoe are shown in this stereoview photograph taken by Rufus Morgan in the 1870s. The Glencoe Mill was located in the Bent Creek area of Buncombe County. (photograph from the Rufus Morgan Photographic Collection #P0057, North Carolina Collection Photographic Archives, Wilson Library, University of North Carolina at Chapel Hill).

1881, and no records of the church remain after that report. However, the lives and movements of the Hatch family give us a clue as to the demise of the church at Glencoe. It started, perhaps, when one of the sisters, Sarah Allen (affectionately called "Sallie"), married James Hardy Lee in 1877. Lee was the son of Col. Stephen Lee, who ran a military boys' school in Asheville for many years. Although J. Hardy Lee was living in Glencoe at the time of his marriage to Sallie, by 1870 the young couple had moved to Asheville, where J. Hardy operated a drugstore.[116]

Records show that the Glencoe post office changed its name to "Brooks" (named for the current postmaster, Samuel Brooks) on February 6, 1882. But then four days later, on February 10, 1882, it was re-established as "Glencoe" with Lewis M. Hatch as postmaster. But that only lasted until May 9, when the "Glencoe" post office was discontinued. Apparently there was also some type of social upheaval in the Glencoe community that caused the breakup of the Glencoe congregation. By 1887, the entire Hatch family had abandoned Glencoe and moved to Asheville, into a house at 98 Bailey Street. This included the two remaining unmarried Hatch sisters (former Glencoe Sunday school teachers), Susan and Emily. Susan Elizabeth Hatch, who had taught the Glencoe day-school, became a teacher at the newly opened Bailey Street Public School, and Emily Julia Hatch became the first librarian at the new Asheville Public Library opened by Thomas Walton Patton in 1894 on Church Street. Col. Lewis Hatch passed away in Asheville on January 12, 1897.

In 1900, the Hatch heirs sold Col. Hatch's vast Glencoe property holdings to George W. Vanderbilt. Vanderbilt had begun buying up all the Bent Creek properties in about 1900, and then in 1914 the Biltmore Estate sold the entire lot to the federal government to become the Pisgah National Forest. The Hatch properties became part of the "Bent Creek Experimental Forest," a subdivided portion of Pisgah Forest.[117]

HAW CREEK MISSION/TRINITY CHAPEL— HAW CREEK, EAST ASHEVILLE

The story of the mission at Haw Creek begins not long after the reorganization of Ravenscroft into an associate mission and training school in 1868. Although it was not originally part of the Ravenscroft Associate Mission, the work at Haw Creek was very closely connected to it.

The Rev. Jarvis Buxton, who was instrumental in the formation of the Ravenscroft Associate Mission, had begun to establish a few outlying mission stations on his own before the associate mission was fully operational. These initial stations, of which Haw Creek was the second, were established and for years maintained by the Rev. Buxton's parish, Trinity Church, Asheville.

The church at Haw Creek is closely tied to George Hamilton Bell. James Sill, in his book *Historical Sketches of Churches in the Diocese of Western North Carolina Episcopal Church*, says that "Mr. Bell was evidently preparing for the ministry, when he and others decided to build a chapel on the Bell estate."[118] Records show that Bell's mother, Catherine Bell, deeded the half-acre lot for the new chapel to the Trinity parish on August 21, 1869, and that on the following day, August 22, Bishop Thomas Atkinson visited and preached "in the Mission House at Haw Creek."[119] The 1871 Convention journal later reported that the previous year, on "July 30th, 1870, George Hamilton Bell received a certificate recommending him to be admitted a candidate for Deacon's Orders."[120] Since candidates for Holy Orders in the Episcopal Church can only apply after completing their theological studies, Sill was no doubt correct in saying that the chapel at Haw Creek was built while Bell was preparing for the ministry. In fact, Bell was one of the first to benefit from the newly established Ravenscroft Training School, initially under the tutelage of the Rev. Buxton.

As a "mission," Trinity Chapel at Haw Creek originally had no full-time rector, and services were only supplied once or twice a month by assigned deacons or priests, including the Rev. Jarvis Buxton. George Bell reported in 1874 that "I preach once a month at this place."[121] Also, the Rev. William F. Rice, another locally trained priest, conducted the Sunday school on occasion, and even acted as "minister-in-charge" for a few years. The Rev. James H. Postell, a local missionary, had oversight of Trinity Chapel during the mid–1880s, as Bell had been sent by the bishop as a missionary priest to Watauga County. But beginning in 1889, and for many years thereafter, the Rev. George H. Bell was reported as "minister-in-charge" at Haw Creek.

In 1894, when the Rev. Alfred H. Stubbs was appointed warden of Ravenscroft, the Haw Creek Mission was put under the oversight of the Ravenscroft Associate Mission, and although the Rev. Bell remained as the minister-in-charge, other missioners also assisted in the work, including the Rev. Stubbs and the Rev. William F. Rice. Looking through the Rev. Stubb's many pages of diaries, we see that some of the family names of Trinity Chapel were West, Reese, Webb, Carter, King, Pressley, Ramsey, and, of course, Bell.

James Sill tells us that later, when the congregation had outgrown the original chapel, they purchased another church "built for the Methodists [now Bethesda United Methodist]."[122] The original chapel was kept and used for years as a "day-school,"[123] apparently run by the Rev. Bell with the assistance of a teacher. "In 1908, there were 87 reported in the Sunday School, and 86 in the Mission School."[124] The Rev. Bell retired in 1918, and the Haw Creek mission station was put under "Diocesan Control," with Bell temporarily serving as the priest-in-charge. J. Burgin Reese, Bell's son-in-law, was then serving as the church warden, with Miss Bird Hess as secretary and Miss Penelope Bell (the Rev. Bell's daughter) as treasurer.[125] The Rev. Cortez Cody was assigned as the priest-in-charge in 1920, and served in that capacity for nine months. But then, in 1921, the Rev. Stubbs (reporting as treasurer of the Board of Trustees of the district) reported that "the Rector of Trinity Church, Asheville has been given charge of the Missions at Grace, Haw Creek, Chunns Cove, in addition to the Church of the Redeemer."[126]

St. John's Episcopal Church, the modern-day descendent of Trinity Chapel, is an active and growing congregation, located on the site of the original chapel along Old Haw Creek Road. Reminders of the old days can be found in the form of familiar street names — Bell Road, Reese Road and Trinity Chapel Road.

LEICESTER MISSION/ST. PAUL'S — LEICESTER

The town of Leicester (pronounced "Lester"), nine miles northwest of Asheville, was originally known as "Turkey Creek." But in 1859, the General Assembly of North Carolina officially incorporated it as "the Town of Leicester," with its boundaries extended "one mile in every direction from the building known as Bascom College."[127] The new name was selected by Leicester Chapman, the principal landowner in the area. Chapman was born in

England and named after the Earl of Leicester (Chapman's father had once served as a captain under the command of the earl).

As a young man, Chapman was sent by his wealthy older brother to be the manager of a sugar plantation in Trinidad, where he met and married Sarah Handfield Carpenter (a native of Ireland). A few years later, the young family decided to move to the United States to seek better educational prospects for their growing family. After landing in Baltimore in the 1840s, they met Thomas Lanier Clingman, a U.S. senator and native of western North Carolina. Clingman convinced the family to move to Buncombe County.[128]

Leicester Chapman and his growing family decided to settle in the Turkey Creek area. In the 1850s Chapman opened a mercantile business near his home in partnership with his brother-in-law, John Carpenter (who must have moved to the area around the same time as the Chapmans).

The first mention of the church at Leicester is in the 1862 Convention journal, where the Rev. Jarvis Buxton, rector of Trinity Church in Asheville, reports that "with several members of the Church," he visited the mission station at Leicester.[129] One of the "several members of the Church" was no doubt Leicester Chapman, who was then a member of Trinity Church. This predates the establishment of the Ravenscroft Associate Mission, which was not formed until 1868. However, the Rev. Buxton's missionary efforts at that time were made in connection with its predecessor, the "Ravenscroft Classical and Theological School," founded in 1854.

The Rev. Buxton was appointed by the Convention in 1866 to be the special agent in charge of soliciting funds for the newly established Ravenscroft Associate Mission. His first official act was to purchase the old "Leicester High School" on December 19, 1867. Buxton reported "that he had received $948.80, out of which he had purchased for the Diocese, for $350, the Leicester High School building (of brick, with five acres of land), near Asheville, which was offered to the Church by the Trustees, on paying that balance of debt due on the building."[130]

Although the Rev. Buxton called it the "Leicester High School," the deed[131] reveals that what he purchased was the former Bascom College, which had been chartered by the Methodist Church in 1859. The deed also reveals two other interesting items. First, it tells us that the land on which Bascom College was situated was originally conveyed to the college by Leicester Chapman and Jonathan Wilson. More importantly, the deed reveals the reason why the trustees felt compelled to sell. Most deeds do not contain such information, but, interestingly, this deed records the following: "Whereas R. L. Gudger refused to act as trustee & L. Chapman elected to fill his vacancy and John T. Palmer is dead & E. M. Stevens was elected to fill his vacancy, and whereas the said corporation has become indebted to an amount they are unable to pay off & discharge & to enable them to pay off the said debts have agreed to sell the land and building aforesaid to the Vestry of Trinity Parish, Asheville."[132] Another source shows that the trustees of Bascom College had first approached the Holston Methodist Conference about purchasing the school, under the same conditions (paying off the remaining debt), but the Conference declined the offer.[133]

It is unclear exactly why the Rev. Buxton purchased the old Bascom College. However, it may have been that he surmised that it could be used as a place of meeting for the fledgling church at Leicester, as well as a parochial school for the local children. And in fact the building eventually was used for those very purposes. Buxton was setting a precedent, as many of the mission churches and schools established by the Ravenscroft Associate Mission were built with funds solicited from interested churches and churchmen (mostly from the North).

The Rev. George T. Wilmer, the first head of the new Ravenscroft Associate Mission, readily acknowledged the foundation for missionary work previously established by the Rev. Buxton. In his report to the 1869 Convention, Wilmer states, "Already the efficient zeal of the Rev. Mr. Buxton and his congregation have established several missionary stations hereafter to be included in this mission."[134] One of those stations, of course, was at Leicester. But the Rev. Buxton maintained supervision of the Leicester mission until 1872, when the Rev. D. H. Buel assumed the headship of the Ravenscroft Association Mission.

In 1873, Leicester Chapman officially donated a one-acre property on Alexander Street to John Carpenter (his brother-in-law and trustee of the church). The deed states that the property was "now enclosed and having on it an Episcopal Church."[135] Apparently the church was built prior to the completion of the property transfer. In fact, this is verified by Bishop Lyman's address of 1873, where he reports that on June 27, 1872, he visited Leicester and "preached in a church recently erected, but not yet completed nor consecrated."[136]

The "Leicester station," which consisted of the school property and the newly erected church on Alexander Street, throughout the 1870s and early 1880s was serviced by various missionaries supplied through the Ravenscroft mission. In 1873–1874, a "the Rev. J. R. Joyner" had charge of the station "for about five months of the year in connection with a school taught at Leicester by him."[137] the Rev. Samuel P. Chandler, who had transferred in from Minnesota, served at Leicester in 1875, followed the next few years by George Hamilton Bell. Bell was a native of Haw Creek in East Asheville and had been trained at the Ravenscroft Training School and was then serving as a roving missioner with the Ravenscroft Associate Mission. Bell officiated once every month at Leicester, and the Rev. Dr. Buel officiated there on every "fifth Sunday" of the month.[138]

Mr. George Bell had charge of the Leicester mission until the fall of 1876, when he was replaced by the Rev. Lucian Holmes, who had been transferred from a diocese in Tennessee. "My work has been mainly confined to Leicester, where I have a large and promising school," reported the Rev. Holmes.[139] Holmes' duties included running the school and pastoring the small congregation of thirty members. He also had hopes of servicing other nearby mission stations, as he further reported: "I have held occasional services at three other points, and expect, in future, to have regular monthly appointments at each of them."[140]

Bishop Lyman visited Leicester on July 17, 1876, and reported that he was "glad to say that the Rev. Lucien Holmes, at the earnest and repeatedly expressed desire of the people, has again taken charge of the church and school there."[141] It is interesting that the bishop said "has again taken charge," implying that the Rev. Holmes had previously had charge of the school at one time. Although we do not find his name directly connected to the Leicester school, records show that there is a distinct possibility that this was the case. Not only had Holmes been the headmaster at the Ravenscroft Classical and Theological School when it had to close its doors in 1864, but, after a brief pastorate in Chatham County, North Carolina, he also returned to Asheville in 1867. Although Holmes was listed in the 1869 journal as "Deacon, teaching in the Associate Mission and Training School, Asheville,"[142] previously in the 1868 journal he was listed as "Deacon, teaching near Asheville."[143] This was the same year that the Rev. Buxton had purchased the "Leicester High School," and probably the

Rev. Holmes was the first instructor of that school, which was "near" Asheville. Unfortunately for the school and mission, the Rev. Holmes' plans were suddenly changed, as within a year of taking charge once again of the work at Leicester, he was transferred to Charlotte to assume the headmastership of Thompson Hall.[144]

The Rev. Charles T. Bland was assigned to Leicester as Holmes' replacement late in 1877. Like Holmes, Bland's duties included not only holding periodic services but also operating the school. His report to the 1878 Convention gives a descriptive picture of the Leicester mission: "We have here a Sunday School, numbering 4 teachers and 14 scholars — white — also a Sunday School for the colored people, numbering one teacher, and 20 scholars. In connection with my Missionary work, I have a School — not properly a Parochial School — numbering about 30 scholars."[145] Also in this report, the Rev. Bland made an appeal for help in repairing the school, which he described as "miserably out of repair."

The Rev. Bland continued running the church and school until April 1881, at which time he vacated his charge and moved to take up work at Marion and Old Fort, North Carolina.[146] One month later, in May 1881, the trustees of the diocese, "after correspondence with Dr. Jarvis Buxton and others," decided to sell the Leicester school property to the Methodist Episcopal Church. In the same report, the trustees of the diocese stated that they also "purchased a lot of 1¾ acres for the erection of a church building at the same place for $50."[147] This new lot was on Church Street in Leicester. Not only was a church never built on this lot, but it also remained vacant for the entirety of the diocese's ownership. The Leicester church continued to meet in the 1872 chapel on Alexander Street.

Ravenscroft missionary the Rev. George H. Bell was again assigned to the Leicester church in December 1883, to fill the vacancy left by the Rev. Bland in 1881. The Rev. Bell continued as minister-in-charge at Leicester for the next eight years, and by 1890 he was seeing a resurgence in attendance. In his 1890 report on "St. Paul's Church–Leicester" (this is the first time the church is given a name), the Rev. Bell writes, "This church is doing better than it has done for years. Attendance better than it has been for fifteen years."[148] This was evidenced by the increase from three families to seven families now in attendance.

In 1892, the Rev. James H. Postell, another Ravenscroft missionary, replaced the Rev. Bell as minister-in-charge. Postell lived in Asheville and did not own a horse, so he had to walk to his charges. Leicester is quite a "walk" at nine miles; therefore, it is not surprising that Postell included in his report an appeal for a horse: "I need a horse to do the work more efficiently. When I walk to Chapel I am too tired to visit on foot the congregation."[149] In the same report Postell also put in an appeal for a rectory to be built (no doubt on the vacant lot purchased in 1881). He states, "We have no Sunday-school at this Chapel for the want of teachers. If I had a rectory here my daughters would help to teach in the Sunday school."[150] But alas, no rectory was built, and we don't know if he ever was given a horse!

The Rev. Postell had charge of St. Paul's for only one year, and then the Rev. Bell was reassigned to the post in 1893. The following year, 1894, the Rev. A. H. Stubbs assumed charge of the Ravenscroft Associate Mission and all of its stations, chapels, and churches. In 1904, the Rev. Stubbs and the Rev. William F. Rice were listed together as "priests-in-charge" at St. Paul's. Mr. J. M. Stevens, M.D., and John H. Hall were listed as the "Committee of the Mission." That meant that they were the lay leaders who had charge of the Leicester mission on the alternate Sundays that either of the priests were not officiating. As most of the missionary priests had multiple charges and could not be at each of their charges fulltime, the lay leaders were vital to the ongoing health and growth of each church/mission.

Unfortunately, the church at Leicester began to decline in the first decade of the twentieth century, and by 1914 it was recorded as having submitted "no report" to the Convention. For the subsequent few years (1915–1919), St. Paul's was on the lists of "missions where no services have been held."

In 1920, the church had deteriorated to such a state that the trustees had to take action. The first action was to sell the vacant lot on Church Street to J. M. Carver for $200.[151] Mr. Haywood Parker reported to the 1921 Convention that the "lot was purchased many years ago when the Mission at Leicester was in a thriving condition, and it was hoped there would eventually be need of a Rectory, and the lot was acquired for that use."[152] Parker went on to give the reason why the trustees decided to act: "The mission however became weakened through the death and removal of the members, and finally ceased to exist. For some years, no member of our Church has been living in that neighborhood."[153]

The second action taken by the trustees in 1920 concerned the fate of the mission property on Alexander Street, on which sat the church and cemetery. Parker reported that the "church had fallen into decay, and was sold last year for old lumber."[154] However, the church lot was not sold, "as it contains the graves of many old residents of the neighborhood, some of whom were communicants and founders of the mission."[155]

In 1938, the diocese, by legal instrument,[156] designated the former church property on Alexander Street as the "Leicester Episcopal Church Yard" and legally established a board of trustees to maintain the property and handle any subsequent burials. The first trustees included Miss Rose Chapman (Leicester Chapman's daughter), Mrs. O. M. Clark, Mrs. L. A. Justice, Burgin A. Patton, and Herman M. Stevens. Then, in 1996, Bishop Robert H. Johnson, then bishop of the Diocese of Western North Carolina, appointed a new board of trustees for the Leicester Episcopal Church Yard. The newly appointed trustees were Nell S. Bell, Jeanette Jenkins, Ivagene Parham, Ronald Rogers, and Bruce Stevens.[157] The church yard and gravesites are all that remains of St. Paul's Episcopal Church–Leicester.

CHURCH OF THE REDEEMER/ST. PHILIP'S — WOODFIN

The Church of the Redeemer, which sits on a lofty bluff on the eastern shore of the French Broad River, four miles northwest of Asheville, is one of the most picturesque churches in the region. Its existence is the result of the work of British ex-patriot Dr. Francis Willis, who built the chapel on his estate in the late 1890s.

Dr. Francis Willis, a practicing physician from Greatford, England, was descended from a long line of physicians and clergymen, beginning with his great-grandfather, also named Francis Willis. The Rev. Dr. Francis Willis (1718–1807), the great-grandfather, first trained as a clergyman and then switched to the study of medicine, and became noteworthy in the field treating mental illness. In 1776, the Rev. Dr. Willis opened an asylum at his estate, Greatford Hall, in Lincolnshire, England. He became famous in 1788 for having treated King George III for his bouts of mental illness. Modern-day readers may be familiar with the popular movie *The Madness of King George* (1994), in which Francis Willis' character is played by actor Ian Holm. The Rev. Dr. Willis' sons John and Robert Darling also worked with their father, and assumed the leadership of the practice following their father's death in 1807. A third son, Thomas, became a clergyman; he later had a son, also named Francis Willis (1792–1859). This Francis Willis, who became a physician, married Henrietta Lowe in 1830 and went into practice with his Uncle John at Greatford. Dr. John Willis, along with his nephew Francis, moved the practice from Greatford Hall to nearby Shillingthorpe in 1830.[158] Francis and Henrietta subsequently produced thirteen children, one of whom was a son named Francis Willis, who is the subject of this sketch.

Dr. Francis Willis (1838–1906) married Catherine Maria Willis on May 19, 1861, at Cuckfield, West Sussex, England. Catherine was Francis's double first cousin. Her father, the Rev. Thomas Willis, was the brother of Francis Willis (her father-in-law) and her mother, Augusta Maria Lowe Willis, was the sister of Henrietta Lowe Willis (her mother-in-law).[159] The couple produced four daughters and a son. Around 1883, Dr. Willis, after many years as a practicing physician in Braceborough, Lincolnshire, England, moved his family to America and settled on the banks of the French Broad River north of Asheville. This area was first called Rockwood, and later Owenby, then Craggy, and now it is part of the Woodfin community of Buncombe County. Shortly after his arrival Dr. Willis began accumulating land for an estate. In just a few years he managed to purchase 100 contiguous acres along the banks of the French Broad River. Using the model of his home country, with its parish churches sponsored by the local landed gentry, Willis built a private stone chapel on the estate for his family, estate workers, and the local people surrounding his estate. Some accounts say that the chapel was built in 1887–1888 and called St. Philip's Chapel, and that it was built for whites and blacks to worship together. Although I believe that they did worship together at times, the only records I could find from that period indicate that St. Philip's Mission was established by Dr. Willis for the African American families on his estate and in the nearby neighborhood.

The first record we have is a parochial report in 1888 filed by the Rev. Henry S. McDuffey, who was the rector of Trinity Chapel, an African American congregation in downtown Asheville: "I also have charge of St, Philip's Mission, four miles north of Asheville. I have given them three services a month. This is a new work. It was begun by Dr. Willis and family. This work is getting on nicely. There have been 21 persons baptized and 6 confirmed."[160] And from the same year, Bishop Theodore Lyman reported, "On the afternoon of the same day [May 6, 1887], the Rt. Rev. The Bishop of Honolulu, in the room occupied by St. Philip's Mission, near Asheville, confirmed, at my request, twelve persons, seven being from St. Philip's Mission, and five from the Colored Chapel in Asheville. This new mission was inaugurated by Dr. Willis, the brother of the Bishop of Honolulu, near his own residence, some three miles from Asheville. The members of his family have taken a very active interest in this good work, and the Rev. Mr. McDuffey, in charge of the colored congregation at Asheville, has been holding services at this mission on Sunday afternoons."[161] The bishop's statement that the service was held in a "room occupied by St. Philip's Mission" implies that they were not in a "chapel." Author the Rev. James Sill substantiated this years later when he wrote of St. Philip's, "A cottage on the Willis land was given for the purpose, where a Church room was furnished for worship."[162]

The bishop also reported that the "Rt. Rev. The Bishop of Honolulu" officiated at the service. And although the bishop mentioned that the bishop of Honolulu was the brother of Dr. Willis, the relationship of the visiting bishop to the church in western North Carolina was even stronger than what appeared to be just a passing visit. the Rt. Rev. Albert Willis, the bishop of Honolulu, was not only the brother of Dr. Willis but also the father of Henrietta Willis Wainwright, who was the wife of the Rev. Richard Wainwright, the priest-in-charge at Gethsemane Church at Bowman's Bluff in nearby Henderson County (another Ravenscroft Associate Mission church).

St. Philip's Mission only appears in the Convention journals for two more years (1889 and 1890), and even then no parochial reports were filed, and the name of the mission merely appeared under the list of the Rev. McDuffey's charges. St. Philip's Mission does not appear at all after 1890.

No mention of a stone church or chapel at the Willis estate occurred until 1894. In that year's Convention journal, the first parochial report for "Rockwood, Church of the Redeemer" was filed by Deacon William Francis Rice. Rice, a local man from Bull Creek (now called Riceville), was a missionary and student at the Ravenscroft Associate Mission and Training School. In his report, Rice records that the new church, which he says is "one of the most beautiful and substantial in this end of the State," was opened by Bishop Lyman on the afternoon of Sunday, September 17, 1893.[163]

Assistant Bishop J. B. Cheshire, who was then assuming many of the duties of the ailing Bishop Lyman, visited Church of the Redeemer again in November of 1893 during his visit to the mountains. Cheshire became bishop just one month later upon the passing of Bishop Lyman on December 13. In his first address to the 1894 Convention, Bishop Cheshire reported on his visit to Redeemer. In addition to officiating at the service, Cheshire stated that he also "dined with Dr. Willis, whose liberality has erected this beautiful stone chapel."[164]

The small congregation continued for many years under the care of the Ravenscroft Associate Mission. Although Dr. Willis provided the bulk of the lay leadership, the sacramental duties were performed by various Ravenscroft missionaries assigned to the church. It seems that mostly the Rev. Rice acted as "priest-in-charge" for many years, assisted by his superior, the Rev. A. H. Stubbs, the warden of Ravenscroft. The Rev. Stubbs, who kept a diary of his ministry, often mentioned his visits to the church during these years. On Thursday, January 6, 1898, the Rev. Stubbs noted that he "walked out to Rockwood." That's almost a four-mile walk in the dead of winter! Fortunately, he also noted that he stayed overnight at the Willis home and enjoyed a "magic lantern show and punch." Mr. Willis drove him back to Asheville the next morning.[165] Later in that year, after noting that he had spent the night at the Willis home, the Rev. Stubbs recorded that "Dr. Willis wishes Rockwood changed to Owenby, the new post office."[166] After that, and for many years, the church was listed as "Owenby–Church of the Redeemer."

In 1899, Dr. Willis and his wife Catherine officially transferred the church building and property to the newly formed Missionary District of Asheville.[167] And in 1901, the church was officially accepted as an "organized mission,"[168] meaning that its financial and spiritual needs were to be met by the diocese, since it was unable to be a self-supporting parish church.

In 1902, Dr. Willis was successful in persuading his son and namesake, the Rev. Francis Willis, to return from the West to be the priest of the Church of the Redeemer. The Rev. Willis, who had received his seminary training at Seabury Divinity School in Minnesota, had been serving among the Native American mission churches in Minnesota and Nebraska since 1889.[169] Even though the Rev. Willis was the fulltime priest, the church remained a "mission church" under the care of the Ravenscroft Associate Mission. Willis acted as a missionary priest, receiving his pay through the diocesan missionary fund. The Rev. Willis' mother, Catherine, passed away in 1902, shortly after his arrival.

During the Rev. Willis' tenure, the church did not grow, and in fact in 1904 it reported[170] having only nine communicants, down one from 1895.[171] Sadly, Dr. Francis Willis, who had been the primary benefactor of the church, passed away on November 10, 1906, just four years after his son's return. Dr. Willis was buried beside his wife in the cemetery behind his beloved chapel. The Rev. Willis only remained for two more years before returning to his ministry in the western lands.

Following the Rev. Willis' departure, the Church of the Redeemer continued under the care of the Ravenscroft Associate Mission, with the Rev. William F. Rice returning as priest-in-charge, though only able to provide occasional services. The church soon went into a decade of decline and was almost closed. But around 1916, the Rev. Willis G. Clark, rector of Trinity Church, Asheville, and lay leader Col. Garland A. Thomasson took an active and aggressive interest in the church.[172] The church was soon revived and on the road to being the active and growing congregation that it is today.

St. Andrew's Chapel — West Asheville, near the French Broad River

The first recorded mention of St. Andrew's is by the Rev. Francis Murdoch in 1871. The Rev. Murdoch was a local boy who was trained for the ministry at Ravenscroft by the Rev. Jarvis Buxton. By 1871, Murdoch was heading up the Ravenscroft Associate Mission and Training School as a temporary replacement for the Rev. George Wilmer, who had left his post after only a year. Murdoch's report to the 1871 Convention stated, "A Chapel has been built at this point, which is about three miles west of Asheville.... A liberal Layman of Connecticut subscribed largely towards this Chapel, and also selected the name for it. The labors of our faithful Sunday School Teachers at this point will doubtless be rewarded in due season. The Rev. J. Buxton holds service at this Chapel once a month."[173] Mr. A. E. Smith conveyed a one-half acre lot "on the waters of the French Broad River ... for the purpose of erecting a chapel of the Protestant Episcopal Church."[174] The location of this first chapel was on Gorman's Bridge Road, just north of Patton Avenue, in present-day West Asheville. At that time West Asheville was a separate community.

By 1874, another Ravenscroft-trained missionary, the Rev. George Bell, was the minister-in-charge of St. Andrew's: the Rev. Bell had been assigned to mission work in Watauga County by Bishop Atkinson, but had recently been transferred back to Asheville (his hometown) and put under the supervision of the Rev. Dr. David Hillhouse Buel, who had been newly appointed to head up the Ravenscroft Associate Mission in 1872. Bell reported to the 1874 Convention, "At this mission there are twenty-five Sunday School pupils. I preach here twice a month, the congregation is large and the people are beginning to take an interest in the Church."[175]

The Rev. Buxton took over the oversight of St. Andrew's in 1876 as one of the mission churches of Trinity parish, where he was the pastor. Buxton visited the St. Andrew's chapel once a month. During the early 1880s, the chapel fluctuated from twenty to forty pupils in its Sunday school classes, and it had only a handful of communicants.

In September of 1882, Ephraim Clayton, Asheville's premier builder, donated a one-acre parcel near his home in Emma for a new chapel. This lot was closer to the French Broad River than the old site. The new lot was just north of Smith's Mill Creek, at Silver Springs. The 1883 *Gazetteer of Buncombe County* described Silver Springs as "a suburb of Asheville, situated on the W[est] bank of French-Broad river, which is here crossed by a fine iron bridge. Contains a good hotel, two stores, and several other industries."[176] The new property was tucked in the corner at the junction of the "Paint Rock and Ducktown branches of the Western North Carolina Railroad." Today this junction is known as the "Murphy Junction," as the railroad was only completed to Murphy, North Carolina, instead of Ducktown, Tennessee, as originally planned. Today this property would be described as on the north side of Emma Road, next to the railroad trestle that crosses over Emma Road near the French Broad River, just north of Patton Avenue behind the Crowne Plaza Resort in West Asheville.

Bishop Atkinson visited St. Andrew's in the following August of 1883 and submitted this encouraging report to the 1884 Convention: "At 4 P.M. in St. Andrew's Church, near the French Broad River, after Evening Prayer by the Rev. Dr. Buxton, I preached, confirmed seven persons and addressed them. This Church has been removed from its old site to a more convenient and acceptable spot and the congregations are now much larger, and the interest has materially increased."[177]

The Rev. James Harvey Postell, a former Methodist minister, was ordained as an Episcopal priest on November 28, 1884, by Assistant Bishop Theodore Lyman.[178] The bishop immediately assigned Postell to missionary work under the Rev. Buxton at Trinity in Asheville, and one of his charges was the chapel of St. Andrew's.[179] Postell happily reported to the 1884 Convention that the congregation now was comprised of "32 families."[180]

Mr. Postell was the minister-in-charge at St. Andrew's for the next few years, and although he reported in 1885 that the congregation was "generally good and well behaved,"[181] by 1887 the number of families had dropped to six, causing Postell to lament, "This congregation is not doing as I would wish. The outside influence is very great, but we hope to do better in the future. We live in hope."[182] Postell's discouragement was no doubt exacerbated by his personal problems. In his report to the Convention that same year, he morosely reported in the third person that "having the severe affliction of losing his wife, his work has been materially affected."[183] To add to his burden, he was continuing his theological studies at the Ravenscroft Training School. The Board of Fellows reported that "Mr. Postell is doing good work in preparing for the Priesthood, to which he will probably be admitted in the ensuing autumn."[184] Interestingly, Postell's son, James C., was also pursuing theological studies at Ravenscroft at this same time.

By 1888, the number of families had increased to ten, up from the previous year, yet well below the thirty-two of 1884. Nonetheless, Mr. Postell was encouraged enough to give a rather long and hopeful report to that year's Convention: "St. Andrew's is more prosperous now than at any previous time since my administration. There is a debt of thirty dollars on this Chapel. Last summer we had it ceiled. The congregations are good and I have hopes to be able to do more for the Mission after this. We are helped very little by people outside of the congregation, and the Church at this point has had very serious opposition, but this is not so bitter now, and I have great hopes that the work at this point will succeed. We have 35 Sunday School scholars, and the average attendance is 20."[185]

However, in 1889, when it was apparent that the number of families attending St. Andrew's was continuing to decrease, "on account of the Methodists," Mr. Postell recommended the following to the Convention: "I think it would be better to sell St. Andrew's and build in the neighborhood of new depot. We have the offer of a lot, and St. Andrew's can be sold for eight hundred or one thousand dollars, and with what can be procured from the people we will be able to build a neat chapel near the new depot." The "new depot" was the recently built Asheville depot of the Southern Railway on the eastern shore of the French Broad on Depot Street.

In 1891 the Rev. Postell established a "St. Andrew's Guild" in an attempt to aid in the growth of the dwindling St. Andrew's congregation. The "Guild," correctly called "The Brotherhood of St. Andrew," was a missionary and evangelism ministry of the Episcopal Church, whose goal was to bring men and boys to Jesus Christ.[186]

St. Andrew's continued to struggle on under the Rev. Postell's leadership for the next few years, with Postell making yearly pleas for assistance and support for the fledgling church. In 1893 he pleaded, "This Chapel has no Sunday-school for the want of teachers. There are about thirty scholars who could be reached very easily if we had teachers. If we had on the lot a Parish school-room we could procure the teachers, and the Chapel would soon be a success. This has been the misfortune of my work; if I had school-rooms on each Chapel lot we would look for almost immediate fruit as the result of this plan. Will not some liberal-minded person or persons help us in this matter?"[187]

That same year the Rev. J. A. Deal, fellow missionary and dean of the Convocation of Asheville, made a tour of the mission works in the western counties. Deal gave the following report and recommendation to the 1893 Convention: "I have visited the Missionary work around Asheville and at other points west. In my judgment the truly rural districts which we occupy must, for the present, be worked simply for the work's sake, without hope of material gain. As education increases and these places come into contact with the busy world, they will be strong centers. We can hasten this by a system of schools and by the Missions above suggested. I believe it would be wise to sell St. Andrew's in West Asheville, secure a lot by gift near Glen Rock Hotel, and with money obtained from sale, build a new church in the midst of a larger population."[188] Deal's recommendation was a reiteration of Postell's 1889 proposal, as the Glen Rock Hotel was across the street from the Asheville depot.

In 1895, Postell was listed in the Convention journal as a missionary with the Ravenscroft Associate Mission, which was then under the leadership of the Rev. A. H. Stubbs, who had recently been appointed "warden of Ravenscroft." Even the Rev. Stubbs gave a negative report of the state of St. Andrew's Chapel: "This church is very badly situated for effective work. Thanks to Miss Postell, however, the Sunday-school is maintained under very adverse circumstances."[189] "Miss Postell" was one of James's daughters (Eunice or Laura), who directed the Sunday school.

The Rev. James Harvey Postell died in 1896. Men of the Ravenscroft Associate Mission maintained services at St. Andrew's Chapel occasionally over the next few years, but by 1904, when the diocese sold part of the land as a right-of-way to the railroad, it was reported as "land formerly occupied by St. Andrew's Church."[190] The remainder of the vacant property, which "was in an isolated place, and was badly cut into by the widening of the railroad, was not suitable for any church purposes,"[191] and so it was sold in 1916 for fifty dollars.[192]

St. Andrew's Church was established in nearby Canton, North Carolina, in 1906 on land donated by the Champion Fibre Company, but it had no connection to the former St. Andrew's Chapel, except that they were both in the same diocese (though not at the same time).

Cherokee County

CHURCH OF THE MESSIAH — MURPHY

The mission church at Murphy was one the first missions established in western North Carolina, and yet it was one of the last missions to be maintained by the Ravenscroft Associate Mission. In telling this story, we are indebted to a 1970s interview with the Rev. A. Rufus Morgan, who not only was a former Episcopal priest, but whose family was also instrumental in the founding of the church at Murphy. The Rev. Morgan's account, from family lore, supplements the published records of the events.

The start of the Episcopal ministry at Murphy began long before the railroad came to the mountains of western North Carolina. As travel through the remote mountainous terrain was very difficult during those days, the story of the church at Murphy is a remarkable tale of hard work and perseverance.

In the fall of 1855, the Rev. H. H. Prout, a missionary in Caldwell County, was sent by Bishop Thomas Atkinson to begin services in Cherokee County. At Murphy, the capital of Cherokee County, the Rev. Prout began holding regular services, first in churches borrowed from other denominations, then later "in a building fitted up as a Chapel."[193] the Rev. Prout's presence at Murphy was due to the request of Prof. William Beal and his wife, Fannie Chipman Beal, who, as former British subjects from Canada, had previously been members of the Church of England. Fannie's half-sister, Joanna Chipman (who was the Rev. A. Rufus Morgan's grandmother), had also recently moved to the area and had married Albert Siler, who hailed from one of the pioneering families of Cherokee and Macon counties.

The Rev. Prout used a great deal of space in his parochial report to the 1856 Convention to make an appeal for more workers to be sent to this remote region of the state:

> Cherokee County, as well as Macon, Jackson and Haywood, is at present unoccupied ground so far as concerns our Church, and it is a broad field upon which the good seed should be sown. Generally the Missionary finds a ready attention, a desire to read, and a willingness to examine our claims. If duly and judiciously followed up, this would in many cases ripen into a direct approval of our doctrine, and a consistent Christian practice. This distant portion of the Diocese may therefore be said to have at least some claim on the active sympathy of Churchmen in other parts of it. Though four hundred miles from the Capital of the State, it is yet our own territory, highly beautiful and possessing abundant resources.[194]

Unfortunately, the Rev. Prout lasted only a year or so before being called back to his former parish in Caldwell County. And then, due to the onset of the Civil War and its aftermath, the church at Murphy would have to wait another twenty years before any ongoing Episcopal ministry was again sent to that remote part of the state.

Bishop Atkinson visited Murphy during August of 1874 and conducted services. On this trip the bishop was hosted by the Rev. D. H. Buel, who had recently assumed the headship of the Ravenscroft Associate Mission and Training School, which the bishop had established in Asheville in 1868 to train local priests for ministering in the mountains of western North Carolina. In his report to the 1875 Convention, Bishop Atkinson reiterated his appeal for missionaries: "We need at once two active Missionaries for this promising field, but we are straitened in finding the requisite means for their maintainance [sic]. I have not the slightest doubt that if they could be sustained, chiefly by outside help for a single year, their support after that time could and would be provided by those enjoying the benefit of their services."[195]

By the summer of 1876, the bishop was ecstatic to report that "The Rev. J. A. Deal is now settled at Murphy, being our first resident minister. The congregation is, at present, very small, but both minister and people anticipate a considerable increase before long, and I should think on very reasonable grounds."[196] John Archibald Deal, a graduate of Trinity College, Hartford, Connecticut, had been trained for missionary service by the Rev. Buxton at Ravenscroft (before the arrival of the Rev. D. H. Buel). After his ordination at Trinity Church, Asheville, in 1872, the Rev. Deal served churches in Wilson, High Shoals, and Wadesboro before being sent to Murphy.

Years later, the Rev. Deal wrote a personal account of those early days as a pioneer missionary:

> On May 30th, 1876, I started with my wife to take up the pioneer missionary work in North Carolina. Murphy is in Cherokee County, in the extreme western part of the State. The greater part of the journey from Wadesboro was made by private conveyance and it took almost a week to make the journey. We were entertained at the home of Mr. Beal upon our arrival in Murphy, later going to a log cabin on the edge of town, which was given us rent free. It was in poor condition and in the hard winter which followed, the bed, chairs and floor were frequently covered with snow. The Bishop provided a salary of $100 per year and the Missionary Committee of the Diocese pledged the same amount. I taught school at five cents per day per pupil, part of which I was unable to collect. In addition to other work I edited the local paper for which I received $6 per month.[197]

The Rev. Deal's host in 1876 was again Prof. William Beal. Prof. Beal's wife Fannie, who in the 1850s had been instrumental in persuading the bishop to send a priest (the Rev. Prout) to Murphy, had died in 1865, and by 1876, Beal was a widower with five children still at home. Beal's maiden sister Sarah also lived in the household.

Although it looked like the church at Murphy would finally be established and supplied with regular ministerial services after the arrival of the Rev. Deal, the congregation was soon to be disappointed again. After only sixteen months at Murphy, the Rev. Deal was transferred to Macon County to establish a church at Franklin. This must have been disappointing to the Beals, especially considering that the Rev. Deal was going to live with Prof. Beal's brother-in-law, Albert Siler, in Franklin. Deal was probably transferred to Franklin because the bishop felt that the prospects of establishing a work at Franklin were more promising than at Murphy. He no doubt made the decision following his 1877 summer visit, about which he later reported, "Several members of the Church who were residing here [at Murphy] two years ago, have since removed, so that the present prospects of the Church in Murphy are very discouraging."[198]

Although the Rev. Deal continued to provide an occasional service at Murphy from his new base at Franklin, the prospect of ever establishing a church at Murphy seemed rather grim. "This Mission is yet under my charge," reported the Rev. Deal in 1878, "but, owing to the fact that I am living 45 miles from Murphy, and it is very difficult to obtain transportation, I am able to give it very little attention. There has been no improvement in this Mission since my last report, indeed, with the present population, it seems impossible to do anything towards advancing the interests of the Church."[199] However, the Rev. Deal continued to show an interest in the mission at Murphy, and throughout the 1880s he would occasionally visit, and sometimes he would even make an appeal in his Convention reports for someone to be sent to Murphy to help the church. And finally, in 1890, over a decade after leaving the church at Murphy, the Rev. Deal began a concerted campaign of appeals for help for the church at Murphy. He appealed to the delegates at the 1890 Convention: "At Murphy we have eleven communicants and a few brought up under Church influences, but not yet confirmed. Murphy is a growing town, quite an important place. The people are anxious for a clergyman, and will do all they can to provide for one and to build a church. Something must be done or the ground will be lost to us."[200]

The Rev. Jarvis Buxton, as the dean of the Asheville Convocation of Churches, joined in the campaign in 1891: "The Dean visited Murphy, Cherokee County, and spent several days in that town, with a Sunday service, in survey of the field. The Convocation expressed the opinion that the Church ought, by all means, to be established at Murphy where we have already a valuable lot, the purchase of the Rev. Mr. Prout in years gone by. The town is only waiting for the presence of a zealous resident minister to be stirred up to a hearty co-operation with him. Nothing will be done in that place without the lead of a devoted missionary, but much will be done with him. The laborer must be sent here and not wait to be called and supported by the few scattered Church people at the outset."[201] Unfortunately, during the same Convention, the bishop put a damper on the efforts of the Rev. Deal and the Rev. Buxton, announcing in his yearly address that "I had hoped to take steps for the establishment of regular services at this point [Murphy]; but after careful enquiry I did not feel that there was, just now, sufficient encouragement to undertake it. The place is so remote from any other missionary centre which could be united with it, that I decided to postpone for a while longer the carrying out of this plan."[202]

But the Rev. Deal and the Rev. Buxton did not give up, and for the next couple of years, they continued making appeals for the church at Murphy. The appeals came to a crescendo in 1893, when the Rev. Deal sounded the alarm that something needed to be done immediately: "It is very necessary that the status of the church property in Murphy should be examined. The old store building has been condemned by the town authorities and pulled down. From the best information I can get, the property was deeded to Bishop Atkinson, Dr. Ramsaur, and Prof. Wm. Beal as Trustees. Prof. Beal, the only surviving Trustee, is getting well up in years; even now he is very infirm in health, and should he die without transferring the property to the Diocese, there might be difficulty in recovering it."[203] Prof. Beal, who in 1893 was 73 years old, was no doubt tired after almost 40 years of seeing little progress made toward establishing an Episcopal church at Murphy. But fortunately, Prof. Beal had been joined over the years by others who were desirous of continuing the work of the church. And in fact, although Bishop Joseph B. Cheshire (who had succeeded Bishop Lyman) visited Murphy during the autumn of 1893 and discouragingly reported to the 1894 Convention that "we have very few of our people here,"[204] the Rev. Deal reported that he too had visited Murphy, and that he had found that not only were there "ten or twelve communicants, all anxious for the service,"[205] but there also were "several of the citizens, not of our communion, [who] express a desire for us to build a church and carry on regular work in the town."[206]

Finally, after years of work by the Rev. Buxton and the Rev. Deal, their ardent appeals convinced Bishop Joseph B. Cheshire to act. His first decision, in September of 1894, was to appoint the Rev. Frederick W. Wey as a missionary priest with the Ravenscroft Associate Mission. The bishop placed the Rev. Wey at Waynesville and appointed him as the missionary priest for Haywood, Jackson (except for some churches still under the charge of the Rev. Deal), Swain and Cherokee counties. Then, on December 27, 1894, the bishop officially organized the congregation at Murphy into a mission church to be called "Church of the Messiah."[207]

Despite being assigned a large area of service, the Rev. Wey was able to concentrate on helping the newly organized mission at Murphy to get firmly established. In his first parochial report for the Church of the Messiah, submitted in 1895, the Rev. Wey reported that the congregation had grown to four families, with sixteen communicant members. The Rev. Wey also reported on the physical conditions of the small church: "Here we have no church property, and worship in a room over a store, furnished with a few old seats left from a former chapel, and the rest of the furniture made of dry goods boxes and rough planks. The people appreciate the Church privileges and do all they can towards the maintenance of the services. A chapel is greatly needed, and much more could be done for the Church had we a proper place of worship, but without outside help this is impossible."[208]

The store mentioned in Wey's report was obviously a different store from the store property that the church had previously owned, which was torn down in 1892 or 1893. And from the Rev. A. Rufus Morgan's account (in the 1970s) we learn that the "store" mentioned in the Rev. Wey's report was a furniture store in downtown Murphy that the Rev. Morgan's father, Alfred Morgan, had secured for the church's use. The Rev. Morgan also recalled that an old "piano box served as the altar." the Rev. Morgan's parents were instrumental leaders in the new church. Alfred Morgan (a farmer and printer) was the lay reader and officiated at the services three Sundays a month, or whenever a Ravenscroft priest was not available. The Rev. Morgan's mother, Fannie Eugenia Morgan, was the organist and Sunday school teacher.[209]

"The necessity [of] having a church building was apparent to all," wrote the Rev. Wey in 1897, "but the great problem to be solved was, how and where to obtain the means to erect a suitable edifice."[210] the Rev. Wey decided to raise the funds through some of his Northern contacts, and, as he wrote, "Kind friends came to his rescue, and when he came home from his 'begging' trip, he had sufficient funds."[211] To save money, the Rev. Wey designed the church himself. Ground was broken to begin the foundations in June of 1896, and a few months later, on August 9, Bishop Cheshire laid the cornerstone. The first service was held in the almost completed building on Palm Sunday (April 11) in 1897. However, the new church was not completed and consecrated until August 17, 1902.

Around 1900, the Church of the Messiah's oversight was transferred to the Waynesville Associate Mission. Also during that time, Alfred Morgan became senior warden of the church, and Prof. Beal's son, Ralph R. Beal, became the treasurer of the church. By this time the congregation consisted of ten families, with seventeen communicants.

In 1909, oversight of the mission at Murphy was transferred back to the Ravenscroft Associate Mission, with the Rev. A. H. Stubbs, warden of the Ravenscroft, acting as the priest-in-charge. On June 8, 1913, during the Rev. Stubbs' oversight of the Church of the

Messiah, Albert Rufus Morgan, son of Warden Alfred Morgan, was ordained as a deacon of the Episcopal Church, and then on July 12, 1914, he was ordained as a priest.[212] The Rev. A. Rufus Morgan went on to be a long-time Episcopal priest, dying in 1983 at the age of 97. Among his achievements was the foundation of the Penland School of the Arts and the rebuilding of the Church of the Incarnation in Franklin, North Carolina.

The Rev. Alfred Houghton Stubbs continued as the priest-in-charge at the Church of the Messiah until his death in 1924, making the mission at Murphy one of the last missions served by the Ravenscroft Associate Mission. Today, services are still held each Sunday in the 1897 chapel.

Haywood County

MICADALE MISSION/ST. MARY'S — MICADALE

"Micadale Church" today is an official geographical place name in Haywood County, recognized by the National Geospatial–Intelligence Agency. Ironically, it is named for a church that no longer exists. However, the church at Micadale was once one of the fastest-growing mission churches of the Ravenscroft Associate Mission.

During the nineteenth century, the mountains of western North Carolina were looked upon as a source for mining mica. "A promising mine was opened on Lickstone mountain, from which a large quantity of merchantable mica of fine quality has been taken. It is a granite dike about 100 feet wide and 100 yards long. It yielded some crystals which cut plates nine by twelve inches. It is owned jointly by W. F. Gleason and the Love estate. No work has been done on this mine for some time past, though practical miners still consider it a good property,"[213] wrote author Wilbur Zeigler in his 1883 guidebook, *The Heart of the Alleghenies*. Zeigler was describing "Micadale," an area in Haywood County, three miles southwest of Waynesville.

Mr. W. F. Gleason, a U.S. commissioner, and his wife moved to Haywood County in 1877 to "engage in mining."[214] The Gleasons were Episcopalians and desirous of starting a congregation in this rural area of the mountains. Soon after moving to the area, they started their own Sunday school "in an old frame house, fitting it up with rough seats."[215]

The first mention in the Convention journals of the work at Micadale occurred in 1879, although it was not mentioned by name. In his parochial report for the Waynesville church, the Rev. Dr. D. H. Buel of the Ravenscroft Associate Mission tells of the church starting two Sunday schools, "one at Waynesville and the other three miles distant."[216] In the 1880 journal, Bishop Atkinson gives the outlying mission station a name as he reports on his 1879 summer visit: "At Mica Vale, only a few miles from Waynesville, and in quite a populous neighborhood, a Sunday School has been established, chiefly through the active zeal of two earnest members of our Church. I visited this place in the afternoon of the day of my service at Waynesville. I met there a large concourse of children, accompanied by their parents, and after making a brief address to them, in the open air, in connection with the presentation of a Sunday School Banner, I preached to them in a schoolhouse nearby, which was kindly offered for our service. If a small chapel could be erected in this neighborhood, we should soon be able to gather in a goodly number of those who are now looking with much interest upon our Church and its services."[217]

Upon the bishop's next visit the following summer, the rented room in the schoolhouse was "insufficient to accommodate the large numbers who regularly gather there."[218] The bishop and the Rev. Dr. Buel both reported that year that because of the huge growth of the mission work, plans were already underway to erect a chapel at Micadale.[219] A suitable lot was purchased and construction begun in 1882. The Rev. Dr. Buel reported that "on November 19th [1882] the Missionary [Dr. Buel], by commission from the Bishop, laid the corner-stone of a chapel and school-room at Mica Dale."[220]

In 1883, while construction on the new chapel and school room was progressing, the church at Micadale "suffered a great loss first, in the temporary removal of Mr. and Mrs. Gleason and then, shortly before their expected return in the sudden death of Mr. Gleason."[221] "The Church rarely, if ever, has a more efficient and useful layman than our departed brother," wrote Dr. Buel in his report "His Pastor is happy to bear testimony that in all his ministerial life he has never had more single hearted, judicious and earnest helpers in his work than Mr. Gleason and his excellent wife."[222]

Construction of the new chapel progressed very slowly, and although a service was held in the chapel during the bishop's 1884 summer visit, he reported that the chapel was not yet complete.[223] In fact, Dr. Buel reported that the congregation first began to use the "annex (or Transept)" on Easter day in 1886, though it was still not completed.[224]

The Rev. Dr. Buel, along with the bishop, not only raised the funds for the construction of the chapel, but was also successful in recruiting helpers for the work. Buel reported (in 1886) that "we have now at Micadale a very valuable teacher, Miss Mary B. Skellie, who is sustained by kind friends at the north. She conducts admirably the very large Sunday school, and the large day school of this Mission, and she and her friend, Miss Birdsall, are most useful helpers in the church work of this mountain valley."[225] A contemporary article from their hometown newspaper, in Rochester, New York, announced, "Under the auspices of a home mission society connected with St. Luke's church of Rochester, Misses Delphenia Birdsall and Beile Skellie, formerly of Mumford [New York], have been sent to Micadale, North Carolina where they are now established in the instruction of the 'poor white.'"[226]

The church at Micadale was originally named "Grace Church in the Mountain Valley," but was soon changed to "St. Mary's." Perhaps its first name was too close to the name of its mother-church, "Grace Church in the Mountains," in nearby Waynesville.

The Rev. W. S. Barrows, who had replaced Dr. Buel as principal of the Ravenscroft Associate Mission, filed the first parochial report for St. Mary's for the 1891 Convention. Previously its report was always included with Waynesville as "an outlying station." By 1891, the St. Mary's congregation consisted of ten families. The Sunday school had seven teachers and eighty scholars, and the parish day-school, which boasted forty-two students, was under the direction of Miss Sybil Carter.[227]

St. Mary's Chapel was finally consecrated by Bishop Lyman on August 20, 1891, after a decade of construction. The Rev. Dr. Buel, who was in poor health, and the Rev. Barrows participated in the celebration. The Rev. Barrows' report, which was submitted to the 1892 Convention, contained many of the particulars of the building of the chapel and, as a valuable historical record, is thus resubmitted below:

> It is sealed throughout in oak. The furniture and trimmings are of cherry. A Parish school-room to match opens into it by sliding doors. Its erection is due to the indefatigable efforts of Dr. Buel and its completion to generous offerings received through Bishop Lyman in response to his

St. Mary's Chapel and School at Micadale was built in the Allen's Creek area, three miles southwest of Waynesville, North Carolina. The church and school are shown in this photograph from the early twentieth-century (courtesy of the Episcopal Diocese of Western North Carolina, Asheville).

appeal two years ago. Among the gifts to St. Mary's should be specially mentioned the land from Mr. Eldridge Medford — the lumber from Bishop Lyman; $100 from St. Mary's School, Raleigh, the windows, font and altar cloth from the Rev. Dr. Chas. H. Hall, of Brooklyn; the altar from the Rev. Chas. A. Jessup, of Garden City; valuable drawings for the same from Wills Bros., Architects of Asheville — curtains from Mrs. Chas. Goodyear; furniture coverings from the Woman's Auxiliary of Waynesville; altar cross from the Rev. John C. Lord, of New Jersey alms basins from the Boys' Missionary Guild of Waynesville; altar linen from Mrs. Chas. Hewlett and The Faithful Endeavor Society of Asheville; and Bible and Prayer Books from the New York Bible and Prayer Book Society. Out of the fund raised by the guests at the Sulphur Springs Hotel, $37.34 was used for completing the interior furnishings of the Chapel, and the remainder, $18.26, is still in hand.[228]

In 1893 it was reported that "the little house and farm of thirty acres upon which the teacher of the day school lived, through the kindness of the late Dr. Buel, free of rent, were during the past year sold."[229] The owners had offered it to the diocese for $500, but after a number of subsequent years, the money could not be raised.

In 1894, Bishop Joseph B. Cheshire reorganized the mission work in the region, and at that time St. Mary's was removed from the care of the Ravenscroft Associate Mission and put under the care of the Rev. Frederick W. Wey, the rector of the Waynesville church.

In 1898, western North Carolina became the Missionary District of Asheville, under its own bishop, the Rev. Junius Horner. Horner and his family not only resided at Asheville but also lived in Shoenberger Hall with the Rev. A. H. Stubbs, who had assumed the headship of the Ravenscroft Associate Mission just four years earlier. Thus Bishop Horner had first-hand knowledge of the missionary work in his district. Shortly after his appointment,

Bishop Horner published a "Statement of the Work" in the May 1899 issue of *The Spirit of Missions*. In his report, Horner gives a detailed report of the work at Micadale:

> At Micadale, for instance, under the Rev. Frederick W. Wey, we have had a school for four years. The settlement has some three hundred people. Four years ago the Sunday-school had an average daily attendance of about twenty-five. On the roll now are 130 names, with an average attendance of nearly one hundred. The day-school has an average daily attendance of sixty. Within the four years about fifty persons have been confirmed and as many more baptized. Since last fall an industrial department for girls has been added to the school, and the girls have taken much interest in the sewing, cooking and general domestic work taught them. The moral tone of the whole community is greatly improved. The children who have attended this school for four years show such improvement in general appearance and bearing as to call forth special remark. Miss Butler, a deaconess, is in charge of this school, assisted by Miss Eichbaum. We have a school building there of three rooms, a dwelling for our deaconess and her assistant, and a pretty little chapel. At first there was much opposition to the work; there are instances where parents forbade their children to enter the Sunday school or day school grounds, who now not only send their children to both schools, but have themselves become communicants.[230]

After the departure of the Rev. Wey around 1900, St. Mary's was put back under the care of the Ravenscroft Associate Mission, directed by the Rev. A. H. Stubbs. However, by 1904 St. Mary's had dwindled to "unorganized mission" status and returned to the care of the Waynesville Associate Mission. And by 1916, it began to show up on the yearly lists of "Missions Where No Services Have Been Held." James Sill records that services were occasionally held at St. Mary's during the 1920s, but that shortly thereafter any record of the work at Micadale ceased.

WAYNESVILLE MISSION/ST. JAMES/GRACE IN THE MOUNTAINS — WAYNESVILLE

The heyday of the work of the Ravenscroft Associate Mission at Grace Church in the Mountains was in the mid–1870s to the late 1880s, under the leadership of the indefatigable the Rev. Dr. David Hillhouse Buel. Though the church at Waynesville was begun prior to that time, it greatly benefited from this fruitful time in the life of the mission.

"In 1847, Mr. James Norwood and family moved from Hillsboro, NC to Haywood County and settled on a farm one mile west of Waynesville.... Both Mr. and Mrs. Norwood were devoted church people and keenly felt the deprivations of their former church. On hearing that the Reverend Jarvis Buxton, then a young minister located at Rutherfordton, held services once a month in Asheville, Mr. Norwood met him there and brought him over to Waynesville to baptize his infant son."[231]

"Ministrations from Dr. Buxton continued at times, and a congregation was formed, of sufficient members to apply to the diocese for admission as a parish in 1866, which was granted two years later."[232] The application for admission into the diocese was signed by the following: William L. Norwood, Samuel L. Love, Joseph N. Benners, W. L. Tate, Thomas S. Lenoir, W. W. Lenoir, S. F. Norwood, George C. Hanson, M. H. Love, and R. A. Norwood.

The newly formed church was accepted in 1868 under the name of St. James Church–Waynesville. This was the same year that the Ravenscroft Associate Mission and Training School was opened in Asheville, and the fledgling church of St. James was soon put under its care. There are records that the Rev. Francis J. Murdoch, during his brief period as head of the Ravenscroft mission (1870–1872), ministered at St. James on a few occasions. But the Rev. D. H. Buel, who became the principal of Ravenscroft in 1872, was responsible for putting the fledgling church on the course to becoming a vibrant and growing congregation.

In his parochial report to the 1873 Convention, the Rev. Dr. Buel stated that he visited St. James one Sunday in each month, and that the church gained three new communicants that year, bringing the total number of church members to eight. The church slowly gained new members during the ensuing years, and by 1876 it could report 15 members.[233]

In that same year, Buel was happy to report that "Col. Robert Love has presented a very eligible lot, and about $500 have been subscribed toward building a Church at this place."[234] Buel, the consummate fund-raiser, also included an appeal for more funds to the Convention: "Five hundred dollars more are needed to accomplish the object. A Church is most urgently needed here, and with a Church building, the promise of growth is most encouraging. Will not our brethren throughout the Diocese send us aid to build a Church in Waynesville?"[235]

The work of the Ravenscroft Training School was beginning to bear fruit as well, as one of its graduates, George H. Bell, was now able to help the Rev. Buel with the missionary work. In fact, Bell officiated at the Easter service at St. James in 1876.

In 1877, an interesting situation came to light. It was reported to the Convention that "it appears from the report of the committee appointed to prepare a list of the parishes that have been received into union with the Convention, and also from the testimony of the oldest members of the Church at Waynesville, that St. James' Church, Waynesville, Haywood county, was not completely organized and was never admitted into union with the Convention."[236] A resolution was therefore made by the Rev. Dr. Buel, and duly passed, to "remove the name of St. James,' Waynesville, from the Journal of the Diocese."

Despite being removed from the roles of the diocese, the church at Waynesville continued to grow. Construction began on their new church in 1878 on the lot previously donated by Col Love. On July 20, 1878, Bishop Thomas Atkinson, along with the Rev. Dr. D. H. Buel, laid the cornerstone for the new church. The Rev. Buel reported that the building of a church was "a heavy undertaking for this feeble mission flock."[237] In the same report, Buel tells of the tremendous Sunday school work being undertaken by the church both at Waynesville and at the "other three miles distant [Micadale]." He reports that they had ten teachers and ninety scholars.

The new church was almost completed by the bishop's next visit in the summer of 1879. On August 17, 1879, the bishop visited Waynesville, and after conducting a service in the Methodist chapel (where the congregation had been meeting for a number of years), the bishop toured the almost completed church. He later gave a glowing report of his visit in his address to the 1880 Convention:

> It afforded me much pleasure to find in this place, a very beautiful and attractive church edifice, rapidly advancing towards completion. It reflects great credit upon the architect who designed it, and the skillful builder who has carried out the plan, with many judicious suggestions of his own. The interior finish is made up wholly of the exquisitely beautiful varieties of wood which so abound in that region, and which will be preserved in their original colour and texture. I have not seen the building since its completion, but I feel sure that for elegance of taste and

architectural propriety, no wooden church building in our State will be at all comparable with it. Great credit is due to the Rev. Dr. Buel for the self-sacrificing zeal and energy with which he has urged forward this noble work.[238]

In 1880 the new church at Waynesville was completed and officially organized under the canon as "The Mission of Grace Church in the Mountains." The new church, which now boasted 45 members, was consecrated on July 29, 1880, by Bishop Lyman. Unfortunately, the bishop was quite ill and, as the Rev. Buel later reported, was "not able to participate in the services as he earnestly desired; for he had felt a deep interest in the work, and contributed largely towards the building. All but one of its beautiful windows are his gift."[239] The Rev. Buel also stated, "The church is very much admired for the excellence of its work and its beauty. These are greatly owing to its builder, Mr. S. T. Jones, who by his very superior skill shown in executing the admirable plans of the Rev. Professor Babcock, our architect, has made Grace Church in the Mountains what it is — the gem of the mountains."[240]

The congregation continued to grow into its new facilities. By 1884 it had sixty-nine members and was the base for two "outlying mission stations," at Micadale and Forks of the Pigeon (Canton, North Carolina). In 1888, the Rev. Buel was saddened to report the death of Dr. Samuel Love, one of the beloved members of the church.[241] Dr. Love was the grandson of Col. Robert Love (who had donated the lot for the church) and a local physician and politician.

The Rev. Dr. D. H. Buel, who was in failing health, became incapacitated upon the death of his beloved wife in 1890, and had to relinquish his mission work to his assistant, the Rev. Mr. William S. Barrows. The Rev. Barrows reported to the 1891 Convention that "Dr. Buel, to whom the Church in Waynesville owes almost everything, has not been able to come out since September. Services are maintained regularly every Lord's Day and both the congregation and Sunday-school are growing with the growth of the town."[242]

The Rev. Barrows was listed in the 1892 report as "Officiating Priest" at Waynesville, while the Rev. Dr. Buel was listed as "Priest In Charge." The Rev. Barrows also reported that the mission-minded congregation had formed a number of benevolent societies, including the Ladies' Missionary Society, Boys' Missionary Guild and Children's Guild, and "Missionary Gleaners," and that there were "several gifts made by the Ladies' Missionary Society, including coverings for the chancel furniture at Micadale. The Boys' Society has given alms basins for Micadale and subscribed for the *Dawn of Day* for a colored Sunday-school."[243] The Rev. William F. Rice, another Ravenscroft-trained priest, who was in charge at Grace-Beaverdam, often assisted Barrows at Waynesville.

The Rev. Dr. D. H. Buel died in 1893, and shortly thereafter the Rev. Barrows left the diocese. Coincident with these events were the death of Bishop Lyman and the election of Joseph B. Cheshire as the new bishop of North Carolina. One of the first acts of the new bishop was the reorganization of the mission work in the western regions of the state. As a result of the reorganization, Grace Church in the Mountains was removed from the Ravenscroft Associate Mission and assigned as its own mission under the directorship of the Rev. Frederick W. Wey, who was appointed to the position by the bishop.

In 1900, Grace Church in the Mountains officially changed from an organized mission to a self-supporting parish. The church remains today as a growing and active congregation.

Henderson County

BOWMAN'S BLUFF MISSION/GETHSEMANE CHAPEL — BOWMAN'S BLUFF, SOUTH OF ETOWAH

The church at Bowman's Bluff was not only reported to be "an attractive little chapel,"[244] but its story is also unique in that it was built in a specific location for a very specific congregation.

Around 1880, sixteen English families settled at Bowman's Bluff, twenty-five miles southwest of Asheville, in a beautiful valley of the French Broad River. These families were not of the usual immigrant type but rather belonged to the landed gentry class and originated from Wales, Derbyshire and southern England.[245] Bowman's Bluff, as its name implies, was on a bluff overlooking the French Broad, northwest of Hendersonville, the county seat. The more prominent family names were Valentine, Holmes, Evans and Jeudwine.

Thomas Atkinson, bishop of the Episcopal Church in North Carolina, reported in his address to the 1885 Convention that on Monday, August 11, 1884, during his visit to Hen-

Interior of Gethsemane Chapel, Bowman's Bluff, North Carolina, circa 1887 (courtesy David S. Mallett).

derson County, he stopped "at a private house, near the French Broad river, in the same county." He went on to further report that "the Rev. Dr. Buel conducted the service, and I preached, and confirmed two persons. The congregation was too large to find room in the house, and we held the service upon the front porch, while many sat under the shade trees near the house. We found in this neighborhood a very encouraging field for the establishment of a mission, and I trust we may soon have a Church erected in the vicinity."[246] Although it is not known for certain where this location was, I strongly suspect that the bishop was speaking of Bowman's Bluff, because the following year (1885), the bishop appointed the Rev. Richard Wainwright to begin conducting services for the small community. The Rev. Wainwright, who had been serving as a priest in Honolulu, Hawaii, since 1881, moved to Bowman's Bluff with his third wife Henrietta Willis (the daughter of the bishop of Honolulu) and his son Eric (from his second marriage). Eric was later enrolled as a boarding student at the Ravenscroft High School (around 1890).

The Rev. Wainwright reported in 1886, "Services held statedly in a school house until a church can be erected."[247] During that first year, he conducted 73 services, with an average attendance of 50 persons. However, he reported that on Easter Day of 1886, "the room was suitably decorated, and we had about 70 at the morning service, and at 3:30 P.M. we had about 90."[248]

In 1886, Prof. Frank Valentine "gave land on a knoll in the center of the settlement"[249] on which to erect the new church building. "Mr. Frank Valentine, who had graduated with highest honors and several degrees from Cambridge, England, was known as one of the finest educators in North Carolina," writes Sadie Smathers Patton "He and his family were perhaps more closely associated with the citizens of Henderson County than any others of the Bowman's Bluff community. He was connected with the city schools for several years, and a son, Prof. T.W. Valentine, was also a member of the faculty during the later part of his life."[250]

The Rev. Wainwright was quite successful in raising the money to build the new church. Most of the money came from the parishioners, as the Rev. Wainwright reported to the bishop: "Subscriptions as follows: Messrs. Holmes $250; Valentine $75; Evans, Stone, Jeudwine, $25 each; myself $200; total raised in Mission [from the congregation] $600, which, with your $200, made a total of $800. Mrs. Wainwright, mother, brother and sisters $125. Having been chosen to superintend the building I guaranteed to find all required above the $800 raised in the Diocese. The total cost will be $1,300, and the church will be free from debt and ready for consecration at your fall visitation."

The new church was completed by the following year and was opened on Easter Day (April 10) in 1887. Bishop Cheshire, who had visited the congregation the previous summer while the new church was being erected, was very pleased and excited about its prospects, and thus submitted this glowing report to the Convention in May of 1887: "With a zealous and cultured clergyman, and a congregation, though small in numbers, yet active and earnest, I feel sure that a leavening power will make itself manifest in the surrounding neighborhood. It gratifies me to say that the Church thus erected is out of debt, and they desire its Consecration during my visit to the mountain region, the coming summer."[251] Indeed, the church was consecrated as "Gethsemane Church" on Thursday, September 8, 1887. Mr. George Holmes, a lay leader of the church, and the Rev. Dr. D. H. Buel, of the Ravenscroft Associate Mission and Training School, assisted Bishop Lyman in the consecration ceremony.[252] The new church's "stained glass windows were brought from his ancestral home in Wales, by Mr. Morgan Evans, one of the group who formed it's congregation."[253]

For the next few years, the church's progress remained steady, each year reporting a congregation of eight families. Then, in 1891, the Rev. Wainwright became so ill that he was not even able to file a parochial report for the Convention. The Rev. W. S. Barrows, who had replaced Dr. Buel as head of the Ravenscroft Associate Mission, officiated once at Bowman's Bluff in 1892, to a congregation diminished to five families. But the bulk of leadership of the congregation was assumed by lay leader Holmes, with oversight from the Rev. Scott Rathburn of St. John's-in-the-Wilderness, Flat Rock, North Carolina, who officiated two Sundays in each month.[254] The bishop visited Bowman's Bluff on November 17, 1893, where he preached, confirmed two persons and administered communion. However, the bishop was sad to report that "the Rev. Richard Wainwright, Priest in charge of this church, was present, but was unable to take part in the service, except to present the Candidates for Confirmation."[255]

In 1894, the Rev. A. H. Stubbs, newly appointed warden of Ravenscroft, was instrumental in getting Gethsemane Church admitted "into union with the Convention of the Diocese" as an "organized Mission."[256] As an official "mission church," the bishop became the rector of the church, but the actual day-to-day oversight was performed by "ministers-in-charge" appointed by the bishop. This meant that Gethsemane was not self-supporting and could not afford to pay a minister's salary.

The bishop appointed the Rev. A. H. Stubbs "minister-in-charge" of Gethsemane Church in 1894. However, the Rev. Wainwright and the Rev. Stubbs were both listed as "Ministers-In-Charge" on that year's report. Samuel Rhodes and William F. Rice, deacons who were studying at Ravenscroft and missioners under the Rev. Stubbs, also assisted at Bowman's Bluff on occasion.

The extension of the railroad to Brevard in 1895 made it easier and more convenient to visit Gethsemane. The Rev. Stubbs often made entries in his diary of visits to Bowman's Bluff for services. In 1894 he records, a number of times, dining, staying with, and being driven around by "Mr. Jeudwine" (John Wynne Jeudwine, a Cambridge graduate who was a successful barrister in England until, as the *Cambridge Alumni Cantabrigienses* says, he "went to Bowman's Bluff, N. Carolina, U.S.A., and grew oranges").[257] In another diary entry, Stubbs records that on Saturday, January 12, 1895, he started out for Bowman's Bluff in a "cold snow storm."[258] Apparently he arrived safely at Bowman's Bluff, as he records performing the Sunday service the following day, though he notes that the temperature was "6 below zero"!

On August 11, 1895, the Rev. Stubbs officiated at a service at Bowman's Bluff with a visiting "Bishop Capers," who confirmed three children: William Meade Stone (13 years old), Charlotte Catherine Stone (12 years old), and Leonard Ernest Jenkins (16 years old).[259]

In 1898, the Rev. Stubbs records that "Wainwright calls to ask me to give up Bowman's Bluff in case Henderson secures a clergyman from Texas."[260] Stubbs immediately follows his entry with a confession—"was glad for the chance."[261] Although I'm not sure if the "clergyman from Texas" ever arrived, by 1904, the Rev. Reginald Wilcox was listed as the minister-in-charge at Bowman's Bluff. The Rev. Wilcox was the priest at St. James Church in Hendersonville. George and John S. Holmes are listed as the "committee of the Mission."

George Holmes, who was from Birmingham, England, was one of the prominent citizens of the Bowman's Bluff community. John S. Holmes, a "State Forester of the North Carolina Department of Conservation and Development,"[262] was one of his sons.

The Rev. Richard Wainwright died in 1902 and was buried in the Riverside Cemetery in Asheville. James Sill, in his sketch of Gethsemane Church, writes that "on account of the moving away of families who were the ones chiefly interested in the Church, the congregation was finally disbanded in 1907."[263] It is interesting to note that the "Bowman's Bluff–Gethsemane Church" continued to show up in the Convention journals for a few more years, and in 1914–1916 it was listed as "Attached to the Ravenscroft Associate Mission." In 1918 the church showed up on a list of "Missions where no services have been held,"[264] and by 1921 it disappeared from the records forever.

CALVARY EPISCOPAL CHURCH/MT. CALVARY MISSION — FLETCHER

The founding of Calvary Episcopal Church predates the establishment of the Ravenscroft Associate Mission; in fact, it was the second Episcopal church to be built in western North Carolina. Its founding families were former members of St. John-in-the-Wilderness, an Episcopal church established in Flat Rock whose congregation was almost solely made up of wealthy planters from the low country of South Carolina who summered in the mountains. A number of these families (notably, the Blakes, Robertsons, Pyatts, Heywards, and Molyneaux) had moved further north from Flat Rock, along the Buncombe Turnpike, and built their large estates in the area now known as Fletcher.[265] "It was in 1857 that Mr. & Mrs. Daniel Blake gathered a few others together one evening at their home 'The Meadows,' to form plans for the building of a Church."[266] Although the church was not officially admitted into union with the diocese until 1860, Bishop Thomas Atkinson consecrated the completed church on July 30, 1859, and subsequently made the following report:

> I consecrated Calvary Church, in Henderson County, preaching on that occasion. There were present of the Clergy, the Rev. Dr. Hanckel, Messrs. Reed, Keith and Davis, of South Carolina, and Mr. Buxton of our own Diocese, who all took part in the services, in the course of which the Holy Communion was administered. The Church, which is a handsome one, of brick, was built by some gentlemen from South Carolina, who have summer residences near it, and who design it not for their own convenience merely, but for the benefit of a populous and improving neighborhood in which regular Church services are likely, with God's blessing, to accomplish immense good.[267]

The bishop appointed the Rev. N. Collin Hughes as the first rector of Calvary Church on September 1, 1860.[268] The Rev. Hughes also had charge of St. James, a newly formed congregation in nearby Hendersonville. On the bishop's next visit to Calvary on October 1, 1861, he confirmed six persons, "two of whom," he reported, "were colored."[269] It is most likely that these were slaves rather than freedmen.

The Rev. Hughes remained in charge of Calvary during the duration of the Civil War, except for a six-week period during the summer of 1862, at which time the church was under the leadership of Thomas F. Davis. It is unclear why Davis had charge for those six weeks, but, interestingly, his is the only report submitted for Calvary during that year. In his report to the 1863 Convention, Davis gave an astute summation of the work of the Episcopal Church in western North Carolina:

All my observations convince me that the progress of our Church among the indigenous population of the mountains will be exceedingly and tryingly slow; but we can, under God retain and increase the hold already obtained upon the minds of a few among the most intelligent residents — and the Church seems strongly called upon, especially in view of the great conservative reaction in political and other opinions which has guided the existing revolution, and seems likely in time to come to characterize the Southern people, to keep herself and her worship represented and visible over as wide an extent as possible, and with all the zeal and ability which we can command, that God in His good time may cause those whom His grace may predispose and call, to enter in and spiritually abide with us.[270]

No reports were submitted for Calvary from 1863 until 1867. The Rev. George M. Everhart, who was put in charge of Calvary in November of 1866, reported to the 1867 Convention that the church was in a sad state of affairs. He stated that "the effects of the war are visible even here, not only in the impoverishment of once very wealthy persons, and the thinning down the number of Communicants to the few reported, but the beautiful Gothic brick Church Building has been no little injured by soldiers; the stained-glass windows are nearly all broken, and the carpets and furniture stolen or defaced."[271] And then to add to this disheartening situation, by the end of the year the Rev. Everhart had resigned his position and moved back to his hometown of Louisville, Kentucky.[272]

Noting the difficulty of obtaining and retaining a minister for Calvary, it is not surprising that in 1869 we find that the Rev. George T. Wilmer, who was in charge of the newly formed Ravenscroft Associate Mission and Training School, reported that plans were underway to add Calvary Church to its list of mission stations.[273] However, in 1870 the bishop decided to appoint the Rev. Thomas A. Morris as the minister-in-charge of Calvary, which now numbered twelve communicants and forty-five Sunday school pupils.[274] The Rev. Morris served for two years, until ill health caused him to resign as Calvary's minister in 1872.[275]

Perhaps the bishop finally realized that this parish needed greater stability in its leadership, for we find that in 1873 it was put under the supervision of the Rev. D. H. Buel, principal of the Ravenscroft Associate Mission and Training School. In 1874, the parochial report for Calvary is recorded under the reports from the Ravenscroft Associate Mission "Stations," submitted by the Rev. Dr. Buel. The church could now boast thirty-one communicants and sixty pupils in its Sunday school. The Rev. Buel praised the congregation, whom he reported "have expended much money and labor in beautifying the church yard."[276] Also that year, Dr. Buel was saddened to report the death of Daniel Blake, whom he described as "one of the founders of the Parish, its generous and devoted supporter; for a long time its lay reader and a Parishioner revered and beloved by the Church and the whole community."[277]

Calvary Church continued under the supervision of the Ravenscroft Associate Mission for a number of years, but, due to a lack of missionaries, it only had the services of a priest on occasion. However, in 1877 Mr. Edwin A. Osborne, an ordained deacon, was assigned as the rector of Calvary Church. The church, like all mission churches in the Episcopal Church, was under the direction of the bishop, yet it also remained under the Rev. Dr. Buel's oversight. Buel explained the arrangement in his 1878 report: "Since the first of November two stations of the Ravenscroft Mission have enjoyed the efficient and acceptable services of a Deacon, the Rev. E. A. Osborne, who resides at Calvary, Henderson county, and devotes three-fourths of his time to that Parish, and one-fourth to St. John's, Rutherfordton. But under the direction of the Bishop, I retain charge of these stations, as Presbyter, until Mr. Osborne shall take priest's orders, and I officiate stately at both places — on the first Sunday of every other month at Calvary."[278]

From his own report, we know that Mr. Osborne was paid "$400 per annum" and that, in addition to officiating at Calvary and St. James in Hendersonville, Osborne also held "missionary services" in nearby neighborhoods.[279] In a later report, from 1881, Osborne elaborates on these "missionary services":

> In addition to the services reported as having been held at Calvary Church, I have held services once a month at a place of meeting known as Boiling Springs, about three miles from the church, and about once a month at the village of Arden, about one mile and a half distant. I also hold occasional services at Hendersonville, about ten miles distant, and at a place called the "Mill Pond," five miles distant, and once a month at Bat Cave, eighteen miles east. This is all purely missionary work, and presents a most encouraging field if one only had the time and means to improve it as it should be done. The congregations are all encouraging, the people who have never before heard of the Church, as is the case with many of them, taking much interest in the work, and joining in the services quite heartily.[280]

In later reports from 1882 to 1884, we learn that Osborne also held services at a place called "Smoky Hollow, six miles distant" and "at Mt. Calvary, eight miles distant."[281] Mt. Calvary, which was located in Pinners Cove, eventually became a mission church with its own property and church building, and was for many years an official mission station of the Ravenscroft Associate Mission.

The Rev. Osborne resigned the rectorship of Calvary Church in 1885 and was replaced by the Rev. William Shipp Bynum. By then Calvary was an established parish church and no longer in need of the help of the Ravenscroft Associate Mission.

Calvary Episcopal Church continues to be a growing and vibrant congregation, and although the original chapel was replaced in 1935 and a new parish hall built in recent years, it remains one of the most picturesque churches in this region.

ST. JAMES — HENDERSONVILLE

The story of St. James Episcopal Church of Hendersonville is much like the story of a middle child, caught between its parents' memories of their first child and the excitement of their newest and latest child.

St. John-in-the-Wilderness Church was established in nearby Flat Rock, just south of Hendersonville, in 1836. St. John's, the first Episcopal church established in western North Carolina, was founded by families from the coastal regions of South Carolina who began "summering" in Flat Rock beginning in the late 1820s. St. John's predated the establishment of Hendersonville, which was chartered in 1847. In fact, St. John's predated the work of the North Carolina Episcopal Diocese, and therefore, in its early days, was maintained by priests from South Carolina who were among the seasonal residents of the community.

The Rev. James Sill, in his book *Historical Sketches of the Churches of the Diocese of Western North Carolina Episcopal Church*, tells us that the work at St. James was started when the Rev. John Drayton of St. John-in-the-Wilderness began holding services in Hendersonville in 1843. But the first published record in the Diocesan Convention journals is from 1855, where Bishop Atkinson reported that on October 11, 1854, he preached in Hendersonville at a Methodist Church, which he said "was kindly offered for our use."[282] The bishop was visiting the area to consecrate the newly completed brick church of St. John's (on October 12) in nearby Flat Rock. The bishop acknowledged that St. John's was not yet fully "connected' to the diocese but that he "hoped that it will be yet more so, by means of assistance rendered by them in our efforts to spread the Gospel in the region around them."[283] Obviously they had already been providing that assistance by beginning work in Hendersonville.

The congregation at Hendersonville was made up of mostly permanent residents, which put it at a disadvantage, as it was relying on ministerial assistance from the seasonal parishioners of St. John's. For the next few years the church at Hendersonville slowly grew, despite having ministerial services provided only during the summer seasons. The only records from those first few years are those of the bishop's yearly visits, and of occasional services provided by the Rev. Jarvis Buxton of Asheville. Buxton was rector of Trinity Church, and also principal of the newly established Ravenscroft Classical and Theological School, which opened in 1855 to train future church leaders for the area. Yet, by 1860, Bishop Thomas Atkinson announced that during his summer visit to the mountains services were held in the new church at Hendersonville. The church was not yet completed, though, and therefore could not be consecrated at that time.

Sadie Smathers Patton, a local author and historian, writes that Mr. and Mrs. William Shipp were not only some of the earliest members of the church, but that Mrs. Shipp also "appears to have been the strongest influence in the ultimate organization of the congregation and completion of the church building."[284] Other early members included the Henry Farmer family (proprietors of the Farmer Hotel in Flat Rock), W. D. Miller, T. E. Evans, W. E. Massie, and Col. and Mrs. John D. Hyman.

The Rev. N. Collin Hughes became the first rector of the church at Hendersonville in September of 1860, and the church was newly named "St. James." the Rev. Hughes filed the church's first parochial report in the 1861 Diocesan Convention journal. He reported that the church had eight communicants at that time.[285] The church was fortunate that the Rev. Hughes established his residency in Hendersonville, and though he also had charge of Calvary Church in nearby Fletcher, St. James did not have to play "second fiddle" to either Calvary or St. John's.

"Lincoln was inaugurated shortly after the Rev. Hughes came to Hendersonville," writes Sadie Patton, "and the strife and dissention of the Civil War was not long in fastening its grip on the parish, town and country."[286] Patton also tells us that the "troops of the North and South often marched through the streets,"[287] and that they were occasionally quartered in some of Hendersonville's larger buildings. No doubt this is why St. James, though completed enough to be used for services in 1860, was not duly consecrated until September 19, 1863.[288] This gave the church the distinction of being one of the few churches actually consecrated as part of the Confederacy.

However, the Civil War had a devastating effect on the fledgling parish of St. James. By the end of the war, in October of 1865, the Rev. Hughes resigned his post and moved his family to the eastern part of the state. Apparently this was not done to accept another pastorate, as Hughes acknowledged that he was several months without a parish.[289]

The Rev. George Everhart, whose broken health had brought him "to this salubrious region," took charge of St. James and Calvary Church in November of 1866. Everhart resided closer to Calvary and thus gave the majority of his time to that parish. But the church at

St. James was in such a sad state that the Rev. Hughes was discouraged to have to report, "I have found not one Communicant belonging to this Parish. Two or three persons, at one time in their lives, did commune, but they decline now to avail themselves of this Holy Sacrament. The prospect for building up the Church in this place is not encouraging, though my congregations are usually very good."[290] Within a year, the Rev. Everhart also resigned the post and moved to Kentucky.[291]

It is not surprising that the next parochial report to be filed for St. James was filed by the Rev. Francis J. Murdoch, who was then in charge of the newly formed Ravenscroft Associate Mission and Training School, located in Asheville. Ravenscroft was formed by Bishop Atkinson in 1868 to train local men for the ministry and also for the purpose of providing missionaries to establish and maintain churches in the mountains of western North Carolina. But even then the Rev. Murdoch had to report that he had "not been able to hold services here since last Fall."[292] It might be expected that being put under the charge of the Ravenscroft Associate Mission would have been advantageous for St. James, but in fact it had little effect on it at all. For the next decade, no parochial reports for St. James were submitted to the Conventions; in fact, the only mention of the parish in that decade was occasionally made in the bishop's reports, where he would report on his yearly visits to the mountains, but even then the report would merely read, "I preached at Hendersonville." the Rev. Drayton of South Carolina, who officiated at St. John's, and who had officiated at St. James in the early days, would occasionally provide ministerial assistance during this time.

For the first time in over a decade, a parochial report for St. James appeared in the 1877 Convention journal. The report was filed by the Rev. D. Hillhouse Buel, head of the Ravenscroft Associate Mission and Training School, as one of the six mission stations under his charge. Also that year, some relief finally appeared with the arrival of deacon Edwin A. Osborne. Osborne was appointed by the bishop to officiate at Calvary Church in Henderson County and at St. John's in Rutherford County, but because he was not yet ordained, he was put under the oversight of the Rev. Buel of the Ravenscroft Associate Mission. Fortunately for St. James, Osborne resided at nearby Calvary (rather than in Rutherford County) and so was soon asked to also provide ministerial assistance to St. James along with his other charges. In 1880, Osborne reported that during the preceding year he was able to officiate at St. James on a few Sundays during the summer and also occasionally on a fifth Sunday. For the first time in many years, we read an encouraging report. Besides reporting that he baptized four children and confirmed one person, Osborne presented a hopeful outlook for the parish: "There is a respectable brick church there, and since the railroad has reached that point, the town is improving, and a fine opening presents itself there for a splendid work for the Church. The people attend the services well, the situation of the town is beautiful, and the climate as fine as the State affords."[293]

In 1881, St. James was officially designated by the Convention as an "organized mission." This meant that it was now financially dependent on the diocese and under the oversight of the presiding bishop, who, although officially now the rector of the church, would assign a "priest-in-charge" to actually fill the post.[294] This guaranteed not only financial stability for the church but also more steady ministerial services. Also in 1881, the regenerated congregation of St. James started a small parochial school for the neighborhood children.

The Rev. Osborne was appointed as the priest-in-charge. Osborne resigned his post at Rutherfordton, but retained his charge at Calvary. However, apparently his appointment to St. James was thought of as temporary, as in his report to the 1882 Convention he advertised for someone to come and be the fulltime rector of St. James: "This mission was organized by authority of the Bishop since last Convention, and is an exceedingly fine field for Church work. Hendersonville is at the present terminus of the S. & A. Railroad, and is a growing little town. There is a good brick church there, which only needs a little repair to make it quite comfortable, while the membership is increasing rapidly. A minister with a small family, who could devote all of his time to the work there would find a support, and soon build up a good Parish. And there can hardly be found a more desirable climate in North Carolina. It is a favorable point for the building up of a good school for girls, which is much needed there."[295]

In the ensuing few years, the Rev. Osborne was able to build up the work at St. James and managed to put it on the road to becoming a healthy, self-supporting parish. He reported eight communicants in 1882, and by 1885 the number had swelled to thirty. However, in that same report from 1885, Osborne also stated, "I withdrew from the Mission the first of October, 1884, and the Rev. Mr. Tracy took my place at that time."[296] The Rev. U. T. Tracy was a visiting priest who was filling in temporarily at St. John-in-the-Wilderness for the Rev. Drayton that year.

The Rev. Drayton seems to have been the only minister providing occasional services at St. James from late 1884 until 1887, at which time the bishop was able to secure the services of the Rev. Arthur Wrixton. Wrixton officiated at St. James and other nearby mission stations (Tryon City, Whitesides and Seagles).[297] But unfortunately, as seemed to be the lot of St. James, Wrixton gave the work back to the Rev. Drayton and left the parish in 1889. The Rev. Hobart C. Brayton of Mississippi, whose address was given as "Hot Springs, NC," briefly took charge of St. James following the Rev. Wrixton.[298]

The Rev. William Stanley Barrows, who had assumed the headship of the Ravenscroft Associate Mission from the Rev. Dr. Buel, stepped in as priest-in-charge of St. James in January of 1891. Barrows reported that the congregation had twenty-three communicants. Although this was reduced from the thirty reported in 1885, the parish remained active. In fact, Barrows was delighted to report that "services are now maintained regularly every Lord's Day."[299]

The Rev. Scott Rathburn, who was appointed rector of St. John-in-the-Wilderness following the death of the Rev. Drayton, assumed the leadership of St. James in 1892. He was followed by the Rev. Hardy Phelps, who officiated briefly at St. James in conjunction with his charge at Calvary Church, until the Rev. Thomas C. Wetmore became the rector in 1895. The Rev. Wetmore remained at St. James until his departure to found Christ School in nearby Arden in 1900.

Perhaps the story of St. James was best summed up in the Rev. Wetmore's 1898 parochial report, where he wrote, "There are many people here from the South [Carolina] during the summer months who take great interest in this Church and give liberally towards its support. There has always existed much prejudice towards the Church in the town, but it is very gratifying to know that now there exists a kinder feeling towards it than has ever been before."[300]

St. James continued to have a succession of rectors over the years, but survives today as a communing parish church.

Jackson County

CULLOWHEE MISSION/ST. DAVID'S — CULLOWHEE

The Episcopal Church's work in Jackson County began in 1874, when Bishop Theodore Lyman visited the county seat of Webster during his yearly visit to the western regions of the state. For the next three or four summers, the bishop included Webster on his visit to the mountains. During his visits the bishop would hold services either in the local schoolhouse or in the courthouse, where crowds of onlookers would gather "to see the 'show,' as the robes of the Minister attracted much interest."[301]

One of those who attended the bishop's services with great interest was local businessman and British ex-pat, Mr. D. D. Davies, who lived in the Cullowhee valley, southwest of Webster. Daniel David Davies was born in Carmarthenshire, Wales, to David and Anna Davies in 1826. According to his own account, he left home at the age of twelve and "wandered into the mining districts." Ten years later, in 1848, at the age of twenty-two, Davies departed from his native land to seek his fortune in America. Being a miner, he naturally immigrated to western Pennsylvania, where there were large mining interests and consequently a large Welsh community. While working for John D. Gray & Company of Pittsburg in the 1850s, Davies was sent by Mr. Gray to explore the southern Appalachians for coal and other mineral deposits. After exploring in east Tennessee, Davies visited Jackson County in 1856, where he discovered large mica and copper deposits. Unable to convince Gray to buy the mineral rights to these deposits, Davies moved on to other company projects in Tennessee and Georgia. But in 1857, still unable to convince Gray to purchase the mineral rights in Jackson County, Davies quit the Gray Company and moved to Jackson County, forming a copper mining partnership with William H. Bryson, William Coleman, John Walker, William Cowan and William Higdon. Although this group was unsuccessful in extracting much copper before its dissolution (caused by the interruption of the Civil War), Davies remained in Jackson County and settled at Cullowhee. Over the years he became involved in other copper and mica mining interests in the area.[302]

Davies had been brought up in the Church of England, but since moving to Cullowhee in the late 1850s he had been a member and leader in the Methodist Episcopal Church, South, since, as he once related, "during that time the Protestant Episcopal Church was a stranger in the land."[303] But in August of 1882, while Bishop Lyman was visiting the area, Mr. D. D. Davies invited the bishop, who was accompanied by the Rev. Dr. Buel of the Ravenscroft Associate Mission, to dine and lodge at "Forest Hill," his estate in Cullowhee.[304] During the overnight stay Davies suggested to the bishop that Episcopal services should be extended to Cullowhee and that a church be erected.[305]

The bishop agreed to begin a mission at Cullowhee, and assigned the ministerial oversight to Dr. Buel and the missionary priests of the Ravenscroft Associate Mission and Training School in Asheville. The new mission first shows up in the Convention journals in 1884, under the parochial report for Webster, where "Cullawhee [sic]" is described as an "outlying station." Also reported that year was the news that while "occasional services" were being supplied to Cullowhee, construction was well underway on a new church, on a suitable lot donated by Mr. Davies and his business partner, Mr. David F. Brown. Bishop Lyman had laid the cornerstone of the new church, "St. David's" (named after Mr. Davies' childhood church in Wales), on December 23, 1883.[306] Services were being held at the nearby "Speedwell schoolhouse" while the new church was under construction.[307]

The rugged terrain of the mountains, combined with poorly maintained dirt roads, made nineteenth-century travel difficult and often dangerous. Today, we often underestimate the significance to those of the nineteenth and early twentieth centuries of having a "neighborhood" church that could be reached without great difficulty. This fact was underscored in Bishop Lyman's report of his visit to the Cullowhee church in August of 1884. After visiting and preaching in Charleston, North Carolina, in Swain County, the bishop and the Rev. Buel set out on Saturday morning, August 23, on the 36-mile journey south to Cullowhee. They hoped to stop at Webster for a visit and arrive at Cullowhee to perform the Sunday morning service. They had not traveled but a few miles before difficulties set in, as the bishop related in the following report:

> We found the road in a very bad condition, and when about five miles from Charleston met with an accident to the carriage, which occasioned us considerable delay. With the assistance of some young men who were passing, we endeavored to remedy the break, as far as possible, and then got on very comfortably for some miles; but when passing over a spur of the mountains, we came upon a sideling, rocky bed, and the carriage turned completely over into a deep hollow on the right side of the road. The horses very providentially stopped at once, or we might have received serious injuries. Dr. Buel escaped unhurt, but I was stunned by the fall, and received severe bruises and a heavy strain. By the help of strangers who were passing, we soon got our carriage back on the road, and finding that it had received no considerable injuries, we soon started on again. We were unable to find any shop where repairs could be had, and consequently we made but very slow progress. We did not reach Webster until 8 P.M., so that we were about twelve hours making the twenty miles. We secured another vehicle at once, so that we might be ready for an early start the next morning, as we were most anxious, on no account, to miss the appointment for that day.[308]

Though a bit shaken and weary, the bishop and the Rev. Buel managed to make their appointment, and when they arrived at Cullowhee on Sunday morning they "found a large congregation gathered in the school house [Speedwell]."[309]

The bishop also reported that the following day (Monday) he "spent visiting several families in the neighborhood and inspecting the neat brick Church in course of erection there, the walls of which were nearly raised. The site is a very beautiful one, near the base of a mountain spur, and overlooking the lovely Cullowhee Valley. The building, it is expected, will be ready for services at my visitation this summer."[310] The bishop remained at Cullowhee another day, and on Tuesday, August 26, he and the Rev. Buel traveled around the mountain to the village of "East La Porte," where they held services in a small schoolhouse. It was hoped that this community could soon be serviced by the new Cullowhee church because, as the bishop reported, "a new road will soon be made over the mountain gap, bringing them within about two miles of the new Cullowhee Church."[311]

The Bishop expected in May of 1885 that St. David's would be "ready for services" by his summer visit (August of 1885), but although it was being used for services, the church was barely "under roof" and quite unfinished. In fact, two years later, in September of 1887, after visiting the church, the bishop regrettably reported that "this Church still stands in an unfinished state, as we have not been able to command the funds requisite for its completion. We greatly need a resident Minister and a Parochial School at this point, and could these desirable plans be carried out we might reasonably look for very decided progress."[312]

Not only were the Davies family regular attendees, but so were the Rogers and Cox families. On October 27, 1887, St. David's first marriage ceremony, officiated by the Rev. Buel, was performed for Thomas A. Cox and Cora Kate Davies, the daughter of Mr. D. D. Davies. Thomas Augustus Cox had moved to Cullowhee in 1886 from Greenville, South Carolina, with his mother and three sisters. Thomas and his new family soon became active members and leaders of the congregation.

An interesting note is that during this time (1888–1889) Cullowhee High School, which would eventually become today's Western Carolina University, was begun by Robert Lee Madison on land near the church. The new institution, in an effort to promote widespread support for its programs, formed a board of directors comprised of representatives from the various religious denominations in the area. Of the nine board members, two were Episcopalians — Mr. Daniel D. Davies and his son-in-law Thomas Cox, both of whom were also leaders of St. David's.[313]

In May of 1891, the Rev. William Stanley Barrows, who was assisting the Rev. Buel at Ravenscroft, reported, "During the past year the Church has been nearly completed through funds secured by the Bishop for that purpose, and will probably be ready for consecration next summer."[314] Despite the church being unfinished, the St. David's congregation was continuing to grow, and in 1891 they were able to report twelve communicants (four families) and twenty-eight scholars in their Sunday school. Also, it was reported that during the year 1891 that "a vestry room has been added and most of the interior of the church finished, besides repairing roof, arranging belfry and hanging bell. The number of public services (47) includes our regular fourth Sunday service, and other Sundays lay reading with Sunday-school."[315]

The church was finally completed in 1892, after eight years of construction. On August 17, 1892, Bishop Theodore B. Lyman consecrated St. David's Church, and subsequently made the following report of the ceremony: "The request for consecration was read by Mr. Thomas A. Cox, and the sentence of consecration by the Rev. J. A. Deal. Morning Prayer was said by the Rev. Messrs. Deal and Barber. The sermon was preached by me, and I also administered the Holy Communion. It was a day of great rejoicing in this lovely valley, and we trust that this attractive Church may avail to draw multitudes into the paths of truth and of righteousness."[316] Unfortunately, the Rev. Dr. David Hillhouse Buel of the Ravenscroft Associate Mission, who had been instrumental in the formation of St. David's, was not able to attend the consecration, as he had been incapacitated for over a year as a result of the death of his wife and the onset of ill health.[317] The previous year (1891) the Rev. W. S. Barrows, who was the Rev. Buel's assistant and later replacement, acknowledged Dr. Buel's contribution to the success of St. David's in his Convention report: "As an instance of 'patient continuance in well doing,' it may be interesting to note that Dr. Buel, who has continued in charge ever since he began this work, more than eighteen years ago, before the day of railroads, was long accustomed during the greater part of the year, to drive once a month regularly from Asheville, more than sixty miles away."[318]

Around 1895, the oversight of St. David's was assumed by the nearby Waynesville Associate Mission, which, using the pattern of the Ravenscroft Associate Mission, was established to supply ministers to the mission churches in its immediate vicinity. But after the turn of the century, St. David's went into a slow decline. Lay leader Thomas Cox tried to keep the church going as communicants died or moved away. But in 1925, with a congregation of only three, Cox appealed to the diocese for financial aid so that St. David's could better serve the spiritual needs of the local college students. But alas, no money was available, and by 1933, the church had only seven or eight members. It finally closed in 1941 and was deconsecrated in 1942.[319]

The church building stood unused for seventeen years, and its furnishings were lent to other churches. However, in the late 1950s, the Rev. Dr. A. Rufus Morgan, who was serving other churches in the area at this time, thought that St. David's should be reactivated as a student center to serve the growing Episcopal population at the nearby Western Carolina University. Through Dr. Morgan's influential efforts, St. David's was reconsecrated on May 9, 1959, and reopened as a student center.[320] Incidentally, Dr. Morgan, who lived to be 97 years old and was an icon of the Episcopal ministry in the mountains of western North Carolina, was born in Franklin and obtained his early schooling at the mission school at Micadale, near Waynesville. Dr. Morgan's ministry was a direct result of the work of the Ravenscroft Associate Mission. Morgan's grandparents had been instrumental in founding the church at Franklin, and his parents had been leaders of the church at Murphy. Also, the Micadale school that he attended was one of the earlier established missions of the Ravenscroft Associate Mission.

In 1961, regular services were resumed at St. David's, and today it is a growing and vibrant congregation.

LOVE'S SCHOOL HOUSE/WEBSTER/ST. JOHN'S — SYLVA

The earliest published record of the Episcopal Church's work in Jackson County is from the Rev. David Hillhouse Buel's report, "Work In North Carolina," published in the June 1875 issue of *The Spirit of Missions*. The Rev. Buel reported that after leaving Assistant Bishop Theodore Lyman at Waynesville (during his autumn 1874 visit) to be attended by the Rev. Huske, "the Bishop, thus attended, went on twenty miles to Webster, the county seat of Jackson County."[321] Buel further stated that while at Webster, "leading gentlemen of the place, lawyers and others, came to see the Bishop and begged him to provide Missionary Services for them. They told him that they had not in their town religious Services of any sort so often as once a week."[322]

The bishop made subsequent visits to Webster during the summers of 1876, 1877, and 1878. During his 1877 visit he had a harrowing experience. In the afternoon of Friday, August 10, the bishop and Dr. Buel departed from Franklin to go to Webster, where they, as the bishop later reported, "arrived just before midnight, after a very dreary and perilous journey over the intervening mountain."[323] Except for the bishop's occasional visits, no concerted effort to form a congregation at Webster was made until 1879. Bishop Lyman visited the Webster station in August of 1879 and subsequently made the following report:

> On Monday, August 18th [1879], accompanied by the Rev. Dr. Buel, I proceeded on to Webster, the county-seat of Jackson county, and the next day, Tuesday, August 19th, in a schoolhouse which is used by different denominations as a place of worship, I preached and confirmed two persons. I urged the importance of an effort to build here, as speedily as possible, a plain and simple church edifice; and I was glad to find, among many of the citizens, a readiness to cooperate in such a work. With a little outside help, this much needed object may easily be accomplished. I endeavored to make arrangements for occasional services at Webster, which Dr. Buel very kindly consented to undertake, although quite heavily burdened already with mission-

ary duties. He greatly needs a co-worker in his large field, and I hope we may soon find a suitable person to be associated with him.[324]

The "school-house" mentioned in the report was Love's Meeting House (a.k.a. Love's Chapel), which was located on the site of an earlier log meeting house originally built around 1840 by Daniel Payne on land donated by John B. Love.

The two persons who were confirmed by the bishop were Dillard L. Love and his niece Sarah. I suspect that Mr. Love was one of those "leading gentlemen of the place, lawyers and others," who in 1874 had begged the bishop to supply missionary services to their town. Mr. Dillard L. Love, who was both a lawyer and businessman, would become the founder and major benefactor of the church at Webster/Sylva for the next three decades of its existence.

Dillard Lafayette Love was born on October 15, 1838, to John Bell and Margaret Coman Love. John Bell Love operated a trading station/store in Webster and owned a substantial amount of property in the Scott's Creek area.[325] John's father (Dillard's grandfather) was Col. Robert Love, the founder of nearby Waynesville.

Dillard served in the Confederate Army as a first lieutenant in Company A of the 16th North Carolina regiment for one year (1861–1862) before having to resign due to "bad health." He then served under appointment from Judge Asa Biggs as "receiver" for Haywood, Jackson, and Macon counties.[326] In August of 1861, the Confederate Congress had enacted the "Act of Sequestration," which enabled authorities to confiscate the property of "enemy-aliens" living in their jurisdictions. One of the new governmental positions established by the act was that of "receiver." The receivers were appointed by Confederate district court judges, and their responsibilities were to track down, seize, and then auction off property belonging to alien enemies.

By the time of his confirmation (and the start of the church), Dillard was a 42-year-old bachelor living at home with his widowed mother and two unmarried brothers (Calhoun and Thomas).[327] He was listed in the census as a lawyer, but records show that he was also a businessman. An 1890 business directory shows that at that time he also owned and operated a flour mill in Webster.

The bishop was finally successful in 1879, shortly after his visit, in persuading the Rev. Buel to begin providing services to Webster. The Webster mission station appears on the Ravenscroft Associate Mission report for the first time in 1880. In the report the Rev. Buel announced that "during the past six months, stated services have, for the first time, been given to this place; and with a very encouraging reception."[328] The report also stated that there were two confirmations (Dillard and his niece) and four communicants at the time, and that the church hoped to soon erect a building to house the fledgling congregation.

The Rev. Dr. Buel, assisted on occasion by Ravenscroft missionary priest George Bell (of Haw Creek, Asheville), continued to provide ministerial services and oversight to the Webster church during the 1880s. And although the congregation increased over those years to almost 15 communicants, by 1890 the church was still meeting in the Webster school house (except when the bishop would visit—then it would have to meet in the courthouse), and had no permanent home of its own.

In 1890, the donation of a suitable lot brought a renewed hope of sustainability to the small congregation. The Rev. Buel reported to the 1891 Convention that "Mr. John Macomb has offered a site for a church at this point, and as the work can be carried on in connection with Cullowhee it would appear to be a most desirable point at which to build." The "point" mentioned in the report was Sylva, which was three miles north of Webster. The new town was being established around the newly opened depot along the Western North Carolina Railroad. In 1890, Sylva had only 35 residents compared to Webster's 267,[329] but because of its railroad connection it was quickly becoming an attractive location to live and work. The lot donated by "Mr. John Macomb" was on the north side of Sylva in what is now known as the "College Hill" area.[330] A new mission at nearby Cullowhee had begun in 1884, and so it seemed that Sylva would be a better location for a church than Webster. Dillard Love also became a property owner in the new town, buying property on the south side of town.[331]

By 1891 the congregation had moved from Webster to Sylva and was meeting in "the Academy" (which was the "Jackson Academy" operated by Robert Lee Madison).[332] In 1892 the Rev. John Deal, as head of the Asheville Convocation, made an urgent appeal to the yearly Convention: "I would advise that a missionary be placed at Sylva, on W. N. C. R. R., from which point five Stations can be reached regularly and with less cost than from any other point. It is important that this matter receive immediate attention, as every month of delay robs us of opportunities and increases the difficulty."[333]

Dillard's mother, Margaret E. (Coman) Love, passed away on April 1, 1893. Margaret, "who as a girl, had been a member of Bishop Ravenscroft's congregation in Raleigh,"[334] had been a strong influence in Dillard's interest in the Episcopal Church and a major supporter of the Sylva church.

Although the church was in need of a missionary priest to hold regular services, the lack of a suitable meeting place also seemed to be a hindrance to the growth of the church

St. John's Church is shown in this early twentieth-century photograph. The church was built on Jackson Street in downtown Sylva, North Carolina, in 1912 on land donated by Dillard L. Love (courtesy of the Episcopal Diocese of Western North Carolina, Asheville).

at Sylva. But then Dillard Love came to the rescue. The Rev. W. S. Barrows, who had taken charge of the Ravenscroft Associate Mission and Training School following the demise of the Rev. Dr. Buel, reported in 1893 that the church now had a dedicated space to meet: "The chapel, or hall, which is over a store, was used for the first time on the third Sunday after Easter [April 23, 1893]. Mr. Dillard L. Love, who is indefatigable in his efforts to advance the interests of the Church at Sylva, is about to begin Lay Services."[335] This was just a few weeks after the death of Dillard's mother. An 1895 report of the Rev. Frederick Wey (at missionary priest who then had general oversight of the Sylva church) gives a clearer explanation of the situation: "Here we have no church property; the hall which we use, and which has been fitted up as a chapel, is the private property of Mr. Dillard L. Love, our efficient Lay Reader, who is doing good service for the Church."[336] Mr. Love had not only provided a place for the congregation to meet anytime they desired to do so, but he also was ordained as a lay leader,[337] thereby providing leadership for the church to be able to hold services every Sunday. In fact, the Rev. Wey reported in 1895 that during the preceding year he had conducted only seven services at Sylva, but that the church had held "Lay Service[s] all other Sundays by Mr. Dillard L. Love."[338]

By the turn of the century, many of the Ravenscroft Associate Mission churches in the more remote counties were reassigned to come under the oversight of newly formed local associate missions, which operated from the larger, more established churches in their respective areas. The Sylva church, which by that time was named "St. John's," was reassigned to the Waynesville Associate Mission, which operated from Grace Church, Waynesville.

However, St. John's continued to be primarily operated under the lay leadership of Dillard Love. Around 1900, Mr. Love started a mission day-school at his personal residence, and by 1901 the school had grown to include fifty-five pupils. In a church-wide appeal letter, the Rev. Clarence Buel (brother of the deceased the Rev. D. H. Buel) reported that in order to be able to serve more students, Mr. Love was "now building an addition, to cost about $1,000, which he has borrowed in the hope that this venture of faith will be generously sustained."[339] The Rev. Buel urged the church to help to support the work at St. John's, specifically the building of the addition to the day-school: "Surely this zealous layman ought to be relieved from the financial obligation which he has been compelled to assume in order to provide accommodations for the children of these hardy mountaineers."[340] Buel added, "Mr. Love writes me that he needs also fifty school desks for the addition which is being built."[341] The day-school operated from Mr. Love's residence at the corner of Walnut and West Main Streets in downtown Sylva. Apparently this was a separate location from the church hall, which was over Dillard Love's business.

The church gained an additional communicant in 1907 when the "old bachelor," Mr. Dillard L. Love, who was then 68 years old, married 46-year-old Mary Louise ("Mollie") Walker of Statesville, North Carolina. Mollie was a professional nurse, who at the time of their marriage was working at Lyon's View Hospital in Knoxville, Tennessee. The couple was married in a small ceremony held at the home of Mollie's sister (Julia Walker McLain) in Statesville on October 15, 1907.[342]

Mollie and Dillard lived in the house on Main Street and were active in the work of St. John's until Dillard's death at the age of 84 on July 11, 1923. But perhaps Dillard Love's greatest contribution to St. John's was the donation of a lot on Jackson Street and the construction of a church building in 1912. This single act finally put the church on a path to sustainability. And although the original frame building was replaced by the current brick church in 1956, St. John's active congregation continues to minister from that very same site in downtown Sylva.

Madison County

ST. JOHN'S — HOT SPRINGS

The earliest published record of the Ravenscroft Associate Mission and Training School is the Rev. David Hillhouse Buel's report, "Work In North Carolina," published in the June 1875 issue of *The Spirit of Missions*. In his report, the Rev. Buel takes his readers along on a "missionary tour" that he and Assistant Bishop Theodore B. Lyman conducted through western North Carolina in the autumn of 1874. This happened to coincide with the start of the work of the Ravenscroft Associate Mission in Hot Springs (then known as Warm Springs). "Returning to Asheville," records the Rev. Buel, "the Bishop next visited Warm Springs in Marshall [Madison] County, forty miles north-west of Asheville down the valley of the French Broad. This is an important watering-place, noted for the medicinal virtue of its warm springs, and there is a large and yearly increasing number of visitors here, many of whom always are Church people. A considerable sum of money has been raised toward a church, and a Missionary is urgently needed for this important point."[343]

William Neilson was the first owner and developer of "Warm Springs," building his inn on the property sometime around 1804. The springs surrounding the inn were reported to have a temperature of 105° and possess healing powers.

The opening of the Buncombe Turnpike in 1828, which connected Tennessee and Kentucky to East Coast markets, put Warm Springs on the map. It soon became a popular stop, both for drovers taking their livestock to market and for passengers and drivers using the newly established stagecoach line that followed the same route. And soon thereafter, it also became a popular destination spot for tourists and those seeking the respite and healing offered by the springs. No doubt that is why, in 1831, brothers James W. and John E. Patton of Asheville (developers of the turnpike) purchased the valuable property. Following an 1838 fire, the brothers rebuilt the inn and added its famous portico of thirteen white columns (supposedly to represent the thirteen original colonies). They named it the "Warm Springs Hotel." But in 1875, when the work of the Ravenscroft Associate Mission began, the Warm Springs property was then owned and operated by Colonel James H. Rumbough.

James Henry Rumbough was born on July 21, 1832, to Jacob and Martha Southerland Rumbough of Woodstock, Virginia. His father, a railroad contractor, had moved the family to Greeneville, Tennessee, in the 1850s, after completing the construction of a railroad line from Lynchburg, Virginia, to Greeneville. James Henry, like his father, was an entrepreneur, and while a young man, he purchased the stagecoach line that ran along the Buncombe Turnpike from Greeneville, Tennessee, to Greenville, South Carolina. On December 12, 1854, Rumbough married Caroline Turpin Powell (of Greeneville) at St. James Episcopal Church in Greeneville.

When the Civil War erupted in the early 1860s, J. H. Rumbough joined the Confederate Army as an officer. Wanting to safeguard his young family, away from the Unionist sympathies of Greeneville, Rumbough purchased the Warm Springs Hotel in 1862 and moved the family into the "Wade Hampton Cottage" on the property. During the war years, while Rumbough was away fighting and being held as a prisoner of war, his wife Carrie not only managed the hotel but was also successful in thwarting a number of Union assaults on the property. In addition, Carrie Rumbough went on to produce eight children with the colonel.[344] Mrs. Rumbough was also the prime mover of the establishment of the Episcopal mission at Warm/Hot Springs.

Although the 1875 report mentioned that "a considerable sum of money has been raised toward a church," except for the mention of the bishop's visit in 1877, no further work toward the establishment of a mission or church was accomplished at Warm Springs until a decade later. The Rev. George H. Bell, a native of Asheville and deacon missionary with the Ravenscroft Associate Mission, submitted the following report to the 1886 Convention: "I began holding services at this place last summer, but had to discontinue them during the winter, there being no place that I could procure for that purpose. I am now using an upper room, kindly furnished me by a Baptist. This work is an important one. A church is much needed here."[345]

Much had changed during that intervening decade. The railroad had reached Warm Springs in 1882, prompting Col. Rumbough to enlarge the 1838 hotel (built by the Pattons). Tragically, the newly enlarged hotel was destroyed by fire in 1884. Col. Rumbough, deciding not to rebuild, sold the property to a group of Northern investors called "The Southern Improvement Company," who built the "Mountain Park Hotel" on the property in 1886. Rumbough went into semi-retirement at his nearby home, "Rutland," just across the Spring Creek.

Construction of a small wooden chapel was begun around 1886 on a parcel of land adjacent to "Rutland" (the Rumbough family home). Although the details are a bit sketchy, for some now unknown reason, the new chapel was constructed on land that had previously been deeded by Rumbough to the Southern Improvement Company. But finally, in 1888, the Rev. Bell could happily announce that "after long and persistent efforts I have recently obtained possession of the Chapel at this place."[346] The Rev. Bell further reported that a Sunday school had been established, and that funds were being raised to complete the still unfinished chapel. The Rev. Jarvis Buxton (of Asheville) reported that during the same year, three of the ten priests of the area, along with other visitors, held their convocation in the unfinished chapel.[347]

Services continued in the unfinished chapel, with the congregation growing from four families in 1886 to nine families. Efforts were made over the ensuing year to complete the chapel. At last, in 1889, the Rev. Bell could gladly report, "The people of the congregation have worked very hard during the past year to finish the church; now we have a nice, comfortable church. Mrs. B. W. Hill has been untiring in her efforts to accomplish this desired end of the many difficulties under which we have labored."[348] "Mrs. B. W. Hill," whom Bell commended for her work, was Mary Lee Rumbough Hill, one of Col. Rumbough's daughters, who had married a local man named Beverly W. Hill.

The finished chapel was consecrated by Bishop Theodore B. Lyman on July 28, 1889. In his 1890 address, the Bishop gave the particulars of the consecration: "The request for consecration was read by Mr. A. G. Doolittle, and the sentence of consecration by Archdeacon Moore, of the Diocese of Louisiana. I preached, confirmed two persons and celebrated the Holy Communion. The Rev. Geo. Bell assisted in the service. The next day I prepared a paper duly organizing the Mission and appointing the proper officers."[349]

The new mission was organized as "St. John's Church," and the bishop appointed the Rev. William Stanley Barrows as the priest-in-charge. The Rev. Barrows, who had just transferred into the diocese from the Diocese of Long Island, New York, was also assigned as an instructor at the Ravenscroft Training School in Asheville. The Rev. Barrows reported the following list of gifts that were donated to the newly opened church: "A solid silver Communion set, from Mrs. Harry Morris; a Caen Stone Font from Mr. and Mrs. James Herman Aldrich; an Oak Prayer Desk, from Mrs. Theodore F. Vail; an Oak Credence Bracket from Mrs. Phelps, of New Orleans; 75 Prayer Books and 75 Hymnals from the New York Bible and Prayer Book Society; a Bible and Alms-Basin from Mr. and Mrs. Wm. G. Doolittle; a new Fence from Mr. John G. Baker; Brass Altar Vases from Sister Cecelia and Mr. Wm. Bispham; a Wardrobe from Miss Skinner; a Cassock from Mr. P. S. Parker, and Altar Linen and Chancel Books from an anonymous benefactor."[350]

The Rev. W. S. Barrows remained as the minister-in-charge for the next few years. Although the church only had a small number of communicants (10–15), the services (which Barrows held 2 or 3 times each Sunday) were well attended, for, as the Rev. Barrows reported in 1891, "This congregation is largely composed of visitors, mostly guests of the Mountain Park Hotel, who come to Hot Springs for recreation or to be benefited by the invigorating climate and the baths. Their gifts are the chief support of the Mission."[351] The gifts reported that year included "an altar cloth from Mrs. J. H. Aldrich, of New York; books and presents for the Sunday-school from Mrs. F. B. Carter, of Montclair, N. J., and Miss Louise A. Millar, of Utica, a surplice from Mrs. Sutton, of Louisville, and lamps with brackets from Mr. Milligan, of Brooklyn."[352]

In 1891, the Rev. Barrows, who had been residing at Warm Springs, moved to Asheville to officiate at other nearby stations, and enlisted the aid of the Rev. William F. Rice and lay reader Harry Rumbough to assist at St. John's. "Harry Rumbough" was Henry Thomas Rumbough, an adult son of Col. and Mrs. Rumbough.

The Rev. Barrows continued, with occasional assistance from other missionary priests, to provide ministerial oversight and services to St. John's until he was replaced in 1894 by the Rev. A. H. Stubbs, who had recently been appointed warden of the Ravenscroft Associate Mission and Training School. The Rev. Stubbs' appointment coincided with the establishment of the Missionary District of Asheville in 1895. The Rev. Stubbs resided at Shoenberger Hall on Church Street in Asheville, which had been built in 1887 on the Ravenscroft campus.

The Rev. Stubbs, who would provide the oversight for St. John's for the next two-and-a-half decades, kept an extensive diary each year, in which he recorded his various ministry services, tasks and travels (and on occasion the weather and temperature). We see from his entries that he would take the train from Asheville to Hot Springs, get off at the depot, and then have to walk across the bridge spanning Spring Creek to get to the chapel. The logistical lay of the land would often provide physical impediments to the Rev. Stubbs' visitations. He often recorded such entries as this 1901 entry: "River high. No bridge. Bridges all down

St. John's Church in Hot Springs, North Carolina, is pictured in this rare photograph from the early twentieth century. The church was built next to Col. Rumbough's residence, which is now a bed and breakfast. The church is no longer in existence (courtesy of the Episcopal Diocese of Western North Carolina, Asheville).

over creek. People have to walk over the railway tresses. Going around makes a serious difference, otherwise dangerous."[353]

The Rev. Stubbs' visits were further complicated by the fact that he apparently did not have a key to the chapel, and so would have to retrieve a key from Mrs. Carrie Rumbough at Rutland, next door to the church. Although he would usually send telegrams prior to his visits, he often encountered difficulties once he arrived. For instance, on July 27, 1901, Stubbs recorded that he "could not use the church as Mrs. Rumbough had been called to the bedside of her daughter, Mrs. Baker, and keys could not be obtained."[354] And there was also a smallpox scare during the first few months of 1903. On January 25, the Rev. Stubbs recorded, "People [at Hot Springs] alarmed about the small pox at Asheville," and although he visited in subsequent weeks, the situation became so severe that on February 25 he recorded, "Small pox scare. People avoid gatherings."[355]

Also from the Rev. Stubb's dairies, we learn of some of the prominent church members. On February 24, 1901, Stubbs recorded that "Mr. Beverly Hill died on the 16th, and was buried in Asheville, Monday 2–18. Mrs. Hill returned to New York yesterday — could not reach Mrs. Weir, and Mrs. Royce, on account of bridge being down and ice in river."[356] Beverly W. Hill, a former mayor of Hot Springs, was the husband of Col. Rumbough's daughter, Mary Lee. Apparently, the couple was living in New York at the time, although Mr. Hill was buried in the riverside cemetery at Asheville. "Mrs. Weir and Mrs. Royce" refers to Mrs. Sally Royce Weir and her mother, Martha Broyles Royce,[357] who, as author Della Hazel Moore writes, "had a unique house built on the mountain opposite the warm springs, overlooking the French Broad River."[358] The ladies did most of the construction of their unique reinforced concrete house. A photo and floor plans of the house were published in 1909 by the Atlas Portland Cement Company — Martha Royce was listed as the "architect."[359] According to accounts in the Rev. Stubbs diary, Martha and Sally often helped lead the worship by playing the organ and/or singing.

Also mentioned in the Rev. Stubbs' diary, and in other sources, are the Lance sisters. Susan, Georgiana, Fannie and Mamie Lance were the daughters of the Newton Jasper Lance family of Calvary Episcopal Church in Fletcher (south of Asheville). Three of the sisters, Georgie, Fannie and Mamie, operated a boarding house on Lawson Street for many years and were noted for "their old time way of cooking."[360]

In 1904, Mrs. Carrie Rumbough donated a chancel window to the church in memory of her son Harry, who had passed away in 1897. Harry, a former member of St. John's, had married Harriet Olivia Sackett of Ohio in 1895, just two years prior to his death.

In 1913, Col. Rumbough, who had reassumed ownership of the Mountain Park Hotel from the Southern Improvement Company years earlier, finally sold the hotel to his son, James Edwin of Asheville. Shortly thereafter the hotel was commandeered by the U.S. government during World War I to house German detainees. Tragically, the hotel was destroyed by fire in 1920. The Rev. Stubbs continued to provide ministerial oversight to St. John's up until his death in 1924.

One of the last recorded major social events to have been held at St. John's was the marriage of Elizabeth Rumbough Baker (Col. Rumbough's granddaughter) to Henry Dotterer (of "Sparkleberry Farm," Charleston, South Carolina) on Monday, February 20, 1939. *The News and Courier*, of Charleston, reported that the ceremony was performed by "the Rev. Arthur W. Farnum, rector of St. Mary's Protestant Episcopal Church, Asheville," and that "the church was decorated with hemlock boughs, magnolia and ivy leaves and white cathedral candles."[361] Records indicate that the Rev. Arthur W. Farnum, former rector of St. James Episcopal Church in Hendersonville, who had assumed the rectorship of St. Mary's in 1928, provided ministerial oversight to St. John's–Hot Springs through the 1930s and 1940s. Services at St. John's were suspended shortly thereafter, and the church was demolished around 1953.[362]

Rutherford County

ST. JOHN'S — RUTHERFORDTON

St. John's Episcopal Church in Rutherfordton was one of the earliest Episcopal congregations to be established in the western part of the state. Although it was not originally founded as a mission of the Ravenscroft Associate Mission and Training School, St. John's was for a time maintained by missionaries of Ravenscroft, and it was further connected with Ravenscroft through its associations with its former rector, the Rev. Jarvis Buxton.

The Town of Rutherfordton was formed in 1787 to serve as the seat of government for Rutherford County. Both county and town are the namesakes of General Griffith Rutherford, a noted western North Carolina politician and military general during the Revolutionary War era.[363]

The work of the Episcopal Church at Rutherfordton can be traced back to the early 1840s, when Bishop Levi Silliman Ives began his great missionary thrust to the western regions of North Carolina. At that time the Episcopal Church in North Carolina was still rather small. In fact, there was less than twenty "clergy" attending the 1840 Convention, and only about fifteen churches represented by lay delegates.

In 1841, the bishop received a request for Episcopal services in Rutherfordton. The bishop had recently received a gift of "a small legacy, left by a pious lady,"[364] which was to be used for missionary purposes. Bishop Ives used the money to support a small band of twelve missionaries throughout the state. Bishop Ives decided to send missionary John S. Kidney to Rutherfordton. Deacon Kidney had recently been appointed assistant to missionary the Rev. Edward M. Forbes at Lincolnton. Forbes and Kidney's missionary territory included Mecklenburg, Lincoln, Rutherford, Caldwell, and Burke counties.[365] Beginning in November of 1842, Deacon Kidney began holding morning and evening services at Rutherfordton once a month. He reported that the fledging congregation only had two communicants.[366]

Meanwhile, in 1842, Bishop Ives visited "Wataga Valley" in Watauga County upon the recommendation of a botanist friend from New York. He named the area "Valle Crucis" (Valley of the Cross) for the shape made by the junction of three streams. Having a heart for missions and for spreading the Gospel of Jesus Christ, and seeing the vast need in the western regions of diocese, the bishop decided to use Valle Crucis as a base for training and sending missionaries to those regions. Shortly after his visit to Watauga County, the bishop established an "Associate Mission and Training School" at Valle Crucis, based on the model of the first associate mission that had recently been established in Nashotah, Wisconsin. The "ministry model" for the Valle Crucis mission included a classical school for the general education of the neighborhood boys, a "training school" for training those seeking "Holy orders" to be ordained as Episcopal lay leaders and priests, and a "mission" from which outlying churches could be established and maintained. One of the first candidates in the training school was Jarvis B. Buxton Jr.

Jarvis Barry Buxton Jr. was born on February 20, 1820, near Washington, North Carolina. Soon after his birth Buxton's father, the Rev. Jarvis Barry Buxton, Sr., moved his family to Fayetteville to take up the position of rector of St. John's Church. After Buxton's primary education, he was sent to school in Flushing, Long Island, where he studied under

Doctor Muhlenberg, founder of St. Luke's Hospital in New York City. He was prepared for college and, returning to North Carolina for his collegiate course, entered the State University at Chapel Hill. He graduated in 1839 and then, proposing to enter the ministry, became a student at the General Theological Seminary in New York, where he graduated in 1842.[367] Shortly thereafter, he began his training for Holy Orders at Bishop Ives' new diocesan school at Valle Crucis.

After sufficient training, in 1846, Buxton was appointed as head of the classical school at Valle Crucis. But in 1847 Bishop Ives quietly established (in conjunction with the mission) a monastic order called "The Society of the Holy Cross." He first asked Jarvis Buxton to be the "superior" in charge of the Order. But Buxton declined the offer, instead accepting a missionary post as rector of the fledging work at Rutherfordton. On the "Ninth Sunday after Trinity" (August 1, 1847) twenty-seven-year-old Jarvis Buxton was ordained a deacon in the Episcopal Church of North Carolina by Bishop Ives at the Valle Crucis mission. Deacon Buxton immediately moved to Rutherfordton to take up his new charge.

Deacon Buxton replaced the Rev. Lewis Taylor, who had been in charge of the mission at Rutherfordton since taking it over from Mr. Kidney in 1845. In his report to the 1848 Convention less than a year later, Deacon Buxton reported that the small congregation of seven at the Rutherfordton church had begun meeting for public worship in various places such as the courthouse and Female Academy, but had already contracted to have a church building constructed.[368] In the same report, he also tells the Convention that he has begun work in Asheville as well.

By May of 1849, the Rev. Buxton could report that not only was the new church building complete and ready for consecration, but the new congregation had also been "received into union with the Convention of the Diocese, under the name of St. John's Church."[369] And then, on June 17, 1849, Bishop Ives officially ordained Jarvis Buxton as "priest" at Rutherfordton.

A list of the delegates to the 1849 and 1850 Conventions gives the names of some of St. John's early church leaders: "Matthew W. Davis, Jason Carson, K. J. Williams, J. W. Calloway, F. J. Wilson, and B. H. Stammire."[370] Author James B. Sill notes that records show that other family names of those early members included: "Duffy, McDowell, Miller, Carrier, Britton, Twitty, Mills, Coxe, Davis, Ford and Shipp."[371]

St. John's at Rutherfordton, which had grown to nineteen communicant members, was finally consecrated on June 29, 1851, by Bishop Ives.[372] The Rev. Jarvis Buxton continued to provide ministerial services to St. John's along with his church planting work in Asheville. But concluding that Asheville would make a more strategic base for missionary work to the mountain regions, Buxton decided to establish his residence at Asheville. And by 1851, the Rev. Buxton was only spending "one-third' of his time at Rutherfordton, which he reported was "41 miles distant" from his Asheville residence. Not surprisingly, in 1852, the Rev. Buxton resigned his post at Rutherfordton. Buxton, with his experience at Valle Crucis and Rutherfordton, went on to establish the Ravenscroft Classical and Theological School at Asheville in 1854, and later the Ravenscroft Associate Mission and Training School.

For the remainder of the 1850s St. John's was ministered to first by missionary priest the Rev. R. H. Mason and then by the Rev. C. T. Bland. The Rev. Bland would later be the priest in charge of a number of other local churches, such as Leicester, Marion and Old Fort. But by 1859, the Rev. Buxton had to be called upon from Asheville to provide temporary ministerial oversight to St. John's. The Rev. Buxton was relieved by the Rev. John Tillinghast in 1861. Tillinghast remained at his post through the Civil War, but by 1868, St. John's had dwindled to only eleven communicants and was without any ministerial oversight. In fact, the church's 1868 parochial report was mysteriously signed, "REPORTED BY A LADY."[373]

Fortunately, the Ravenscroft Associate Mission, which was begun in Asheville by the Rev. Buxton in 1868, stepped in to provide ministerial oversight to St. John's. In 1872, the Rev. D. H. Buel was appointed principal of the Ravenscroft Associate Mission, and although he was able to provide steady oversight to the small congregation, his other duties and charges only permitted him to hold services at St. John's on a "fifth Sunday" of each month.[374]

In 1877, Mr. Edwin A. Osborne, an ordained deacon, was assigned the charge of Calvary Church, Fletcher (south of Asheville), as well as St. John's, Rutherfordton. However, both churches were still under the oversight of the Rev. Buel and the Ravenscroft Associate Mission. Buel explained the odd arrangement in his 1878 report of the Ravenscroft Associate Mission: "Since the first of November two stations of the Ravenscroft Mission have enjoyed the efficient and acceptable services of a Deacon, the Rev. E. A. Osborne, who resides at Calvary, Henderson County, and devotes three-fourths of his time to that Parish, and one-fourth to St. John's, Rutherfordton. but under the direction of the Bishop, I retain charge of these stations, as Presbyter, until Mr. Osborne shall take priest's orders, and I officiate statedly at both places [...] and on every fifth Sunday of the month at St. John's."[375] the Rev. Dr. Buel further reported that the bulk of the work at St. John's was done by Deacon Osborne, but, more importantly, Buel noted that "this Church has within the last two years lost heavily in communicants and members, and in financial ability by removals from the place."[376]

In the summer of 1881, the Rev. Osborne resigned his charge at Rutherfordton to concentrate on his missionary efforts "at Hendersonville and other points west of the Blue Ridge."[377] For the next few years, St. John's was left with no ministerial oversight, except for occasional visits by the bishop. Even the bishop acknowledged the sad situation: "This Parish has become very much weakened, and has been now for a long time, without any regular services. I have used every means to secure a supply, but thus far without any success."[378] And following the bishop's visit in September 1884, he was saddened to have to report, "I regret that this Parish is still destitute of any regular ministrations. The congregation has been so sadly reduced by deaths and removals that we have only a little handful remaining. Still it is most important that the witness of the Church should be maintained, and I trust brighter days may yet be in store for the Parish."[379]

Finally, in the fall of 1887, Bishop Lyman asked the Rev. E. A. Osborne to resume ministerial services to St. John's. The Rev. Osborne had several years earlier moved from Hendersonville to Charlotte to assume the leadership of the Thompson Orphanage. Osborne provided services to St. John's once a month in addition to his duties at the orphanage and his other missionary work. In 1888, the Rev. Osborne submitted the following report concerning the struggling congregation at St. John's: "There are only a few members here with their families, and they are doing what they can to maintain the services of the Church in their midst."[380]

The Rev. Osborne was replaced in 1889 by the Rev. Arthur N. Wrixon, who also had charge of the churches at Shelby and Tryon. The Rev. Wrixton held services at St. John's on each first and fifth Sundays of the month. He also established a weekday service on Wednesday afternoons, "so that there may be an opportunity — at least once a week for all to join in public worship."[381] Wrixton additionally held monthly services at St. Joseph's Chapel, six miles from Rutherfordton. St. Joseph's Chapel had been built on the Green River Plantation, former home of Joseph McDowell Carson. Carson and his family were among the founding families of St. John's, and it is reported that Joseph Carson provided the funding for the construction of St. John's in the early 1850s. St. Joseph's Chapel was built next to the family graveyard by Carson's daughter, Matilda Carson Thruston, as a memorial to her father and her only child (also called Joseph).[382]

The Rev. Wrixton was replaced in 1892 by the Rev. Girard W. Phelps. The Rev. Phelps served at St. John's for a few years, before being replaced around 1897 by the Rev. Charles J. Wingate. But in 1899, Col. Franklin Coxe, who had married Margaret Carson Mills, the granddaughter of Joseph McDowell Carson of Green River Plantation, completed a stone chapel "for the use of the mission."[383] St. John's Church was soon sold to the Lutherans, and its congregation transferred to the new stone chapel, named St. Francis.

St. John's Church is today the home of the Rutherford County Historical Society. A damaging fire in 2011 has left the church badly in need of repair.

Transylvania County

St. Paul's-in-the-Valley — three miles west of Brevard

This predecessor to St. Philip's was established in 1856 for a group of families from Charleston, South Carolina, who had built a permanent colony three miles east of the village of Brevard. Bishop Atkinson visited this new work in the summer of 1856 and was excited to report:

> I preached at Mr. Frank Johnston's, on the French Broad River. This congregation is a new and promising one, consisting mainly of gentlemen and their families from South Carolina, who have been attracted to the locality by its possession of such advantages, and so combined, of health, fertility, and magnificence of scenery, as I certainly have never seen paralleled elsewhere. The congregation differs from that at Flat Rock in that its members generally are, by birth, or have become, permanent residents of the State, instead of merely occupying summer homes in it. On this account, they of course offer better hopes of increasing the strength of the Church. During the past summer, they enjoyed the very acceptable and useful services of the Rev. Stuart Hanckel of South Carolina. They have determined to build a Church, which they hope to have ready for consecration if Providence should permit me to visit them again this ensuing summer or autumn.[384]

Francis Withers Johnstone, a native of Charleston, was one of a group of wealthy South Carolina low-country planters who had established summer residences in the mountains of western North Carolina in the 1850s. Most of these planters settled in Flat Rock, south of Hendersonville, but Johnstone and a few other families established mini-plantations further north along the banks of the French Broad River in what would later become Transylvania County. Johnstone built his modest one-and-a-half-story home, called "Montclove," around 1850. "The area did not have a plantation economy by any means, but some of the wealthier landowners did own slaves. Francis Johnstone of Montclove was one of the fifty largest slaveowners in western North Carolina and owned the most slaves in Transylvania County, with thirty-nine slaves and $70,000 in real and personal property."[385]

A parson from England, who in 1862 was visiting Frank's brother Andrew Johnstone at Flat Rock, gives us a contemporary account not only of Frank Johnstone but also of his vast estate and lands:

> Another brother, Mr. Frank Johnstone, lives about four miles up the river; he counts his domain by miles, not by acres. He is one of the handsomest and finest-grown men I ever saw; and I heard his sons and daughters were as fine as he. He raised a whole regiment of North Carolina, and some time served with it; but either from wounds or illness he was forced to take furlough. He is going to turn the river from its windings by a cut of a quarter of a mile, so as to make it shoot over an immense wheel for his mill. The American name for this river is "Zalika." I asked Mr. Johnstone how he did for a market? "Oh," he said, "the dealers come to me." He sells his corn at $1¼ per bushel; an acre yields from sixty to eighty bushels. I never saw neater fencing or better draining than at the farms at "French Broad." It is the garden of the mountains.[386]

The frame church was begun in 1856, and by the bishop's visit the following summer, he could report that "a Church was then nearly finished, and a site for a Parsonage had been given."[387] Meanwhile, the Rev. James Stuart Hanckel, an Episcopalian priest from Charleston, South Carolina, who summered in the region, became the officiating minister. Hanckel had built his summer residence, Chestnut Hill, close to Johnstone's Montclove. He officiated at morning services in Johnstone's carriage-shed and then at afternoon services held at the nearby Methodist campground.[388]

The progress on the building of the church was slow and thus the church was not completed and consecrated until April 28, 1860. The new church, named "St.-Paul's-in-the-Valley," was "open" for services from June until November each year, which was the season when most of communicants were in the area. Most of the colony would vacate their summer residences and move back to South Carolina in November for the winter months.

In 1859, the Rev. Hanckel accepted a professorship at the Theological Seminary in Camden, South Carolina, which required him to stay in South Carolina into June to finish the school term; it also required him to leave the church at the end of September to begin the fall term. In the summer of 1860, "the Rev. Mr. Lucas" covered the services from May until the Rev. Hanckel arrived in late June, and then the Rev. Mr. Porter officiated in October until the closing of the church in early November.[389] Despite these minor inconveniences, the new church thrived under the Rev. Hanckel's leadership. Hanckel was delighted to report in 1861, "Besides those reported, several residents attached to other Communions commune also with us. The number of occasional Communicants last Summer was also quite large. The attendance of visitors and of country people was also more numerous than ever before."[390]

However, just as the church was starting to flourish, the Civil War broke out, causing a major upheaval across the South. Although no major battles were fought in the region, the mountains of western North Carolina were not exempt from the ravages of war. The church struggled on for a few years, but by the end of the conflict little remained of the fledgling congregation of St. Paul's-in-the-Valley. The Rev. Hanckel gave the discouraging details of the demise of the church in his report to the 1864 Convention:

> A sad and I fear in great measure a permanent change, has occurred in this neighborhood since the Bishop's last visit [September 22, 1863]. It was so sudden and unexpected that it has been difficult to realize its extent even on the spot. Of the 13 Low-Country families, 7 have removed permanently; others are now absent, and their return (at least in several instances) is doubtful, and the probability is, that by the Fall not one will be left in this Valley. Of the 32 Communicants reported last year, 16 have certainly and permanently (and 10 more probably) removed. Six only remain. Within a fortnight our Church has been entered at night by robbers, and stripped of carpets, cushions, hangings, surplice, &c. The books alone were left. The Communion Service I had at my house.[391]

The colony was broken up and the church abandoned and the altar vessels and books were taken to Camden by the Rev. Hanckel for safekeeping.[392]

In 1873, the Rev. David Hillhouse Buel, who had just months before become principal of the newly formed Ravenscroft Associate Mission and Training School, visited St. Paul's during a visit to nearby Brevard (3 miles distant). A small group of church people in Brevard had requested that Episcopal services be resumed in the area. While helping to form a new congregation in downtown Brevard, the Rev. Buel and the bishop decided to revive St. Paul's-in-the-Valley. Assistant Bishop Theodore B. Lyman visited in the summer of 1874 and submitted the following report: "This is a very neat Church, and prettily situated in the Valley of the French Broad. Formerly there was a good congregation here in the summer, chiefly composed of families from Charleston. But since the war, only a small number reside in the neighborhood. No services had been held in the Church for ten years. The prospect is now good for reviving the congregation, if only occasional services can be provided. But thus far we have been unable to make the needed provision."[393]

For the ensuing decade, the parochial report for St. Paul's-in-the-Valley was written in conjunction with the church in Brevard. The church at Brevard, named St. Philip's, met in the courthouse for many years until a new church building was completed in 1885. At that time the remaining families of St. Paul's transferred their memberships to St. Philip's. No mention is made of St. Paul's-in-the-Valley in the journal reports after 1886.

Although St. Paul's-in-the-Valley is no longer in existence, its adjacent cemetery remains to this day along the Greenville Highway (US 276) and is under the perpetual care of the St. Philip's congregation.

St. Philip's — Brevard

The Rev. David Hillhouse Buel, who had just months before become principal of the newly formed Ravenscroft Associate Mission and Training School, first visited Brevard in 1873 upon the request of some parishioners who desired to establish a parish church in the town. An earlier church, St. Paul's-in-the-Valley, had been formed before the Civil War, three miles outside of the town.

A few months after the Rev. Buel's visit, Bishop Thomas Atkinson visited Brevard during his yearly visit to the western regions of his diocese. "At Brevard, a place I had never before visited, I met a good congregation, preached and administered the Holy Communion,"[394] reported the bishop to the 1874 Convention. It is surprising that Bishop Atkinson, who was so instrumental in spearheading the missionary endeavors to the western regions, and who had visited the area many times during the previous decades, had never before visited Brevard.

The Rev. Buel's first parochial report for Brevard was in 1874, when he reported having a congregation of three communicants. The subsequent reports over the next few years also included the communicants at St. Paul's-in-the-Valley Church, which the Rev. Buel had reopened. In 1875 Buel reported having eight communicants[395] for both churches, so we can assume that three communicants were at Brevard and five at St. Paul's.

For the next eight years the fledgling congregation at Brevard continued to meet in borrowed or leased spaces — sometimes at the Methodist chapel, sometimes at the Baptist church, and often in a hall at the courthouse. But finally, in 1883, the Rev. Buel was delighted to announce, "We are about to build a church in the village of Brevard which is three miles distant from St. Paul's in the Valley, and we hope by God's blessing to complete it during the ensuing year."[396] With the Rev. Buel's experience in building mission churches, it's surprising that he actually thought the church would be completed in a year!

Bishop Theodore B. Lyman laid the cornerstone of the new church on Tuesday, August 7, 1883, at five o'clock in the afternoon.[397] The church was being erected on a lot that had been donated by Mrs. Jane Hume, a recent widow.[398] Robert and Jane Hume originally moved to Transylvania County from Charleston, and were among the first members of St. Paul's-in-the-Valley. The Humes and the William Johnstone family were about the only families remaining when St. Paul's was reopened by the Rev. Buel in 1873. The Humes, whose home was originally in the Dunn's Rock area near St. Paul's, had since relocated to Brevard, following the burning of their home. Unfortunately, Robert Hume had passed away in September of 1880, just four weeks after being confirmed as a communicant member by Bishop Lyman.[399]

The progress on the construction of the new church was much slower than the Rev. Buel had predicted. But, although it would actually take eight years to fully complete the construction, by the summer of 1885 the congregation was able to begin using it for services. Bishop Lyman was to have officiated at the first service to be held in the new church on August 23, 1885. However, after arriving in Brevard with the Rev. Buel on Friday, following a harrowing ride from Cashiers, North Carolina, during which they were attacked by a swarm of yellow jackets, the Bishop received news of the sudden death of his daughter.[400] He departed immediately for home and left the Rev. Buel to officiate at the first service at the newly built church. The wood-framed church, with a seating capacity of 120 people, was named St. Philip's in homage to the historic St. Philip's Church in Charleston, which was the home church of the founders of the church at Brevard. At this time, the few remaining communicants at St. Paul's-in-the-Valley transferred their membership to St. Philip's. St. Paul's Church is no longer standing, but its adjacent cemetery remains and is still in use.

The Rev. Buel continued to provide ministerial oversight and monthly services over the next few years. In 1888, the Rev. William F. Rice, a Ravenscroft Associate Mission priest, took over as the minister-in-charge. Construction on the new church was halted due to lack of funds. But when Bishop Lyman visited in the summer of 1890 and observed the still unfinished state of the church, he decided to make a public appeal for help. By the next Convention, in the spring of 1891, the bishop was able to report that because of the generous gifts from interested individuals, "Valuable improvements are now going on under the special supervision of a Layman of the Congregation who is thoroughly skilled in all such work."[401] St. Philip's was officially consecrated by Bishop Lyman on Thursday, October 22,

1891, with the Rev. Edward Bradley and the Rev. Scott B. Rathbun assisting in the service.[402] The Rev. Bradley had been officiating at Brevard for a few months, but left the diocese shortly after the consecration. The Rev. Rathbun was the rector at St. John-in-the-Wilderness in nearby Flat Rock. Soon after the consecration and the departure of the Rev. Bradley, the bishop assigned the ministerial oversight of St. Philip's to the Rev. Rathbun, who continued in that capacity until the Rev. A. H. Stubbs took over in 1894. During these years, the lay leadership was assumed by Albert Jenkins. The Jenkins family had moved to the area in 1872 and had been some of the few remaining former members of St. Paul's-in-the-Valley.

The Rev. Alfred H. Stubbs was assigned as the warden of Ravenscroft in 1894. As warden, he was in charge of the Ravenscroft Associate Mission and Training School, taking over for the Rev. D. H. Buel, who had passed away in 1893.

The Rev. Stubbs was assisted at Brevard by veteran Ravenscroft missionary priest the Rev. W. F. Rice, who had served the church at Brevard in years past. In 1895, the Rev. Stubbs, who was overtaxed with the charges of the training school and other Ravenscroft mission churches, made an appeal[403] for a resident minister to come and live in Brevard and serve fulltime at St. Philip's and other nearby mission churches such as Bowman's Bluff and Etowah. The Rev. Stubbs knew that the railway would soon be extended to Brevard, and in his opinion, "It will make Missionary work here far more practical and effective."[404]

The Rev. Chalmers Durant Chapman was the result of the Rev. Stubbs' appeal. In 1896, the Rev. Chapman became the first resident priest at St. Philip's, arriving after having served pastorates in New Jersey. St. Philip's was now on the road to sustainability.

Although the wooden church of 1883 burned in 1925 and was replaced by a stone church in 1927, St. Philip's today is still located on its original property in downtown Brevard, and has an active and growing congregation.

Missions Miscellanea

FORKS OF THE PIGEON MISSION — CANTON

Among the numerous mission stations and churches established by the Ravenscroft Associate Mission and Training School, there are a handful of missions that were very short-lived and/or for which there are but scant records of their existence.

"The Forks of the Pigeon" is the original name for the area surrounding modern-day Canton in Haywood County. This is also the area recently made famous by Charles Frasier's novel *Cold Mountain*. "The Forks of the Pigeon" mission first shows up in the Convention journals in 1882, listed in the report of the Ravenscroft Associate Mission Stations within the parochial report for Grace Church, Waynesville: "Grace Church in the Mountains, Waynesville, Haywood County, with two Outlying Stations, Mica Dale and The Forks of the Pigeon."[405] The exact same entry appears for the next six years (last entry 1888), with no additional information about the mission. At that time the Waynesville church was also a mission of Ravenscroft and maintained by the Rev. Dr. David H. Buel (and later by the Rev. William Stanley Barrows).

Following the 1888 entry, there is no mention of "Forks of the Pigeon" until 1895. By that time, the Rev. Frederick W. Wey was the priest-in-charge at Grace Church in the Mountains at Waynesville. The Rev. Wey, a missionary priest, had recently been assigned to Grace Church by Bishop Cheshire. In his parochial report for Grace Church in 1895, the Rev. Wey included the following statement: "Besides the above services I went up the Pigeon river near Springdale, thirteen miles from Waynesville, where we have three communicants, to give them a service and administer the Holy Communion."[406] The "Springdale" community is a small community just south of Canton and is now called Cruso. This is probably the same location as the "Forks of the Pigeon" mission mentioned in the previous Ravenscroft reports. No further records of "The Forks of the Pigeon" mission appear after 1895. Although there is no direct link, author the Rev. James Sill, in his 1955 book, suggested that St. Andrew's Church in Canton, which was founded in 1906 by the Champion Fiber Company, may have had its foundational roots in the former mission work of the "Forks of the Pigeon."

RICEVILLE MISSION — EAST OF ASHEVILLE

The most mysterious of all the Ravenscroft missions was the mission at Riceville, just east of Asheville. There are spotty records spanning from 1871 to 1911 that show that a Ravenscroft Associate Mission church was established at Riceville, yet there is very little recorded of the actual families involved or of the number of services held.

The founding of Riceville goes back to the 1780s, when Joseph Marion Rice first settled along the banks of Bull Creek in what is now Swannanoa Township in Buncombe County. The settlement that grew up around Rice's farm was first known as "Bull Creek"—named for the creek, which was supposedly named for the buffalo that used to roam the area. Legend has it that Joseph Rice killed the last buffalo in the area in 1799.

Any discussion of the work of the Episcopal Church at Riceville must begin with its hometown boy, the Rev. William Francis Rice, who, as a Ravenscroft Associate Mission–trained missionary, was active as a deacon and priest in the early work of the Episcopal Church in western North Carolina.

"Billy" Rice was born in 1847 to John Longmire Rice and his wife Martha Roseanne Stephenson Rice, descendents of Joseph Marion Rice. Sometime between 1870 and 1875, Billy Rice met and married Margaret Henrietta Lindsay of nearby Haw Creek. The Rice family were mostly Presbyterians, but the Lindsays were devout Episcopalians, belonging to Trinity Chapel of Haw Creek, one of the earliest missions of the Rev. Jarvis Buxton and the Ravenscroft Associate Mission. The first published record of Rice as an Episcopalian was in 1875, when he was reported to be the Sunday school superintendent at Trinity Chapel, Haw Creek.[407] Shortly thereafter, Billy, who was a farmer by occupation, felt the call of God to the ministry and enrolled as a postulant at the Ravenscroft Associate Mission and Training School at Asheville in 1876.[408] Under the guidance of the Rev. Dr. David Hillhouse Buel at the training school, Billy not only received religious educational training but also gained practical experience as a missioner with the accompanying Ravenscroft Associate Mission.

However, the beginning of the Ravenscroft Associate Mission work at Riceville predates Billy Rice's call to the ministry. In 1871, Francis Murdoch, a native from Asheville being trained at Ravenscroft, presented the first (and only) parochial report for "Bull Creek Mission": "Services have been held here once a month since January 1st. A lot has been purchased

The Reverend William Francis Rice was one of the first local men to be trained for the priesthood at the Ravenscroft Associate Mission and Training School. The Rev. Rice served as a Ravenscroft missionary priest for almost 40 years (courtesy of Sybil Fox).

for a Church. As soon as funds can be collected, and a small Chapel built, a Sunday School will be opened."[409] Oddly, there are no subsequent reports ever submitted for "Bull Creek" or Riceville after this. However, a half-acre lot for a church was purchased from E. F. Clarke in 1871.[410] The lot was "about 100 yards from Clark's Mill" on the east side of Bull Creek Road, across from the old Stephenson family home, just north of the intersection of Shope Creek Road.

The only other record of the Riceville mission we have before 1914 is from 1889, when the Rev. Rice, in his parochial report for Beaverdam Chapel (where he was the minister-in-charge), reported, "The following is a list of the other places at which I hold services: At the Presbyterian Church near my home [...]."[411] The Riceville Presbyterian Church was very near the Episcopal property, and so it appears that whatever fledgling Episcopal congregation there may have been in Riceville, they were never able to organize and construct their own church building, and therefore any occasional services they may have held were held in nearby churches. The lot on Bull Creek Road was sold out of the diocese to Alfred Stephenson in 1911.[412]

GOOD SHEPHERD MISSION — TURNPIKE

"The Church of the Good Shepherd" mission was started around 1898 at Turnpike, North Carolina, on the border of Buncombe and Haywood counties in the Upper Hominy Valley.

The village of Turnpike was 15 miles west of Asheville and centered around a popular stop on the Western Turnpike. George Smathers established the Turnpike (Toll Road) stop in the early 1800s, and his son John Charles Smathers built a tavern at the stop in the 1860s. Prior to the coming of the railroad in the 1880s, "Smather's Hotel" was a popular noontime stop and overnight accommodation for patrons of the stagecoach lines. Then, with the arrival of the railroad, it became a popular station along the Ducktown branch of the Western North Carolina Railroad. A contemporary advertisement from the mid–1880s touted Turnpike's attractions: "It is frequented by visitors in the summer, and is certainly a very desirable place to linger at during the heated term. A fine spring of mineral water, recently discovered, adds to its many features."[413]

The mission called Good Shepherd, was located at Turnpike, on the western border of Buncombe County, adjacent to the Haywood County line. The small mission centered around the Capt. John Keais Hoyt family. Capt. Hoyt was born in Washington, North Carolina, but lived and worked in New York City before moving to Turnpike in the early 1880s. In an 1893 parochial report of St. Clement's Church, the Rev. George Bell reported that "Miss M. L. Hoyt is doing a noble work in that community." St. Clement's was another Ravenscroft Associate Mission church at Candler, which was only five miles from Turnpike. "Miss M. L. Hoyt," then a single woman aged 31 years old, was actually Marie Louise Brush, the stepdaughter of Capt. John K. Hoyt. Marie was the second-oldest daughter of Dr. Francis Vinton Brush and Mary Elizabeth Bensell.[414] In 1873, Mary divorced Dr. Brush,[415] who was an alcoholic, and later married Capt. Hoyt in Hoboken, New Jersey in 1877.[416] Capt. Hoyt, along with his wife Mary, stepdaughters Bell, Marie Louise, and Minnie, and daughter Mary Bricknell, moved to Turnpike in 1883. In 1885, Hoyt built his mansion, "Engadine," on land next to the Turnpike (Smather's) Hotel. Capt. Hoyt developed one of the first professional vineyard operations in this region. At the time of the 1893 report, Miss Marie Louise Brush was living at Engadine with her parents and commuting to St. Clement's. Miss Brush was probably the prime motivator for starting a new church at Turnpike in 1898, and no doubt was one of the few communicants of Good Shepherd.[417]

The Rev. A. H. Stubbs, who had assumed the leadership of the Ravenscroft Associate Mission in 1894, had charge of the small mission at Turnpike, with occasional assistance from missionary priest the Rev. W. F. Rice. The Rev. Stubbs recorded in his diary that on August 20, 1899, the Rev. William F. Rice officiated at the baptism of Alva Blanche Muse, the daughter of King and Mattie Muse, at the schoolhouse at Turnpike. "Marie Louise

Hoyt" is listed as the infant's sponsor.[418] Apparently the Ravenscroft priests were unaware that Marie's last name was Brush, not Hoyt.

The mission at Turnpike was so small that in the Rev. Stubbs' report to the 1901 Convention, it is listed as having only two communicants, and the Rev. Stubbs reported that he had only held five services at the mission from September 1, 1899, to September 1, 1900—the fewest number of services for any of the fourteen mission churches on the list.[419]

From what little records we have, it appears that Good Shepherd Mission, Turnpike, was in existence from about 1898 to about 1910. The 1910 census shows that Capt. Hoyt and his wife Mary, and their daughter Mary Bricknell, and Marie Louise had returned to the captain's hometown of Washington.[420] Capt. Hoyt died in Washington in 1912, and although his wife Mary returned to their home at Turnpike shortly thereafter, the church was never revived. Marie Louise Brush, who had moved to Washington with the family in 1910, never married and eventually moved back to Asheville and worked for many years as a nurse at Ottari Sanitarium. She bought a house at 530 Biltmore Avenue, where she later died at the age of 86 in 1954.[421]

ETOWAH MISSION — ETOWAH

Another short-lived Ravenscroft mission was at Etowah in Henderson County. The completion of the "Hendersonville and Brevard Railroad" in 1894 not only provided easier access to the Ravenscroft mission churches at Brevard and Bowman's Bluff, but also resulted in the opening of a mission church at Etowah, which was one of stops on the new rail line. The Rev. A. H. Stubbs would get off at the Etowah station when visiting the church at Bowman's Bluff, which was just three miles south of the station.

Records indicate that the Etowah mission was established sometime in 1899. Services were held in a schoolhouse at Oak Forest, which was a public school built around 1872. The school was located along the modern-day School Road, just across the highway from the present-day Oak Forest Cemetery.[422]

Apparently the congregation at Etowah was very small; in fact, during the mission's short lifespan there were never any communicant members. The 1901 report of the Ravenscroft Associate Mission stated that in the previous year (September 1899–September 1900), thirteen services were held at Etowah, but there were no baptisms, no confirmations, no marriages, no burials and no communicants![423]

Services were held regularly at Etowah beginning in 1899, but it was not until the September 7, 1902, service that "an offertory [was] received for the first time"[424] and the mission officially named St. Paul's. St. Paul's was maintained by the Rev. Stubbs and lay readers from Gethsemane Church at nearby Bowman's Bluff. Frank Valentine, an Englishman from Bowman's Bluff who also was a headmaster at Ravenscroft High School in Asheville, would often play the organ during services at St. Paul's. But by 1904, the mission at Etowah had been handed over to the Rev. R. N. Wilcox, rector at St. James in downtown Hendersonville. Sometime after 1906 the mission ceased to exist.

ST. JOHN'S–BUXTON MEMORIAL — ASHEVILLE

One final mission that remains a bit of a mystery is St. John's–Buxton Memorial Chapel in the city of Asheville. Its roots seem to stem from the work of the Rev. James H. Postell, a former Methodist minister who converted to Episcopalianism and became a Ravenscroft missionary priest in 1883. In 1884, the Rev. Postell reported that, along with his other assignments, he ministered to 15 families with 50 children in the "northern suburbs of Asheville." "I have great hopes of the work commenced in the northern suburbs of Asheville," reported Postell. "The people are a working class, intelligent, industrious and thrifty. They are anxious for us to commence preaching to them, which I hope we will be able to do in a short time. We have a hired room, and during the summer hope to be able to build a neat chapel."[425]

From all indications, this new work was in the "Doubleday Addition," which was one of the first planned suburbs of Asheville, predating Montford. This new community was developed in 1883 by General Ulysses Doubleday, who was a retired Civil War general and the younger brother of the famed General Abner Doubleday, the founder of the sport of baseball. Doubleday had moved to Asheville (for his health) in 1882 after a long career as a banker and broker in New York City.[426] In Asheville he went into the lumber and building business with a business partner named George F. Scott. In April of 1883, Doubleday commissioned civil engineer (and academy founder) S. F. Venable to draw up the official plat for his new community.[427] I suspect that Doubleday immediately began building spec houses on the lots, as the 1883–1884 Asheville City Directory records over twenty residents occupying houses in the "Doubleday Addition," which only contained forty-five lots. Just as the Rev. Postell observed, most of the new residents were of the working class.—their occupations, which were listed in the 1883 directory, were mostly carpenters, painters, laborers, and a number of "wagoners."

In 1885, after two years of trying to establish a church in the "northern suburbs," the Rev Postell sadly reported, "This section of Asheville has seventeen or eighteen Sunday School scholars, and for the want of Sunday School supplies the school went down, and I have failed from this circumstance to build a chapel there, as I expressed fully in my report to last Convention."[428] Oddly, the 1886 Convention journal index contains a listing for "Northern Asheville" on "page 82," but alas, there was no report or mention of "Northern Asheville"[429] on page 82 or anywhere else in the journal.

No further parochial reports can be found after 1885, and in fact the next reference to this work comes a decade later, when, in 1895, Charles Woolsey sold a portion of his lands, across East Street from his home ("Witchwood"), to the parties of George W. Pack, A. J. Lyman and Oliver Gideon for the purpose of erecting an Episcopal chapel. George W. Pack was a wealthy citizen and benefactor of Asheville, who had moved to this city in 1882 and built his mansion on the corner of Hillside and Merrimon Avenue. Augustus Julian Lyman, the youngest son of Bishop Theodore Lyman, was a prominent lawyer and real estate broker who also lived on Merrimon Avenue. Oliver Gideon was a carpenter who lived at 37 East Street[430] near the donated lot, which was on the northeast corner of the intersection of East and Hillside Streets.

In 1902, the three men listed on the 1895 deed, along with Charles Woolsey (the grantor on that deed), transferred the lot to the trustees of the Missionary District of Asheville.[431] By this time Charles Woolsey and A. J. Lyman, although still residents of the northern suburb of Asheville, were lay leaders at All Soul's Church in Biltmore Village on the southside of town.

In 1908, noted local architect Richard Sharp Smith was commissioned (by whom we don't know) to design a chapel for the lot. The drawings[432] show that the proposed chapel would have its main entrance and front facing west on East Street. The new chapel was to be one story with a raised basement, and was to be built of either all stone or a combination of stone and half-timbering with pebbledash stucco (Smith drew three different options, one of which even had a crenulated three-story bell tower). The drawings are all labeled as "St. John's Chapel," but the 1908 and 1909 Asheville City Directories refer to it as "St. John's–Buxton Memorial."

However, just a few years after the completion of the drawings, in 1913, the Diocese abandoned the project and decided to sell the vacant lot. Haywood Parker, then Secretary of the District Trustees recorded the particulars of the end of St. John's-Buxton Memorial Church in his report to the 1913 Convention:

> Mrs. Woolsey recently executed a deed to the trustees, releasing the lot on East Street, in Asheville, from the conditions and limitations contained in the deed by which that lot was conveyed to the trustees by the late Col. Woolsey. There were large assessments against this lot on account of street paving, sidewalks, etc., and as the trustees had no hopes of a church being built thereon at any time in the near future, and even doubted if it was a suitable location for a church, they decided to sell the lot, and have sold the same to Mr. Guthrie for $1,000.[433] Mr. Guthrie paid one-third cash, and executed notes secured by purchase money mortgage for the remainder.[434]

The Ravenscroft Associate Mission and Training School was responsible for much of the growth of the Episcopal denomination in the mountains of western North Carolina. And although many of the churches that they established are still active and growing congregations to this day, some, like the few mentioned above, were short-lived and many of their stories remain a mystery.

Timeline

1783	James Patton immigrates to America from Ireland.
1797	Asheville is incorporated and named for Governor Samuel Ashe.
1807	James Patton moves to Swannanoa, North Carolina.
1812	Joseph Roland Osborne is born in Haywood County, North Carolina.
1814	James Patton moves to Asheville and opens the Eagle Hotel.
1823	John Stark Ravenscroft elected first bishop of the Episcopal Diocese of North Carolina Church.
1828	The Buncombe Turnpike is chartered; Charlestonians establish a colony in nearby Flat Rock.
1830	The "Greek Revival" sweeps the country.
1831	Levi Silliman Ives elected second bishop of the Episcopal Diocese of North Carolina Church.
1842	A. J. Downing publishes *Cottage Residences*.
1845	Joseph Osborne purchases 73 acres from his brothers; Valle Crucis Mission is established in Watauga County.
1846	James Patton dies.
1847	Jarvis Buxton assumes the charge at Rutherfordton and begins ministering at Asheville.
1848	Joseph Osborne completes his brick mansion (author's estimate).
1850	Joseph Osborne's mansion appears in F. S. Duncanson's painting of Asheville.
1851	Architect Frank Wills' designed church for Trinity Episcopal Church is completed at Asheville.
1852	Bishop Ives resigns and Valle Crucis Mission closes.
1853	Bishop Atkinson elected third bishop of the Episcopal Diocese of North Carolina Church.
1854	Diocesan Convention votes to establish a classical and theological school at Pittsborough, but changes to Asheville; Joseph Osborne sells his property to William Patton.
1855	William Patton sells the Osborne property to Jarvis Buxton for a "Classical and Theological School."

1856	Ravenscroft Classical and Theological School opens under the direction of the Rev. Jarvis Buxton.
1861	The Rev. Lucien Holmes assumes headmastership of Ravenscroft School.
1864	Ravenscroft School closes because of the Civil War.
1868	Ravenscroft reopens solely as an associate mission and training (theological) school, with Headmaster Rev. George T. Wilmer.
1869	The Rev. Francis Murdoch replaces Wilmer as headmaster.
1872	The Rev. Dr. David Hillhouse Buel replaces Murdoch as headmaster.
1873	The Rev. Theodore Benedict Lyman elected assistant bishop of the Episcopal Diocese of North Carolina Church.
1880	Railroad arrives at Asheville.
1881	Bishop Atkinson dies, and Rev. Lyman becomes the fourth bishop of the Episcopal Diocese of North Carolina Church.
1883	Diocese of East Carolina separates from the Diocese of North Carolina.
1885	The Board of Fellows of Ravenscroft is established and the Diocesan Convention calls for the re-establishment of a "Classical School."
1886	Board of Fellows builds classroom/chapel building and a small two-story addition to Ravenscroft to fit it for a high school.
1887	Ravenscroft High School for Boys opens with Henry Axtell Prince as headmaster.
1888	Prince resigns and Haywood Parker assumes headmastership; Shoenberger Hall is completed as the new home of the Ravenscroft Associate Mission and Training School.
1889	Ronald MacDonald replaces Parker as headmaster of the Ravenscroft High School.
1890	Headmaster MacDonald's wife, Louise Blandy MacDonald, dies in their second-floor bedroom in Ravenscroft.
1891	Dr. D. H. Buel's wife, Mary Mayo Atkinson Buel, dies in Shoenberger Hall; Dr. Buel is totally incapacitated as head of the Ravenscroft Associate Mission and is replaced by Rev. W. S. Barrows.
1893	Dr. D. H. Buel dies at Baltimore in January; Rev. Joseph B. Cheshire elected as assistant bishop in June, and becomes fifth bishop of the Episcopal Diocese of North Carolina Church upon the death of Bishop Lyman in December.
1894	The Rev. W. S. Barrows resigns as head of Ravenscroft Associate Mission, and Bishop Cheshire appoints Rev. A. H. Stubbs to the new position of "warden of Ravenscroft Associate Mission and Training School," and a portion of Shoenberger Hall is rented to Mrs. Kepler for one year; Ronald MacDonald resigns as headmaster of Ravenscroft High School and is replaced by T. H. Toynbee Wight.
1895	The "Missionary Jurisdiction of Asheville" separates from the Diocese of North Carolina.
1896	Wight resigns and Frank Valentine becomes the new headmaster of Ravenscroft High School.

1898	The Rev. Junius Moore Horner is appointed the first bishop of the Missionary Jurisdiction of Asheville and moves into Shoenberger Hall.
1899	The title and covenants of the Ravenscroft property are cleared and the trustees build two new cottages and refurbish the old chapel into a cottage as well.
1901	Ravenscroft High School for Boys closes.
1902	Ravenscroft first opens as a boarding house; the Rev. Jarvis Buxton dies, and his daughter Mary opens their home as "Buxton Place."
1910	Trustees decide to subdivide Ravenscroft property and hire Biltmore Nursery to draw up a plat.
1911	Ravenscroft, now on Lot #27 of the new plat, is sold for $4,000 to Roger Lamson, Jr.
1912	Nellie Hyman buys Lot #28 and signs agreement to manage "The Belvedere" boarding house in the old Ravenscroft house; John and Elizabeth Roberts open the North State Fitting School in a portion of Buxton Place, with Thomas Wolfe as one of the first students.
1914	Six additional lots of the Ravenscroft property are sold; Roger Lamson, Jr., dies.
1919	Remaining lots are sold; Mabel Lamson, Roger's widow, sells Ravenscroft house to E. H. Luckett, while it continues operating as "The Belvedere."
1922	Missionary District of Asheville becomes the Diocese of Western North Carolina.
1924	The Rev. A. H. Stubbs dies at Shoenberger Hall.
1926	Buxton Hill removed, lowered and developed as a commercial subdivision.
1931	Lena Buckner assumes management of the Belvedere.
1933	Bishop Junius Horner dies at Shoenberger Hall.
1938	Buckner changes name of the Belvedere to "The Buckner Home."
1934	Bishop Robert Emmett Gribben elected second bishop of the Diocese of Western North Carolina and moves into Shoenberger Hall.
1943	W. H. and Nellie Nollman purchase Ravenscroft and open it as "Chateau Nollman."
1947	Bishop Gribben resigns and moves out of Shoenberger Hall, leaving it vacant.
1951	Junius and Laura Lee Horner purchase Shoenberger Hall and open it as "The Women's Exchange Gift Shop and Gay-Nineties Tea Room."
1966	Nollmans sell Ravenscroft to Asheville Acceptance Corporation, owned by Walter Deal.; Preservation Society of Asheville–Buncombe County is chartered.
1976	Laura Horner Fowler sells Shoenberger Hall property to Groves Printing, owned by Richard Whittington.
1977	State and local preservationists seek alternatives to demolition of Shoenberger Hall.

1978	Shoenberger Hall is demolished; David Black alerts state and local preservationists that Ravenscroft is threatened; National Register nomination submitted and approved.
1979	Preservation North Carolina's Historic Preservation Fund of North Carolina secures option on Ravenscroft, and then sells it to Dr. and Mrs. Stuart D. Tauber with protective covenants in the deed.
1980	Ravenscroft is restored and adapted into a professional office complex.
1981	Asheville City Council passes Ordinance #1213, declaring Ravenscroft a designated local historic property.
1995	Stuart Tauber sells Ravenscroft to MTM Investments.

Appendix
Chronology of Joseph Roland Osborne
COMPILED BY MARSHALL RAMSEY JONES

- September 5, 1812. Joseph Roland Osborne is born.
- January 18, 1840. John Osborne of Buncombe and Ephraim Osborne of Haywood buy 73 acres (less Methodist land) and including John Osborne's and J.M. Alexander's houses from J.M. Alexander for $3,000.00. October 23, 1840.
- John of Buncombe sells a young slave girl to Joseph Osborne for $200.00.
- 1840. Joseph does not appear on the Buncombe census.
- April 27, 1842. Andrew Jones of Buncombe executes a deed of trust to John of Buncombe for a debt owed to "F&M Patton" of Buncombe.
- April 28, 1842. Jones' deed of trust is recorded.
- 1842. Asheville Female Seminary is established.
- 1842. Andrew Jackson Downing's book containing the pattern for Ravenscroft is first published.
- November 1, 1843. Solomon King executes a deed of trust to Joseph of Buncombe for a debt owed to James W. Patton.
- November 6, 1843. King's deed of trust is recorded.
- January 11, 1844. (Haywood County) "This is to certify that Ephraim Osborne or his agent is at liberty to use our names with Polly Ann Edmonston in connection with his in any suit in law or equity or chancery which he may commence in the State of Tennessee to recover a five thousand acre tract of land in Shelby County [Tennessee] granted to John Strother and John Gooch on the waters of Wolf River. Signed N. Edmonston and Polly A. Edmonston. Witness: John Osborne of Buncombe."
- January 13, 1844. The Edmonstons' power of attorney is recorded.
- March 1844. Joseph Osborne purchases the 73 acres (less Methodist land) from John Osborne of Buncombe and Ephraim Osborne for $2,700.00, "including the buildings occupied by John Osborne."
- November 1, 1844. The bill of sale by John Osborne of the young slave girl to Joseph is recorded.
- February 23, 1845. J.M. Alexander's deed to John and Ephraim for the 73 acres (less Methodist land) is recorded.
- February 24, 1845. John and Ephraim's deed to Joseph for the 73 acres (less Methodist land) is recorded.
- October 6, 1845. Joseph Cordell executes a deed of trust to Joseph.

- October 6, 1845. Joseph sells Lot #1 in Asheville, at the north end of his 73 acres, to William Patton of Charleston and Ephraim Clayton of Buncombe for $250.00. This tends to establish that Joseph knew Ephraim Clayton, who was a sophisticated and prolific builder, and to whom the construction of Ravenscroft has been credibly attributed.
- October 10, 1845. Joseph's mother, Martha Roland Osborne, dies in Haywood County.
- October 25, 1845. E.H. Cunningham of Buncombe executes a deed of trust to Joseph.
- October 1845. Cunningham's deed of trust to Joseph is recorded.
- November 1, 1845. Joseph Osborne and James W. Patton buy five acres in downtown Asheville from Joseph M. Rice for an unstated consideration. Perhaps this includes the land on which the Patton & Osborne store stood just north of Aston Street on Biltmore Avenue (then called Main Street).
- February 4, 1846. Joseph Osborne's deed to William Patton and Ephraim Clayton is recorded.
- April 25, 1846. Rice's deed to Joseph Osborne and James W. Patton is recorded.
- November 2, 1847. Joseph Osborne sells a lot from the 73-acre tract near the Methodist church to James W. Patton for $75.00. This could be part or all of the land of the Presbyterian or Episcopal church.
- April 13, 1848. Joseph sells a lot from the 73-acre tract to John Lyle of Washington County, Tennessee, for $350.00. This might also be church land.
- May 31, 1848. Joseph's deed to John Lyle is recorded.
- October 30, 1848. Joseph's deed to James W. Patton for the $75.00 lot is recorded.
- October 16, 1850. W.W. Davis executes a deed of trust to Joseph Osborne for a debt owed to E.H. Cunningham.
- 1850. Joseph appears on the Buncombe census.
- 1850. Ravenscroft appears on the Duncanson painting.
- February 22, 1851. (Haywood County) "R. Osborn, Thomas Osborn and Joseph Osborn pay $1,040.96 to Ephraim Osborne for a male slave. Witnessed by E.M. Osborne and W. Osborne."
- October 9, 1851. After public sale, Joseph conveys the land covered by W.W. Davis' deed of trust to W.W. Davis.
- October 9, 1851. Davis' deed of trust to Joseph is recorded.
- July 1852. Ephraim's bill of sale for the male slave to R. Osborne, Thomas Osborne and Joseph Osborne is recorded.
- October 2, 1852. Joseph Osborne and James W. Patton convey part or all of the five-acre tract near the "College" (Asheville Female Seminary, which at some point changed its name to Holston Conference Female College, then to Asheville College, then to the University of North Carolina at Asheville) and near the "Stewards Hall" for $150.00 to the "Trustees of the Holston Conference Female College ... for the purpose of founding, carrying on and perpetuating a Female college to be under the control, patronage and management of said Conference.... If the said Conference shall cease to use the property aforesaid for the purpose of Female education as aforesaid and shall withdraw their patronage, the said land shall be held by the Trustees above named for the benefit of the Citizens of Asheville & Vicinity to be used by the for educational purposes as they may deem proper." This land was located at the corner of Oak and Woodfin and a large dormitory was erected there in 1856. The Holston Conference Female College closed during the Civil War, but reopened afterward and the dormitory building was used as a boarding house for faculty members. In the late nineteenth century, it ceased to be used directly for education and was operated as a hotel, which failed. In 1899 it was reopened as a hotel and christened "The Oaks," which also failed. It was reopened again in 1908 as a hotel and christened the "Cherokee Inn."

ASHEVILLE FEMALE COLLEGE. Around 1850 or 1851 this college was established on the land now bounded on the north by Woodfin, on the east by Locust, on the south by College and on the west by Oak. Part of it is used as a hotel and the remainder is now the high school's property. At first it was Holston Conference Female College, but was afterward known as the Asheville Female College, and subsequently as the Asheville College for Women. It prospered and had a large patronage from the start under the presidency of Dr. John M. Carlisle, Dr. Anson W. Cummings, Dr. James S. Kennedy, Dr. R. N. Price, Dr. James Atkins, and Mr. Archibald Jones.

- November 3, 1852. Joseph Osborne buys 20 acres on the Swannanoa River from William Patton of Charleston for $507.50.
- October 14, 1853. Joseph Osborne purchases several large tracts on the Swannanoa River at a public court sale for $7,550.00.
- October 15, 1853. Joseph Osborne sells the large Swannanoa River tracts purchased the day before to William Patton of Charleston for $7,550.00.
- October 31, 1853. Joseph Osborne purchases a one-half interest in the large Swannanoa tracts from William Patton for $5,500.00.
- December 26, 1853. Henry Carter Massey and Martha Jane Osborne are married.
- January 14, 1854. Joseph Osborne sells two tracts, consisting of one 2½-acre tract just south of the Methodist land, and one 13½-acre tract just south of the 2½-acre tract, for a total of 16 acres. This land must have come from the original 73-acre tract. The sale was to William Patton of Charleston for $5,500.00. The lower of the two tracts included the land on which Ravenscroft stands. Unfortunately, the deed does not specifically mention the brick house. However, as noted above, the brick house had previously appeared on the Duncanson painting of 1850, which was painted during Joseph Osborne's ownership.
- January 1854. Joseph's deed to the Ravenscroft tracts is recorded.
- February 1854. William Patton's deed to Joseph for the half interest in the large Swannanoa tracts is recorded.
- March 1, 1854. Joseph Osborne sells a lot remaining from the 73-acre tract, near Cordell's, to James W. Patton for $100.00 "Reserving this, that the Spring is to be enjoyed by the lot holders adjoining and the citizens generally, but it is understood that when it is abused and not used properly, the said J.W. Patton shall have the right to prohibit the use of it to any such person or persons."
- March 1854. Joseph's deed to the Spring lot is recorded.
- March 31, 1854. The court's deed to Joseph for the large Swannanoa tracts is recorded.
- March 31, 1854. Joseph's deed to William Patton for the large Swannanoa tracts is recorded.
- July 13, 1854. Joseph sells 47 acres, possibly including part of the original 73-acre tract, and possibly including the 20-acre Swannanoa tract, for $210.16 to James W. Patton. Although the price is suspiciously low, this is apparently a genuine transaction, as it was promptly recorded. It is possible that the transaction also settled a debt that was not mentioned, or the consideration was figured to balance a division of assets.
- July 24, 1854. Joseph's deed to the 47 acres is recorded.
- October 7, 1854. Joseph supposedly sells one acre from the original 73-acre tract, near the Spring lot, to William L. Hilliard for $4,000.00. If this was fair market value, no doubt it contained at least one building. What is suspicious is that the deed was not recorded until 13 years later, three years before Joseph's death in 1870 and long after he had moved to Tennessee. Did Joseph or his family ever get the $4,000.00?
- November 11, 1854. Joseph Osborne sells a lot from the original 73-acre tract, near Ephraim Clayton and William Patton's lot, for $230.80 to Edward Hughes of Buncombe.
- February 8, 1855. Joseph purchases a lot near the Methodist church from James W. Patton for $125.00.

- February 8, 1855. Joseph sells the lot purchased that day from James W. Patton to John W. Willson for $225.00.
- February 24, 1855. Patton's deed to Joseph for the $125.00 lot is recorded.
- February 24, 1855. Joseph's deed to Willson for the $225.00 lot (same lot) is recorded.
- March 31, 1855. Joseph Osborne and William Patton supposedly sell the large Swannanoa tracts to John H. Murphy of Buncombe for $14,000.00, with $7,500.00 to Joseph and $6,500.00 to William Patton. However, the deed is not recorded until 29 years later, 14 years after Joseph's death in 1870, and it does not bear Joseph Osborne's original signature.
- July 1855. Joseph's deed to Edward Hughes for the $230.80 lot near Clayton and Patton's lot is recorded.
- January 17, 1856. Joseph sells a lot from the original 73 acres on Second Street to Thomas Goodlake of Buncombe for $500.00.
- January 18, 1856. Joseph's deed to Goodlake is recorded.
- January 31, 1856. Joseph marries Penelope Lucretia Twitty in Asheville. R.H. Chapman performs the ceremony.
- January 1856. Joseph prepares a summary of the debts, dating back to 1840, of John M. Kinzy to "Patton & Osborne," totaling $446.82 including interest. This may represent a division of the assets of Patton & Osborne, but previous research led me to conclude that the Patton & Osborne store changed to Patton & Summey closer to 1850. The debts appear to be business debts rather than for dry goods.
- July 1856 (approximately). Joseph Osborne and his pregnant wife Penelope travel to John Osborne's near Germantown in Shelby County, Tennessee.
- October 9, 1856. Joseph supposedly sells a small strip of land from the original 73 acres to Erastus Rowley for $1.00. However, the deed is not recorded until 29 years later, 15 years after Joseph's death in 1870.

NEWTON ACADEMY. From 1797 to 1814 the Rev. George Newton taught a classical school at this place [Newton Academy] which was famous throughout several States.[7] Mr. Newton was a Presbyterian minister, reported to the Synod at Bethel Church, South Carolina, October 18,1798, as having been received by ordination by the Presbytery of Concord (Foote's Sketches on North Carolina, 297). He lived on Swannanoa until 1814, when he removed to Bedford county, Tennessee. There for many years he was principal of Dickson Academy and pastor of the Presbyterian church in Shelbyville, and there he died about 1841.[7] "At that time there was a building which had been used for church and school purposes, known as Union Hill Academy. The house, which was a log one, was removed and in 1809 a brick house took its place. In the same year its name was changed to that of Newton Academy."[8] Here for many years the people resorted to preaching and sent their children to school, and buried their dead. In 1857 or 1858 the brick building between the present academy and the grave yard was removed and the brick academy now there was erected. (See Clayton v. Trustees, 95 N. C., 298.)

DR. ERASTUS ROWLEY. "The old Newton Academy was the only institution in the county which, up to 1840, had ever been dignified with as big a name as that of Academy. This was a very old structure when I first entered it in 1844. Dr. Erastus Rowley taught here that year. The house was a very long one and rather wide — one story, divided into two rooms — one very long room and one small one. It was built of brick and stood on the top of the knoll some distance above where the present one stands. Many of the older men of this section received their education at this widely known institution and its fame has always been almost co-extensive with that of Asheville."[9]

> 7. Asheville Centenary. NOTE. Newton Academy is on the east side of South Main Street, Asheville, and nearly opposite the Normal and Collegiate Institute.

8. From Judge S. C. Pritchard's address before Normal and Collegiate Institute, 1907.
9. "Reminiscences" of Dr. S.S.T. Baird, 1905.

- October 26, 1856. Joseph's son Joseph is born in Asheville.
- February 27, 1857. Joseph arrives in Shelby County, Tennessee.
- February 28, 1857. Joseph writes:

> Shelby County, Tennessee 28 Feb 1857
>
> My dear wife,
>
> I arrived here on yesterday, so you see it took me longer to come than we expected. Although the staging has been reduced by one half since we traveled the road, yet owing to the state of the road, it takes longer to pass over it now than it did last summer. We did not travel any at night, so as we had much walking to do, we could see to pick our way through the muck. I was pleased to hear the president of the company say that the entire connection would be made by the first of April. Then, we can pass in short time.
>
> I am now at brother John [Morrison Osborne, Sr.]'s where I shall remain a few days. I will go down to Memphis, I suppose, on Monday and see the great Mississippi once more. The weather has been very warm since I left there, and yesterday was like a summer day; the peach trees in bloom, and the oak timber will be budding out and showing leaves if this weather remains one week longer. Brother John's family are all well and have a very comfortable place a little farther from Germantown than where they were last year. I have seen all the family except Emily [Matilda Osborne]; she is at school. Not yet been to Mr. [Henry Carter] Massey's. Alice [Massey Osborne] is looking quite well and talks aplenty; frequently speaks of your sisters. Says that she would have been highly pleased to have seen you. She has made many inquiries after you and the dear little babe. She is still as kind as ever.
>
> Our dear little Jose and wife, how often I have thought of you I can't tell. I feel that it has been a long time since we parted. I hope that your health is still improving and you will soon be quite well. You must not get low spirited but keep up. Look at our dear little laughing boy, how sweet he is, and good. And growing so finely. Should be calculated to keep up your spirits and make you cheerful. I hope you will go down to brother Thomas [Osborne]'s and spend some time if you think well of it. I feel there they will do all they can to make your visit pleasant. Do take sister Lou[isa Jane Twitty McDowell] and the Doctor [William Joseph "Joseph" McDowell]'s advice in taking anything that would be of benefit to your health. I feel sure they will be kind and do everything they can for you. It was a hard trial for me to leave for as long a time and I feel there you will miss me but you know it was strictly necessary for me to come out here.
>
> I know nothing as yet what my movements will be but will in a few days, and then will write you again. You must write me about what Harriet [Elizabeth Osborne] says about our little babe and tell her she must help you to nurse it while I am gone and say to her that a gentleman of no particular age [Walter Franklin Lenoir] was making very earnest inquiries as to who the young lady was who had just arrived from the west. I think he will lay by the old beaver for a while. See if he does not. Sister [Elizabeth Elvira Jones Osborne] was just asking me if I was writing to you. I told her I was. She says give her love to you and say that she would have been glad to have seen you and the little babe here. She is a kind, good woman. Well now my dear I must close and will promise to try to make my next more interesting. I will think of you often and will think the time long before I see you and our dear little blue eyed babe. It seems I can almost see him now as he looks when laughing. You must all take care of the little babe and Sister Lou[isa Jane Twitty] must take care of you. I shall look for a letter from you every few days. Give my love to all our friends there. Your affectionate husband,
>
> J.R. Osborne
>
> You must not forget me when you offer up petitions to our Heavenly Father. Tell Violet she must be obedient and take good care of the little babe and she must have some little present

when I come home. I had almost forgotten to tell you to kiss our little boy for me at least one dozen times a day and talk to him about me. I know you will. Has sister Ellen found her trunk? They are planting corn in this country now.

- March 4, 1857. George W. Shackelford executes a deed of trust for a female slave to Joseph to secure a debt owed to "Patton & Burgin."
- March 22, 1857. Joseph writes:

    Shelby County, Tennessee, 22nd March 1857
    My dear dear wifie,

    Yours dated the 15th came to hand in due time. I wrote you on the 17th in answer to yours of the 8th and 11th and this beautiful morning I will devote some time in writing to my dear one far away. You don't know how much pleasure it gives me to read your letters. I had a hope from your last that your health is improving and that you will soon be quite well and how I love to hear you talk of our dear little boy. Bless his little self. Kiss him for his papa. How I would like to see you and him. It seems a very long time since I left you but you may be sure I think of you often and have not yet forgotten how our dear little laughing boy looks. Methinks I can almost see him. Don't you suppose that you could deceive me with some other little one as you seem to think. You say you hope I will soon get through so I can come back to my lonely wife and little boy that any place is lonely without me. I am satisfied that you are with kind friends but it is not like being with those we love dearly. I can and fully appreciate your feeling and sympathize with you for I feel today that there is a dear one absent. I feel lonely and very often cast my mind back to where I left my dear ones and if it was consistent with my business here I would soon join them there again providence permitting. You ask me to write when you may look for me. You may be sure it would be one of the happiest moments for sure to be able to write you the day I would start home to be with my dear ones but I am sorry that I can't say yet as to when I can leave. I still think that I shall be able to accomplish in a good degree the objects of my visit here. I was perfectly satisfied when I parted with you that I could not get back in so short a time as you seem to give me. There is no use to go back and leave my business half done so as to incur the expense of another trip. I want to be done with it and now my dear let me assure you I will do all I can to hasten back for I want to get back perhaps quite as badly as you wish me, for you know I am not the one to be from home and never will be unless it is strictly necessary. I am not yet decided about going to Arkansas but I guess I had not better wait until you get ready to. So write me if so we would best begin soon. I am much obliged to Dr. McDowell naming the farm that is to be sold there but I think I will not give any directions about it. If when I return we have any inclinations to settle there (which I think uncertain) we will look around and see if we can find a place to suit our fancy. I would think well if you could hire a vehicle and ride frequently. It would be of great service to you, and now spring seems to have set in you can take your evenings and mornings walk with little Soney. It will be good for you both. How I am delighted to hear that Soney is growing so fast. I don't think tea good for him if you mean stone tea. Tell Violet I have not yet raked off any bowls or pitchers but often think of little Soney when lying in bed if he is watched as close as he was when I was there. Tell her that she must take good care of Soney as I gave him to her to nurse and not to let him trouble you and I hope she will not allow Miss Betsy to be troubled much at night. Write me if his hair is growing and if black. Give my love to the family. I will write you again soon my dearest and may heaven's blessings rest upon you.

    Your devoted husband J.R. Osborne

    I will expect to get a letter from you this evening.

- March 23, 1857. Joseph writes (only fragment of letter remains):

    I have been thinking about your suffering from heartburn and may it not be caused in some degree from the too free use of water while you are eating. Talk to Dr. McDowell about it. You know that you will sometimes drink as much as two glassfuls of water for dinner and eat scarcely anything and then repeat it at supper and breakfast. Now think of it my dear and suppose you leave off the use of it as much as you can for a few times and see how you feel afterward. I think if you will try it for a few days you will find your appetite better and instead of water use porter if not to be had there get someone to send to Knoxville for one or two dozens and use it freely. I feel anxious about you and hope your health will improve. Let me hear from you after you have tried it a few days. I hope to make my next letter more interesting. Will write you again in a few days.

- March 24, 1857. Joseph writes:

    Shelby County, Tenn. 24 Mar. 1857
    My Darling Wifie,

   Yours dated the 18th inst. came to hand in due time and on the 22nd I answered yours of the 15th. I now hasten to answer your last. I am truly sorry to hear that your health is no better and perhaps not so well. My dear it places me in an awkward predicament to see you write in such low spirits. Of course I have great uneasiness about you, fearing you may get worse. I scarcely know what to be at from the way you write. It seems that you will be looking for me you say this week. My dear I would not be here one day longer if I did not think it was for the interest of you and our dear little one. Then I know it is for you that I am absent. Before I left there I tried to make the impression on your mind that I could not return half so soon as you seem to think. If however your health is decidedly worse and you should so inform me I will leave my business and return at once. My duty, first of all is to be with and take care of you and our dear little one. More especially when you are sick. And I would not allow anything to prevent me being with you when you are sick or in trouble, and let me repeat what I have written before that I may be well understood. If you think I ought to return on account of your health being worse write me so and I will start at once, but if I go now I leave my business undone and would return here to look after it again so soon as I could find you well enough so I could leave you. This I wish to avoid. I wish to finish all before I leave here, so I may not have to leave you and our dear little one again soon. If I am to be happy it is to be at home with those I love.

   I feel sad today to think I am so far from my dear ones and them sick. What to do I know not but for the present I must bear it hoping by the next letter I get from you will bring me better news. That you and little Soney are both out walking and riding this beautiful weather and both feeling much improved. With regard to weaning Soney I would not advise it unless you should find it strictly necessary for you might find trouble in doing so in drying up the little milk that you have. I was just talking with Martha about it and she says that you will have to be very careful or your breasts will become sore, that hers gave her great pains and had to be lanced and she feels so uneasy for fear that you might undertake to wean the babe and have sore breasts, that she sends you a receipt which she asked me to copy but I will send it as it is.

   Think of what I wrote you in my last about the use of so much water while you are eating. Try to abandon the use of it as much as you can for a few days and see if you will not be rid of the heartburn and have more appetite. And anything that you may fancy that you could eat, don't spare pains or money in procuring it. I am sorry now that I had not left you more but I know you can get anything you may desire if in the country. Now my dear I hope you will write me in answer to this that you have much improved and that I must remain here until I have finished my business so I will not have to leave my darling ever again soon. Don't quit writing until I tell you. Your letters come to me very quick now in about three days. Give my love to Sister Lou and tell her she must have you out walking a little every day when it will suit. May heavens blessing rest upon you and our little one.

   Your Devoted Husband J.R. Osborne

   Tell Violet that I am glad to hear that she has got little Jose so fat — that she must keep him so until I come.

   Sister and Martha send their love to you. They seem to sympathize with you and make many inquiries after you and our darling little one. All is very well with them. We now seem to have spring in earnest. The trees has taken a fresh start to put out their leaves in earnest since the warm weather. Martha says she can't send much word that would interest you unless something about the poultry. Would that she has gathered about ninety dozens of eggs this spring and has a great many young chickens. She says that she must try and raise enough to spare the rouges some.

- March 1857. Shackelford's deed of trust for the female slave is recorded.
- April 17, 1857. Joseph writes (only fragment of letter remains):

My darling I am so fearful that the use of that horrible practice using snuff is injuring you that I don't know what to do about it. You know how I object to it and there is nothing that I would not do for you if you would just abandon it at once. Let me make a bargain with you that I quit the use of the horrible stuff if you will. Say if you will my dear wifie. And to begin when you get this. Let me know my darling how you get on without it in your next. Look at that sweet little babe and for his and my sake and the sake of your health try it. I feel a deep interest in the restoration of your health and let us try in every way that the use of the stuff is injurious to I have not a doubt.

- April 23, 1857. Joseph writes:

Shelby County Tenn. 23d April 1857
My Darling Wifie,

Yours dated the 15th inst came to hand in due time and I wrote you I believe on the 17th or 18th and not mailed until the 19th. I told you in that I thought in my next I would let you know what time I would start home. Now my darling wifie you have been so good not to complain of my absence more than to wish my return, that if I should remain three of four days longer than I expected than when I last wrote you, that you will bear with me. I tell you that if I could only leave this day to meet my dear little family it would be a happy moment in my life. I know you have had a trial in taking care of our darling little boy and that too in such a bad state of health. My absence from you so long is to try and better the condition of you and our darling little one. So my darling help me to bear my trouble. You can do much in that way. Yes you will and then I hope we will again very soon be permitted to see each other. I now think that I will leave for home on next Monday or Tuesday the 27th or 28th and I would like to make a little stop in Chattanooga on my way. I was in Memphis on Tuesday the 21st. The little boy was still low, very much reduced, but clear of fever and with good nursing he may perhaps get well, but I regard it as doubtful if he will recover.

The apples is nearly all gone. I fear I shall not be able to bring any but if to be had I will certainly do so. It has been so cold here all throughout April up to this time that we have had fire nearly all the time. The farmers are very much out of heart about their crops. Some are plowing up and planting over.

Well I hope soon to see you and our darling little Soney bird. You can't imagine how much I wish to see him. It is just two months this day since I left you and I can still almost see him in imagination. Kiss the dear little one for his papa a dozen times. How I love to hear you speak of him growing and doing so well. I hope his little ear is well by this time. You must take good care of yourself and try and keep up in good cheer and I will soon be there. I will not ask you to write any more now. You have been so good to write all the time that it will bring me in debt. I guess I will write you again before I reach there. May you and our dear little one be preserved is the prayer of your devoted

Husband J.R. Osborne

- April 26, 1857. Joseph writes:

Shelby County Tenn. 26th April 1857
My darling Wifie,

My last to you was on the 23rd and yours last received was dated the 15th inst. This morning our darling little boy is just six months old and it has been the rise of two months since I left him. How I would love to be with you and him today. But if I am not there in person, I am there much in mind. I just thought I would write you a few lines this morning my darling and tell you of my movements. I intend to go down to Memphis in the morning and start for home from there. I wrote you that I hoped to start on Monday or Tuesday, but if I should see any reasonable probability of accomplishing anything in by business it seems to me that I ought to remain even until the middle of the week as much as it would be against my inclination. I never in all my life felt so anxious to get on my journey home. I don't know what to do with myself. But I feel that I should do all that I can. Then if I do nothing I will be satisfied that I have done my duty to you. What troubles me most is that I am away from you and your health so bad I know it is my duty to be with you to try and doctor you up and to relieve you with our darling little babe. But I feel sure that you are much relieved by the kind assistance of our dear friends. If I had not been satisfied of this I would have been there long since regardless of my business. Well I will surely take my leave (if well) in the morning and go to Memphis and will see there if I can accomplish anything. You see I could not do anything on account of the sickness of the negroes. The little boy is improving slowly, able to sit up very little. I thought perhaps that he might get up by the middle of the week so I could do something is the reason why I think it may be best for me to remain a day or two longer, for if I go off and leave them just so I doubt if ever I receive anything for them. Now my dearest, believe and think and say that your husband is trying to do the best he can and kiss our precious little Soney many time for his papa. I will write you again if I don't start in a day or two. So don't be looking until I tell you. I fear I shall not get any more letters from you until I see you. Give my love to all our friends and may you be protected and taken care of is the prayer of your husband

J.R. Osborne

This is the only paper I had. It is raining today and seems a little like spring.

- May 1857. Joseph returns to [East Tennessee]?
- May 19, 1857. Cassius Faulkner Osborne writes:

  Dear Uncle,

  I was pleased to learn from your letter of the 12th inst that you had reached your family in good health, and finding those so dear to you in an improving condition. Our friends here are usually well. Nothing new or wondrous I believe since you left. Pa [John Morrison Osborne, Sr.] has been gone to Paris [Tennessee] about eleven days. He expected to return tomorrow or next day. He told me when he left to be ready when he got back to start to E.T. with these negroes. They are doing very well at this time. I think they have all improved since they were brought home. The second boy (Bill) has been a little unwell a few days but is about well again.

  The weather is still unfavorable to crops, cold and wet; tolerable stands of cotton, though there is a probability of a good deal of it dying. There was a very destructive hail storm past near Collierville a few days since.

  I cannot tell when I will start yet till Pa returns. I will hurry all I can, and write you again.

  Your Nephew
  C.F. Osborn[e]

- July 18, 1857. Joseph purchases one acre adjoining his own line and Smith's for $125.00 from Charles Moore.
- July 18, 1857. Moore's deed to the $125.00 lot is recorded. This would appear to be the purchase of a lot for a new house for the young family.
- August 20, 1857. Joseph's young son dies.
- December 7, 1857. Joseph writes:

  Germantown 7th Dec. 1857

My darling wifie,

Yours dated the 27th and 30th inst both came to hand the same time. I was becoming very anxious to hear from you. Your first spoke of being unwell but I hope you was not much sick and now quite well. Your letters was so good that they was of great service to me as I was a little unwell. But I am now feeling pretty well and looking after my business. I hope to accomplish something in a very few days. I will do or not soon and leave here. I have been all the time at Mr. Massie's and Robert Love has been here with me a few days. Today he and Brother John goes over the river to return tomorrow and when they return I will know more of my business. Love wants me to go with him to Arkansas but I do not know or even think seriously of it. After a few days, I will know more then I will write you. I do hope my dearest that you are enjoying yourself and have good health . I suppose you are now at Brother Thomas.' I am away from you greatly against my will. I will so arrange my affairs that I can be with my dear wife and how my thoughts run to our darling little one that I used to love to write about so much but happy little one he so much better off than we are. Write me in your next if you have heard of anything from North Carolina since we left. Martha has been quite unwell the last few days but better now. All send their love to you, and now my dearest try and be as content as you can and I promise your old man will not stay away any longer than he is obliged to and write me as soon as you get this. And give my love to all our friends. I don't know where you will be when I return, at the Doctor's or Brother T's. Think of your husband far away and pray for your devoted husband.

J.R. Osborne

- July 7, 1858. Walter Franklin Lenoir and Hattie Elizabeth Osborne are married.
- October 2, 1858. Joseph's son Edward Chapman Osborne is born.
- September 21, 1859. Joseph Osborne and James W. Patton's deed for the Female College is recorded.
- July 27, 1860. Joseph's daughter Mary is born.
- May 26, 1862. Joseph's daughter Clara Innis Osborne is born.
- July 3, 1864. Joseph's daughter Mary dies.
- November 9, 1864. Joseph's daughter Delia Massie Osborne is born.
- May 14, 1866. Joseph's son George Roland Osborne is born.
- September 1867. Joseph's deed for the $4,000.00 lot to Hilliard is recorded. It does not appear to bear Joseph's original signature.
- September 7, 1868. Joseph's son Frank Lenoir Osborne is born.
- March 10, 1870. Joseph dies in Tennessee and is buried in Old Sweetwater Baptist Church cemetery between Sweetwater and Philadelphia, Tennessee.
- 1870. Joseph's widow Penelope is listed on the Monroe County, Tennessee, census as owning no real estate and only $700.00 in personal property.
- June 16, 1884. Joseph Osborne's and William Patton's deed to the large $14,000.00 Swannanoa tracts is recorded. The deed does not bear Joseph Osborne original signature.
- April 29, 1885. Joseph's deed for the $1.00 strip of land to Erastus Rowley is recorded. It does not bear Joseph's original signature.

Chapter Notes

Preface

1. Norman Tyler, Ted J. Ligibel, and Ilene Tyler, *Historic Preservation: An Introduction to Its History, Principles, and Practice* (New York: W. W. Norton, 2009), 15.

Chapter One

1. From information submitted to Old Buncombe County Genealogical Society by Dr. Helen Patton — see http://www.obcgs.com/patton.htm.
2. F. A. Sondley and Theodore F. Davidson, *Asheville and Buncombe County* (Asheville, NC: Citizen Company, 1923), 144.
3. See David Coleman Bailey's *Fashionable Asheville*, especially volume 1, part 1, chapter 3, "The Influence of Charleston."
4. Baring, of Baring Bros., London was sent by Lord Ashburton to arrange a matrimonial match between Lord Ashburton and distinguished Charleston widow Susannah Tudor Heyward. However, Baring decided that a better match would be one between himself and Mrs. Heyward.
5. Alice Middleton Trenholm, *Flat Rock, North Carolina: A Sketch of the Past* (Asheville, NC: Inland Press, 1908), 21.
6. Catherine W. Bishir, *North Carolina Architecture* (Chapel Hill: University of North Carolina Press, 1990), 251.
7. Ibid., 254.
8. John Preston Arthur, *Western North Carolina: A History from 1730–1913* (Raleigh, NC: Edward Buncombe Chapter of the Daughters of the American Revolution, 1914), 221.
9. James Patton, *Biography of James Patton* (Chapel Hill, NC: Call number CB P332p 1850 [North Carolina Collection, UNC-CH]), 22.
10. Ibid., 18.
11. Hamilton Jones, *Reports of Cases of Equity Argued and Determined in the Supreme Court of North Carolina: From December Term, 1854 to August Term 1856, Inclusive*, vol. II (Salisbury, NC: J. J. Bruner, 1856), 494.
12. A search of the records at the office of the Buncombe County Register of Deeds reveals that between 1840 and 1849, Osborne was involved in at least 8 property transactions.
13. Arthur, *Western North Carolina: A History*, 147. "Patton & Osborne" may have been owned by Thomas Taylor Patton (or his brother James W.) and Joseph Osborne, and "Patton & Summey" was a later partnership of Thomas Walton Patton (James W.'s son) and Albert T. Summey.
14. See www.familysearch.org — 1850 slave schedule for Buncombe County, dated December 12, 1860.
15. Catherine W. Bishir, Charlotte V. Brown, Carl R. Lounsbury, and Ernest H. Wood III, *Architects and Builders in North Carolina: A History of the Practice of Building* (Chapel Hill: University of North Carolina Press, 1990), 142.
16. Actually, as Downing acknowledges, Design IX was by John Notman, an architect of Philadelphia, Pennsylvania.
17. Actually, Philadelphia architect and author Samuel Sloan used Downing's "Design IX" (though not acknowledged) for the basis of "Design I — An Italian Villa" in his 1852 publication of *The Model Architect*.
18. Bishir et al., *Architects and Builders in North Carolina*, 144.
19. In March of 1851, Joseph Osborne and George Shackleford secured a deed of trust, whereby Osborne agreed to pay Shackleford's $600 debt owed to John Burgin and J. E. Patton for the purchase of a "negro girl named Lizzie." In return, Osborne kept the negro girl as collateral until Shackleford paid the debt now owed to Osborne (Deed Book 24, page 434 in the records of the Buncombe Register of Deeds). Also, on October 6, 1845, Joseph Osborne sold Lots 2 and 3 at the north end of his 73 acres to William Patton and Ephraim Clayton for $250 (Deed Book 23, page 255 in the records of the Buncombe Register of Deeds).
20. *North Carolina Architects and Builders: A Biographical Dictionary*, online at http://ncarchitects.lib.ncsu.edu/people/P000070 (North Carolina State University).
21. *North Carolina Architects and Builders: A Biographical Dictionary*, online at http://ncarchitects.lib.ncsu.edu/people/P000072 (North Carolina State University).
22. Bishir et al., *Architects and Builders in North Carolina*, 138.
23. Asher Benjamin, *The Architect or Practical House Carpenter* (1830; repr., Mineola, NY: Dover, 1988), 26.
24. Ibid.
25. "Joseph Osborne to William Patton," January 14, 1854 (Deed Book 25, page 244 in the records of the Buncombe Register of Deeds).
26. On January 31, 1856, Joseph Osborne married Penelope Lucretia Twitty, a music teacher at the Asheville Female College and the daughter of the owner of the "Twitty Hotel" in Rutherfordton, North Carolina. Around 1860 Joseph moved his family to Sweetwater, Tennessee, where he died on March 10, 1870, leaving his widow with their five surviving children (they had seven children). For more detailed information on Joseph Osborne, see the appendix.
27. Laurence Foushee London, *The Episcopal Church in North Carolina: 1701–1959*, "The Formation of the Diocese

of North Carolina: 1817–1830," by Henry S. Lewis (Raleigh, NC: Episcopal Diocese of North Carolina, 1987), 96.

28. Ibid., 121.

29. Ibid., 116–20.

30. *Journal of the Ninth Annual Convention of the Protestant Episcopal Church in the State of North Carolina* (Fayetteville, NC: Edward J. Hale, 1825), 10.

31. *Journal of the Twenty-Eighth Annual Convention of the Protestant Episcopal Church in the State of North Carolina* (Fayetteville, NC: Edward J. Hale, 1844), 18.

32. William West Skiles.

33. *Journal of the Twenty-Ninth Annual Convention of the Protestant Episcopal Church in the State of North Carolina* (Fayetteville, NC: Edward J. Hale, 1845), 15–17.

34. Susan Fennimore Cooper, *William West Skiles: A Sketch of Missionary Life at Valle Crucis in Western North Carolina, 1842–1862* (New York: James Pott & Co., 1890), 18–19.

35. *Journal of the Thirtieth Annual Convention of the Protestant Episcopal Church in the State of North Carolina* (Fayetteville, NC: Edward J. Hale, 1846), 17.

36. *Journal of the Thirty-First Annual Convention of the Protestant Episcopal Church in the State of North Carolina* (Fayetteville, NC: Edward J. Hale, 1847), 25.

37. Ibid.

38. For more detailed explanation of Bishop Ives' "Anglo-Catholicism" and the Society of the Holy Cross," see Lewis Wright's essay "Anglo-Catholicism in Antebellum North Carolina: Levi Silliman Ives and the Society of the Holy Cross," *Anglican and Episcopal History* LXIX, no. 1 (2000): 44–71.

Chapter Two

1. Samuel A. Ashe, *Biographical History of North Carolina: From Colonial Times to the Present*, vol. 5 (Greensboro, NC: Charles L. Van Noppen, 1906), 38.

2. *Journal of the Thirty-Second Annual Convention of the Protestant Episcopal Church in the State of North Carolina* (Fayetteville, NC: Edward J. Hale, 1848), 29.

3. Ibid.

4. *Journal of the Thirty-Third Annual Convention of the Protestant Episcopal Church in the State of North Carolina* (Fayetteville, NC: Edward J. Hale, 1849), 19.

5. *Journal of the Thirty-Fifth Annual Convention of the Protestant Episcopal Church in the State of North Carolina* (Fayetteville, NC: Edward J. Hale, 1851), 38.

6. Ibid.

7. "Charles Moore to Jarvis Buxton." Deed dated December 3, 1851 (Deed Book, page 430 in the records of the Buncombe County Register of Deeds).

8. *Journal of the Thirty-Seventh Annual Convention of the Protestant Episcopal Church in the State of North Carolina* (Fayetteville, NC: Edward J. Hale, 1853), 28.

9. *Journal of the Thirty-Eighth Annual Convention of the Protestant Episcopal Church in the State of North Carolina* (Fayetteville, NC: Edward J. Hale, 1854), 44.

10. Ibid., 49.

11. Ibid.

12. *Journal of the Thirty-Ninth Annual Convention of the Protestant Episcopal Church in the State of North Carolina* (Fayetteville, NC: Edward J. Hale, 1855), 21.

13. Ibid.

14. Ibid., 22.

15. Ibid.

16. "William Patton to Rev. Jarvis Buxton," July 11, 1855 (Deed Book 25, pages 544–45 in the records of the Buncombe Register of Deeds).

17. The date of the addition and the builder are conjectural on the author's part, though based on comparison with other Clayton/Shackleford projects, especially the 1856 building for Mars Hill College (see photo in Chapter 1 of this book).

18. Rev. Buxton reported to the 1857 Convention that recent improvements included a "tenant's house, with well and cistern."

19. *Journal of the Fortieth Annual Convention of the Protestant Episcopal Church in the State of North Carolina* (Fayetteville, NC: Edward J. Hale, 1856), 47–48.

20. J. G. DeRoulhac Hamilton, *The Papers of Thomas Ruffin*, vol. II (Raleigh, NC: Edwards & Broughton Printing Co., 1918), 520.

21. Ibid., 16–17.

22. The first instance of the name "Ravenscroft School" appears in Rev. Buxton's report to the 1858 Convention on page 36 of its published journal.

23. *Journal of the Forty-First Annual Convention of the Protestant Episcopal Church in the State of North Carolina* (Fayetteville, NC: Edward J. Hale, 1857), 34–35.

24. *Journals of Girard W. Phelps, Journal #1— School days June 1857–June 1861* (transcribed July 6–August 10, 1995, by Christine Phelps). These journals are now in the possession of Thomas and Christine Phelps of Bostic, North Carolina.

25. St. Luke's Episcopal Church, Roper, North Carolina—a North Carolina historical marker near the former church reads, "Original site 1836. Built on Edward Buncombe property purchased from the estate for one dollar. De-consecrated and torn down in 1918. The Church of the Advent Episcopal Church in Roper renamed St. Luke's Episcopal Church. It became St. Luke's–St. Ann's Episcopal Church in 1987." This is interesting considering that Ravenscroft School was in "Buncombe County," named for Gen. Edward Buncombe, this same famed Revolutionary War hero from Washington County, North Carolina.

26. *Journals of Girard W. Phelps, Journal #1*, "The First Twelve Months In Asheville."

27. *Journals of Girard W. Phelps, Journal #1*, December 29, 1859. After three years at Asheville, Phelps returned to Washington County. His journal entry reads, "I returned from the mountains. I reached home on the 13th of the month having been on the road 8 days."

28. *Journals of Girard W. Phelps, Journal #1*, "The First Twelve Months In Asheville."

29. *Journals of Girard W. Phelps, Journal #1*, July 27, 1857.

30. *Journals of Girard W. Phelps, Journal #1*, August 7, 1857.

31. *Journals of Girard W. Phelps, Journal #1*, August 8, 1857.

32. Letter from Josiah Collins, III, to Girard Phelps, dated April 13, 1858. Transcription by Thomas M. Phelps, March 1995 (rev. August 2012). Letter book, 1858–1861, 10–11, PC.417.2, Josiah Collins Papers, State Archives of North Carolina, Raleigh, North Carolina.

33. *Journals of Girard W. Phelps, Journal #1*, September 8, 1857.

34. *Journals of Girard W. Phelps, Journal #1*, February 7, 1858.

35. *Journals of Girard W. Phelps, Journal #1*, October 9, 1857.

36. *Journals of Girard W. Phelps, Journal #1*, January 10, 1858.

37. Joseph Blount Cheshire, *The Church in the Confederate States: A History of the Protestant Episcopal Church in the Confederate States* (New York: Longmans, Green and Co., 1912), 104.

38. *Journals of Girard W. Phelps, Journal #1*, October 13, 1857.
39. *Journals of Girard W. Phelps, Journal #1*, December 11, 1857.
40. *Journals of Girard W. Phelps, Journal #1*, December 12, 1857.
41. *Journals of Girard W. Phelps, Journal #1*, January 15, 1858.
42. *Journals of Girard W. Phelps, Journal #1*, December 20, 1858.
43. *Journal of the Forty-Second Annual Convention of the Protestant Episcopal Church in the State of North Carolina* (Fayetteville, NC: Edward J. Hale, 1858), 36.
44. Ibid.
45. Ibid.
46. *Journal of the Forty-Fifth Annual Convention of the Protestant Episcopal Church in the State of North Carolina* (Fayetteville, NC: Edward J. Hale, 1861), 12.
47. Ibid.
48. Ibid., 16.
49. Ibid., 17.
50. Ibid., 18.
51. Fanny L. Patton, *Thomas Walton Patton: A Biographical Sketch* (Asheville, NC: Published by Fannie L. Patton, 1908), 14.

Chapter Three

1. *Journal of the First Annual Council of the Protestant Episcopal Church in the State of North Carolina* (Fayetteville, NC: Edward J. Hale, 1863), 20.
2. Ibid.
3. Ibid., 21–22.
4. Ibid., 28.
5. *Journal of the Forty-Eighth Annual Council of the Protestant Episcopal Church in the State of North Carolina* (Fayetteville, NC: Edward J. Hale, 1864), 16.
6. *Journal of the Fiftieth Annual Convention of the Protestant Episcopal Church in the State of North Carolina* (Fayetteville, NC: Edward J. Hale, 1866), 29.
7. Donald S. Armentrout and Robert Boak Slocum, *An Episcopal Dictionary of the Church: A User-friendly Reference for Episcopalians* (New York: Church Publishing Incorporated, 2000), 30.
8. *Journal of the Fifty-First Annual Convention of the Protestant Episcopal Church in the State of North Carolina* (Fayetteville, NC: Edward J. Hale, 1867), 57.
9. *Journal of the Fifty-Second Annual Convention of the Protestant Episcopal Church in the State of North Carolina* (Wilmington, NC: Wm. H. Bernard's Printing and Publishing House, 1868), 34.
10. *Journal of the Fifty-Third Annual Convention of the Protestant Episcopal Church in the State of North Carolina* (Raleigh, NC: M. S. Littlefield, Printer and Binder, 1869), 27.
11. Ibid., 84.
12. Ibid., 84–85.
13. Current residents of Asheville are familiar with "Murdoch Avenue," named for the Murdoch family.
14. Edward McCrady and Samuel A. Ashe, *Cyclopedia of Eminent and Representative Men of the Carolinas of the Nineteenth Century*, vol. 2 (Madison, WI: Brant & Fuller, 1892), 394–95.
15. These mission stations in Murdoch's charge included Waynesville, Haywood County; Glencoe Mission, St. Andrews Chapel, and Bull Creek Mission, all in Buncombe County; Hendersonville, Henderson County; and St. John's Church, Rutherfordton, Rutherford County. Murdoch also mentions in his report that he held services in several other locations: St. John's Church, Gaston County; Leicester, Calvary Church (Henderson County); Trinity Chapel (African American church in Asheville); Haw Creek; and Beaverdam Chapel.
16. *Journal of the Fifty-Fifth Annual Convention of the Protestant Episcopal Church in the State of North Carolina* (1871), 25.
17. *Journal of the Fifty-Sixth Annual Convention of the Protestant Episcopal Church in the State of North Carolina* (1872), 36. Shortly after giving up his labors at Ravenscroft, in 1872 Rev. Murdoch accepted a call to be the pastor of St. Luke's in Salisbury, North Carolina, where he served for 37 years until his death in 1909.
18. See London, *The Episcopal Church in North Carolina*, "The Episcopal Church in North Carolina: 1883–1900," by James S. Brawley, 301–2.
19. Ibid.
20. See Phoebe B. Stanton, *Gothic Revival & American Church Architecture: An Episode in Taste, 1840–1856* (Baltimore, MD: The John Hopkins University Press, 1968), 280–81. Also see Constance M. Greif, *John Notman, Architect* (Philadelphia, PA: Athenaeum of Philadelphia, 1968), 30 and Figure 46.
21. Maryland State Archives, *MSA SC 5496–10599*, http://www.msa.md.gov/megafile/msa/speccol/sc5400/sc5496/010500/010599/html/010599bio.html.
22. Glencoe was a few miles west of Asheville, in the Candler area.
23. John Archibald Deal, candidate for the priesthood, and George Bell, candidate for Deacon's Orders. Bell was finally ordained a priest ten years later, and both men went on to serve charges in western North Carolina for many years.
24. *Journal of the Fifty-Seventh Annual Convention of the Protestant Episcopal Church in the State of North Carolina* (1873), 59.
25. *Journal of the Fifty-Fifth Annual Convention of the Protestant Episcopal Church in the State of North Carolina* (1871), 25.
26. Ibid.
27. London, *The Episcopal Church in North Carolina*, "The Diocese of North Carolina: 1861–1883," by James W. Patton, 261.
28. Ibid., 264.
29. Ibid., 265–66.
30. Ibid., 266.
31. http://www.digitalhistory.uh.edu/database/article_display.cfm?HHID=141.
32. Buxton's mission churches included Chapel at Haw Creek (now St. John's); Beaverdam Chapel; St. Andrew's Chapel; and Trinity Chapel (now St. Mathias).
33. D. Hillhouse Buel, "Work In North Carolina," *The Spirit of Missions* (June 1875), 339.
34. Ibid.
35. Ibid.
36. *Journal of the Sixty-First Annual Convention of the Protestant Episcopal Church in the State of North Carolina* (Goldsboro, NC: J. B. Messenger Power Press Print, 1877), 43.
37. *Journal of the Sixty-Fifth Annual Convention of the Protestant Episcopal Church in the State of North Carolina* (1881), 40.
38. Ibid., 48.
39. Ibid., 57.
40. Ibid., 114.
41. Ibid.
42. *Journal of the Sixty-Sixth Annual Convention of the Protestant Episcopal Church in the State of North Carolina* (1882), 112–13.

43. Article by Rev. E. W. Dixon in *The Church Advocate*, February 24, 1945.
44. "Uncle Isaac Dickson Died Here This Week," *Asheville Citizen*, March 20, 1919.
45. *Journal of the Sixty-Seventh Annual Convention of the Protestant Episcopal Church in the State of North Carolina* (1883), 76.
46. London, *The Episcopal Church in North Carolina*, "The Diocese of North Carolina: 1861–1883," by James W. Patton, 269.
47. *Journal of the Sixty-Seventh Annual Convention of the Protestant Episcopal Church in the State of North Carolina* (1883),38.
48. London, *The Episcopal Church in North Carolina*, "The Episcopal Church in North Carolina: 1883–1900," by James S. Brawley, 299.
49. London, *The Episcopal Church in North Carolina*, "The Diocese of North Carolina: 1861–1883," by James W. Patton, 273.

Chapter Four

1. *Journal of the Sixty-Seventh Annual Convention of the Protestant Episcopal Church in the State of North Carolina* (1883), 35.
2. Ibid., 37.
3. Ibid., 148.
4. *Journal of the Sixty-Eighth Annual Convention of the Protestant Episcopal Church in the State of North Carolina* (Raleigh, NC: P. W. Wiley & Co. Book and Job Printers, 1884), 20.
5. This is sometimes spelled "Hicks" and sometimes "Hix" in the Convention journals.
6. Ibid., 21.
7. Ibid.
8. Ibid., 22.
9. Ibid.
10. Ibid., 23.
11. Ibid., 23–24.
12. Ibid., 25.
13. Ibid., 75.
14. Ibid., 48.
15. Born April 1, 1860, to Robert and Georgiana Keerl Atkinson in Baltimore, Maryland. He graduated from the University of Virginia. Following his time at Ravenscroft, he served as priest at St. John's, Fayetteville, North Carolina, and Free Church of St. Barnabas, Baltimore, Maryland, and also as archdeacon of Baltimore.
16. *Journal of the Sixty-Ninth Annual Convention of the Protestant Episcopal Church in the State of North Carolina* (Raleigh, NC: P. W. Wiley & Co. Book and Job Printers, 1885), 57–58.
17. Ibid., 9–10.
18. Ibid., 10.
19. Ibid., 11.
20. Ibid., 36.
21. Ibid., 29.
22. This is sometimes spelled "Hicks" and sometimes "Hix" in the Convention journals.
23. Ibid.
24. Ibid., 39–40.
25. Ibid., 41.
26. Ibid., 48.
27. *Journal of the Seventieth Annual Convention of the Protestant Episcopal Church in the State of North Carolina* (Raleigh, NC: Edwards & Broughton, Power Printers and Binders, 1886), 41.
28. Ibid.
29. Ibid.
30. Ibid., 42.
31. Ibid., 40.
32. Ibid., 45.
33. Ibid., 48.
34. *Journal of the Seventy-First Annual Convention of the Protestant Episcopal Church in the State of North Carolina* (Raleigh, NC: Edwards & Broughton, Power Printers and Binders, 1887), 37.
35. Ibid.
36. Ibid., 38.
37. Edward P. Greene, Wm. L. Reaney, and Percy R. Eubanks.
38. *Journal of the Seventieth Annual Convention of the Protestant Episcopal Church in the State of North Carolina* (Raleigh, NC: Edwards & Broughton, Power Printers and Binders, 1886), 61.
39. Ibid., 39.
40. Ibid., 39–40.
41. Ibid., 63.
42. Ibid., 64.
43. Ibid.
44. Ibid
45. Ibid.
46. *Journal of the Seventy-Second Annual Convention of the Protestant Episcopal Church in the State of North Carolina* (Raleigh, NC: Edwards & Broughton, Power Printers and Binders, 1888), 39.
47. Ibid.
48. Information from John Leonard, ed., *Who's Who in New York* (New York: L. R. Hamersley, 1907), 1065–66.
49. The Bingham Military School (originally the Bingham School) was located near Mebane Station, North Carolina, 1865–1891. Interestingly, it moved to Asheville in 1891. It closed in 1928.
50. "Form" is synonymous with our word "grade." The use of "form" still continues in England and traditional boarding schools.
51. *Journal of the Seventy-Second Annual Convention of the Protestant Episcopal Church in the State of North Carolina* (1888), 40.
52. Ibid.
53. Ibid., 5–6.
54. Henry Hall, *America's Successful Men of Affairs* (New York: New York Tribune, 1895–1896). Electronic reproduction. New York: Columbia University Libraries, 2008. JPEG use copy available via the World Wide Web. Master copy stored locally on [10] DVDs#: ldpd_6221441_000 01 to 10 (Columbia University Libraries Electronic Books, 2006), 597.
55. *Journal of the Seventy-Second Annual Convention of the Protestant Episcopal Church in the State of North Carolina* (1888), 32.
56. *Journal of the Seventy-Third Annual Convention of the Protestant Episcopal Church in the State of North Carolina* (Raleigh, NC: Edwards & Broughton, Power Printers and Binders, 1889), 51.
57. Milton Harding was a local contractor. We know that also at one time he formed a partnership with Peter Demens of Asheville "to bid on government construction projects. By early May, 1890, they had won the contract for the United States Courthouse and Post Office building in Asheville, followed in June with the contract for a similar project in Statesville. In July, Demens was compelled to dissolve the partnership when Harding proved to be 'an incorrigible drunkard.' As Demens wrote that month to Treasury Department officials in Washington: 'he began to drink and for two weeks nobody knew where he was or what he was doing, and up to today he is not himself yet,

Notes — Chapter Four

the result of such a protracted spree'" (Michael T. Southern from http://ncarchitects.lib.ncsu.edu/people/P000068).

58. *Journal of the Seventy-Third Annual Convention of the Protestant Episcopal Church in the State of North Carolina* (1889), 51–52.

59. Ibid., 53.

60. Although Parker was not the board's choice, Thomas Patton continued his admiration for Haywood Parker by permitting him, in 1899, to marry his daughter Josephine (Josie) Buel Patton. Parker left Ravenscroft in 1889 to pursue a law degree. He later returned to Asheville, where he subsequently opened his law practice. Haywood and Josie had four children, including Mary Parker, to whom this book is dedicated.

61. Ibid., 52.

62. Asheville's *The Daily Citizen*, July 30, 1889. Microfilm at Pack Library, Asheville, North Carolina.

63. *Journal of the Seventy-Fourth Annual Convention of the Protestant Episcopal Church in the State of North Carolina* (Raleigh, NC: Edwards & Broughton, Power Printers and Binders, 1890), 69. This was also verified by family letters and their listing as passengers in the records of the *State of Nevada*, which arrived in the port of New York on September 4, 1889. Of course, they then had to travel down to Asheville.

64. F. M. Huntington Wilson, *The Memoirs of An Ex-Diplomat* (Boston: Bruce Humphries, 1945), 27.

65. *Journal of the Seventy-Fourth Annual Convention of the Protestant Episcopal Church in the State of North Carolina* (1890), 68–69.

66. Ibid., 69.

67. Ibid.

68. Ibid., 8.

69. Ibid., 49.

70. Ibid., 68.

71. Ibid., 69–70.

72. Her full name was Winifred Varina Jefferson Davis Blandy — she was named for former Confederate president Jefferson Davis and his wife Varina, who were lodging with the Blandys when she was born in 1869.

73. Letter from Ronald MacDonald to Louisa MacDonald, July 9, 1890 — George MacDonald Collection. General Collection, Beinecke Rare Book and Manuscript Library, Yale University.

74. Ibid.

75. Ibid.

76. "Louise Virenda, wife of Ronald McDonald, of Ravenscroft school, died suddenly this morning. Mrs. MacDonald had been in poor health for some time, but her death will be a sad surprise to her many friends. She was a member of the Episcopal church, an earnest and faithful worker, and beloved by all who knew her. Notice of the funeral will be given later." *The Daily Citizen*, August 27, 1890 (front page). Microfilm: Pack Library, Asheville, North Carolina. The funeral notice was published the next day, after the funeral had occurred.

77. Non-boarding, also called "day scholars."

78. Probably Bingham Military School.

79. Letter from Lilia MacDonald to Winifred MacDonald, September 21, 1890 — George MacDonald Collection. General Collection, Beinecke Rare Book and Manuscript Library, Yale University.

80. Letter from Lilia MacDonald to MacKay MacDonald, October 5, 1890 — George MacDonald Collection. General Collection, Beinecke Rare Book and Manuscript Library, Yale University.

81. Letter from Lilia MacDonald to Winifred MacDonald, December 15, 1890 — George MacDonald Collection. General Collection, Beinecke Rare Book and Manuscript Library, Yale University.

82. Letter from Lilia MacDonald to Louisa MacDonald, November 5, 1890 — George MacDonald Collection. General Collection, Beinecke Rare Book and Manuscript Library, Yale University.

83. Ibid.

84. Letter from Lilia MacDonald to Winifred MacDonald, undated (c. October 1890) — George MacDonald Collection. General Collection, Beinecke Rare Book and Manuscript Library, Yale University.

85. Ibid.

86. Letter from Lilia MacDonald to Winifred MacDonald, undated (c. November 1890) — George MacDonald Collection. General Collection, Beinecke Rare Book and Manuscript Library, Yale University.

87. Letter from Lilia MacDonald to Louisa MacDonald, November 5–6, 1890 — George MacDonald Collection. General Collection, Beinecke Rare Book and Manuscript Library, Yale University.

88. Tom Bush.

89. Francis Mairs Huntington Wilson.

90. Vardry Echols McBee, Jr., and Charlton C. Millard.

91. Letter from Lilia MacDonald to Louisa MacDonald, November 5–6, 1890 — George MacDonald Collection. General Collection, Beinecke Rare Book and Manuscript Library.

92. Winnie Blandy, Ronald MacDonald's sister-in-law, who was visiting from England.

93. Letter from Lilia MacDonald to Louisa MacDonald, November 5–6, 1890 — George MacDonald Collection. General Collection, Beinecke Rare Book and Manuscript Library, Yale University.

94. Ibid.

95. Letter from Lilia MacDonald to Winifred MacDonald, January 21, 1891 — George MacDonald Collection. General Collection, Beinecke Rare Book and Manuscript Library, Yale University.

96. Letter from Lilia MacDonald to Louisa MacDonald, December 6, 1890 — George MacDonald Collection. General Collection, Beinecke Rare Book and Manuscript Library, Yale University.

97. Benjamin Lee was the coachman and his wife Emma Lee was the Ravenscroft cook. A search of the 1890 Asheville City Directory shows the servant staff also included Jeff Blair, porter; Lizzie Moorhead, housemaid; and Annie Bangle, nurse. However, Jeff Blair and Annie Bangle were later fired after they "were discovered drinking together at 9:00 A.M. by Emma, the cook ... to the several neglect of the horse, the cow & the baby."

98. Letter from Lilia MacDonald to Louisa MacDonald, December 6, 1890 — George MacDonald Collection. General Collection, Beinecke Rare Book and Manuscript Library, Yale University.

99. This may have been Charles W. Knuckles, who is listed in the 1896/1897 Asheville directory as a "barber." Two other brothers, Harry and James S., are also listed in the directory, but I suspect this reference was to Charles.

100. Letter from Lilia MacDonald to Louisa MacDonald, December 6, 1890 — George MacDonald Collection. General Collection, Beinecke Rare Book and Manuscript Library, Yale University.

101. Letter from Lilia MacDonald to Louisa MacDonald, January 15, 1891 — George MacDonald Collection. General Collection, Beinecke Rare Book and Manuscript Library, Yale University.

102. Letter from Lilia MacDonald to Louisa MacDonald, January 22, 1891 — George MacDonald Collection. General Collection, Beinecke Rare Book and Manuscript Library.

103. Rev. Buxton had recently stepped down as rector

of Trinity Church. In his semi-retirement he took charge of the struggling church at Rutherfordton, where he had served fifty years earlier.

104. Letter from Lilia MacDonald to Louisa MacDonald, February 5, 1891—George MacDonald Collection. General Collection, Beinecke Rare Book and Manuscript Library, Yale University.

105. Ibid.

106. *Journal of the Seventy-Fifth Annual Convention of the Protestant Episcopal Church in the State of North Carolina* (1891), 68.

107. Ibid., 69.

108. Ibid., 50.

109. Ibid., 114.

110. Ibid., 133.

111. Ibid., 96.

112. Letter from Ronald MacDonald to George MacDonald, November 27, 1890—George MacDonald Collection. General Collection, Beinecke Rare Book and Manuscript Library, Yale University.

113. Letter from Lilia MacDonald to Louisa MacDonald, November 9, 1890—George MacDonald Collection. General Collection, Beinecke Rare Book and Manuscript Library, Yale University.

114. *Thirty-Third Annual of the Association Graduates of the United States Military Academy at West Point, New York. June 9th 1902* (Saginaw, MI: Seemann & Peters, Printers & Binders, 1902), 43–45.

115. Lilia Scott MacDonald.

116. Probably Winnie Blandy, Louise MacDonald's younger sister, or possibly Jessie Sharman, a cousin of Ronald MacDonald's mother who came to replace Lilia as matron and housekeeper.

117. Letter from Jessie Sharman to Winifred MacDonald, January 25, 1892—George MacDonald Collection. General Collection, Beinecke Rare Book and Manuscript Library, Yale University.

118. Letter from Lilia MacDonald to Winifred MacDonald, undated—George MacDonald Collection. General Collection, Beinecke Rare Book and Manuscript Library, Yale University.

119. *Journal of the Seventy-Seventh Annual Convention of the Protestant Episcopal Church in the State of North Carolina* (Raleigh, NC: Edwards & Broughton, Power Printers and Binders, 1893), 93.

120. Ibid., 67.

121. London, *The Episcopal Church in North Carolina*, "The Episcopal Church in North Carolina: 1883–1900," by James S. Brawley, 292–93.

122. These included St. Martin's, St. Michael's, All Angels, St. Mark's, and St. Paul's (in Monroe).

123. "Biographical information" from the "Joseph Blount Cheshire Papers," Collection Number: 00146 at the University of North Carolina, Chapel Hill, www.lib.unc.edu/mss/inv/c/Cheshire,Joseph_Blount.html.

124. *Journal of the Seventy-Eighth Annual Convention of the Protestant Episcopal Church in the State of North Carolina* (1894), 52.

125. Ibid. The board also reported that "the Rev. Samuel Rhodes, Rev. W. F. Rice, Mr. John H. Gilreath and Mr. John C. Seagle have been pursuing their studies under Mr. Barrows."

126. Ibid., 82.

127. *Journal of the Seventy-Ninth Annual Convention of the Protestant Episcopal Church in the State of North Carolina* (1895), 48.

128. Rev. Andrew David Stowe, *Stowe's Clerical Directory of the American Church: 1920–21* (Minneapolis, MN: Andrew D. Stowe, 1920), 254.

129. *Journal of the Seventy-Ninth Annual Convention of the Protestant Episcopal Church in the State of North Carolina* (1895), 65.

130. Samuel F. Rhoades, deacon. Stubbs' other assistant, William F. Rice, was living at the Grace community just north of Asheville.

131. Ibid., 69–70.

132. Ibid., 48. The expenses expended for the costs of repairs and improvements were reported to be as follows:
Connection with city water-works and sewer $155.00
Repairing roof and gutters 21.00
Putting in grates and repairing walls 17.86
Balance in hand 6.14
$200.00

133. *Journal of the Seventy-Eighth Annual Convention of the Protestant Episcopal Church in the State of North Carolina* (1894), 52.

134. *Record Book, Board of Fellows of Ravenscroft, 1894–1916*, Diocese of Western North Carolina Records, W.L. Eury Appalachian Collection, Special Collections, Appalachian State University, Boone, North Carolina, 4.

135. *Record Book, Board of Fellows of Ravenscroft*, 17.

136. "Women's Edition," *Asheville Citizen*, Thanksgiving Day 1895.

137. Letter from Ronald MacDonald to Winifred MacDonald, January 16, 1892 — George MacDonald Collection. General Collection, Beinecke Rare Book and Manuscript Library, Yale University.

138. Marshall DeLancey Haywood, *Lives of the Bishops of North Carolina: From the Establishment of the Episcopate in that State Down to the Division of the Diocese* (Raleigh, NC: Alfred Williams, 1910), 157.

139. *Record Book, Board of Fellows of Ravenscroft*, 13–14.

140. His actual initials were "Mr. T. H. Toynbee Wight." At the Convention of 1895, they further misspelled it as "Mr. J. H. F. Wight." That's what happens to one who has too many initials in his name!

141. From familysearch.org—England and Wales Census, 1881, National Archives ref #RG11, 268/38, 8, and Great Britain Deaths and Burials, 1778–1988, for Thomas H. Wight, ref #Pt2,sh687, page 209, line 33.

142. R. M. Grier and F. A. Hibbert, *The Register of S. Chad's College Denstone from the Opening of School in February 1873 to April 1904* (Shrewsbury, UK: W. O. Wilding [O. D.], 1904), 71.

143. *Journal of the Seventy-Ninth Annual Convention of the Protestant Episcopal Church in the State of North Carolina* (1895), 48.

144. Ibid., 3.

145. Ibid., 44.

146. London, *The Episcopal Church in North Carolina*, "The Episcopal Church in Western North Carolina: 1894–1948," by Elizabeth N. Thompson, 467.

147. *Journal of the Eightieth Annual Convention of the Protestant Episcopal Church in the State of North Carolina* (Raleigh, NC: Edwards & Broughton, Power Printers and Binders, 1896), 67–69.

148. Ibid., 42.

149. Ibid., 45.

150. *Journal of the Second Annual Convention of the Protestant Episcopal Church in the Missionary Jurisdiction of Asheville* (Asheville, NC: Asheville Printing Company, 1896), 86.

151. Found in the July 25, 1895, issue of *The Nation*.

152. *Journal of the Board of Fellows of Ravenscroft*, 24.

153. After receiving his degree from the Harvard Medical School in 1901, Dr. Thomas Henry Toynbee Wight served as lecturer on embryology and demonstrator of uri-

nology and pathology at the University College of Medicine in Richmond, Virginia. Soon thereafter he relocated to California and had a distinguished career as a physician and author in the field of pathology. He served as an officer in the Medical Reserve Corps in both the Spanish-American War and World War I. His son Ronald T. Wight, who was born in Asheville in 1896, died at Malta in 1915 while serving in the British Army during World War I. Toynbee Wight died of pneumonia at Carmel, California, at age 65, on May 11, 1936.

154. Sadie Smathers Patton, *The Story of Henderson County* (Asheville, NC: Miller Printing Company, 1947), 159.

155. According to the *Alumni Cantabrigienses* (compiled by J. A. Venn in 1954 and published by Cambridge University Press), 273, Frank Valentine obtained his B.A. in 1862 and his M.A. degree in 1883.

156. Arthur, *Western North Carolina: A History*, 184.

157. *Journal of the Eighty-First Annual Convention of the Protestant Episcopal Church in the State of North Carolina* (Raleigh, NC: Edwards & Broughton, Power Printers and Binders, 1897), 64–65.

Chapter Five

1. *Journal of the Second Annual Convention of the Protestant Episcopal Church in the Missionary Jurisdiction of Asheville* (Asheville, NC: Asheville Printing Company, 1897), 30.

2. London, *The Episcopal Church in North Carolina*, "The Episcopal Church in Western North Carolina: 1894–1948," by Elizabeth N. Thompson, 470.

3. Info from Stowe, *Stowe's Clerical Directory 1920–21*, 137, and John Leonard, ed., *Who's Who in America*, vol. 3, *1903–05* (Chicago: A. L. Marquis, 1903), 726.

4. London, *The Episcopal Church in North Carolina*, "The Episcopal Church in Western North Carolina: 1894–1948," by Elizabeth N. Thompson, 471.

5. *Journal of the Fourth Annual Convention of the Protestant Episcopal Church in the Missionary Jurisdiction of Asheville* (Asheville, NC: Asheville Printing Company, 1898), 84.

6. "William Patton to Rev. Jarvis Buxton," July 11, 1855 (Deed Book 25, pages 544–45 in the records of the Buncombe Register of Deeds).

7. *Journal of the First Annual Convention of the Protestant Episcopal Church in the Missionary Jurisdiction of Asheville* (Asheville, NC: Asheville Printing Company, 1895), 47.

8. *Journal of the Fourth Annual Convention of the Protestant Episcopal Church in the Missionary Jurisdiction of Asheville* (1898), 84.

9. *Journal of the Fifth Annual Convention of the Protestant Episcopal Church in the Missionary Jurisdiction of Asheville* (Asheville, NC: Asheville Printing Company, 1899), 16.

10. Ibid.
11. Ibid., 16.
12. Ibid., 16–17.
13. Ibid., 16.

14. This article was discovered and brought to my attention by Zoe Rhine of the NC Collection at Pack Memorial Library, Asheville, North Carolina. This "cottage" is still extant at #75 Church Street.

15. *Journal of the Fifth Annual Convention of the Protestant Episcopal Church in the Missionary Jurisdiction of Asheville* (1899), 17.

16. *Journal of the Eighth Annual Convention of the Protestant Episcopal Church in the Missionary Jurisdiction of Asheville* (Asheville, NC: Asheville Printing Company, 1902), 29–30.

17. Patton, *The Story of Henderson County*, 158.
18. Ibid., 160.

19. Letter from Lilia MacDonald to Louisa MacDonald, February 17, 1891—George MacDonald Collection. General Collection, Beinecke Rare Book and Manuscript Library, Yale University.

20. Charles Lee Smith, *The History of Education in North Carolina* (Washington, DC: Government Printing Office, 1888), 170–71.

21. Tyson Gray Gibson, "A Loss in the Community: Integration and the End of a Unique Educational Heritage" (senior thesis at the University of North Carolina, Asheville, 2003).

22. Martha Kepler and her son (from her first marriage), Thomas J. Wooldridge, and his family moved to 114 Montford Avenue in late 1905 or 1906.

23. *Journal of the Sixteenth Annual Convention of the Missionary Jurisdiction of Asheville* (Asheville, NC: Hackney & Moale Company, 1910), 24.

24. *Journal of the Twenty-First Annual Convention of the Protestant Episcopal Church in the Missionary Jurisdiction of Asheville* (Asheville, NC: Asheville Printing Company, 1915), 25.

25. "Episcopal Church, Missionary District of Asheville to Roger Lamson, Jr.," July 6, 1911 (Deed Book 172, page 396 in the records of the Buncombe Register of Deeds).

26. The 1912 Asheville City Directory listing: Lamson Roger, Jr., capitalist, bds "Ravenscroft."

27. "Agreement between Roger Lamson, Jr. and Mrs. Nellie W. Hyman," March 15, 1912 (Deed Book 173, page 530 in the records of the Buncombe Register of Deeds).

28. *Journal of the Twenty-Fifth Annual Convention of the Protestant Episcopal Church in the Missionary Jurisdiction of Asheville* (Asheville, NC: Asheville Printing Company, 1914), 48). The following lots were sold: #1—Asheville Country Club; #19—Lena N. Buckner; ##20 and 21—W. B. Davis; #22—Lina B. Davis; #25—Dr. E. B. Glenn; #26—Mr. Miles.

29. *Journal of the Twenty-Fourth Annual Convention of the Protestant Episcopal Church in the Missionary Jurisdiction of Asheville* (Asheville, NC: Asheville Printing Company, 1919), 54.

30. "Lease between W. K. Howe and Leon & Mary St. John," March 30, 1917 (Deed Book 212, page 269 in the records of the Buncombe Register of Deeds).

31. London, *The Episcopal Church in North Carolina*, "The Episcopal Church in Western North Carolina: 1894–1948," by Elizabeth N. Thompson, 508.

32. Thomas Wolfe, *Look Homeward Angel* (New York: Charles Scribner's Sons, 1929), 173.

33. "Buxton Hill Investment Company"—Incorporation, February 6, 1926 (Deed Book C008, page 217 in the records of the Buncombe Register of Deeds). The company stockholders were James A. McKay, W. E. Crown, and Otto E. Stockington.

Chapter Six

1. "Episcopal Diocese of WNC to Laura Lee Horner," April 28, 1951 (Deed Book 705, page 455 in the records of the Buncombe Register of Deeds).

2. Internal memo from John Kinney to Janet Seapker, December 15, 1976, from Shoenberger Hall file—National Register Nomination Western Office of NCSHPO.

3. John Robinson, staff writer, "Schoenberger Hall:

Efforts to Save It Are Unsuccessful," *Asheville Citizen-Times*, March 25, 1978.

4. From personal email from J. Myrick Howard to Dale Slusser, February 29, 2012.

5. John Campbell, Jr., staff writer, "Old Ravenscroft School Is Purchased," *Asheville Citizen-Times*, September 8, 1979.

6. "Stuart Tauber to Whom it may Concern," Ordinance #1213, May 15, 1981 (Deed Book 1271, page 728 in the records of the Buncombe County Register of Deeds).

7. Purchased by MTM Investments on May 3, 1995 (Deed Book 1847, page 386 in the records of the Buncombe County Register of Deeds).

8. "Stuart Tauber to Whom it may Concern," Ordinance #1213, May 15, 1981 (Deed Book 1271, page 728 in the records of the Buncombe County Register of Deeds).

Chapter Seven

1. "Midshipman Drops Dead," *The Sun*, New York, February 29, 1905.

2. Frederick W. Cogburn, *A History of Lowell and Its People* (New York: Lewis Historical Publishing Company, 1920), 160.

3. Ibid.

4. Patent number: 941671; filing date: February 17, 1908; issue date: November 30, 1909.

5. From familysearch.org.

6. Letter from Lilia MacDonald to Winifred MacDonald, undated (c. November 1890) — George MacDonald Collection. General Collection, Beinecke Rare Book and Manuscript Library, Yale University.

7. Biographical information from the Southern Historical Collection at the Wilson Library of the University of North Carolina at Chapel Hill — Collection Number: 03248-z "Philip Charles Cocke Speeches, 1907–1948."

8. Letter from Lilia MacDonald to Louisa MacDonald, December 18, 1890 — George MacDonald Collection. General Collection, Beinecke Rare Book and Manuscript Library, Yale University.

9. Margaret "Grits" Davis recollections, http://edwinpascaldavis.blogspot.com/2009/01/margaret-grits-davis-recollections.html.

10. "Edwin Pascal Davis from Davis Bros. Photographers Portsmouth, NH," http://edwinpascaldavis.blogspot.com/2009/01/edwin-pascal-davis-from-davis-bros.html.

11. Their property appears to have been on the north side of the river near the intersection of what is now Glendale Avenue. It crossed "Rossi's Creek" and went up toward "Beaumont" (Beaucatcher Mountain) into what is now "Kenilworth." I think "Rossi's Creek" is what was dammed up to form Kenilworth Lake.

12. *Harvard Class of 1900: Second Report* (Cambridge, MA: Harvard University Press, 1906), 61; *Harvard Class of 1900: Fourth Report* (Cambridge, MA: Harvard University Press, 1915), 113–14; *Harvard Class of 1900: Fifth Report* (Cambridge, MA: Harvard University Press, 1921), 128–29.

13. Henry T. and Harriet Rosenbury Collins. Harriet Rosenbury Collins was the twin sister of William J. Erdman's wife, Henrietta Rosenbury Erdman. The Collins family had moved to Asheville the previous year (1887). Henry Collins became a prominent local businessman, founding the Asheville Ice & Coal Co. and Asheville Milling Co. (information courtesy of Pack Library).

14. Letter from Lilia MacDonald to Louisa MacDonald, January 1, 1891 — George MacDonald Collection. General Collection, Beinecke Rare Book and Manuscript Library, Yale University.

15. From a biographical portrait of "Frederick Erdman" by his son Frank Erdman (www.erdman.org).

16. Henry T. and Harriet Rosenbury Collins.

17. The Folsom property was near what is now the intersection of US 70 and Maple Springs Road, near Bull Mountain Road in East Asheville.

18. *Electrical World*, February 17, 1912, issue, 353–54.

19. http://fl-genweb.org/gadsden/Social-1925_Jun25.html.

20. Patton, *The Story of Henderson County*, 94–95. Note: Sadie Smathers Patton was the wife of the son of Ellen Patton Hyman's brother, Preston Fidelia Patton, II. Sadie's husband, to whom her book was dedicated, was Preston Fidelia Patton, III, also a Ravenscroft High School graduate.

21. http://files.usgwarchives.net/ca/inyo/cemeteries/eastline-dh.txt.

22. *Thirty-Third Annual of the Association Graduates of the United States Military Academy at West Point, New York. June 9th 1902*, 43–45.

23. From a memoir by L. B. Slattery, published in the *Proceedings of the American Society of Civil Engineers* XXXVI, no. 6 (August 1910), 1240.

24. From obituary in *Asheville Citizen-Times* (undated) — NC Collection, Pack Library, Asheville, North Carolina.

25. From obituary in *Asheville Citizen-Times* (undated) — NC Collection, Pack Library, Asheville, North Carolina.

26. *Yearbook of the Young Men's Christian Associations of North America, for the Year May 1, 1920 to April 30, 1921* (New York: Association Press, 1921), 91.

27. See "Historical Sketch of the Fund Raising Profession," by A. C. Marts, http://www.martsandlundy.com/pdf/history/ML_Historical_Sketch.pdf.

28. From obituary in *Asheville Citizen-Times*, September 9, 1947 — NC Collection, Pack Library, Asheville, North Carolina.

29. From obituary in *Asheville Citizen-Times*, September 28, 1955 — NC Collection, Pack Library, Asheville, North Carolina.

30. "Eugene Sawyer, 94, Still In Gear After Long Automotive Career," *Asheville Citizen-Times*, October 15, 1965; and from obituary in *Asheville Citizen-Times*, October 24, 1966 — NC Collection, Pack Library, Asheville, North Carolina.

31. "History of Kiawah Island," Town of Kiawah, http://www.kiawahisland.org/client_resources/background%20%282%29.pdf.

32. Ashton Cobb, *Kiawah Island: A History* (Charleston, SC: History Press, 2006), 100–101.

33. *New York Times*, April 8, 1918; and *Asheville Citizen-Times*, April 8, 1918.

34. Frederic E. J. Lloyd, ed., *The American Church Clergy and Parish Directory for 1903* (Cleveland, OH: Frederic E. J. Lloyd, 1903), 301.

35. Letter from Lilia MacDonald to Winifred MacDonald, undated (c. 1890) — George MacDonald Collection. General Collection, Beinecke Rare Book and Manuscript Library, Yale University.

36. Geddings Hardy Crawford, ed., *Who's Who In South Carolina* (Columbia, SC: McCaw of Columbia, 1923), 205–6.

37. "F.M.H. Wilson Dies; Former Diplomat," *New York Times*, January 1, 1947.

Chapter Eight

1. Buel, "Work In North Carolina," 339.

2. *Journal of the Sixty-Ninth Annual Convention of the*

Protestant Episcopal Church in the State of North Carolina (1885), 78.
  3. Ibid.
  4. Jonathan H. Poston, *The Buildings of Charleston* (Columbia: University of South Carolina Press, 1997), 268–69.
  5. J. P. Davison, compiler, *The Asheville City Directory and Gazetteer of Buncombe County for 1883–84* (Richmond, VA: Baughman Brothers Printers, 1883), 80.
  6. From notations on Image L574-DS of the NC Collection of Pack Memorial Library, Asheville, North Carolina.
  7. *Journal of the Seventy-First Annual Convention of the Protestant Episcopal Church in the State of North Carolina* (1887), 102.
  8. *Journal of the Seventy-Second Annual Convention of the Protestant Episcopal Church in the State of North Carolina* (1888), 112.
  9. Ibid.
  10. "John W. Lorick and his wife, M. C. Lorick, to Theodore B. Lyman, Bishop and W. E. Anderson, and R. H. Battle, Trustees of the Diocese of North Carolina of the Protestant Episcopal Church. Deed dated August 26, 1888" (Deed Book 68, page 534 in the records of the Buncombe County Register of Deeds).
  11. "T. J. Candler & his wife, H. E. Candler, to Joseph Roberson, John W. Lorick, and Robert F. Bryson, Trustees of Loricks View Baptist Church." Deed dated August 28, 1883 (Deed Book 60, page 514 in the records of the Buncombe County Register of Deeds).
  12. *Journal of the Seventy-Third Annual Convention of the Protestant Episcopal Church in the State of North Carolina* (1889), 105.
  13. *Journal of the Seventy-Seventh Annual Convention of the Protestant Episcopal Church in the State of North Carolina* (1893), 97.
  14. *Journal of the Seventy-Ninth Annual Convention of the Protestant Episcopal Church in the State of North Carolina* (1895), 74.
  15. "Rev. A. H. Stubbs Diaries," ID #MS033 — NC Collection, Pack Memorial Library, Asheville, North Carolina. Journal entry: Friday, July 5, 1895.
  16. *Journal of the Twenty-Fourth Annual Convention of the Protestant Episcopal Church in the Missionary Jurisdiction of Asheville* (1918), 210.
  17. *Journal of the Twenty-Sixth Annual Convention of the Missionary Jurisdiction of Asheville* (Asheville, NC: Asheville Printing Company, 1920), 36.
  18. Sondley and Davidson, *Asheville and Buncombe County*), 152.
  19. *Biographical Dictionary of the United States Congress*, http://bioguide.congress.gov.
  20. *Journal of the Sixtieth Annual Convention of the Protestant Episcopal Church in the State of North Carolina* (Goldsboro, NC: J. B. Whitaker, Jr., Book and Job Printer, 1876), 43.
  21. *Journal of the Sixty-Ninth Annual Convention of the Protestant Episcopal Church in the State of North Carolina* (1885), 57–58.
  22. "Pedigree Resource File," http://familysearch.org/pal:/MM9.2.1/9CQD-249, accessed April 26, 2012 (entry for Francis Randolph Curtis).
  23. *Catalogue of the Officers and Students of Trinity College: 1880–1881* (Hartford, CT: Trinity College, 1880), 43.
  24. *Catalogue of the Officers and Students of Trinity College: 1883–1884* (Hartford, CT: Trinity College, 1883), 42–43.
  25. "Richmond Pearson & his wife, Gabrielle, to F. Randolph Curtis, and Gen. J. G. Martin, ET AL." Deed dated November 1882 (Deed Book 44, page 15 in the records of the Buncombe County Register of Deeds).
  26. Davison, *The Asheville City Directory and Gazetteer of Buncombe County for 1883–84*, 71.
  27. "F. Randolph Curtis, Estate." Plat dated June 1, 1906 (Deed Book 147, page 206 in the records of the Buncombe County Register of Deeds).
  28. *Journal of the Sixty-Ninth Annual Convention of the Protestant Episcopal Church in the State of North Carolina* (1885), 78.
  29. "Stubbs Diaries," October 15, 1898.
  30. *Medical Department of the University of Nashville and the University of Tennessee: Sixtieth Session, 1910–1911* (Nashville: University of Nashville and the University of Tennessee, 1910), 49 (shows Plato Herman Lee, Class of 1886).
  31. See www.familysearch.org — United States Census, 1900. Shows Plato and Eugenia Lee having been married for 6 years, with three children: Catie, John and Marian.
  32. See www.familysearch.org — United States Census, 1880. Household of John W. and Mary Lee of Bull Creek, Madison County, North Carolina. Shows Elizabeth Lee as 12 years old.
  33. "Stubbs Diaries," March 18, 1900: *"Alexander's Union Chapel*—Miss Lee not there. Neither Mrs. Coxe."
  34. See www.familysearch.org — United States Census, 1900. Household of James N. Vance, French Broad Township, Buncombe County, North Carolina. Mary later married Alex Wilbar in Tennessee in 1902, and died in Judson, North Carolina, in 1918 (see her death certificate at familysearch.org). Mary and Alex are both buried at Riverside Cemetery in Asheville.
  35. "Stubbs Diaries," November 28, 1899.
  36. "Stubbs Diaries," July 21, 1901.
  37. "Stubbs Diaries," December 29, 1901.
  38. "Stubbs Diaries," February 15, 1903.
  39. *Journal of the Tenth Annual Convention of the Protestant Episcopal Church in the Missionary Jurisdiction of Asheville* (1904), 80.
  40. http://www.heritagewnc.org/WNC_natural_disasters/1916_flood.htm.
  41. *Journal of the Fifty-First Annual Convention of the Protestant Episcopal Church in the State of North Carolina* (1867), 57.
  42. "Aftermath of the Civil War," by Erika Lindemann, "Chapter 6: 1860–1869" of *True and Candid Compositions: The Lives and Writings of Antebellum Students at the University of North Carolina* (http://docsouth.unc.edu/true/).
  43. Compiled from the following sources: Benjamin B. Winborne, *The Colonial and State Political History of Hertford County, N.C* (Raleigh, NC: Edwards & Broughton Co., 1906), 120; *A Catalogue of the Officers and Students of Harvard University for the Academical Year of 1853–54, Second Term* (Cambridge, MA: Metcalf and Company, 1854), 66; Nathaniel Cheairs Hughes, Jr., *Yale's Confederates: A Biographical Dictionary* (Knoxville: University of Tennessee Press, 2008), 115; and William Stevens Powell, *Dictionary of North Carolina Biography, Volume 3* (Chapel Hill: University of North Carolina Press, 1988), 361–62.
  44. *Journal of the Fifty-First Annual Convention of the Protestant Episcopal Church in the State of North Carolina* (1867), 57.
  45. Ibid.
  46. *Journal of the Fifty-Second Annual Convention of the Protestant Episcopal Church in the State of North Carolina* (1868), 92.
  47. *Journal of the Seventieth Annual Convention of the Protestant Episcopal Church in the State of North Carolina* (1886), 104.

48. See www.familysearch.org — United States Census, 1880 (https://familysearch.org/pal:/MM9.1.1/MC68-RD7).
49. *Journal of the Seventy-First Annual Convention of the Protestant Episcopal Church in the State of North Carolina* (1887), 104.
50. *Journal of the Seventy-Sixth Annual Convention of the Protestant Episcopal Church in the State of North Carolina* (Raleigh, NC: Edwards & Broughton, Power Printers and Binders, 1892), 52.
51. Ibid., 86.
52. Ibid.
53. *Journal of the Seventy-Seventh Annual Convention of the Protestant Episcopal Church in the State of North Carolina* (1893), 109. Rice notes that the lectern, prayer desk, and bishop's chair were given by Mr. Charles W. Woolsey.
54. *Record of the Class of 1845 of Yale College, Containing Obituaries of Deceased, and Biographical Sketches of Surviving members*, prepared by the Secretary at the Request of the Class (New York: Jenkins & Thomas, 1881), 39–44.
55. John Leonard, ed., *Women's Who's Who in America*, (New York: American Commonwealth Company, 1914), 506.
56. "College Settlement Work: The Lofty Aims of This Late Form of Philanthropic Effort," *New York Times*, October 1, 1893.
57. Susan Guion Chester, "Woman's Place and Work: College Settlements and Their Relation to the Church," *The Churchman*, March 11, 1893, 342.
58. Robert A. Woods and Albert J. Kennedy, eds., *Handbook of Settlements* (New York City: Charities Publications Committee, 1911), 249.
59. Bulletin of the Bureau of Labor, No. 55, November 1904, "The Revival of Handicrafts in America: I. Domestic Weaving and Rug Making — Asheville, NC," by Max West, Ph.D (Washington, DC: Government Printing Office, 1904), 1576.
60. *Journal of the Seventy-Eighth Annual Convention of the Protestant Episcopal Church in the State of North Carolina* (1894), 110.
61. Ibid., 111.
62. *Journal of the Seventy-Ninth Annual Convention of the Protestant Episcopal Church in the State of North Carolina* (1895), 86.
63. The Lymans continued at Grace Church until Mr. Lyman's death from pneumonia in 1902. Susan (who then became known as Mrs. Chester Lyman) remained in Asheville and at Grace until her mysterious disappearance from a New York–bound steamer in 1917. See David E. Whisnant Papers, 1893–1967 Collection at the University of North Carolina at Chapel Hill (http://www.lib.unc.edu/mss/inv/w/Whisnant,David_E.html).
64. Leonard Wilson, *Makers of America: Biographies of Leading Men of Thought and Action*, vol. II (Washington, DC: B. F. Johnson, 1916), 377–78.
65. "A. H. Lyman and C. E. Lyman to Susan G. Chester." Deed dated April 13, 1894 (Deed Book 90, page 328 in the records of the Buncombe County Register of Deeds).
66. *Journal of the Seventy-Fifth Annual Convention of the Protestant Episcopal Church in the State of North Carolina* (Raleigh, NC: Edwards & Broughton, Power Printers and Binders, 1891), 90.
67. *Journal of the Seventy-First Annual Convention of the Protestant Episcopal Church in the State of North Carolina* (1887), 104.
68. *Journal of the Seventy-Second Annual Convention of the Protestant Episcopal Church in the State of North Carolina* (1888), 115.
69. Arthur, *Western North Carolina: A History*, 426–27.
70. *Journal of the Seventy-Seventh Annual Convention of the Protestant Episcopal Church in the State of North Carolina* (1893), 109.
71. *Journal of the Seventy-Ninth Annual Convention of the Protestant Episcopal Church in the State of North Carolina* (1895), 76.
72. Ibid., 86.
73. Rex Redmond, *Beaverdam: Historic Valley of the Blue Ridge Mountains: A Nostalgic Look at a Valley and Its People* (Greenville: SC: Postal Instant Press, 2011), 111–12.
74. *Journal of the Sixth Annual Convention of the Protestant Episcopal Church in the Missionary Jurisdiction of Asheville* (1900), 56: "Rev. Alfred H. Stubbs, Warden, Rev. Jarvis Buxton, D. D. and William F. Rice, Associate Priests, temporarily assisted by Rev. L. F. Hindry of Southern Florida [serving at Church of the Redeemer, Craggy], and Messrs. Child, Holmes, Kimberly, Law, Parker, Patton, Seagle and valentine, Lay Readers."
75. *Journal of the Tenth Annual Convention of the Protestant Episcopal Church in the Missionary Jurisdiction of Asheville* (1904), 41 and 47. The proposal to sell the St. Titus property in 1904 was cancelled by the trustees — yet in 1905 the sale went through. See "Junius M. Hunter, Rodney R. Swope, W. T. Capers, Thomas W. Patton, Haywood Parker, and Frederick W.W. Graham, Trustees of the Protestant Episcopal Church in the Missionary District of Asheville to Board of Education, Buncombe County." Deed dated May 30, 1915 (Deed Book 139, page 112 in the records of the Buncombe County Register of Deeds).
76. Frank Roberson recalls that the school was called the "Haynes School," possibly named after Rev. Washington Haynes, first pastor of Beaverdam Baptist Church.
77. "The County Board of Education of Buncombe County to C. B. Scarborough, Buncombe County." Deed dated September 21, 1920 (Deed Book 243, page 115 in the records of the Buncombe County Register of Deeds).
78. James B. Sill, *Historical Sketches of Churches in the Diocese of Western North Carolina Episcopal Church* (Asheville, NC: Publishing Office, Church of the Redeemer, 1955), 159.
79. *Journal of the Seventy-Fourth Annual Convention of the Protestant Episcopal Church in the State of North Carolina* (1890), 108.
80. "Black Mountain Hotel Company — Plat." Deed dated January 1, 1904 (Deed Book 5, page 3 in the records of the Buncombe County Register of Deeds).
81. Sill, *Historical Sketches*, 160. Rev. Sill writes, " F. M. Osborne, (sic Rev. E. A. Osborne, likely)," but it was not Rev. E. A. Osborne, but more likely Rev. Francis Moore Osborne, who was then priest in charge at St. Martin and Holy Comforter Chapels in Charlotte, North Carolina. See *Journal of the Ninetieth Annual Convention of the Protestant Episcopal Church in the Diocese of North Carolina* (Raleigh, NC: Edwards & Broughton, Printers and Binders, 1906), 8.
82. "Annie Allred and husband, J. J. Allred, to Junius Horner, R. R. Swope, A. H. Stubbs, Haywood Parker, W. Vance Brown, and C. D. Beadle, Trustees in the Protestant Episcopal Church in the Missionary District of Asheville." Deed dated April 4, 1917 (Deed Book 214, page 118 in the records of the Buncombe County Register of Deeds).
83. *Journal of the Twenty-Third Annual Convention of the Protestant Episcopal Church in the Missionary Jurisdiction of Asheville* (Asheville, NC: Asheville Printing Company, 1917), 33: "The Trustees have received a deed from J. J. Allred and wife, Ann E. Allred, for a triangular lot adjoining the church lot at Black Mountain, on the west. This lot was paid for by the members of the church at Black Mountain, and was purchased so that this triangle and a small

part of the church lot could be utilized as a Rectory lot. At the request of the members of the church at Black Mountain, the Trustees voted to mortgage this Rectory lot for a sum not to exceed $1,500, the proceeds to be used in part payment of the Rectory which is now being built.—*Haywood Parker, Secretary to the Trustees.*"

84. J. L. Mashburn, *Hominy Valley: The Golden Years* (Enka, NC: Colonial House, 2008), 10–11.

85. Ibid., 15.

86. *Journal of the Sixty-Ninth Annual Convention of the Protestant Episcopal Church in the State of North Carolina* (1885), 53.

87. Ibid., 11.

88. *Journal of the Seventieth Annual Convention of the Protestant Episcopal Church in the State of North Carolina* (1886), 73.

89. *Journal of the Seventy-First Annual Convention of the Protestant Episcopal Church in the State of North Carolina* (1887), 75.

90. Ibid., 47. He reports, "Has raised money at Candler's to pay for ground and Church originally owned by Methodists."

91. "Dr. W. W. Clark to Rt. Rev. T. B. Lyman, W. E. Andersen, R. H. Battle, and Gen. Cox, Trustees for the Episcopal Church, the Diocese in North Carolina." Deed dated January 7, 1887 (Deed Book 57, page 389 in the records of the Buncombe County Register of Deeds).

92. *History of Montmorenci Methodist Church*, 5.

93. Recollections of Mrs. Jennie E. Clarke as recorded in the *History of Montmorenci Methodist Church*, 5.

94. Ibid.

95. *Journal of the Seventy-Second Annual Convention of the Protestant Episcopal Church in the State of North Carolina* (1888), 16–17.

96. *Journal of the Seventy-Seventh Annual Convention of the Protestant Episcopal Church in the State of North Carolina* (1893), 98.

97. Ibid.

98. *Journal of the Tenth Annual Convention of the Protestant Episcopal Church in the Missionary Jurisdiction of Asheville* (1904), 87.

99. Mashburn, *Hominy Valley: The Golden Years*, 293.

100. *Journal of the Twentieth Annual Convention of the Protestant Episcopal Church in the Missionary Jurisdiction of Asheville* (1914), 78.

101. "Dr. A. P. & Eloise Willis to the Trustees for the Protestant Episcopal Church, the Diocese in North Carolina." Deed dated May 21, 1915 (Deed Book 203, page 46 in the records of the Buncombe County Register of Deeds).

102. Sill, *Historical Sketches*, 28 and 66–67.

103. *Journal of the Seventy-Seventh Annual Convention of the Protestant Episcopal Church in the State of North Carolina* (1893), 101.

104. Sill, *Historical Sketches*, 28.

105. Ibid., 67.

106. See "United States Census, 1900," William Owen, ED 132 Asheville township, Beaverdam & Haw Creek Voting Precincts Ramoth and Montford towns, Buncombe, North Carolina, United States (https://familysearch.org/pal:/MM9.1.1/MST5-2HQ).

107. "Stephen Lee and his wife, S. R. Lee, to William Thomas Owen." Deed dated February 2, 1872 (Deed Book 34, page 453 in the records of the Buncombe County Register of Deeds).

108. *Journal of the Seventy-Eighth Annual Convention of the Protestant Episcopal Church in the State of North Carolina* (1894), 105.

109. Rev. William Francis Rice was ordained as a priest on June 10, 1900.

110. "Glencoe Mill, 1872" in the Rufus Morgan Photographic Collection #P0057, North Carolina Collection Photographic Archives, The Wilson Library, University of North Carolina at Chapel Hill.

111. William A. Nesbitt, *History of Early Settlement and Land Use on the Bent Creek Experimental Forest* (Asheville, NC: Appalachian Forest Experiment Station, 1941), 36.

112. Ibid.

113. These were the daughters of Colonel Lewis M. Hatch: Susan Elizabeth Hatch, Emily Julia Hatch, and Sarah ("Sallie") Allen Hatch.

114. Susan Elizabeth Hatch—in the 1870 census, her occupation is listed as "Teaching."

115. Buel, "Work In North Carolina," 342–43.

116. The 1870 federal census shows the Lee family as living in Asheville, and Lee's occupation as "druggist."

117. Nesbitt, *History of Early Settlement and Land Use on the Bent Creek Experimental Forest*, 18.

118. James B. Sill, *Historical Sketches*, 77.

119. *Journal of the Fifty-Fourth Annual Convention of the Protestant Episcopal Church in the State of North Carolina* (Raleigh, NC: M. S. Littlefield Printer & Binder, 1870), 16.

120. *Journal of the Fifty-Fifth Annual Convention of the Protestant Episcopal Church in the State of North Carolina* (1871), 44.

121. *Journal of the Fifty-Eighth Annual Convention of the Protestant Episcopal Church in the State of North Carolina* (Raleigh, NC: Daily News Print, Fayetteville Street, 1874), 84.

122. Sill, *Historical Sketches*, 78.

123. Ibid.

124. Ibid.

125. *Journal of the Twenty-Fifth Annual Convention of the Protestant Episcopal Church in the Missionary Jurisdiction of Asheville* (Asheville, NC: Asheville Printing Company, 1919), 111.

126. *Journal of the Twenty-Seventh Annual Convention of the Protestant Episcopal Church in the Missionary Jurisdiction of Asheville* (Asheville, NC: Asheville Printing Company, 1921), 28.

127. *Public Laws of the State of North Carolina Passed by the General Assembly at the Session of 1858-'9* (Raleigh, NC: Holden and Wilson, Printers to the State, 1859), 274.

128. *The Leicester Leader*, January 13–January 19, 2011, vol. 4, no. 2 (published by the Tribune/Leader).

129. *Journal of the Forty-Sixth Annual Convention of the Protestant Episcopal Church in the State of North Carolina* (Fayetteville, NC: Edward J. Hale, 1862), 39.

130. *Journal of the Fifty-Second Annual Convention of the Protestant Episcopal Church in the State of North Carolina* (1868), 34.

131. "Episcopal Church, Missionary District of Asheville to Roger Lamson, Jr.," July 6, 1911 (Deed Book 172, page 396 in the records of the Buncombe Register of Deeds).

132. "TR Bascom College: John J. Roberts, F. Sluder, George W. Hampton, R. L. Gudger, and John T. Palmer to the Vestry of Trinity Parish: N. W. Woodfin, J. G. Martin, J. L. Bailey, T. W. Patton, and F. J. Murdoch." Deed dated December 19, 1867 (Deed Book 28, page 366 in the records of the Buncombe County Register of Deeds).

133. R. N. Price, "Methodism in East Tennessee: Before, During, and Since the War," *Methodist Review Quarterly* (April 1908), 298.

134. *Journal of the Fifty-Third Annual Convention of the Protestant Episcopal Church in the State of North Carolina* (1869), 85.

135. "Leicester Chapman and his wife Sarah to John Carpenter." Deed dated April 14, 1873 (Deed Book 35,

page 325 in the records of the Buncombe County Register of Deeds).

136. *Journal of the Fifty-Seventh Annual Convention of the Protestant Episcopal Church in the State of North Carolina* (Raleigh, NC: Edwards & Broughton, Power Printers and Binders, 1873), 19.

137. *Journal of the Fifty-Eighth Annual Convention of the Protestant Episcopal Church in the State of North Carolina* (1874), 87.

138. *Journal of the Sixtieth Annual Convention of the Protestant Episcopal Church in the State of North Carolina* (1876), 94.

139. *Journal of the Sixty-First Annual Convention of the Protestant Episcopal Church in the State of North Carolina* (1877), 144.

140. Ibid.

141. Ibid., 43.

142. *Journal of the Fifty-Third Annual Convention of the Protestant Episcopal Church in the State of North Carolina* (1869), 3.

143. *Journal of the Fifty-Second Annual Convention of the Protestant Episcopal Church in the State of North Carolina* (1868), 3.

144. *Journal of the Sixty-Second Annual Convention of the Protestant Episcopal Church in the State of North Carolina* (Published by order of the Convention, 1878), 44.

145. Ibid., 78.

146. *Journal of the Sixty-Fifth Annual Convention of the Protestant Episcopal Church in the State of North Carolina* (1881), 111.

147. *Journal of the Sixty-Sixth Annual Convention of the Protestant Episcopal Church in the State of North Carolina* (1882), 41.

148. *Journal of the Seventy-Fourth Annual Convention of the Protestant Episcopal Church in the State of North Carolina* (1890), 80.

149. *Journal of the Seventy-Sixth Annual Convention of the Protestant Episcopal Church in the State of North Carolina* (1892), 105.

150. Ibid., 104.

151. *Journal of the Twenty-Seventh Annual Convention of the Protestant Episcopal Church in the Missionary Jurisdiction of Asheville* (1921), 31. See also "Episcopal Church, Missionary District of Asheville to J. M. Carver, April 30, 1920" (Deed Book 239, page 284 in the records of the Buncombe Register of Deeds).

152. Ibid.

153. Ibid.

154. Ibid., 32.

155. Ibid.

156. "Robert H. Gribbin, Haywood Parker, William W. Redwood, R. H. McDuffie, Kingsland Van Winkle and David B. Harris, Trustees for the Protestant Episcopal Church in the Diocese of Western North Carolina to Miss Rose Chapman, Mrs. O. M. Clark, Mrs. L. A. Justice, Burgin A. Patton, and Herman M. Stevens," June 27, 1938 (Deed Book 513, page 141 in the records of the Buncombe Register of Deeds).

157. "Certificate Regarding Appointment of Trustees for Leicester Episcopal Church Yard," March 19, 1998 (Deed Book 2014, page 011 in the records of the Buncombe Register of Deeds). This indenture was recorded in 1998, but the trustees were appointed on May 24, 1996 (two years earlier).

158. "The Willis Houses," Asylum Index, http://studymore.org.uk/4asylums.htm.

159. *Blain Biographical Directory of Anglican Clergy in the Diocese of Honolulu 1862–1902* (final edition, 2012, at http://anglicanhistory.org/hawaii/blain_directory.pdf).

160. *Journal of the Seventy-Second Annual Convention of the Protestant Episcopal Church in the State of North Carolina* (1888), 105.

161. Ibid., 34–35.

162. Sill, *Historical Sketches*, 49.

163. *Journal of the Seventy-Eighth Annual Convention of the Protestant Episcopal Church in the State of North Carolina* (1894), 129.

164. Ibid., 69.

165. "Stubbs Diaries," January 6, 1898.

166. "Stubbs Diaries," October 9, 1898.

167. "Francis Willis and his wife Catherine Willis to J. M. Horner, T. W. Patton, Churchill Satterlee, McNeely DuBose, Charles McNamee, and Haywood Parker, Trustees of the Missionary District of Asheville." Deed dated October 2, 1899 (Deed Book 114, Page 56 in the records of the Buncombe County Register of Deeds).

168. Sill, *Historical Sketches*, 68.

169. Stowe, *Stowe's Clerical Directory 1920–21*, 288.

170. *Journal of the Tenth Annual Convention of the Protestant Episcopal Church in the Missionary Jurisdiction of Asheville* (1904), 106.

171. *Journal of the Seventy-Ninth Annual Convention of the Protestant Episcopal Church in the State of North Carolina* (1895), 110–11.

172. Sill, *Historical Sketches*, 68.

173. *Journal of the Fifty-Fifth Annual Convention of the Protestant Episcopal Church in the State of North Carolina* (1871), 67.

174. "A. E. Smith to Rt. Rev. Thomas Atkinson, W. H. Battle, and Gen. Cox, Trustees of Diocese of North Carolina of the Protestant Episcopal Church." Deed dated August 22, 1871 (Deed Book 69, page 241 in the records of the Buncombe County Register of Deeds).

175. *Journal of the Fifty-Eighth Annual Convention of the Protestant Episcopal Church in the State of North Carolina* (1874), 83.

176. Davison, *The Asheville City Directory and Gazetteer of Buncombe County for 1883–84*, 87.

177. *Journal of the Sixty-Eighth Annual Convention of the Protestant Episcopal Church in the State of North Carolina* (1884), 49.

178. Ibid., 56.

179. Ibid., 109.

180. Ibid.

181. *Journal of the Sixty-Ninth Annual Convention of the Protestant Episcopal Church in the State of North Carolina* (1885), 77.

182. *Journal of the Seventy-First Annual Convention of the Protestant Episcopal Church in the State of North Carolina* (1887), 102.

183. Ibid., 48.

184. Ibid., 37.

185. *Journal of the Seventy-Second Annual Convention of the Protestant Episcopal Church in the State of North Carolina* (1888), 111.

186. http://www.brotherhoodstandrew.org/.

187. *Journal of the Seventy-Seventh Annual Convention of the Protestant Episcopal Church in the State of North Carolina* (1893), 97.

188. Ibid., 145.

189. *Journal of the Seventy-Ninth Annual Convention of the Protestant Episcopal Church in the State of North Carolina* (1895), 78.

190. *Journal of the Tenth Annual Convention of the Protestant Episcopal Church in the Missionary Jurisdiction of Asheville* (1904), 126.

191. Ibid., 53.

192. "J. M. Horner, R. R. Swope, A. H. Stubbs, W.

Vance Brown, Haywood Parker and C. D. Beadle, Trustees for the Episcopal Church in the district of Asheville to Richard E. Kiibler." Deed dated March 17, 1916 (Deed Book 206, page 523 in the records of the Buncombe County Register of Deeds).

193. *Journal of the Fortieth Annual Convention of the Protestant Episcopal Church in the State of North Carolina* (1856), 49.

194. Ibid.

195. *Journal of the Fifty-Ninth Annual Convention of the Protestant Episcopal Church in the State of North Carolina* (J. B. Whitaker, Jr., Book and Job Printer, 1875), 43.

196. *Journal of the Sixty-First Annual Convention of the Protestant Episcopal Church in the State of North Carolina* (1877), 43.

197. Rev. Norvin C. Duncan, *Pictorial History of the Episcopal Church in North Carolina: 1701–1964* (Asheville, NC: Miller Printing Company, 1965), 122–23.

198. *Journal of the Sixty-Second Annual Convention of the Protestant Episcopal Church in the State of North Carolina* (1878), 48.

199. Ibid., 84.

200. *Journal of the Seventy-Fourth Annual Convention of the Protestant Episcopal Church in the State of North Carolina* (1890), 89.

201. *Journal of the Seventy-Fifth Annual Convention of the Protestant Episcopal Church in the State of North Carolina* (1891), 138.

202. Ibid., 62.

203. *Journal of the Seventy-Seventh Annual Convention of the Protestant Episcopal Church in the State of North Carolina* (1893), 145.

204. *Journal of the Seventy-Eighth Annual Convention of the Protestant Episcopal Church in the State of North Carolina* (1894), 66.

205. Ibid., 141.

206. Ibid.

207. *Journal of the Seventy-Ninth Annual Convention of the Protestant Episcopal Church in the State of North Carolina* (1895), 56, 60, 62–63.

208. Ibid., 102–3.

209. Elliot Wigginton, *Foxfire 4: Water Systems, Fiddle Making, Logging, Gardening, Sassafras Tea, Wood Carving, and Further Affairs of Plain Living* (New York: Anchor Books, 1977), 408–9.

210. Rev. Frederick W. Wey, *Historical Sketches of the Missions in Charge of the Rev. Fred'k W. Wey in the Missionary Jurisdiction of Asheville, N.C.* (Murphy, NC: Alfred Morgan, 1897), 16.

211. Ibid.

212. *Journal of the Twenty-First Annual Convention of the Protestant Episcopal Church in the Missionary Jurisdiction of Asheville* (Asheville, NC: Asheville Printing Company, 1915), 69.

213. Wilbur G. Zeigler and Ben S. Grosscup, *The Heart of the Alleghenies or Western North Carolina* (Raleigh, NC: Alfred Williams, 1883), 203.

214. Sill, *Historical Sketches*, 113–14.

215. Ibid.

216. *Journal of the Sixty-Third Annual Convention of the Protestant Episcopal Church in the State of North Carolina* (Raleigh, NC: Uzzell Wiley & Co. Printers and Binders, 1879), 110–11.

217. *Journal of the Sixty-Fourth Annual Convention of the Protestant Episcopal Church in the State of North Carolina* (Raleigh, NC: Uzzell Wiley & Co. Printers and Binders, 1880), 76–77.

218. Ibid.

219. Ibid., 114.

220. *Journal of the Sixty-Seventh Annual Convention of the Protestant Episcopal Church in the State of North Carolina* (1883), 88.

221. *Journal of the Sixty-Eighth Annual Convention of the Protestant Episcopal Church in the State of North Carolina* (1884), 74.

222. Ibid.

223. *Journal of the Sixty-Ninth Annual Convention of the Protestant Episcopal Church in the State of North Carolina* (1885), 11.

224. *Journal of the Seventieth Annual Convention of the Protestant Episcopal Church in the State of North Carolina* (1886), 60.

225. Ibid.

226. *Rochester Democrat and Chronicle*, January 2, 1886, http://www.fultonhistory.com.

227. *Journal of the Seventy-Fifth Annual Convention of the Protestant Episcopal Church in the State of North Carolina* (1891), 114.

228. *Journal of the Seventy-Sixth Annual Convention of the Protestant Episcopal Church in the State of North Carolina* (1892), 111.

229. *Journal of the Seventy-Seventh Annual Convention of the Protestant Episcopal Church in the State of North Carolina* (1893), 123.

230. Rt. Rev. Junius Horner, "Missionary District of Asheville—Statement of the Work," *The Spirit of Missions* LXIV, no. 5 (May 1899), 225.

231. W. Clark Medford, *The Middle History of Haywood County* (Johnson City, TN: Overmountain Press, 2004), 76–77.

232. Ibid., 36.

233. *Journal of the Sixtieth Annual Convention of the Protestant Episcopal Church in the State of North Carolina* (1876), 94.

234. Ibid.

235. Ibid.

236. *Journal of the Sixty-First Annual Convention of the Protestant Episcopal Church in the State of North Carolina* (1877), 40.

237. *Journal of the Sixty-Third Annual Convention of the Protestant Episcopal Church in the State of North Carolina* (1879), 110–11.

238. *Journal of the Sixty-Fourth Annual Convention of the Protestant Episcopal Church in the State of North Carolina* (1880), 96.

239. *Journal of the Sixty-Fifth Annual Convention of the Protestant Episcopal Church in the State of North Carolina* (1881), 114.

240. Ibid.

241. *Journal of the Seventy-Second Annual Convention of the Protestant Episcopal Church in the State of North Carolina* (1888), 79.

242. *Journal of the Seventy-Fifth Annual Convention of the Protestant Episcopal Church in the State of North Carolina* (1891), 133.

243. *Journal of the Seventy-Sixth Annual Convention of the Protestant Episcopal Church in the State of North Carolina* (1892), 131.

244. Patton, *The Story of Henderson County*, 235.

245. Theodore L. Fitzsimons, "An Elizabethan Colony in North Carolina," *International Studio* 59 (1916), 191–92.

246. *Journal of the Sixty-Ninth Annual Convention of the Protestant Episcopal Church in the State of North Carolina* (1885), 7.

247. *Journal of the Seventieth Annual Convention of the Protestant Episcopal Church in the State of North Carolina* (1886), 91.

248. Ibid.

249. Ibid.
250. Patton, *The Story of Henderson County*, 235.
251. *Journal of the Seventy-First Annual Convention of the Protestant Episcopal Church in the State of North Carolina* (1887), 8.
252. *Journal of the Seventy-Second Annual Convention of the Protestant Episcopal Church in the State of North Carolina* (1888), 14.
253. Patton, *The Story of Henderson County*, 235. These windows were later installed in St. James, Upward, after Gethsemane closed, and then, when St. James was closed, the windows were bought by the Mallet family and installed in a private chapel at their estate in Bowman's Bluff. A copy of a photo taken of the windows in the Mallet chapel is stored in box 59 at the offices of the Western North Carolina Diocese in Asheville, North Carolina.
254. *Journal of the Seventy-Seventh Annual Convention of the Protestant Episcopal Church in the State of North Carolina* (1893), 96.
255. *Journal of the Seventy-Eighth Annual Convention of the Protestant Episcopal Church in the State of North Carolina* (1894), 96.
256. *Journal of the Seventy-Ninth Annual Convention of the Protestant Episcopal Church in the State of North Carolina* (1895), 28–29 and 50.
257. J. A. Venn, *Alumni Cantabrigienses: Part II, From 1752 to 1900*, vol. III, *Gabb–Justamond* (Cambridge: Cambridge University Press, 1947), 573.
258. "Stubbs Diaries," January 12, 1895.
259. "Stubbs Diaries," August 11, 1895.
260. "Stubbs Diaries," April 29, 1898.
261. Ibid.
262. Patton, *The Story of Henderson County*, 235.
263. Sill, *Historical Sketches*, 62.
264. *Journal of the Twenty-Fourth Annual Convention of the Protestant Episcopal Church in the Missionary Jurisdiction of Asheville* (1918), 210.
265. Rev. James Sill, in *Historical Sketches*, writes that Dr. G. W. Fletcher was "a native resident, who became the first Junior Warden of the vestry" (15).
266. Sill, *Historical Sketches*, 15. Sill ends the sentence as follows: "which was consecrated on August 21, 1859 by Bishop Atkinson." I omitted this portion because the date of consecration is incorrect.
267. *Journal of the Forty-Fourth Annual Convention of the Protestant Episcopal Church in the State of North Carolina* (Fayetteville, NC: Edward J. Hale, 1860), 17.
268. *Journal of the Forty-Fifth Annual Convention of the Protestant Episcopal Church in the State of North Carolina* (1861), 38.
269. *Journal of the Forty-Sixth Annual Convention of the Protestant Episcopal Church in the State of North Carolina* (1862), 13.
270. *Journal of the First Annual Council of the Protestant Episcopal Church in the State of North Carolina* (1863), 40–41.
271. *Journal of the Fifty-First Annual Convention of the Protestant Episcopal Church in the State of North Carolina* (1867), 60.
272. *Journal of the Fifty-Second Annual Convention of the Protestant Episcopal Church in the State of North Carolina* (1868), 96.
273. *Journal of the Fifty-Third Annual Convention of the Protestant Episcopal Church in the State of North Carolina* (1869), 85.
274. *Journal of the Fifty-Fifth Annual Convention of the Protestant Episcopal Church in the State of North Carolina* (1871), 66.
275. *Journal of the Fifty-Seventh Annual Convention of the Protestant Episcopal Church in the State of North Carolina* (1873), 86.
276. *Journal of the Fifty-Eighth Annual Convention of the Protestant Episcopal Church in the State of North Carolina* (1874), 27.
277. Ibid.
278. *Journal of the Sixty-Second Annual Convention of the Protestant Episcopal Church in the State of North Carolina* (1878), 81.
279. Ibid., 82–83.
280. *Journal of the Sixty-Fifth Annual Convention of the Protestant Episcopal Church in the State of North Carolina* (1881), 81.
281. *Journal of the Sixty-Seventh Annual Convention of the Protestant Episcopal Church in the State of North Carolina* (1883), 120–21.
282. *Journal of the Thirty-Ninth Annual Convention of the Protestant Episcopal Church in the State of North Carolina* (1855), 15.
283. Ibid.
284. Patton, *The Story of Henderson County*, 193.
285. *Journal of the Forty-Fifth Annual Convention of the Protestant Episcopal Church in the State of North Carolina* (1861), 37.
286. Patton, *The Story of Henderson County*, 192.
287. Ibid.
288. *Journal of the Forty-Eighth Annual Council of the Protestant Episcopal Church in the State of North Carolina* (1864), 11.
289. *Journal of the Fiftieth Annual Convention of the Protestant Episcopal Church in the State of North Carolina* (1866), 40.
290. *Journal of the Fifty-First Annual Convention of the Protestant Episcopal Church in the State of North Carolina* (1867), 60.
291. *Journal of the Fifty-Second Annual Convention of the Protestant Episcopal Church in the State of North Carolina* (1868), 28.
292. *Journal of the Fifty-Fifth Annual Convention of the Protestant Episcopal Church in the State of North Carolina* (1871), 67.
293. *Journal of the Sixty-Fourth Annual Convention of the Protestant Episcopal Church in the State of North Carolina* (1880), 150.
294. John Wall, *A Dictionary for Episcopalians* (Lanham, MD: Rowman & Littlefield, 2000), 82.
295. *Journal of the Sixty-Sixth Annual Convention of the Protestant Episcopal Church in the State of North Carolina* (1882), 145.
296. *Journal of the Sixty-Ninth Annual Convention of the Protestant Episcopal Church in the State of North Carolina* (1885), 74.
297. *Journal of the Seventy-Second Annual Convention of the Protestant Episcopal Church in the State of North Carolina* (1888), 14 and 128.
298. *Journal of the Seventy-Fourth Annual Convention of the Protestant Episcopal Church in the State of North Carolina* (1890), 6 and 30.
299. *Journal of the Seventy-Fifth Annual Convention of the Protestant Episcopal Church in the State of North Carolina* (1891), 103.
300. Sill, *Historical Sketches*, 19.
301. Wey, *Historical Sketches*, 13.
302. The biographical material on Davies came from the following sources: Wey, *Historical Sketches*, 13, and Max R. Williams, ed., *The History of Jackson County* (Sylva, NC: Jackson County Historical Society, 1987), 138, 153, 156–57.
303. Wey, *Historical Sketches*, 13.

304. *Journal of the Sixty-Seventh Annual Convention of the Protestant Episcopal Church in the State of North Carolina* (1883), 54.
305. Wey, *Historical Sketches*, 13.
306. *Journal of the Sixty-Eighth Annual Convention of the Protestant Episcopal Church in the State of North Carolina* (1884), 75.
307. Wey, *Historical Sketches*, 13.
308. *Journal of the Sixty-Ninth Annual Convention of the Protestant Episcopal Church in the State of North Carolina* 1885), 9–10.
309. Ibid.
310. Ibid.
311. Ibid., 10.
312. *Journal of the Seventy-Second Annual Convention of the Protestant Episcopal Church in the State of North Carolina* (1888), 16.
313. William Ernest Bird, *The History of Western Carolina College: The Progress of an Idea* (Chapel Hill: University of North Carolina Press, 1963), 10.
314. *Journal of the Seventy-Fifth Annual Convention of the Protestant Episcopal Church in the State of North Carolina* (1891), 96.
315. *Journal of the Seventy-Sixth Annual Convention of the Protestant Episcopal Church in the State of North Carolina* (1892), 91.
316. *Journal of the Seventy-Seventh Annual Convention of the Protestant Episcopal Church in the State of North Carolina* (1893), 74.
317. Rev. Dr. Buel had retired to Baltimore, Maryland, to live with his daughter. He died there shortly thereafter on January 13, 1893.
318. *Journal of the Seventy-Fifth Annual Convention of the Protestant Episcopal Church in the State of North Carolina* (1891), 96.
319. From the "History of St. David's" at the church website: http://www.st-davids.org.
320. Ibid.
321. Buel, "Work In North Carolina," 344.
322. Ibid.
323. *Journal of the Sixty-Second Annual Convention of the Protestant Episcopal Church in the State of North Carolina* (1878), 48.
324. *Journal of the Sixty-Fourth Annual Convention of the Protestant Episcopal Church in the State of North Carolina* (1880), 77.
325. Arthur, *Western North Carolina: A History*, 192.
326. Amnesty letter written September 23, 1865, from Dillard L. Love to Andrew Johnson; see http://dla.acaweb.org/cdm/singleitem/collection/berea/id/837/rec/1. This letter was written by Dillard L. Love to President Andrew Johnson in response to the president's Amnesty Proclamation of May 29, 1865.
327. See www.familysearch.org — United States Census, 1880. Household of Margaret E. Love, Webster, Jackson County, North Carolina. Shows Dillard L. as 42 years old, with the occupation of lawyer.
328. *Journal of the Sixty-Fourth Annual Convention of the Protestant Episcopal Church in the State of North Carolina* (1880), 122.
329. Levi Branson, *Branson's North Carolina Business Directory: 1890*, vol. VII (Raleigh, NC: Levi Branson, 1889), 389.
330. Williams, *The History of Jackson County*, 119. It says, "J. N. McCombs bought what is now known as College Hill."
331. Ibid.
332. Madison soon thereafter was chosen to be the first president of the Cullowhee Institute, which eventually became Western Carolina University.
333. *Journal of the Seventy-Sixth Annual Convention of the Protestant Episcopal Church in the State of North Carolina* (1892), 137.
334. *Journal of the Seventy-Seventh Annual Convention of the Protestant Episcopal Church in the State of North Carolina* (1893), 138.
335. Ibid.
336. *Journal of the Seventy-Ninth Annual Convention of the Protestant Episcopal Church in the State of North Carolina* (1895), 117.
337. In the 1874 journal, Dillard L. Love is listed as a "Lay Reader" with the Ravenscroft Associate Mission and Training School (97).
338. *Journal of the Seventy-Ninth Annual Convention of the Protestant Episcopal Church in the State of North Carolina* (1895), 116.
339. Rev. Clarence Buel, "Appeal: A Good Layman and His Good Work," *The Churchman*, March 30, 1901, 31.
340. Ibid.
341. Ibid.
342. "Marriage of Miss Mollie Walker and Col. Dillard L. Love," in *The Landmark*, Statesville, North Carolina, Friday, October 18, 1907.
343. Buel, "Work In North Carolina," 343.
344. The above background material on the Rumbough family was mostly gleaned from the following two sources: Della Hazel Moore, *Hot Springs of North Carolina* (Johnson City, TN: Overmountain Press, 2002), and Jacqueline Burgin Painter, *The German Invasion of Western North Carolina* (Johnson City, TN: Overmountain Press, 1992).
345. *Journal of the Seventieth Annual Convention of the Protestant Episcopal Church in the State of North Carolina* (1886), 58.
346. *Journal of the Seventy-Second Annual Convention of the Protestant Episcopal Church in the State of North Carolina* (1888), 77.
347. Ibid., 129.
348. *Journal of the Seventy-Third Annual Convention of the Protestant Episcopal Church in the State of North Carolina* (1889), 73.
349. *Journal of the Seventy-Fourth Annual Convention of the Protestant Episcopal Church in the State of North Carolina* (1890), 8–9.
350. Ibid., 79.
351. *Journal of the Seventy-Fifth Annual Convention of the Protestant Episcopal Church in the State of North Carolina* (1891), 105.
352. Ibid.
353. "Stubbs Diaries," August 25, 1901.
354. "Stubbs Diaries," July 27, 1901.
355. "Stubbs Diaries," January 25, February 8, and February 25, 1903.
356. "Stubbs Diaries," February 24, 1901.
357. Martha Royce's great-granddaughter, Judith Riker Damon, has recently published *A Genteel Spy*, which is an account of Martha's Civil War experiences in Franklin, Tennessee. The account was originally written by Martha's daughter Betsy (Damon's grandmother) in 1875.
358. Moore, *Hot Springs of North Carolina*, 56.
359. *Concrete Houses & Cottages* (New York: Atlas Portland Cement Company, 1909), 31.
360. Moore, *Hot Springs of North Carolina*, 119.
361. *The News and Courier* (Charleston, SC), February 25, 1939.
362. Moore, *Hot Springs of North Carolina*, 119.
363. "RUTHERFORDTON, NC: A Brief History," by Robin S. Lattimore, noted historian and author of local history. Information from http://www.rutherfordton.net/history.html.

364. *Journal of the Twenty-Sixth Annual Convention of the Protestant Episcopal Church in the State of North Carolina* (Fayetteville, NC: Edward J. Hale, 1842), 19. Also, on page 36, the bishop reported, "The pecuniary aid afforded these stations, has been derived from the bequest of the late Mrs. Troy of Wadesborough, entrusted to the Bishop for Missionary purposes."

365. Ibid.

366. *Journal of the Twenty-Seventh Annual Convention of the Protestant Episcopal Church in the State of North Carolina* (Fayetteville, NC: Edward J. Hale, 1843), 26.

367. Ashe, *Biographical History of North Carolina*, 38.

368. *Journal of the Thirty-Second Annual Convention of the Protestant Episcopal Church in the State of North Carolina* (1848), 29.

369. *Journal of the Thirty-Third Annual Convention of the Protestant Episcopal Church in the State of North Carolina* (1849), 19.

370. *Journal of the Thirty-Third Annual Convention of the Protestant Episcopal Church in the State of North Carolina* (1849), 5, and *Journal of the Thirty-Fourth Annual Convention of the Protestant Episcopal Church in the State of North Carolina* (Fayetteville, NC: Edward J. Hale, 1850), 6.

371. Sill, *Historical Sketches*, 30.

372. *Journal of the Thirty-Sixth Annual Convention of the Protestant Episcopal Church in the State of North Carolina* (Fayetteville, NC: Edward J. Hale, 1852), 15.

373. *Journal of the Fifty-Second Annual Convention of the Protestant Episcopal Church in the State of North Carolina* (1868), 117.

374. *Journal of the Fifty-Seventh Annual Convention of the Protestant Episcopal Church in the State of North Carolina* (1873), 59.

375. *Journal of the Sixty-Second Annual Convention of the Protestant Episcopal Church in the State of North Carolina* (1878), 81.

376. Ibid., 82.

377. *Journal of the Sixty-Sixth Annual Convention of the Protestant Episcopal Church in the State of North Carolina* (1882), 145.

378. *Journal of the Sixty-Seventh Annual Convention of the Protestant Episcopal Church in the State of North Carolina* (1883), 51.

379. *Journal of the Sixty-Ninth Annual Convention of the Protestant Episcopal Church in the State of North Carolina* (1885), 14.

380. *Journal of the Seventy-Second Annual Convention of the Protestant Episcopal Church in the State of North Carolina* (1888), 108.

381. *Journal of the Seventy-Fourth Annual Convention of the Protestant Episcopal Church in the State of North Carolina* (1890), 127.

382. Hon. John Hugh McDowell, *History of the McDowells, Erwins, Irwins and Connections: Being a Compilation from Various Sources* (Memphis, TN: C. B. Johnston, 1918), 271.

383. Sill, *Historical Sketches*, 126–27.

384. *Journal of the Forty-First Annual Convention of the Protestant Episcopal Church in the State of North Carolina* (1857), 18–19.

385. National Register of Historic Places Multiple Property Documentation Form—"Historic and Architectural Resources of Transylvania County, North Carolina including the incorporated towns of Brevard and Rosman, ca. 1820–1941," prepared by Deborah J. Thompson, 527 Manchester Street, Barbourville, Kentucky—June 21, 1993, 15.

386. Rev. William Wyndham Malet, *An Errand to the South in the Summer of 1862* (London: Richard Bentley, New Burlington Street, 1863), 250.

387. *Journal of the Forty-Second Annual Convention of the Protestant Episcopal Church in the State of North Carolina* (1858), 17.

388. *Journal of the Forty-First Annual Convention of the Protestant Episcopal Church in the State of North Carolina* (1857), 45.

389. *Journal of the Forty-Fifth Annual Convention of the Protestant Episcopal Church in the State of North Carolina* (1861), 33.

390. Ibid.

391. *Journal of the Forty-Eighth Annual Council of the Protestant Episcopal Church in the State of North Carolina* (1864), 41.

392. Sill, *Historical Sketches*, 11–13 and 62–64.

393. *Journal of the Fifty-Ninth Annual Convention of the Protestant Episcopal Church in the State of North Carolina* (1875), 41.

394. *Journal of the Fifty-Eighth Annual Convention of the Protestant Episcopal Church in the State of North Carolina* (1874), 26.

395. *Journal of the Fifty-Ninth Annual Convention of the Protestant Episcopal Church in the State of North Carolina* (1875), 78.

396. *Journal of the Sixty-Seventh Annual Convention of the Protestant Episcopal Church in the State of North Carolina* (1883), 88.

397. *Journal of the Sixty-Eighth Annual Convention of the Protestant Episcopal Church in the State of North Carolina* (1884), 47.

398. Ibid., 75.

399. *Journal of the Sixty-Fifth Annual Convention of the Protestant Episcopal Church in the State of North Carolina* (1881), 67, 113.

400. *Journal of the Seventieth Annual Convention of the Protestant Episcopal Church in the State of North Carolina* (1886), 8.

401. *Journal of the Seventy-Fifth Annual Convention of the Protestant Episcopal Church in the State of North Carolina* (1891), 61.

402. *Journal of the Seventy-Sixth Annual Convention of the Protestant Episcopal Church in the State of North Carolina* (1892), 64.

403. *Journal of the Seventy-Ninth Annual Convention of the Protestant Episcopal Church in the State of North Carolina* (1895), 132.

404. Ibid.

405. *Journal of the Sixty-Sixth Annual Convention of the Protestant Episcopal Church in the State of North Carolina* (1882), 112.

406. *Journal of the Seventy-Ninth Annual Convention of the Protestant Episcopal Church in the State of North Carolina* (1895), 121–22.

407. *Journal of the Fifty-Ninth Annual Convention of the Protestant Episcopal Church in the State of North Carolina* (1875), 80.

408. *Journal of the Sixtieth Annual Convention of the Protestant Episcopal Church in the State of North Carolina* (1876), 9.

409. *Journal of the Fifty-Fifth Annual Convention of the Protestant Episcopal Church in the State of North Carolina* (1871), 67.

410. "E. F. Clark to Rt. Rev. Thos. Atkinson, Geo. W. Mordicai, and W. H. Battle, Trustees," January 2, 1871 (Deed Book 164, page 322 in the records of the Buncombe County Register of Deeds).

411. *Journal of the Seventy-Third Annual Convention of the Protestant Episcopal Church in the State of North Carolina* (1889), 108.

412. "J. M. Horner, R. R. Swope, H. Fred Saumenig,

C. D. Beadle, W. Vance Brown, and Haywood Parker to Alfred L. Stephenson," October 9, 1911 (Deed Book 173, page 439 in the records of the Buncombe County Register of Deeds).

413. Davison, *The Asheville City Directory and Gazetteer of Buncombe County for 1883–84*, 89.

414. William Richard Cutter, *Genealogical and Family History of Central New York*, vol. 1 (New York: Lewis Historical Publishing Company, 1912), 15.

415. *New York Times*, January 21, 1873: "Francis V. Brush, son of the late ex-Mayor Conklin Brush, of Brooklyn, was yesterday divorced by a decree of the City Court from his wife, Mary E. Brush, on her petition. Twenty-four dollars per week are allowed Mrs. Brush as alimony."

416. "New Jersey, Marriages, 1678–1985," https://familysearch.org/pal:/MM9.1.1/FZGS-TJT, accessed August 20, 2012. John K. Hoyt and Mary Elizth. Bensel, 01 Jan 1877; citing reference pg 334, FHL microfilm 494159.

417. Most reports show Good Shepherd as having two communicants — except in 1906, when it is listed as having four communicants.

418. "Stubbs Diaries," August 20, 1899.

419. *Journal of the Seventh Annual Convention of the Protestant Episcopal Church in the Missionary Jurisdiction of Asheville* (Asheville, NC: Asheville Printing Company, 1901), 58.

420. United States Census, 1910, https://familysearch.org/pal:/MM9.1.1/MLMR-J5J, accessed August 20, 2012. Mary L. Brush in household of John K. Hoyt, Beaufort Ward 2, Carteret, North Carolina; citing sheet 13A, family 147, NARA microfilm publication T624, FHL microfilm 1375108.

421. North Carolina, Deaths, 1931–1994, https://familysearch.org/pal:/MM9.1.1/FPZM-P29, accessed August 20, 2012. Marie Louise Brush, 15 May 1954.

422. See http://www.hendersoncountypublicschoolsnc.org/eto/about/school-history/.

423. *Journal of the Seventh Annual Convention of the Protestant Episcopal Church in the Missionary Jurisdiction of Asheville* (1901), 56.

424. "Stubbs Diaries," September 7, 1902.

425. *Journal of the Sixty-Eighth Annual Convention of the Protestant Episcopal Church in the Diocese of North Carolina* (1884), 109.

426. Authority of the State of New York, under the supervision of the New York Monuments Commission, *Major General Abner Doubleday and Brevet Major General John C. Robinson in the Civil War* (Albany, NY: J. B. Lyon, 1918), 61–62.

427. "Profile Map, U. Doubleday Add'tn, Asheville, N. C.," S. F. Venerable, C. E. April 10, 1883 (Deed Book 8, page 2 in the records of the Buncombe County Register of Deeds).

428. *Journal of the Sixty-Ninth Annual Convention of the Protestant Episcopal Church in the Diocese of North Carolina* (1885), 77–78.

429. *Journal of the Seventieth Annual Convention of the Protestant Episcopal Church in the Diocese of North Carolina* (1886), 106.

430. Maloney Directory Company, *Maloney's 1899–1900 Asheville City Directory* (Richmond, VA: J. L. Hill Printing Co., 1899), 184.

431. "George W. Pack, A. J. Lyman, Oliver Gideon, and Charles Woolsey to Rt. Rev. J. M. Horner, McNeely DuBose, Walter Hougson, T. W. Patton, Charles McNamee and Haywood Parker, Trustees of the Protestant Episcopal Church in the Missionary District of Asheville," January 9, 1902 (Deed Book 157, page 22 in the records of the Buncombe County Register of Deeds).

432. These drawings are housed at the Asheville Art Museum, Asheville, North Carolina, but can be viewed in the North Carolina State University Digital Library Collection, at http://d.lib.ncsu.edu/collections/catalog/aam_RS0131_0001.

433. "Rev. J. M. Horner, R. R. Swope, C. D. Beadle, W. Vance Brown and Haywood Parker, Trustees of the Protestant Episcopal Church in the Missionary District of Asheville to N. B. Guthrie," April 1, 1913 (Deed Book 182, page 588 in the records of the Buncombe County Register of Deeds).

434. *Journal of the Nineteenth Annual Convention of the Missionary District of Asheville* (1913), 30.

Bibliography

Books and Periodicals

Armentrout, Donald S., and Robert Boak Slocum. *An Episcopal Dictionary of the Church: A User-friendly Reference for Episcopalians.* New York: Church Publishing Incorporated, 2000.

Arthur, John Preston. *Western North Carolina: A History from 1730–1913.* Asheville, NC: Edward Buncombe Chapter of the Daughters of the American Revolution, 1914.

Ashe, Samuel A. *Biographical History of North Carolina: From Colonial Times to the Present.* Vol. 5. Greensboro, NC: Charles L. Van Noppen, 1906.

Authority of the State of New York, under the supervision of the New York Monuments Commission. *Major General Abner Doubleday and Brevet Major General John C. Robinson in the Civil War.* Albany, NY: J. B. Lyon, 1918.

Bailey, David Coleman. *Fashionable Asheville.* 2 vols. Charleston, SC: BookSurge, 2004.

Benjamin, Asher. *The Architect or Practical House Carpenter.* 1830. Reprint, Mineola, NY: Dover, 1988.

Bird, William Ernest. *The History of Western Carolina College: The Progress of an Idea.* Chapel Hill: University of North Carolina Press, 1963.

Bishir, Catherine. *North Carolina Architecture.* Chapel Hill: University of North Carolina Press, 1990.

———. *Southern Built: American Architecture, Regional Practice.* Charlottesville: University of Virginia Press, 2006.

Bishir, Catherine, Charlotte V. Brown, Carl R. Lounsbury, and Ernest H. Wood III. *Architects and Builders in North Carolina: A History of the Practice of Building.* Chapel Hill: University of North Carolina Press, 1990.

Bishir, Catherine, Michael T. Southern, and Jennifer F. Martin. *A Guide to the Historic Architecture of Western North Carolina.* Chapel Hill: University of North Carolina Press, 1999.

Branson, Levi. *Branson's North Carolina Business Directory: 1890.* Vol. VII. Raleigh, NC: Levi Branson, 1889.

Buel, D. Hillhouse. "Work In North Carolina." *The Spirit of Missions* (June 1875).

Buel, Rev. Clarence. "Appeal: A Good Layman and His Good Work." *The Churchman*, March 30, 1901.

Campbell, John, Jr., staff writer. "Old Ravenscroft School Is Purchased." *Asheville Citizen-Times,* September 8, 1979.

Catalogue of the Officers and Students of Trinity College: 1880–1881. Hartford, CT: Trinity College, 1880.

Catalogue of the Officers and Students of Trinity College: 1883–1884. Hartford, CT: Trinity College, 1883.

Chapin, George H. *Health Resorts of the South: Containing Numerous Engravings Descriptive of the Most Desirable Health and Pleasure Resorts of the Southern States.* Boston: George H. Chapin, 1889.

Chase, Nan K. *Asheville: A History.* Jefferson, NC: McFarland, 2007.

Cheshire, Joseph Blount. *The Church in the Confederate States: A History of the Protestant Episcopal Church in the Confederate States.* New York: Longmans, Green & Co., 1912.

Chester, Susan Guion. "Woman's Place and Work: College Settlements and Their Relation to the Church." *The Churchman*, March 11, 1893.

Cobb, Ashton. *Kiawah Island: A History.* Charleston, SC: History Press, 2006.

Cogburn, Frederick W. *A History of Lowell and Its People.* New York: Lewis Historical Publishing Company, 1920.

Concrete Houses & Cottages. New York: Atlas Portland Cement Company, 1909.

Cooper, Susan Fennimore. *William West Skiles: A Sketch of Missionary Life at Valle Crucis in Western North Carolina, 1842–1862.* New York: James Pott & Co., 1890.

Crawford, Geddings Hardy, ed. *Who's Who In South Carolina.* Columbia, SC: McCaw of Columbia, 1923.

Cutter, William Richard. *Genealogical and Family History of Central New York.* Vol. 1. New York: Lewis Historical Publishing Company, 1912.

Davison, J. P., compiler. *The Asheville City Directory and Gazetteer of Buncombe County for 1883–84.* Richmond, VA: Baughman Brothers Printers, 1883.

Diocese of North and East Carolina. *Sketches of*

Church History in North Carolina: Addresses and Papers by Clergymen and Laymen of the Dioceses of North and East Carolina. Wilmington, NC: Wm. L. DeRossett, Jr., 1892.

Downing, Andrew Jackson. *The Architecture of Country Houses: Including Designs for Cottages, and Farm-Houses and Villas, With Remarks on Interiors, Furniture, and the Best Modes of Warming and Ventilating.* New York: D. Appleton, 1850. Reprinted as *The Architecture of Country Houses.* New York: Dover, 1969.

_____. *Cottage Residences: or, A Series of Designs for Rural Cottages and Adapted to North America.* New York City: Wiley & Putman, 1842. Reprinted as *Victorian Cottage Residences.* New York: Dover, 1981.

Duncan, Rev. Norvin C. *Pictorial History of the Episcopal Church in North Carolina: 1701–1964.* Asheville, NC: Miller Printing Company, 1965.

Dykeman, Wilma. *The French Broad.* Newport, TN: Wakestone Books, 1955.

Ehle, John. *The Road.* Knoxville: University of Tennessee, 1998.

Fitzsimons, Theodore L. "An Elizabethan Colony in North Carolina." *International Studio* 59 (1916).

Gibson, Tyson Gray. "A Loss in the Community: Integration and the End of a Unique Educational Heritage." Senior thesis at the University of North Carolina, Asheville, 2003.

Greenberg, Sue, and Jan Kahn. *Asheville Volume Two (NC).* Mount Pleasant, SC: Arcadia, 1997.

Greif, Constance M. *John Notman, Architect.* Philadelphia, PA: Athenaeum of Philadelphia, 1968.

Grier, R. M., and F. A. Hibbert. *The Register of S. Chad's College Denstone from the Opening of School in February 1873 to April 1904.* Shrewsbury, UK: W. O. Wilding [O. D.], 1904.

Hall, Henry. *America's Successful Men of Affairs.* New York: New York Tribune, 1895–1896. Electronic reproduction. New York: Columbia University Libraries, 2008.

Hamilton, J. G. DeRoulhac. *The Papers of Thomas Ruffin.* Vol. II. Raleigh, NC: Edwards & Broughton Printing Co., 1918.

Harshaw, Lou. *Asheville: Mountain Majesty.* Asheville, NC: Bright Mountain Books, 2007.

Haywood, Marshall DeLancey. *Lives of the Bishops of North Carolina: From the Establishment of the Episcopate in that State Down to the Division of the Diocese.* Raleigh, NC: Alfred Williams, 1910.

Horner, Rt. Rev. Junius. "Missionary District of Asheville — Statement of the Work." *The Spirit of Missions* LXIV, no. 5 (May 1899).

Jones, Hamilton. *Reports of Cases of Equity Argued and Determined in the Supreme Court of North Carolina: From December Term, 1854 to August Term 1856, Inclusive.* Vol. II. Salisbury, NC: J. J. Bruner, 1856.

Lafever, Minard. *The Architectural Instructor: Containing a History of Architecture from the Earliest Ages to the Present Time.* New York: G. P. Putman, 1856.

_____. *The Beauties of Modern Architecture: Illustrated by Forty-Eight Original Plates, Designed Expressly for This Work.* New York City: D. Appleton, 1839.

_____. *The Modern Builder's Guide.* New York City: Paine & Burgess, 1846.

_____. *Who's Who in New York.* New York: L. R. Hamersley, 1907.

_____. *Women's Who's Who in America.* New York: American Commonwealth Company, 1914.

_____. *The Young Builder's General Instructor.* Newark, NJ: W. Tuttle, 1829.

Leonard, John, ed. *Who's Who in America.* Vol. 3, 1903–05. Chicago: A. L. Marquis, 1903.

Lloyd, Frederic E. J., ed. *The American Church Clergy and Parish Directory for 1903.* Cleveland, OH: Frederic E. J. Lloyd, 1903.

London, Lawrence, ed. *The Episcopal Church in North Carolina: 1701–1959.* Raleigh, NC: Episcopal Diocese of North Carolina, 1987.

Malet, Rev. William Wyndham. *An Errand to the South in the Summer of 1862.* London: Richard Bentley, New Burlington Street, 1863.

Maloney Directory Company. *Maloney's 1899–1900 Asheville City Directory.* Richmond, VA: J. L. Hill Printing Co., 1899.

Mashburn, J. L. *Hominy Valley: The Golden Years.* Enka, NC: Colonial House, 2008.

Massengill, Stephen E. *Western North Carolina: A Visual Journey Through Stereo Views and Photographs.* Charleston, SC: Arcadia, 1999.

McCrady, Edward, and Samuel A. Ashe. *Cyclopedia of Eminent and Representative Men of the Carolinas of the Nineteenth Century.* Vol. 2. Madison, WI: Brant & Fuller, 1892.

McDaniel, Douglas Stuart. *Asheville (NC) (Images of America).* Mount Pleasant, SC: Arcadia, 2004.

McDowell, Hon. John Hugh. *History of the McDowells, Erwins, Irwins and Connections: Being a Compilation from Various Sources.* Memphis, TN: C. B. Johnston, 1918.

Medford, W. Clark. *The Middle History of Haywood County.* Johnson City, TN: Overmountain Press, 2004.

Moore, Della Hazel. *Hot Springs of North Carolina.* Johnson City, TN: Overmountain Press, 2002.

Nesbitt, William A. *History of Early Settlement and Land Use on the Bent Creek Experimental Forest.* Asheville, NC: Appalachian Forest Experiment Station, 1941.

Painter, Jacqueline Burgin. *The German Invasion of Western North Carolina.* Johnson City, TN: Overmountain Press, 1992.

Patton, Fanny L. *Thomas Walton Patton: A Biographical Sketch.* Asheville, NC: published by Fannie L. Patton, 1908.

Patton, James. *Biography of James Patton.* Chapel Hill, NC: Call number CB P332p 1850 (North Carolina Collection, UNC-CH).

Patton, Sadie Smathers. *The Story of Henderson County.* Asheville, NC: Miller Printing Company, 1947.

Poston, Jonathan H. *The Buildings of Charleston.* Columbia: University of South Carolina Press, 1997.

Powell, William Stevens, and Jay Mazzocchi. *Encyclopedia of North Carolina.* Chapel Hill: University of North Carolina at Chapel Hill Press, 2006.

Price, R. N. "Methodism in East Tennessee: Before, During, and Since the War." *Methodist Review Quarterly* (April 1908).

Redmond, Rex. *Beaverdam: Historic Valley of the Blue Ridge Mountains: A Nostalgic Look at a Valley and Its People.* Greenville: SC: Postal Instant Press, 2011.

Roberson, T. C., Miss Annie Mae Thrash, and Mrs. John Gilmore. *History of Montmorenci Methodist Church, Candler, North Carolina- 1857–1957.* Candler, NC: Montmorenci Methodist Church, 1969.

Robinson, John, staff writer. "Schoenberger Hall: Efforts to Save It Are Unsuccessful." *Asheville Citizen-Times,* March 25, 1978.

Sill, James B. *Historical Sketches of Churches in the Diocese of Western North Carolina Episcopal Church.* Asheville, NC: Publishing Office, Church of the Redeemer, 1955.

Slusser, Dale Wayne. *In the Near Loss of Everything: George MacDonald's Son in America.* Allentown, PA: Zossima Press, 2009.

Smith, Charles Lee. *The History of Education in North Carolina.* Washington, DC: Government Printing Office, 1888.

Sondley, F. A., and Theodore F. Davidson. *Asheville and Buncombe County.* Asheville, NC: Citizen Company, 1922.

Stanton, Phoebe B. *Gothic Revival & American Church Architecture: An Episode in Taste, 1840–1856.* Baltimore, MD: The John Hopkins University Press, 1968.

Stowe, Rev. Andrew David, ed. *Stowe's Clerical Directory 1920–21.* Minneapolis, MN: A. D. Stowe, 1920.

Tessier, Mitzi Schaden. *Asheville: A Pictorial History.* Marceline, MO: Donning, 1982.

Thirty-Third Annual of the Association Graduates of the United States Military Academy at West Point, New York. June 9th 1902. Saginaw, MI: Seemann & Peters, Printers & Binders, 1902.

Trenholm, Alice Middleton. *Flat Rock, North Carolina: A Sketch of the Past.* Asheville, NC: Inland Press, 1908.

Tyler, Norman, Ted J. Ligibel, and Ilene Tyler. *Historic Preservation: An Introduction to Its History, Principles, and Practice.* New York: W. W. Norton, 2009.

Venn, J. A. *Alumni Cantabrigienses: Part II, From 1752 to 1900.* Vol. III, *Gabb–Justamond.* Cambridge: Cambridge University Press, 1947.

Wall, John. *A Dictionary for Episcopalians.* Lanham, MD: Rowman & Littlefield, 2000.

Wey, Rev. Frederick W. *Historical Sketches of the Missions in Charge of the Rev. Fred'k W. Wey in the Missionary Jurisdiction of Asheville, N.C.* Murphy, NC: Alfred Morgan, 1897.

Wigginton, Elliot. *Foxfire 4: Water Systems, Fiddle Making, Logging, Gardening, Sassafras Tea, Wood Carving, and Further Affairs of Plain Living.* New York: Anchor Books, 1977.

Williams, Max R., ed. *The History of Jackson County.* Sylva, NC: Jackson County Historical Society, 1987.

Wilson, F. M. Huntington. *The Memoirs of An Ex-Diplomat.* Boston: Bruce Humphries, 1945.

Wilson, Leonard. *Makers of America: Biographies of Leading Men of Thought and Action,* Vol. II. Washington, DC: B. F. Johnson, 1916.

Wolfe, Thomas. *Look Homeward Angel.* New York: Charles Scribner's Sons, 1929.

Woods, Robert A., and Albert J. Kennedy, eds. *Handbook of Settlements.* New York: Charities Publications Committee, 1911.

Wright, Lewis. "Anglo-Catholicism in Antebellum North Carolina: Levi Silliman Ives and the Society of the Holy Cross." *Anglican and Episcopal History* LXIX, no. 1 (2000): 44–71.

Yearbook of the Young Men's Christian Associations of North America, for the Year May 1, 1920 to April 30, 1921. New York: Association Press, 1921.

Zeigler, Wilbur G., and Ben S. Grosscup. *The Heart of the Alleghenies or Western North Carolina.* Raleigh, NC: Alfred Williams, 1883.

Convention Journals—State of North Carolina

Journal of the Ninth Annual Convention of the Protestant Episcopal Church in the State of North Carolina. Fayetteville, NC: Edward J. Hale, 1825.

Journal of the Twenty-Sixth Annual Convention of the Protestant Episcopal Church in the State of North Carolina. Fayetteville, NC: Edward J. Hale, 1842.

Journal of the Twenty-Seventh Annual Convention of the Protestant Episcopal Church in the State of North Carolina. Fayetteville, NC: Edward J. Hale, 1843.

Journal of the Twenty-Eighth Annual Convention of the Protestant Episcopal Church in the State of North Carolina. Fayetteville, NC: Edward J. Hale, 1844.

Journal of the Twenty-Ninth Annual Convention of the Protestant Episcopal Church in the State of North Carolina. Fayetteville, NC: Edward J. Hale, 1845.

Journal of the Thirtieth Annual Convention of the Protestant Episcopal Church in the State of North Carolina. Fayetteville, NC: Edward J. Hale, 1846.

Journal of the Thirty-First Annual Convention of the Protestant Episcopal Church in the State of North Carolina. Fayetteville, NC: Edward J. Hale, 1847.

Journal of the Thirty-Second Annual Convention of the Protestant Episcopal Church in the State of North Carolina. Fayetteville, NC: Edward J. Hale, 1848.

Journal of the Thirty-Third Annual Convention of the Protestant Episcopal Church in the State of North Carolina. Fayetteville, NC: Edward J. Hale, 1849.

Journal of the Thirty-Fourth Annual Convention of the Protestant Episcopal Church in the State of North Carolina. Fayetteville, NC: Edward J. Hale, 1850.

Journal of the Thirty-Fifth Annual Convention of the Protestant Episcopal Church in the State of North Carolina. Fayetteville, NC: Edward J. Hale, 1851.

Journal of the Thirty-Sixth Annual Convention of the Protestant Episcopal Church in the State of North Carolina. Fayetteville, NC: Edward J. Hale, 1852.

Journal of the Thirty-Seventh Annual Convention of the Protestant Episcopal Church in the State of North Carolina. Fayetteville, NC: Edward J. Hale, 1853.

Journal of the Thirty-Eighth Annual Convention of the Protestant Episcopal Church in the State of North Carolina. Fayetteville, NC: Edward J. Hale, 1854.

Journal of the Thirty-Ninth Annual Convention of the Protestant Episcopal Church in the State of North Carolina. Fayetteville, NC: Edward J. Hale, 1855.

Journal of the Fortieth Annual Convention of the Protestant Episcopal Church in the State of North Carolina. Fayetteville, NC: Edward J. Hale, 1856.

Journal of the Forty-First Annual Convention of the Protestant Episcopal Church in the State of North Carolina. Fayetteville, NC: Edward J. Hale, 1857.

Journal of the Forty-Second Annual Convention of the Protestant Episcopal Church in the State of North Carolina. Fayetteville, NC: Edward J. Hale, 1858.

Journal of the Forty-Third Annual Convention of the Protestant Episcopal Church in the State of North Carolina. Fayetteville, NC: Edward J. Hale, 1859.

Journal of the Forty-Fourth Annual Convention of the Protestant Episcopal Church in the State of North Carolina. Fayetteville, NC: Edward J. Hale, 1860.

Journal of the Forty-Fifth Annual Convention of the Protestant Episcopal Church in the State of North Carolina. Fayetteville, NC: Edward J. Hale, 1861.

Journal of the Forty-Sixth Annual Convention of the Protestant Episcopal Church in the State of North Carolina. Fayetteville, NC: Edward J. Hale, 1862.

Journal of the First Annual Council of the Protestant Episcopal Church in the State of North Carolina. Fayetteville, NC: Edward J. Hale, 1863.

Journal of the Forty-Eighth Annual Council of the Protestant Episcopal Church in the State of North Carolina. Fayetteville, NC: Edward J. Hale, 1864.

Journal of the Forty-Ninth Annual Council of the Protestant Episcopal Church in the State of North Carolina. Raleigh, NC: J. C. Gorman's Bok and Job Printing, 1865.

Journal of the Fiftieth Annual Convention of the Protestant Episcopal Church in the State of North Carolina. Fayetteville, NC: Edward J. Hale, 1866.

Journal of the Fifty-First Annual Convention of the Protestant Episcopal Church in the State of North Carolina. Fayetteville, NC: Edward J. Hale, 1867.

Journal of the Fifty-Second Annual Convention of the Protestant Episcopal Church in the State of North Carolina. Wilmington, NC: Bernard's Printing and Publishing House, 1868.

Journal of the Fifty-Third Annual Convention of the Protestant Episcopal Church in the State of North Carolina. Raleigh, NC: M. S. Littlefield Printer & Binder, 1869.

Journal of the Fifty-Fourth Annual Convention of the Protestant Episcopal Church in the State of North Carolina, n.p., 1870.

Journal of the Fifty-Fifth Annual Convention of the Protestant Episcopal Church in the State of North Carolina n.p., 1871.

Journal of the Fifty-Sixth Annual Convention of the Protestant Episcopal Church in the State of North Carolina n.p., 1872.

Journal of the Fifty-Seventh Annual Convention of the Protestant Episcopal Church in the State of North Carolina. Raleigh, NC: Edwards & Broughton, Power Printers and Binders, 1873.

Journal of the Fifty-Eighth Annual Convention of the Protestant Episcopal Church in the State of North Carolina. Raleigh, NC: Daily News Print, Fayetteville Street, 1874.

Journal of the Fifty-Ninth Annual Convention of the Protestant Episcopal Church in the Diocese of North Carolina. Goldsboro, NC: J. B. Whitaker, Jr., Book and Job Printer, 1875.

Journal of the Sixtieth Annual Convention of the Protestant Episcopal Church in the Diocese of North Carolina. Goldsboro, NC: J. B. Whitaker, Jr., Book and Job Printer, 1876.

Journal of the Sixty-First Annual Convention of the Protestant Episcopal Church in the Diocese of North Carolina. Raleigh, NC: News Steam Job Print, 1877.

Journal of the Sixty-Second Annual Convention of the Protestant Episcopal Church in the Diocese of North Carolina. Published by order of the Convention, 1878.

Journal of the Sixty-Third Annual Convention of the Protestant Episcopal Church in the Diocese of North Carolina. Raleigh, NC: Uzzell Wiley & Co. Printers and Binders, 1879.

Journal of the Sixty-Fourth Annual Convention of the Protestant Episcopal Church in the Diocese of North Carolina. Raleigh, NC: Uzzell Wiley & Co. Printers and Binders, 1880.

Journal of the Sixty-Fifth Annual Convention of the Protestant Episcopal Church in the State of North Carolina. Raleigh, NC: Uzzell & Gatling Steam Printers & Binders, 1881.

Journal of the Sixty-Sixth Annual Convention of the

Protestant Episcopal Church in the State of North Carolina. Raleigh, NC: Uzzell Wiley & Co. Printers and Binders, 1882.

Journal of the Sixty-Seventh Annual Convention of the Protestant Episcopal Church in the State of North Carolina. Raleigh, NC: P. W. Wiley Job Printer), 1883.

Journal of the Sixty-Eighth Annual Convention of the Protestant Episcopal Church in the Diocese of North Carolina. Raleigh, NC: E. M. Uzzell Power Printer & Binder, 1884.

Journal of the Sixty-Ninth Annual Convention of the Protestant Episcopal Church in the Diocese of North Carolina. Raleigh, NC: E. M. Uzzell Steam Printer & Binder, 1885.

Journal of the Seventieth Annual Convention of the Protestant Episcopal Church in the Diocese of North Carolina. Raleigh, NC: Edwards & Broughton, Power Printers and Binders, 1886.

Journal of the Seventy-First Annual Convention of the Protestant Episcopal Church in the Diocese of North Carolina. Raleigh, NC: Edwards & Broughton, Power Printers and Binders, 1887.

Journal of the Seventy-Second Annual Convention of the Protestant Episcopal Church in the Diocese of North Carolina. Raleigh, NC: Edwards & Broughton, Power Printers and Binders, 1888.

Journal of the Seventy-Third Annual Convention of the Protestant Episcopal Church in the Diocese of North Carolina. Raleigh, NC: Edwards & Broughton, Power Printers and Binders, 1889.

Journal of the Seventy-Fourth Annual Convention of the Protestant Episcopal Church in the Diocese of North Carolina. Raleigh, NC: Edwards & Broughton, Power Printers and Binders, 1890.

Journal of the Seventy-Fifth Annual Convention of the Protestant Episcopal Church in the Diocese of North Carolina. Raleigh, NC: Edwards & Broughton, Power Printers and Binders, 1891.

Journal of the Seventy-Sixth Annual Convention of the Protestant Episcopal Church in the Diocese of North Carolina. Raleigh, NC: Edwards & Broughton, Power Printers and Binders, 1892.

Journal of the Seventy-Seventh Annual Convention of the Protestant Episcopal Church in the Diocese of North Carolina. Raleigh, NC: Edwards & Broughton, Power Printers and Binders, 1893.

Journal of the Seventy-Eighth Annual Convention of the Protestant Episcopal Church in the State of North Carolina. 1894.

Journal of the Seventy-Ninth Annual Convention of the Protestant Episcopal Church in the State of North Carolina. 1895.

Journal of the Eightieth Annual Convention of the Protestant Episcopal Church in the Diocese of North Carolina. Raleigh, NC: Edwards & Broughton, Power Printers and Binders, 1896.

Journal of the Eighty-First Annual Convention of the Protestant Episcopal Church in the Diocese of North Carolina. Raleigh, NC: Edwards & Broughton, Power Printers and Binders, 1897.

Journal of the Eighty-Second Annual Convention of the Protestant Episcopal Church in the Diocese of North Carolina. Raleigh, NC: Edwards & Broughton, Power Printers and Binders, 1898.

Journal of the Eighty-Third Annual Convention of the Protestant Episcopal Church in the Diocese of North Carolina. Raleigh, NC: Edwards & Broughton, Power Printers and Binders, 1899.

Journal of the Ninetieth Annual Convention of the Protestant Episcopal Church in the Diocese of North Carolina. Raleigh, NC: Edwards & Broughton, Printers and Binders, 1906.

Convention Journals — Asheville

Journal of the First Annual Convocation of the Protestant Episcopal Church in the Missionary Jurisdiction of Asheville. Asheville, NC: Asheville Printing Company, 1895.

Journal of the Second Annual Convention of the Protestant Episcopal Church in the Missionary Jurisdiction of Asheville. Asheville, NC: Asheville Printing Company, 1897.

Journal of the Third Annual Convention of the Protestant Episcopal Church in the Missionary Jurisdiction of Asheville. Asheville, NC: The Citizen Company, 1897.

Journal of the Fourth Annual Convention of the Protestant Episcopal Church in the Missionary Jurisdiction of Asheville. Asheville, NC: The Citizen Company, 1898.

Journal of the Fifth Annual Convention of the Protestant Episcopal Church in the Missionary Jurisdiction of Asheville. Asheville, NC: The Citizen Company, 1899.

Journal of the Sixth Annual Convention of the Protestant Episcopal Church in the Missionary District of Asheville. Asheville, NC: The French Broad Press, 1900.

Journal of the Seventh Annual Convention of the Protestant Episcopal Church in the Missionary District of Asheville. Asheville, NC: The French Broad Press, 1901.

Journal of the Eighth Annual Convention of the Missionary District of Asheville. Asheville, NC: Asheville Printing Company, 1902.

Journal of the Ninth Annual Convention of the Missionary District of Asheville. Asheville, NC: Hackney & Moale Company, 1903.

Journal of the Tenth Annual Convention of the Protestant Episcopal Church in the Missionary District of Asheville. Asheville, NC: Hackney & Moale Company, 1904.

Journal of the Eleventh Annual Convention of the Protestant Episcopal Church in the Missionary District of Asheville. Asheville, NC: Hackney & Moale Company, 1905.

Journal of the Twelfth Annual Convention of the Protestant Episcopal Church in the Missionary District of Asheville. Asheville, NC: Hackney & Moale Company, 1906.

Journal of the Thirteenth Annual Convention of the Protestant Episcopal Church in the Missionary District of Asheville. Asheville, NC: Hackney & Moale Company, 1907.

Journal of the Fourteenth Annual Convention of the Protestant Episcopal Church in the Missionary District of Asheville. Asheville, NC: Hackney & Moale Company, 1908.

Journal of the Fifteenth Annual Convention of the Protestant Episcopal Church in the Missionary District of Asheville. Asheville, NC: Hackney & Moale Company, 1909.

Journal of the Sixteenth Annual Convention of the Protestant Episcopal Church in the Missionary District of Asheville. Asheville, NC: Hackney & Moale Company, 1910.

Journal of the Seventeenth Annual Convention of the Protestant Episcopal Church in the Missionary District of Asheville. Asheville, NC: Hackney & Moale Company, 1911.

Journal of the Eighteenth Annual Convention of the Protestant Episcopal Church in the Missionary District of Asheville. Asheville, NC: Hackney & Moale Company, 1912.

Journal of the Nineteenth Annual Convention of the Protestant Episcopal Church in the Missionary District of Asheville. Asheville, NC: Hackney & Moale Company, 1913.

Journal of the Twentieth Annual Convention of the Protestant Episcopal Church in the Missionary District of Asheville. Asheville, NC: Hackney & Moale Company, 1914.

Journal of the Twenty-First Annual Convention of the Protestant Episcopal Church in the Missionary District of Asheville. Asheville, NC: Hackney & Moale Company, 1915.

Journal of the Twenty-Second Annual Convention of the Protestant Episcopal Church in the Missionary District of Asheville. Asheville, NC: Hackney & Moale Company, 1916.

Journal of the Twenty-Third Annual Convention of the Protestant Episcopal Church in the Missionary District of Asheville. Asheville, NC: Hackney & Moale Company, 1917.

Journal of the Twenty-Fourth Annual Convention of the Protestant Episcopal Church in the Missionary District of Asheville. Asheville, NC: Hackney & Moale Company, 1918.

Journal of the Twenty-Fifth Annual Convention of the Protestant Episcopal Church in the Missionary District of Asheville. Asheville, NC: Hackney & Moale Company, 1919.

Journal of the Twenty-Sixth Annual Convention of the Protestant Episcopal Church in the Missionary District of Asheville. Asheville, NC: Hackney & Moale Company, 1920.

Journal of the Twenty-Seventh Annual Convention of the Protestant Episcopal Church in the Missionary District of Asheville. Asheville, NC: Hackney & Moale Company, 1921.

Index

Numbers in ***bold italics*** indicate pages with photographs.

Act of Sequestration 161
Acton, NC 107–109
Alexander, James Mitchell 109–110
Alexander's Mission 49, 109–113
Andrews, W.S. 10
Argyle 5
Atkinson, Bishop Thomas 20–21, 28–29, 31–33, 36, 37, 90, 110, 127, 135–136, 138–140, 146, 148, 151, 153–155, 172, 174, 183–184; death 40; will and estate 46–48, 50–51, 56
Atkinson, Rev. Thomas (grandson of the bishop) 49
Azalea 6

Baker, Elizabeth Rumbough 168
Baring, Charles 5, 15
Baring, Susan Tudor Heywood 5
Barrows, Rev. William Stanley 61, 64–67, 70–71, 106, 143, 147, 150, 156, 159, 163, 166, 176, 184
Bascom College 128–129
Battle, Samuel Westray, Jr. 95
Beal, Fannie Chipman 138–139
Beal, Ralph R. 141
Beal, Prof. William 138–139, 140
Beaver Dam Chapel 33, 113, 114–118, 124, 147, 179
Bell, Rev. George Hamilton 46, 48, 121–124, 127–128, 130–132, 135, 146, 161, 165–166, 179
Bell, Penelope 128
Belvedere 85–87, 185
Benjamin, Asher 11, 13,-14
Bent Creek 124–127
Bigelow, Hamilton Storrs 66, 95
Birdsall, Delphenia 143
Bishir, Catherine 6, 11
"Bishop Atkinson Professorship (or Scholarship)" 41–42
Bissell, Dwight Walter 59–60, 62–63, 66–68
Black, David 92
Blake, Daniel 6, 151–152
Bland, Rev. Charles T. 131, 170
Bonnele, Mr. 68
Bowman's Bluff, NC 78, 104, 107, 119, 134, 148–151, 176, 180
Bowman's Bluff Mission 148–49
Boyd, Wilson 124

Bradley, Rev. Edward 176
Brayton, Rev. Hobart C. 156
Brevard, NC 37, 39, 43, 49, 150, 172, 174–176, 180
Brooklands 5
Brooks, NC 127
Brush, Marie Louise (aka: M.L. Hoyt) 122, 179–180
Buckner, Lena N. 87, 185
Buel, Rev. David Hillhouse 36, ***37***; 38–43, 45–46, 48–49, 52, 55–56, 58, 60–61, 64–67, 70, 84, 106–107, 121–122, 125, 130, 135, 138, 139, 142, 143–147, 149–150, 152, 155–164, 171, 174–177, 184
Bull Creek Mission 107, 134, 177–179; *see also* Riceville Mission
Buncombe Turnpike 5–6, 20, 109, 151, 164, 183
Burnsville, NC 20
Burrage, Alvah Lowell 66, 95–96
Burrage, John Otis 66, 96
Bush, Thomas Frederick 62, 66, 96
Buxton, Anna Nash Cameron 18
Buxton, Rev. Jarvis Barry, Jr. 17, 18–19, ***20***, 21–26, 28–29, 31–35, 39–40, 46, 49–53, 60–61, 63, 65, 75, 80–81, 88, 113–114, 121, 123, 125, 127–131, 135–136, 139–141, 145, 151, 154, 165, 169–171, 176–177, 183–185
Buxton, Mary R. 88, 185
"Buxton Hill" (aka Buxton Place) 88–89, 185
Buxtons Memorial (Asheville, NC) 180–82
Bynum, Rev. William Shipman 51, 53, 153

Cain, Rev. Walter S. 118
Calvary Episcopal Church (Fletcher, NC) 11, 37, 39, 107, 151–156, 168, 171
Campbell, James Winthrop 66, 96
Candler, Thomas J. 108–109
Candler, William Gaston 121–123
Candler's Mission 121–123, 179; *see also* St. Clement's
Canton, NC 138, 147, 176–177

Carpenter, John 129–130
Carson, Joseph McDowell 172
Carver, J.M. 132
Cashiers, NC 72, 175
Chandler, Rev. Samuel P. 130
Chapman, Rev. Chalmers Durant 176
Chapman, Leicester 27, 128–130, 132
Chapman, Sarah Handfield Carpenter 129
Charlestonians 5–6, 11, 15, 183
"Chateau Nollman" 87, 92, 185
Cheesborough, James Walton 66, 98
Cheesborough, Joseph Edmond 66, 98
Cherokee County, NC 72, 138–141
Cheshire, Bishop Joseph Blount 24, 31, 43, 45, 47, 53, 70–72, 75–76, 80, 109, 124, 134, 140–141, 144, 147, 149, 177, 184
Chester, Mrs. Charles T. 115
Christian, Mrs. Anna 87
Chunn's Cove Mission 123, 128
Church of the Good Shepherd (Turnpike, NC) 179–180
Church of the Incarnation (Franklin, NC) 142, 160
Church of the Messiah (Murphy, NC) 138–142, 160
Church of the Redeemer (Woodfin, NC) 90, 128, 132–135
Clark, Rev. Willis G. 135
Clarke, Dr. W.W. 122
Clayton, Ephraim 10–11, 13, 19, 22, 136
Cocke, Phillip Charles 63, 66, 96, ***97***
Cody, Rev. Cortez 121, 128
Coit, Rev. Dr. Henry A. 59
Collins, Josiah, (III) 24–26
Confederate States 28–29, 31, 161
Cox, Mike 91
Cox, Thomas Augustus 159–160
Coxe, Col. Frank 45, 172
Coxe, Mary Vance 111
Croft, John D. 98
Cullowhee, NC 43, 48–49, 67, 157–159, 162
Cullowhee Mission 157

221

Index

Curtis, Francis Randolph 49, 110–111

Davies, Daniel David 157, 159
Davis, Alexander Jackson 5
Davis, Minot 66, 98–99, 100
Davis, Rev. Thomas F. 151
Deal, Rev. John Archibald 72, 137, 139–141, 159, 162
Deal, Walter 87, 92
Denson, Samuel 36
Dick, Judge Robert P. 10
Dickson, David Buel 42
Dickson, Isaac 42, 71, 84
Dickson, Dr. John 13
Diocesan School 21–22, 25, 31, 48, 68, 75
Diocese of East Carolina 43, 79
Doubleday, Ulysses 181
Downing, Andrew Jackson 5–6, 10–11, 13, 183
Drayton, Rev. John 153, 155–156
Drovers (Drover's Road) 5, 109, 164
Dunleith 10

Eagle Hotel **4**–6, 11, 45, 183
East La Porte 158
Edwards, B.P. 87
Engadine 122, 179
Erdman, Frederick 66, 99
Erdman, George L. 99
Erdman, Walter Collins 66, 99–100
Erwin, Andrew 4
Etowah, NC 148, 176, 180
Etowah Mission 180
Evans, Morgan 149–150
Everhart, Rev. George M. 152, 154–155

Farnum, Rev. Arthur W. 168
Flat Rock, NC 5–6, 10–11, 15, 102, 150–151, 153–154, 172–173, 176, 183
Fletcher, NC 6, 11, 30, 107, 151, 154, 168, 171
Folsom, Charles 100
Forbes, Rev. Edward M. 169
Forest Hill 157
Forks of the Pigeon Mission 49, 107, 147, 176–177
French Broad River 6, 37, 91, 100, 109–111, **112**; 113, 114, 125, 132–133, 135–137, 148–149, 164, 168, 172–174
French Broad Union Chapel (aka Trinity Union Chapel) 110–111

General Theological Seminary 18, 29, 31–32, 36, 38, 71, 80, 105, 170
Gethsemane Chapel (Bowman's Bluff, NC) 105, 134, 148–151, 180
Gideon, Oliver 181
Gleason, W.F. 142–143
Glencoe Mill **26**
Glencoe Mission 37, 39, 67, 102, 107, 124–127

Good Shepherd Mission 179–80
Grace Episcopal (Beaverdam) 35, 113–**115**, 116–119, 124, 128, 147
Grace in the Mountains (Waynesville, NC) 49, 66, 143, 145–147, 163, 176–177
Greek Revival 2, 4, 6, 10–11, 13, 26, 34, 94, 183
Gribben, Bishop Robert Emmet 87, 90, 185
Gwyn, James Alfred 66, 100

Hall, John H. 131
Hanckel, Rev. James Stuart 151, 172–174
Harding, Milton 58
Harkins, Margaret Candler 109
Harkins, Thomas Jefferson 109
Hatch, Emily Julia 125, 127
Hatch, James McRae 66, 100–101
Hatch, Col. Lewis Melvin 124–127
Hatch, Susan Elizabeth 125, 127
Haw Creek Mission 114, 121, 123, 127–128, 130, 161, 177
Haywood County 8, 35, 39, 43, 48–49, 57–58, 72, 100, 138, 141, 142, 145–146, 161, 176, 179, 183
Henderson, George T. 118–119
Henderson County 39, 78, 83, 103–104, 119, 134, 148–149, 151–152, 171–172, 183
Hendersonville, NC 26, 78, 83, 101, 103, 148, 150–151, 153–156, 168, 171–172, 180
Henry, J. Thurston 90
Henry, Hannah 118
Herren, James Madison 118
Hess, Miss Bird 128
Hill, Beverly W. 165, 168
Hill, Mary Lee Rumbough 165, 168
Hill School 59, 105
Hix Fund (aka Hicks Fund) 46–48, 50–51, 54, 76, 81
Hoffman, C.L. 61
Holmes, Edward Isaac, Jr. 101
Holmes, George 149–151
Holmes, John S. 149–151
Holmes, Rev. Lucien 29, 33, 130–131, 184
Holt, Erwin Allen 66, 101
Holt, Eugene 66, 101
Holt, Jacob 10
Horner, Bishop Junius Moore 80, 87, 144–145, 185
Horner, Junius Moore, Jr. 89–90
Horner, Mrs. Laura Lee 90–91, 185
Hot Springs, NC 6, 156, 164–**167**, 168
Hoyt, Capt. John Keais 122, 179–180
Hoyt, Marie Louise (aka Marie Louise Brush) 122, 179–180
Hughes, Rev. N. Collins 151, 154–155
Hume, Jane 175

Hume, Robert 175
Hyman, James P. 66, 101
Hyman, Mrs. Nellie 85, 185

Ives, Bishop Levi Silliman 15, 17–18, 20, 47, 169–170, 183

Jackson Academy 162
Jackson County 39, 43, 48–49, 72, 138, 141, 157, 160–161
Jeudwine, John Wynne 150
Johnstone, Francis Withers 172–173
Jones, Charles Earl Johnson 101
Jones, Edward C. 11
Joyner, Rev. J.R. 130

Kepler, Martha C. 72–73, 84, 184
Kepler, Samuel 72–73, 84
Kerr, Andrew 6
Kerr, Elizabeth 6
Kerr, Henrietta 6, 18
Kidney, Rev. John S. 169–170
Kimberly, Dr. John 113–114, 117
Kimberly, Thomas Maney 114, 117
King, Edward 5

Lafever, Minard 11, 13–14
Lamson, Roger 85, 87, 185
Lance, Fannie 168
Lance, Georgiana 168
Lance, Mamie 168
Lance, Newton Jasper 168
Lance, Susan 168
Lee, Eugenia 111
Lee, James Hardy 67, 102, 127
Lee, Dr. Plato Herman 111
Lee, Sara "Sallie" Hatch 67, 102, 127
Lee, Col. Stephen 35, 124, 127
Lee, Walter Hatch 66–67, 102
Leicester Episcopal Church Yard 132
Leicester High School (Leicester Academy) 33, 129–132
Leicester Mission 37, 107, 123, 128–132, 170; *see also* St. Paul's
The Lodge 5
Log Cabin Settlement 116–117
Loricks View Baptist Church 108–109
Love, Dillard Lafayette 161–163
Love, John Bell 161
Love, Margaret Coman 161–162
Love, "Mollie" (nee: Mary Louise Walker) 163
Love, Col. Robert 146–147, 161
Love, Dr. Samuel L. 145, 147
Love's School House (aka: Love's Meeting House) 149, 160–161
Lowndes, Richard Henry 102
Luckett, E.H. 87, 185
Lyman, Alonzo Hunt 117
Lyman, Augustus Julian 181
Lyman, Susan Chester 115–117
Lyman, Bishop Theodore Benedict 36, 38–40, 43, 45, 48–50, 52, 57–58, 60, 65, 68, 70, 76, 80, 106, 110, 114, 121–122, 130, 133–

Index

134, 136, 140, 143–144, 147, 149, 157–160, 164–165, 171, 174–174, 181, 184

MacDonald, George 1, 59, 64, 67–68
MacDonald, Lilia 61–65, 67–68, 83, 96, 98–100, 105
MacDonald, Louise Virenda Blandy 59, 61, 65, 184
MacDonald, Ozella Louise 59
MacDonald, Ronald 1, 59–**66**; 67–68, 73–74, 78, 83, 95, 96, 184
Madison, Robert Lee 159, 162
Madison County 164
Marion, NC 20, 120, 131, 170
Mars Hill College 11
Mason, Rev. R.H. 170
McBee, Vardry Echols, Jr. 62, 66, 102
McDuffey, Rev. Henry S. 133–134
McGhee, L.C. 58–59
The Meadows 6, 151
Mears, Rev. A. DeRossett 120
Methodist Church 6, 10, 14–15, 19, 107, 108, 110–111, 120, 122, 128–129, 131, 136–137, 146, 154, 157, 173, 175, 180
Micadale Mission 43, 49, 66, 107, 142–**144**, 145
Millard, Charlton C. 62, 66, 102
Millard, Herbert R. 62, 66, 102
Missionary District of Asheville (aka Missionary Jurisdiction of Asheville) 75–80, 82, 85, 87, 109, 124, 134, 144, 166, 181, 184–185
Montclove 172–173
Montmorenci Methodist Church 122
Moore, Charles 20, 108
Moore, Bishop Richard Channing 15
Morgan, Rev. A. Rufus 104, 138, 141–142, 160
Morgan, Alfred 141, 142
Morgan, Fannie Eugenia 141
Morgan, Rev. Rufus 8, 124, 126
Morris, Rev. Thomas A. 152
Mt. Calvary Mission (Pinners Cove) 107, 151, 153
Mountain Park Hotel 165–166, 168
Murdoch, Rev. Francis J. 35–36, 114, 125, 135, 146, 155, 177, 184
Murphy, NC 40, 136, 138–142, 160
"Murphy Junction" 136

Nashotah, WI 169
Neilson, William 164
Newington 6
Nollman, Nellie 87, 92, 185
Nollman, W.H. 87, 92, 185
North State Fitting School 88,–89, 185
Norwood, James 145

Osborne, Rev. Edwin A. 107, 152–153, 155–156, 171
Osborne, Ephraim 10
Osborne, John 10
Osborne, Jonathan 8
Osborne, Joseph Roland 1, 7–8, 10–**14**, 19–20–23, 30, 76, 183; chronology 187–196
Osborne, Martha 8
Owen, William T. 124
Owenby, NC 107, 133–134

Pack, George W. 117, 181
Parker, Haywood 57–59, 79, 132, 182, 184
Parker, Phillip Stanley 63, 66–68, 166
Patton, Clara Walton 6
Patton, James, Sr. 3–5, 7–8, 10, 19, 45, 183
Patton, James W. 6–7, 10, 18–19, 22, 27, 29, 42, 164
Patton, John E. 6, 164
Patton, Preston Fidelia, III 66, 103
Patton, Sadie Smathers 103, 149, 154
Patton, Thomas T. 7
Patton, Thomas Walton 29–30, 42, 59, 73, 79, 114, 127
Patton, William 6, 8, 10, 14, 22, 46, 52, 80, 183
Patton & Osborne 8
Patton & Summey 8
Payne, Daniel 161
Penniman, Mrs. Ridgley (Margaret Campbell Allison Penniman) 84
Phelps, Deborah Fortune 25
Phelps, Girard William 25–30, 172
Phelps, Rev. Hardy 156
Phelps, Jeremiah 25
Pinchot, Gifford 60
Pinners Cove 107, 151, 153
Pittsboro, NC 16, 21, 75, 96, 183
Polk County Courthouse 11
Postell, Rev. James H. 107–109, 111, 120–121, 128, 130–131, 136–137, 180–181
Pottstown, PA 59, 105
Prince, Henry Axtell 56–58, 184
Prout, Rev. Henry H. 15, 138–140

Ramseur, Miss 60
Ramseur, Vernon Badham 60, 66, 103
Rathburn, Rev. Scott 150, 156
Ravenscroft, Bishop John Stark 15, 76, 162, 183
Ravenscroft Board of Fellows 50–61, 70–74, 76–79, 136, 184
Ravenscroft Classical and Theological School 1, 22, **23**, 25, 30–31, 33, 46, 52, 81, 129–130, 154, 170, 183–184
Ravenscroft High School for Boys 1, 52–58, 60–**66**, 67–**69**, 71–78, 81–84, 119, 149, 180, 184–185; biographical notes of alumni 95–105

Ravenscroft Training School and Associate Mission 1, 33, **34**, 36–58, 60, 64–67, 70–79, 81–82, 87, 106–107, 109–110, 113–114, 117, 120–121, 123–125, 127–128, 130, 134–136, 139, 145–146, 149, 152, 155, 157, 163–164, 166, 169–170, 174, 176,–178, 182, 184
"Reconstruction Era" 31
Redwood, Harry W. 103
Redwood, William Morris 103–104
Reece, J. Burgin 128
Rhoades, Rev. Samuel 71, 109, 122, 124
Rice, Joseph Marion 177
Rice, Rev. William Francis 71, 78, 114, 117–124, 128, 131, 134–135, 147, 150, 166, 177–**178**, 179
Riceville Mission 107, 134, 177–179
Roberson, Frank David 119
Roberts, John Munsey 88, 185
Roberts, Margaret E. 88, 185
Robertson, Alexander 6, 29
Rockwood 107, 133–134; *see also* Church of the Redeemer (Owenby)
Roebling, John A. 84–85
Royce, Martha Broyles 168
Rumbough, "Carrie" (nee: Caroline Turpin Powell) 165, 167–168
Rumbough, "Harry" Henry Thomas 166
Rumbough, Col. James Henry 164–168
Rutherfordton, NC 17–20, 37, 39, 145, 156, 169, 172, 183
Rutland 165, 167
Rutledge, Frederick 5

St. Andrew's Chapel (West Asheville) 123, 135–138
St. Clement's (Candler, NC) 121–123, 179
St. David's (Cullowhee, NC) 48, 66–67, 157–160
St. James (Black Mountain, NC) 119–121
St. James (Hendersonville, NC) 150–151, 153–156, 168, 180
St. James (Waynesville, NC) 145–147
St. John, Kathryn 85–87
St. John, Leon 85–87
St. John-in-the-Wilderness Episcopal Church 5, 11, 150–151, 153, 156, 176
St. John's (Hot Springs) 164–**167**, 168
St. John's (Rutherfordton, NC) 19, 37, 39, 152, 169–172
St. John's (Webster/Sylva, NC) 48, 160–**162**, 163–164
St. John's–Buxton Memorial (Asheville, NC) 180–182
St. Luke's (Chunn's Cove) 122–124
St. Mark's (Alexander's) 109–113
St. Mary's (Micadale) 43, 66, 142–**144**, 145

St. Mathias Episcopal Church 71
St. Pauls (Acton) 107–109
St. Paul's (Etowah) 180
St. Paul's (Leicester) 128–132
St. Paul's-in-the-Valley (Brevard, NC) 39, 49, 172–176
St. Phillip's (Brevard, NC) 43, 49, 172, 174–176
St. Phillip's (Owenby) 132–135
St. Titus' (also: Upper Beaver Dam) 118–*119*
Sand Hill Academy 107–108
Sawyer, Eugene Colton 104
Shackleford, George Wesley 10–11, 22, 27
Shipp, Catherine LaFayette Cameron 26, 154
Shipp, Judge Marcus William 26, 154
Shoenberger, John H. 57–58
Shoenberger Hall 58, 61, 63–64, 71–*72*, 73, 76, 78, 80–85, 87–92, 106, 144, 166, 184–186
Siler, Albert 138–139
Siler, Joanna Chipman 138
Sill, Rev. James B. 106, 120, 127–128, 132, 145, 151, 153, 170, 177
Silver Springs, NC 107, 136
Skellie, Beile 143
Skiles, Rev. William West 18
Sloan, Samuel 10
Smather's Hotel 179
Smith, Anne E. 7, 135
Smith, Richard Howland 43, 45, 47, 50–52, 98
Smith, Richard Sharp 116–117, 181–182
Smith's Mill Creek 107, 136
"Society of the Holy Cross" 17, 170
"Somerset Place" 25
Southern Improvement Company 165, 168
Speedwell School 158
Stephenson, Alfred 179
Stevens, Dr. J.M. 131
Stevens, Samuel Norman, II 107–108
Struan 6

Stubbs, Rev. Alfred Houghton 71–72, 78, 80, 82, 87, 106, 109, 111–112, 117–118, 120–122, 124, 128, 131, 134, 137, 141–142, 144–145, 150, 166–168, 176, 179–180, 184–185
Sylva, NC 160–164

Tauber, Dr. Stuart Davis 93–94, 186
Taylor, Rev. Lewis 170
Tennent, J.A. 82
Thomasson, Col. Garland A. 135
Thurston, Rev. Henry 16–17
Thurston, Matilda Carson 172
Tillinghast, Rev. John 171
Tracy, Rev. U.T. 156
Transylvania County 37, 39, 49, 172–173, 175
Trescott, Elizabeth 6
Trinity Chapel 71, 133; *see also* St. Mathias Episcopal Church
Trinity Chapel (Haw Creek) 114, 127–128, 177
Trinity Episcopal Church (Asheville, NC) 19–20, 22, 24, 27, 32, 36, 39, 49–50, 59, 61, 63, 65, 71, 75, 80, 85, 103–104, 113–114, 124, 127–129, 135–136, 154, 183
Trinity Union Chapel 110–111; *see also* French Broad Union Chapel
Turnpike, NC 179–180

Valentine, Frank 74, 78, 82, 148–149, 180, 184
Valentine, Thomas 74, 83, 119, 149
Valle Crucis 15–18, 32, 169–170, 183
Vance, Robert Brank 110–111
Vanderbilt, George 40, 60, 104, 127
Vanderhorst V. Arnoldus 66, 104
Von Rock, Silvio 66, 104

Wainwright, Eric Ross 64, 104–105, 149
Wainwright, Henrietta Willis 134, 149

Wainwright, Rev. Richard 64, 104, 134, 149–151
Waite, Herbert 68
Warm Springs, NC 6, 40, 107, 164–168; *see also* Hot Springs, NC
Watauga, NC 15–16, 46, 76, 121, 128, 135, 169, 183
Way, William 105
Waynesville, NC 20, 37, 39, 49, 66, 72, 141–147, 159–161, 163, 176–177
Waynesville Mission 145
Webster, NC 39, 48–49, 157–158, 160–162
Weir, Sally Royce 168
Wetmore, Rev. Thomas C. 50–51, 54, 156
Wey, Rev. Frederick W. 72, 141, 144–145, 147, 163, 177
Wight, Thomas Henry Toynbee 74, 78, 184
Wilcox, Rev. Reginald 150, 180
Wilmer, Rev. George T. 33–35, 130, 135, 152, 184
Willis, Rt. Rev. Albert 133
Willis, A.P. (Arthur Ponder) 123
Willis, Augusta Maria Lowe 133
Willis, Catherine Maria 133–135
Willis, Rev. Dr. Francis (1718–1807) 132
Willis, Dr. Francis (1838–1906) 132–135
Willis, Rev. Francis, Jr. (1864–c1950) 134–135
Willis, Henrietta Lowe 133
Willis, Rev. Thomas 133
Wills, Frank 19, 36, 144, 183
Wilson, Francis Mairs Huntington 62, 66–68, 104–105
Wingate, Rev. Charles J. 172
Witchwood 181
Woodfin, Nichols 27–28
Woolsey, Charles 181–182
Wrixton, Rev. Arthur 156, 172

www.ingramcontent.com/pod-product-compliance
Ingram Content Group UK Ltd.
Pitfield, Milton Keynes, MK11 3LW, UK
UKHW050531150426
5217IPUK00026B/1886